# Follow in the Tigerman's Footprints

Tigerman and Colin Guest

Published by Colin Guest, 2024.

**Follow in the Tigerman's Footsteps**
**Subtitled**

# An Expats experiences of working in fourteen countries

First published in 2015 by Colin Guest
This edition published in 2019 by Tigerman Press.

While every precaution has been taken in the preparation of this book, the publisher assumes no responsibility for errors or omissions, or for damages resulting from the use of the information contained herein.

FOLLOW IN THE TIGERMAN'S FOOTPRINTS

**First edition. May 8, 2024.**

ISBN: 979-8224492381

Written by Tigerman and Colin Guest.

# Also by Tigerman

Follow in the Tigerman's Footprints

Watch for more at https://www.colinguestauthor.com.

# Also by Colin Guest

**1**
Desperation Rules the Day
Suzy's Dilemma

**Standalone**
Desperation Rules the Day
An Unforgettable Cruise
A Dangerous Love Affair
An Expats Experiences of Living in Turkey
Terror Holiday
It Happened in Barcelona
Impending Disaster
Fatal Love
Accidental Death
Follow in the Tigerman's Footprints

Watch for more at https://www.colinguestauthor.com.

*Exploits in Iran*

# Chapter 1
# Part 1

My first experience of working overseas started with a simple phone call back in 1978. When I answered it, I never knew it would result in the start of a new and incredible life. My old company contacted me to inquire if I was interested in a job in Iran. If so, my position would be a joint superintendent, along with my best friend, Ozzer.

The contact was to fit-out the interior of the Royal Hyatt Hotel in Tehran. Until this time, I had never thought about working overseas. However, by accepting this assignment, it would be an exciting and significant step up in my career. It would also enhance my CV.

On talking it over with my wife Jen, she thought it a great idea.

Especially. after I explained it would mean my being able to spend more time with her and the children. Although this might sound absurd, at the time I worked all around England, and only received a weekend off every three weeks. Whereas, if I accepted the Iran contract, I would receive ten days leave every three months. Although nervous about my working abroad, Jen could see the benefits. I thought it an excellent opportunity. The extra money would not only benefit my family but would enable me to buy the car of my dreams. This being a 1969-1972 Ford Mustang, six-cylinder convertible.

At the time of this offer, I worked as a supervisor with a London shopfitting company and drove around in a brand new company car. However, because of the company not paying me the full salary promised, I had little money in my pocket. When I talked to my boss about this, he said he would bring this up at a forthcoming management meeting. Unfortunate;y, instead of increasing my salary as promised, the company promoted my fellow supervisor, Peter, to be my boss. This proved my doubts were correct. A further surprise occurred a short time later when, without reason, Peter sacked me.

After taking my case to the Industrial Tribunal for unfair dismissal, I won, and the company had to pay me compensation.

In the meantime, I phoned my old company and agreed to go to Iran. As they did not agree with the salary I requested, instead of going as a joint superintendent, I took an area foreman position.

At the start of my contract, the Shah of Iran sat on the Peacock Throne. Although all was quiet and peaceful in the country, later events would prove things were not as they appeared.

When I left to start my journey out to Iran, a wave of sadness swept over me. I would not see my wife and children for three long months. Compared to my regular three weeks away, it would seem like a lifetime. However, as it would result in a better life for me and my family, it made me feel better.

My trip out to Tehran started when I met up with around fourteen shop fitters in a hotel near Heathrow Airport. We would stay there the night, then fly out the next morning. As none of us men had worked overseas before, or with Labourers from other countries. Iran promised to be a challenging experience.

During dinner in the hotel restaurant, things became somewhat out of hand. It happened after I, the senior person present, said the lads could have a drink with their meal. Although the company said they could, I should have known better. One bottle of wine led to another, to another, and another. I later heard our drinks bill was excessive. To say the least

The following morning, we nervously boarded the plane for Iran Whatever lay ahead would be an unfamiliar experience for all of us. However, never in my wildest dreams could I have predicted the severity of the danger that awaited us.

Our flight was long, as we had to change planes at Amman, the capital city of Jordan. When we finally came to land at Tehran airport, thousands of lights lit the darkness of the night up. They chris-crossed the city and seemed to go on forever. As the plane swooped lower, I could see masses of houses and shops. I had thought Tehran would be rather small, with perhaps only a few large government buildings.

Once through passport control, we walked out into the busy arrival hall, Here we found some of our fellow workers waiting to meet us who had arrived a month earlier. As it was bitterly cold outside, I was grateful to be wearing a thick parka. Once we were all aboard a mini-bus, the driver set off. Our first stop was at the Rainbow Hotel, where our shop fitters would stay. A short distance on, we came to the Marmara Hotel, where I would stay, along with the other area foremen.

Once checked in, along with Ray who I would share with, we went to our room, and in minutes were fast asleep.

The next morning, excitement, and anticipation ran through me. It would be the start of a new chapter in my working life. To my surprise when we went down for breakfast, I found an English breakfast was available. Once finished, along with the other work supervisors, we boarded a coach. Then, after collecting the lads from the Rainbow Hotel, we set off. To my surprise, the road up towards the mountains where the Hyatt hotel was located, was wide and well surfaced.

Approximately thirty minutes later, the hotel appeared in sight. At twenty-six stories' high, it stood out like a lonely sentinel on the rocky hillside. As we stopped outside, I shrugged. This would be my workplace for the foreseeable future.

As we unloaded our toolboxes from the coach, Ozzer came out and introduced himself to those he had not met before.

He shook my hand. "Welcome to Iran, Col. I hope you brought warm clothing. You're going to need it."

I grinned. "Yes, Jim said I would need them."

Ozzer then took us on a tour of the hotel that included a walk up to the roof level. By the time we reached it, we were all gasping for breath. With Tehran situated at 7000ft above sea level, and the hotel above this, the lack of oxygen made breathing strenuous. As I looked back down the hillside, far below, I could just make out the faint outlines of the city.

I am sure that like me, it shocked the other men when Jeff, one of our labourers, climbed up onto the parapet. Then, with hands in his pockets, he walked around the top of the building. With a drop of twenty-six stories, this was sheer madness. Ozzer shouted at him to get down, which he did, as calmly as though climbing off a chair. Ozzer then pointed behind the hotel at the Evin prison,. This which later became known in the international news, as the largest political prison in Iran. The prison extended across the hillside, with the majority underground. All one could identify were several observation posts set in a high-security fence. Nearer to the hotel was what looked like a parade ground.

Despite the bitter cold and considerable snow at the site, thanks to Jim's advice, I had packed long johns and thermal vests.

To my disbelieve, I learned that the Iranian labourers slept outside in cardboard boxes that once contained the guest room wardrobes. Not until some time later were tents supplied for them.

Once settled into a routine, work went well. In fact, too well, for we would run out of materials. We then had to wait for our containers to arrive with more supplies. These came on huge Mack trucks that struggled to climb the long hill up from the city. On their arrival, we greeted them like a bunch of kids waiting to receive a present.

To unload the crates from the containers, we used a large forklift truck. While unloading one, when one of our Iranian labourers screamed in pain. The forklift had driven onto his foot. His scream alerted the driver, who hastily stopped the machine. Unfortunately, it left the man's foot trapped underneath one of the huge tires. After one man jacked up the wheel, the man, still in shock, was driven to a hospital.

With it an accident, I couldn't understand why the Iranian forklift driver seemed so panic-stricken. The labourer foreperson then explained. Under local law; the driver was liable to support the injured man's family until the man could work again."

The forklift driver and victim were fortunate, as the man's foot was only bruised.

Arnie, another foreperson, was in charge of installing the main lobby ceiling. It comprised a series of octagonal boxes with mirrors fixed inside them. For a joke, Arnie grabbed hold of one labourer and pushed his head down inside one of the boxes. As it gave the impression you were upside down, the poor man screamed aloud until Arnie released him.

I had worked with Arnie before, and knew he loved playing practical jokes. Therefore, his action was not out of character to those like myself who had worked with him before.

I soon found that one big problem on the site were the sandwiches we had for our lunch. These were prepared at the Rainbow Hotel. They consisted of green-looking meat, topped with a piece of stale cheese. Not only that, come lunchtime, the bread rolls containing this mixture had dried up. This was no good, as it was all we had to eat until our return to the hotel in the evening.

I found that the first group of men on-site had made complaints about them to no avail. However, those who had worked with me, knew I was fussy about what I ate. As a result, they hoped I would succeed in my complaint, where they had failed.

I first complained to Ozzer about this, but as he ate almost anything, it proved a waste of time. I then talked to Jim, our admin guy, about them. He said he had tried to get better sandwiches, but been unable to get the hotel to supply them.

Things came to a head when the lads decided to hold a meeting to discuss what action they could take to change things. The men refused to allow any work supervisors to attend the meeting, except me, as they knew I was on their side.

The men realised that if the owner of our company knew of our problem, he would sort it out. As a result, after some discussion, we decided to write him a letter. I stated I would write one, but would not send it unless everyone first signed it. After all, had agreed, I wrote an official letter of complaint. Once all the lads had signed it, I sent a letter to my wife. Inside I explained our problem, and asked her to post the enclosed letter on to our head office.

A short time later, we received a reply . The company would pay us the equivalent amount of money they had been paying for our sandwiches. It meant we could buy whatever we wanted to eat for our lunch. This was great news and boosted both our morale and takings in the local supermarket. We then received more good news. Instead of paying for dinner in our hotels, the company would give us cash instead. I am sure this resulted from complaints from the men staying at the Rainbow Hotel. They had complained numerous times about the quality of meals they received. This new deal allowed some of our men to save a lot ,of money. Instead of buying sufficient food to eat, they ate little and kept the rest of their allowance. One man was rumoured to live on tins of beans. A look at him was proof he saved most of his allowance, for in only a few weeks, he had to tighten his belt by at least four inches.

One day our company boss came out from the UK, and while on-site, called me aside. To my surprise, he said, "Colin, I have a letter for you from your wife." Before I could speak, he continued, "Don't worry, she's okay, but before giving you the letter, I have to talk to you."

He then explained that my wife had called him after a visit to her doctor, who had noticed a large black mole on her neck. A biopsy revealed it was cancerous, and had to be removed. It pleased me when he said I could phone my wife at the company's expense to discuss the situation. Even better, if I thought it necessary to return home, he would arrange it A.S.A.P..

That evening, I called Jen who explained she had sorted everything out regarding the children and could manage okay. She said I should stay until my next scheduled leave. As I knew she was sensible and could cope without me, I agreed. However, I said if she changed her mind, to phone, and I would fly straight home.

In the meantime, the fitted Banquet Hall carpet looked fabulous., but the next morning, we were shocked to find it loose and uneven. After discussion, the fitters decided they had not given the carpet enough time to breathe after they had unrolled it. Given this, they re-stretched and refitted the carpet. To their astonishment, the next morning, it was again found loose and uneven. The men then thought the problem was the air-conditioning, that was not working. Although it sounds incredible, once turned on, we had no further problem with the carpet.

Another problem re carpets arose in the octagonal-shaped Roof Top Restaurant. The carpet had come in sections that had to be sewn together on site. Unfortunately, once done, the shape proved incorrect. I first heard of this problem when informed the restaurant was flooded. On investigation, it turned out the carpet fitters had turned on a fire hose to soak the carpet. As it dried out, incredibly, the carpet shrunk to the correct size and shape.

Another funny incident occurred re the Roof Top Restaurant that would involve many back-breaking hours to apply the various decorative finishes to the ceiling. Ray, however, one of our painters, came up with a novel idea about doing this job. He had a small mobile scaffold set up with a mattress on top to form a kind of hammock. He then laid down in it and painted the ceiling.

As work progressed, we later had over sixty men on-site. We then used a 44 seater coach, plus a minibus to ferry them back and forth to the site. Our coach driver, Carlos, was excellent, whereas the driver of the minibus was a lunatic. If you were nervous, you never went on his minibus, at least not twice.

At one time, our coach followed him as he sped down a side road with deep water channels on each side. To our disbelief, at the bottom of the road, without stopping, he turned onto the main road. Allah must have been with him, for he managed to do this without hitting anyone.

Before setting off each day, we made a check to see who was not on the coaches. This was commonplace, as that Fred, Harry, or someone else was hospitalized and receiving fluids intravenously. By the end of our stay in Iran, most of us had gone down with varying degrees of dysentery.

As I entered our site canteen one day, I found Mike, one of our guys, slumped over. He looked rough and said he felt terrible, so I said he should return to his hotel. While we were standing outside, awaiting a taxi, he collapsed. To my relief, he soon came to, but a few minutes later passed out again. Given this, I had someone call the hotel nurse . She came and after taking his temperature, said he should go to the hospital for a check-up.

While awaiting a taxi, I thought Mike was going to die on me. He kept said, "Don't leave me," and held a vice-like grip on my hand. Fortunately, after being checked out in the hospital, Mike was soon okay.

# Part 2

On the social side, life in Tehran was excellent, with bars, clubs, and cinemas available. However, when I saw posters advertising film, and pictures of people being cut and hacked up, it made me wonder what kind of people these Iranians were. As a result, when I first went with Ozzer to the post office, downtown, I felt nervous. As a result, I carried my open penknife on the end of my finger. However, once used to walking around downtown, I found it not a problem.

Before flying out to Iran, a colleague advised that we buy half a gallon of whisky at the duty-free shop in Heathrow. This he said we could exchange for more than its cost in the local shops. I then did this several times until the price of whisky dropped to the same price as in the UK.

Shopping in Tehran was unusual, as except in supermarkets, you could barter down the asking price. This was not only normal, but expected.

Downtown was an enormous Souk (bazaar), which I later found is the largest in the world. It sold a massive range of goods, from cheap household ware to gold shops full of dazzling jewellery. It was incredible to see so much gold in one area. Moreover, unlike nine ct in England, you could buy 18ct or even 22ct. The quality of items being exceptional.

In one section of the souk was a large footwear section. To our amazement, after you picked out what type of soles you wanted, you then went to another part to pick out the uppers. Then, you took these to another section where skilled craftsmen turned them into shoes.

As clothing in Iran was expensive, it gave a couple of our men an idea of how to make some extra money. On their next home leave, they collected a large suitcase of cast-off clothing and brought it back to Tehran. On their next day off work, they took it to the Souk to sell. They later told us that when people discovered what they were charging, crowds gathered. Despite nervous about everyone pushing and shoving, they sold everything they had.

On finishing work, back at our hotel, some evenings, we foreman would go straight to the lobby bar. One night, five of us walked in, sat at a table and ordered five beers. After the waiter brought them, as he turned to walk away, I ordered five more. This we then did each time he brought our beers. Our table became so full that we had to move some plates and glasses to a nearby table. The two Iranians who sat at our table shook their heads in disbelief. This situation only ended when our waiter refused to serve us anymore.

A grin spread across my face as I said, "If you don't serve us, we'll go upstairs and order from room service." This did not go down well with the waiter, but after a few words, we reached a compromise: He would serve us one more round of drinks, and in return, we would call it a day.

Apart from drinking in the bar, we kept a supply of vodka (which was inexpensive to buy) in our rooms. This went down well with a small bottle of soda that we bought by the crate full. Only later did we learn why the staff never complained about taking away the empties. There was a 50% deposit return on the bottles.

On one of our trips back from leave in England, as usual, we flew to Amman on Jordanian Airways. From here, we would then took an Iran Airways flight on to Tehran. On this trip, along with other passengers, after boarding our plane in Amman, an announcement said everyone had to get off. We all disembarked, then after going through another security check, re-boarded .

Unlike before, they carefully checked the weight of all hand luggage. The amount taken from people and put in the hold was enormous. It showed the lack of adequate control the first time we passed through security. However, this was not the real reason for our having to disembark. A shocked crew member had seen an Arab woman as she prepared to light a gas bottle to boil water and make tea. It seems she carried the gas bottle onto the plane under her burka (dress). The consequences of what could have happened had she lit it up during the flight, was truly frightening.

While in a local bank one day, I observed two staff members taking trays piled high with banknotes to the tellers. As some Iranian bank notes were of high denominations, the value on the plates must have been colossal. Without a doubt, you would never see things like this in a UK bank.

While talking to one of the office staff one day, when I asked why he looked so depressed, he said, "I've sold my scooter."

"That good," I replied. Iit meant the man had some money.

He shook his head. "No, it's not good. The man paid me by cheque, but the bank said there is no money in his account."

"Well, take the scooter back from him."

"He won't give it to me."

"Why don't you go to the police?"

"If I do, they will put him in prison."

"That's not good."

"No! That would be terrible if they put him in prison."

"Why?" I asked in frustration, "I don't understand the problem."

"If I get him put into prison, I have to look after his family until he gets out again."

"What! But that's crazy."

"Yes, it is, but it's the law here."

On another occasion, one of the local staff advised us about driving in Iran. He said if we knocked someone down and they looked dead, to reverse and make sure they were. On seeing our shocked expressions, he then explained why. "The law states that if you knock down and injure someone, you had to look after their family until the injured person can work again. However, if you killed them, you could pay what is called "Blood Money." This usually works out less than what one would pay if someone had to be in the hospital for any length of time. Fortunately, as none of us drove in Iran, this problem did not arise.

On the way back from the site one day, Carlos, our driver, took a different route back to our hotel. As we passed under a low flyover, we heard a loud bang, followed by a scraping sound. The next minute, a car behind us started blasting his horn. The coach's roof rack had been knocked off and hit the car behind. Unbelievably, despite our yells and the blasts from the vehicle behind, Carlos seemed oblivious. He continued until stopped by a set of traffic lights. The driver of the car behind came up and started yelling at Carlos. Given the commotion, a policeman standing at the junction came to investigate. We expected Carlos to pull over when the lights changed, but when they did, Carlos carried on until pulling up outside our hotel. Although we could not believe what he had done, Carlos seemed unconcerned. It did not seem to bother him at all.

At our hotel, one of our waiters had taken a dislike to Ray and me. He also had a habit of reaching across our faces whenever putting down or clearing away our dishes. During dinner one evening, Ray said, "I'll stop him from doing that." As the waiter reached across Ray, he grabbed his arm and pretended to bite it. Ray's action worked, as the waiter never did it again.

On another occasion, the same waiter served a fish dish Ray had ordered. After a few minutes, I could smell the fish was off, so told Ray. He sniffed, and said, "No, it's not," and resumed eating. I again told him the fish was off. This time, after having a good sniff, Ray agreed.

He called the waiter over."The fish is off, would you please change it?"

The server glowers at him, and replies, "It's not off; it's fresh."

"It's off;" I said. "You can smell it from my side of the table."

The waiter had a quick sniff, then said, "It's okay."

I chuckled. "If you think so, then you eat it."

The waiter declined, and still protesting the fish was fresh, took it away.

While out one night, a group of us we met up with some American schoolteachers who worked at an International school. The next day, we went to their school for a game of football. While out drinking, this sounded a great idea, but not come the morning when nursing hangovers. Unfortunately, one of their guys came to our hotel to take us down to the school, so we had no choice but to go.

After buying a couple of crates of beer, we slowly weaved our way down to the school. This involved walking alongside the "Dube," an open water channel that brought water down from the mountains. At the top of town, the water was clean and drinkable, but by the time it reached the Souk at the bottom, was full of rubbish and undrinkable.

At one point, someone decided to cross the channel while holding their end of a crate of beer. Their idea was to pull the guy holding the other end into the Dube. This incident became known as "Dube Wrestling," a usual occurrence on our later trips back and forth to the American school.

On our arrival, the Americans made us welcome, and after a livener of beer, we went out onto the bone-dry earth pitch. It was a hot, rough game with the Americans complaining about the hard-tackling by some of our guys. As they could not compete with the speed of some Americans, they used this tactic to get possession of the ball.

I played out on the wing. Here I kept cool by staying under a tree and soaking myself with a nearby hosepipe. Although it was a good game, because of heat and exhaustion, we frequently had to change players.

Sometime later, the Americans invited us to the school for a funfair, organised to collect money for charity. On arrival, we found two camels, which for a small fee one could ride. This, of course, we had to try. I found it a spectacular experience when the camel raised itself off its knees. Then, while sitting astride it, our camel kept turning its head to bite the feet of the person sat in front. Fortunately, it never managed to do so. Had it been able, its huge teeth would have caused severe injury.

That's Colin on the left.

One night, Ray, Arnie, George, Frank and I called in at 'The German Restaurant' for a drink. We found it set up in the open around a dance floor, with an orchestra playing soft music. Although busy, a waiter led us to a table near the back. Over the next hour, we drank 4-5 bottles of wine. Suddenly, George and Frank, known to us as Fred Astaire and Ginger Rogers, stood up. They then started to dance around our table. For us, this was nothing unusual, however, the staff, did not appreciate their actions.

When a short time later, I saw four waiters converging on us, I exclaimed, "Look out, here comes trouble."

One waiter said, "You're not allowed to dance together here! If you want to dance, you have to dance with a woman."

"We would love to," George said. "However, your women are all accompanied by men. I don't think they would like us to ask their women for a dance."

One waiter nodded. "You're right," he replied. "But you cannot dance here; you must leave."

"Leave!" I exclaimed. "We are excellent customers for you. Just look at the amount of wine we have bought."

After a sideways glance, the water said, "okay! You can stay, but please stay sitting down."

A short while later, a group of men and women came in and sat at a nearby table. They were sat talking when Ray stood up. "I'm going to ask one of the girls for a dance."

As Ray walked over to their table, Frank said bet you don't get one."

Ray spoke to the group, then to our astonishment, he sat down and started talking with them. We could not believe our eyes when, a short time later, Ray and one girl stood up. They walked onto the dance floor and started to dance. After the music finished, Ray took the girl back to her table. We all agreed we would not see him again that night. It was therefore with much surprise, when Ray came back, and without a word, returned to sit with us, then picked up his drink.

"What are you doing here?" I asked. "We thought you were set up there."

He scowled. "Oh! I was. The guy said I could go home with them."

"So, why aren't you still with them? You could have been all right there."

"You're right! However, the dirty S.O.B. made it clear I could go with his wife, as long as he could watch." Ray shrugged. "No way I'm into that sort of thing, so here I am."

On the site, the general attitude of the local workers was indifferent to say the least. One incident occurred when a German worker was laying a latex screed in the Banquet Hall. While doing so, two workers came in and started to grind off some metal steps with an angle grinder.

The German called out, "Stop doing that; this is a dangerous material." The two men stopped and then walked away. However, a few minutes later, they returned and started grinding once more. Suddenly, a spark from their grinding landed on the latex screed. There was a puff of smoke, and the whole floor went up in flames. As everyone nearby started towards the fire to help put it out, someone yells, "Look out, there's a gas bottle in the middle of the floor, it's liable to explode."

In an instant, everyone made a mad dash for the exit doors. Arnie ran to one door leading into the kitchen. I watched as he frantically tried to push it open. Although a dangerous situation, I found it comical to see him desperately struggling to open the door.

"Arnie," I yelled. "It opens in, not out."

He turned. With his mouth wide open and eyes bulging with fear, Arnie's face was a picture of panic. In a flash, he turned back, yanked the door open and shot out through it.

After a few minutes and no explosion, several of us gingerly ventured back to see what had happened. To our surprise, the flames had burned out, and strangely, there was no sign of the gas bottle.

"Where's the gas bottle gone?" someone asked.

"The German guy went into the fire and dragged it outside," someone replies.

"He deserves a medal," I said. "The hotel could easily have gone up in smoke."

At a project management meeting later that week, the incident was mentioned. The Hotel Project Manager announced, "The local company is being fined $50,000."

Serves them right, I thought. The P.M. then dropped a bombshell. "The German company would also receive the same amount of fine."

Their engineer jumped to his feet. "What! If it was not for our guy, we could have had a major fire on our hands."

"Yes, and that's why you're also fined. If your guy had stopped working when the grinding works started, the fire would not have occurred."

Although the local company's men were at fault, politics played a part. To save face, they also found the German company to be at fault.

Because of no working lifts, there were problems in getting both materials and workers up to the higher floors. Also, there was no running water on site. Given this, the only toilets available were portable chemical ones. These were kept on Level 4, that we used as our material storage floor. Fortunately, we soon had one service lift in operation, with one of our men acting as a lift man.

The lift was necessary because because of stomach problems, our workers needed immediate access to the toilet.

One such incident occurred to Geoff, who was working in the Rooftop Nightclub. Despite his frantic banging and calling down the shaft, by the time it did, Jeff needed a change of clothing.

As these toilets were portable, they required emptying every so often. Although an unpleasant job, someone had to do it. To assist in this, the management offered extra money to whoever volunteered for this duty. To our surprise, Arnie volunteered, with help from one labourer.

Arnie went back to the Cocktail Lounge after emptying the toilets and found his team chatting outside.

"What's going on?" he yelled. "Get back to work!"

"Not likely," someone called back. "You try working in there; the smell is terrible."

Puzzled, Arnie went inside, but then reappeared, holding his nose. It turned out he had emptied the toilets near the air intake for the air-conditioning units. These had sucked the strong stench back inside the hotel. As a result, it took several hours before work could proceed.

Because of personal problems back home, Ozzer returned to the UK. .John, our project manager, decided to send the other joint superintendent back to the UK. After a meeting held with all foremen present, it was agreed that I should take over as Superintendent in Charge. This meant I now had the position first offered to me.

# Part 3

I soon found myself spending my days going up and down the floors in our service lift, checking how things were going. If I felt some people were not working hard enough, I would try and catch them out. To do this, after leaving them, I would either go up or down one floor in the lift, then walk back to the working level using the fire escape stairs. I did this when I thought the French Polishers were taking too long to complete one floor. As a result, I caught them playing football in the corridor. It shocked them when I reappeared, as they thought that once gone, I would not be back. I warned them that if I caught them playing around again, I would send them home. As a result, I never had a problem with them or anyone else due to not working hard enough.

All those who had gone out to Tehran during the winter brought a Parka, it being essential to keep one warm. However, once the weather became warmer, they were no longer needed. As a result, the lads started selling them to the Iranian workers. Due to mine being one of the largest, and Iranians much smaller, it was more difficult to sell. As it happened, it was a good job; I couldn't sell it. As one day we were laid out sunbathing on the terrace, the next day it snowed.

Soon, most of the lads were having lunch while sitting outside around a large ornamental fountain. After eating his, Dave would take advantage of the warm sun to sleep on the edge of it. This was fine, but when it was time to return to work, Dave always had to be woken up. As a result, he was always the last back to work.

I decided he needed a sharp, cold lesson to ensure he went back to work along with everyone else. One lunchtime, Brian and I crept up alongside Dave as he slept. We then leapt up and pushed him into the fountain. Brian then ducked down out of sight, leaving me standing there alone. As Dave jumped back up dripping wet, he was so angry; I thought he was liable to kill me.

"You crazy S.O.B," he yelled. "I'm soaked, and what about my watch?" he added, shaking the water from it.

I grinned. "Well, you said it was a good one; now, you'll find out how good."

After a few minutes, Dave calmed down and went to change his clothes. Still, the trick on him worked, as he was never again late back to work after lunch.

Dave later lost his watch, when out one day, he found he did not have enough money for a taxi home. Given this, Dave offered his watch as security of payment to a taxi driver. After accepting it, the driver drove Dave to his hotel. He ran inside to get money to pay the driver, but when he came out again, the taxi and his watch had gone.

On our asking, the company sent a darts board out from the UK. We then made up a surround for the dartboard out of some old packing crates. Had we but known the problem this would cause; we would never have made it. One evening, we put the surround on our coach as we were leaving the site. On seeing this, the security guard came and demanded it taken off. We protested that we had made it from pieces of scrap timber, and not part of the fittings for the hotel. An intense argument broke out between us when we refused to take it off the coach. Suddenly, the guard put his hand on his gun holster. Seeing this, someone said, "If you want it that bad, you can have it." With that, we threw it off the coach and drove away, leaving it lying on the ground.

Our darts activities took place in one guestroom at the top of the Rainbow Hotel. Because of our drinking large quantities of beer while playing darts, the manager was more than happy to accept this.

Although the matches we played were serious, it became difficult to hit the board after drinking a lot of beer. One person who—strange though it seems—was unaffected this way was Ray. When it was his turn to throw, he would stagger up to the line, stand there rocking on his heels, then throw his darts. Unbelievably, somehow, Ray always managed to get a high score.

Because of the amount of beer consumed during our darts evening, things were always somewhat rowdy. One night, for a joke, Paul decided he would put someone into the adjoining bathroom bathtub. He decided that Brian, who had not yet arrived, would be his victim. After his arrival and drinking copious amounts of beer, Paul started to drag Brian towards the bathroom. On realising what Paul was trying to do, Brian decided not to go quietly and put up quite a struggle. By now, a group of lads had enthusiastically joined in, trying to force Brian into the bathroom. Then, as they were getting him through the doorway, Brian jammed a foot against the doorframe. As he pushed violently backwards, a small table loaded with bottles and glasses crashed to the floor. Despite the broken glass and general mess, the boys were still trying to force Brian through the door. Abruptly, he shouted at the top of his lungs, "Hold it!" I've cut my foot."

On looking, we saw Brian's foot was streaming with blood from a nasty cut. It was a pity that what had started as a joke had ended like this.

"That's a hospital job," I said. "You're going to need stitches." With that, a few of us helped Brian downstairs and into a passing taxi.

"Hospital quick," I told the driver.

On our arrival, all was quiet. As it was about 1-30am in the morning, it was not too surprising. With his blood oozing on the floor, a nurse took Brian's details. Once finished, she said, "Right, please give me 1,200 Riyals for his treatment?"

We were stunned. Because of the amount of blood Brian was losing, we expected him to be treated before payment. However, with it normal to pay before receiving hospital treatment, we paid the money. Then with no doctors on night duty, we had to wait while the nurse phoned for one to come to the hospital.

On his arrival, he took Brian for treatment. When he returned, Brian looked grim. "We have a problem," he said. "They want to take X-rays to check if there are any pieces of glass inside the cut."

"So, what's the problem?" I asked, "Get one done."

Brian smiled. "The problem," he said, "is that they want 4,000 Riyals before taking them."

! It was a lot of money. Even after emptying all our pockets, we did not have enough. This was hardly surprising, as we never needed much money when playing darts.

I asked the nurse if they would take the x-ray first, saying we would pay the bill later. "You have our address," I said, "so you know you will receive the money." However, it was a no go.

That kind of money was only available from one person. We knew Dicky Mint, as he was called, had been saving most of his food allowance money. While we sat waiting, one lad went back to the hotel. Although not amused at being woken at around 2-15 am, on hearing the problem, Dick handed over the money. Once we gave it to the nurse, she took Brian off for his x-ray.

A short time later, he returned. Wearing a broad grin, he exclaimed, "It's OK. There was no glass inside the cut."

"What! You mean, we paid all that money for nothing?" I said.

"Listen," Brian snarls. "If it had been your foot, wouldn't you have wanted to be sure?"

Of course, I had nothing to say.

Another startling event occurred during another of our darts nights. Ray and I decided we had had enough to drink, so left to return to our hotel. As we passed the boy on reception, Ray reached up and ruffled his hair. "Night, night, sunshine," he said.

When the boy reached up to fend off Ray's hand, he said something, but we ignored him. We carried on out into the street, with the boy shouting after us. As I turned to say something back to him, I saw he was waving a large stick. Although Ray and I both yelled at him to go away, he took no notice. He continued shouting and threatening us with the stick.

Opposite the hotel was a Lufthansa Airline Office, with two armed guards outside. I called over to them. "Tell the boy to put down the stick, or he will get hurt."

One guard spoke to the boy, who turned, and still shouting, went back inside the hotel. The following evening we learnt why the boy was so angry with us. It seemed while trying to stop Ray from ruffling his hair; his watch broke. As one of our lads had given it to him, it devastated him. Ray apologised to the boy and later managed to get the watch repaired.

One serious incident occurred to one lad after a darts match. It shocked us the next day when in a trembling voice, he recounted his ordeal.

"On the way back to the hotel, someone stopped and asked me for a light. Then, as I went to take out my lighter, someone grabbed me from behind and forced me into a parked car. It then drove off with me, sat on by two men in the back. Although drunk when I left the darts match, I soon sobered up. When the car stopped, and the men dragged me out, I was petrified. A few weeks earlier, I had read an article in the local newspaper. It said about an expatriate worker found tied up with his throat cut. Given this, I thought my time was up."

Arne chuckled, then continued. "Although the men stole my watch and gold chain, they did not get my wallet. By mistake, I had put it in my rolled-up shirt sleeve, thinking it was my pack of cigarettes. Anyway, after beating me up, the men drove off, leaving me lying on the ground. Once they had gone, I got up and looked to see if I recognised where I was, but it was too dark.

As I staggered around trying to find a taxi to take me back to the hotel; I stumbled into a barbed-wire fence. I realised it must be a military zone, so turned and walked away. As I did, I heard someone shout out. Not knowing what they said, I just called back, 'It's okay, I'm going.'

"A few minutes later, a patrol led by an officer who had been called out to investigate, found me. After explaining what had happened, he had me taken back to the hotel. I then had a stiff drink before crashing out in bed and trying not to think about my lucky escape."

Without a doubt, this was a shocking and disturbing incident. One that made us much more careful when out late, especially after drinking.

One night, Paul chatted up a girl in our hotel bar, and later smuggled her upstairs to his room. Management had employed a guard to stop such events occurring, who would not allow her to pass. Only after Paul bribed him, did he let her go up? However, shortly after Paul and the girl entered his room, there was a knock on the door. It was the manager, who informed Paul that girls were not allowed in the rooms. Although Paul said there was no girl in the room, the manager insisted on searching. On checking, he found her hiding in the bathroom and sent her downstairs. The manager's actions annoyed Paul, for after taking his money, the guard had informed the manager. No doubt forgetting to mention Paul had paid him to allow the girl upstairs.

While Ray, Paul, Bobbie and I were out one night, someone suggested a race to see who could drink a litre of beer the quickest. After a short discussion, we agreed Ray and Bobbie would participate. I felt confident Ray would win, so put my money on him.

After said, "Ready steady go," Bobbie lifted his glass and with a few breaks emptied it. Ray, however, just sat there and watched. I was furious.

Could you tell me why didn't you drink?" I said. "You just cost me money."

Ray grabbed his glass, lifted it, and without stopping downed the litre of beer. I was about to ask why he didn't drink before, when Ray started to bring the beer back up. Luckily, he somehow managed to deposit it back into his glass. The three of us laughed at the sight of Ray sat slumped over the table. Then, amidst muttering of utter disgust and baleful eyes, I turned to Paul and Bobbie. "I'll take him home," I said.

This, however, proved easier said than done. Ray managed to walk downstairs and out of the restaurant. However, once in the fresh air, he all but collapsed. Because of being heavy and a dead weight, I couldn't carry him. Plus, in his state, no taxi driver would accept him." I said, "Ray, listen. We will have to walk home."

"It's no good," he blubbered, "I can't."

I chuckled. "Shut up and listen. You love the music of the Floral Dance; well, that's how we are going to get you home." I draped one of his arms over my shoulder and one of mine over his. I then said, "Right, here we go. Da, da, dada da da."

We then set off back towards our hotel,. Still, even with me holding Ray up, he found it hard work to walk. Also, every so often, I had to stop and catch my breath. At last, we arrived at our hotel. As we crashed through the entrance doors; someone called out, "Look at the state of him. He's even worse than usual."

While someone was helping me get him into the lift, Ray fell against the doorframe, hitting his head.

I laughed, "No problem," I said, lifting him up "He won't feel a thing." Between us, we took Ray upstairs to his room and threw him onto his bed to sleep it off.

# Part 3

One night a crowd of us went to one of our local bars that as usual was busy. While standing looking around, an attractive girl came over and asked if I wanted to dance. This was most unusual. No one had been asked this before.

On looking at the girl, I said, "Why not?"

"Okay!" she said, "but before we dance, you must first buy me a drink."

I grinned. "No problem. What would you like?" I thought maybe a gin and tonic, or vodka/tonic.

However, I was shocked when she said, "I would like a bottle of vodka, please."

"You are joking?" I exclaimed. "That's about 800 Riyals. For that money, I'll dance on my own."

Later that same evening, a few of us went to the bar upstairs. We had only been there a few minutes, when one of the staff told us to leave. He said we were too noisy.

I shrugged. "No problem. We'll go back downstairs. They don't mind us being noisy."

I later found myself sat at a table with a group of Swedish guys toasting each other for all sorts of silly reasons.

The next morning Arnie came and thanked me for saving him last night.

I shook my head. "What on earth are you talking about?"

His eyebrows shot up. "Don't you remember me telling you about the Swedish guy who kept pestering me, and wouldn't leave me alone? You said you would go and have a word with him. Well, I don't know what you said, but he got the right message. He left the club shortly after."

Arnie might well have remembered this, but for the life of me, I did not know what he was talking about.

Another funny incident occurred one night at the Gypsy Bar, another late-night bar we frequented. I noticed one of our men had a beer bottle in his jacket pocket , so told him drinks were not allowed outside the bar.

He gave a grim smile. "It's not for drinking, it's empty. I am carrying it as a means of protection. One girl told me that some guy is going to get me on the way out."

"Well, we can't have that can we?" I grinned. "Don't worry; when you leave, some boys will leave with you."

When we later left the bar, we kept a watchful eye open but saw no one lurking around.

As we walked through the grounds of the bar, we passed a large shallow ornamental pond. Dave chuckled. "I know who can go in there," he said. When Ray came out to join us, Dave tried to push him into the pond. However, as Ray was heavier and stronger, it was Dave who ended up in the pond.

Ray laughs and said, "OK, Dave, give me your hand."

Dave caught hold of Ray's outstretched hand and started to pull himself out of the pond. Ray said, "Oh well, as you're already wet." He released Dave's hand, who then fell backwards into the water. When he climbed out, Dave was soaked.

As we walked down the road, when Dave took off his shirt to wring it out, someone grabbed it and threw it up a tree.

"Come on," Dave pleaded as he climbed up to retrieve it. "That's enough."

None of us had a girlfriend while working in Iran. We were all too busy drinking to bother much about them. That is apart from John, who said he needed a woman. He solved his problem by getting one of his hotel waiters to take him down to "Pussy City." It was a walled-in area and full of prostitutes.

John told us of an amusing incident while there one time. "They took me into a room, where I looked through a window as a selection of girls paraded past. After telling the waiter which girl I fancied, he arranged for her to be sent to a bedroom where I was waiting. When she entered the bedroom and found I was a foreigner, she refused to go with me and walked out. Laughing, he said, "To say the least, I was not amused."

While home on leave, a friend I had asked to look out for a Ford Mustang, called to say he had found a Mustang convertible. After going and looking at it, I decided to buy it. However, when I told Jen about the Mustang, she advised me to wait until the completion of my contract. I thought this strange, as before going to Iran, she had wanted me to buy one. As at the time Jen had an MG Midget sports car, I had refused. Given Jen's statement, with reluctance, I decided not to buy the Mustang.

While shopping in Iran, we didn't have a problem, as the shopkeepers were honest. This, however, changed, one Friday afternoon. A group of our men were in our hotel lobby bar drinking and showing off what they had bought downtown. When one guy produced a gold necklace, an Iranian man sitting with them asked to see it.

He looked, and shook his head. "I don't think its gold."

"Of course, it's gold!" the man who bought it snapped back.

The man shrugged. "Sorry, I think not. Still, if you want to come with me, I will check it out for you."

A few of our men went with the man to a shop, where he tested the necklace with some chemicals. Our guy was furious when it turned out he was correct. He took the necklace back to the shop where he bought it and told the shopkeeper the chain was not gold. He said that unless he got his money back, he would go to the police. On hearing this, the shopkeeper became nervous. He then not only handed back the money paid, but gave extra as well. This was the only case I heard where someone cheated one of us.

After my eventual return from Iran. A ring I bought that was supposed to contain rubies and sapphires, turned out to be just pieces of coloured glass.

In our hotel bar one night, Arnie started making eyes at a woman sat nearby. The woman's husband was not amused and came over and had strong words with Arnie. He and his wife then walked out of the hotel. Shortly after, the man returned and to our amazement, he apologised to Arnie for shouting at him. The man then went, leaving Arnie with his mouth wide open.

We later heard that at the time of the incident, a man from Savak (the much-feared secret police) was present. It seems most likely that the man was told that Arnie was a guest in the country. Therefore, he was not to be insulted. The man must have furious about having to apologise, but in the circumstances, he had no choice.

After a heavy night drinking, Arnie had a strange habit of not getting into bed, would sleep lying on the bathroom floor. The maid had found him like this on more than one occasion. This gave one of our guys an idea. One night, while Arnie was busy pouring beer down his throat, he slipped upstairs. He went into Arnie's room and poured the gravel from a floor-mounted ash tray into his bed. On finding this, when he later went to get into bed, Arnie did his usual and slept on the floor.

The next morning, Arnie laughed as he said, "While cleaning the gravel from my bed, the maid walked in. No doubt she told the other maids that I sometimes lie on a layer of gravel in my bed."

One weekend, our driver Carlos took a group of us on a trip up into the mountains. To our delight, he stopped at a village where there were chairlifts taking people up the mountain. We thought it would be fun to go up, but Ray was nervous of heights. However, as he wanted to go up to the snow level with us, he had no choice but to get in a chair. It was funny to hear Ray squeal in alarm as the chairs swung back and forth, with him more than happy to get off at the top. Although to our disappointment, we found only a small patch of snow there, it was good to be up there enjoying the fantastic mountain scenery.

On another trip out with Carlos, he drove a coach load of us to Quom, which at the time, none of us knew who was staying there. The journey across the barren landscape was both long and tiring. Apart from the odd toilet break and a quick drink, we didn't stop until we arrived.

As we explored the area, we grew concerned about the poor condition of the place. Apart from a beautiful mosque, the town was dirty. All sorts of rubbish covered the open sides of the riverbed next to the city, making it a most unhygienic looking place.

While glancing in the shops, armed troops toting riot shields unexpectedly appeared. It seemed things could get dangerous, so we returned to our coach, and Carlos drove us back to Tehran.

Although this was an unsettling experience, it was nothing to what we would later see during our stay in Iran.

Until our visit to Quom, life had been good. Then one ordinary weekend turned out to be a life-changing experience. Several people spat at us as they walked by, said, "Go home, Americans." When we replied we were British, they apologised.

I had heard of massive demonstrations in some cities and wondered if their attitude was anything to do with this. I soon found it was, when these events spread to Tehran. This turned out to be the start of significant problems in the country. In a short time, the situation deteriorated, with martial law declared, followed by a curfew set a few days later.

On the first morning of martial law, we were on the way up to the site. Then, as we rounded a corner, we became shocked to see a tank parked at a strategic road junction. If that was not bad enough, as we then entered a large square, I gasped in alarm. There lying on the ground surrounded by sandbags was a soldier holding a machine gun. This type of situation was something one usually saw in films, not in real life. It made me realise just how dangerous things had become.

In the evening, on our drive back to our hotel, I decided to take some pictures of the tanks and soldiers. As we approached a parked tank, I stood and prepared to take one. However, one of the heavily armed soldiers standing by it must have had a sharp eye. On spotting and taking my action as a threat, he raised his automatic rifle. I realised my mistake and threw myself back down in my seat. As I sat huddled up, I fully expected bullets to come flying in through the window. Luckily for me and my colleagues, this never happened.

One man sat near me yelled, "You crazy S.O.B., you could have got us all killed."

Strange, but after that episode, I never attempted to take any more photos of tanks and soldiers.

Authorities imposed a prohibition on going outside after 9 pm during the curfew. Despite this, Arthur, staying in the Rainbow Hotel decided to go and to see what was going on. It was both stupid and a dangerous thing to do, which Arthur soon found out. No sooner had he stepped outside, when armed soldiers bundled him back in again. An officer warned the reception manager that if Arthur stepped outside again, he was liable to be shot.

Although this incident should have acted as a warning to everyone, it did not. Geoff, another of our guys at the same hotel, decided to go up to the roof and take some photos of the patrolling troops. As they were driving around in heavily armed jeeps, fitted with a machine gun and a gunner ready to open fire. Geoff ought to have been more aware of the situation.

He later told us, "As a patrol approached, I hid on the roof where I thought I couldn't be seen. Then, as I was about to take a photo, I heard a shouted command. The next instant, the troops jumped out of their jeep and took up firing positions towards the roof. I realised I'd been spotted, and they would open fire if I didn't move. Nevertheless, despite the repeated command, I felt frozen in place. Suddenly the roof door burst open, and someone dragged me back inside the building. It was our hotel manager. He had heard the command and realised someone was on the roof." Geff shrugged. "Had it not been for his quick action, they would have shot me."

One morning, a couple of our men found a member of their hotel staff banging his head against the wall. They stopped and asked him what was wrong. They were shocked when he said, "Last night, my father was in a mosque when troops surrounded it and demanded everyone come out. When they did, he and everyone else was shot and killed."

An even more horrifying incident occurred when a cinema, full of people had the doors chained and locked shut. It was then set it on fire, resulting in over 300 people burned to death. I found it hard to believe people could do such a terrible thing to other human beings.

It was about this time when we moved out of our hotels, to stay up at the Hyatt Hotel, where we took over one entire floor. As I was the senior person, I received a suite, that I shared with Ray. This was great, as we were then safely out of town. Plus, we were no longer in danger while travelling back and forth to the site. Because of the large number of men we had, we required an additional room. After some discussion, Peter, one of our ceiling fixers, agreed to stay in town until one was available. However, given the deteriorating situation, we decided it best to bring Peter up with us.

Frank, one of our senior foremen and Alan, another man, offered to go down with Peter to collect his belongings.

On their return, Frank told us of their harrowing ordeal. "I knew it would be no picnic," he said, "but I never realised it would prove so scary. After agreeing to pay double the usual fare, a taxi driver took us to the hotel. He said he would wait while we collected Peter's things.

As our taxi turned the corner by the hotel, we found a mob playing pass the chair." Before anyone could ask what he meant, Frank explained. "They were throwing a chair through our hotel window out into the street. It was then picked up and thrown through the window of the bank opposite. Anyway, getting out of the taxi, we ran inside and up to Peter's room. While I stood guard at the top of the stairs holding a Bullworker exercise bar for protection , Alan helped Peter pack his possessions. Suddenly, I heard someone coming up the stairs. I was about to lash out with the Bullworker when I noticed it was our hotel manager. Although shocked at seeing me about to hit him, he helped get us out of the hotel and into our waiting taxi. We then made a hasty retreat up here."

"Wow," I said. "That's one situation I feel lucky not to have been part of."

That same night, without informing management, one of our men flew back to the UK. Despite the gravity of the situation, he was the only one who left this way

As the troubles in Iran grew daily, it made the headlines back home. Some parents called for their sons to be brought home. Given the seriousness of the situation, our company contacted John, our Project Manager. They informed him that the choice to stay or leave was up to us men, as we were the only ones who knew just how dangerous the situation was.

John then held a meeting with all our men present. In a sombre voice, he said, "Right, you all know the situation is far from good. Given this, the company has left it up to you guys to decide if you want to stay or go home." He chuckled. "For anyone agreeing to stay on, the company is offering an increased bonus."

That raised a laugh when someone called out, "Is that Bullet Money?"

I stated that we were in no danger as we were well up out of town, and as long as we stayed up here, we would be okay.

The lads then discussed the options. The offer of what was then known as "Bullet Money" was a good one. Despite this, like me, most thought there was little likelihood of the troubles reaching us. After a show of hands, the majority decided to stay and carry on working. The few lads who opted to leave, returned to the UK a few days later.

# Part 4

Living in the Hyatt was better than when living in the hotel's downtown. Here we could have whatever we wanted for breakfast. A tasty fried breakfast followed by croissants and coffee was a great way to start the day. Some lads, however, took advantage of this situation. When they went in for breakfast, they carried bags that they loaded up with a selection of croissants to eat at snack time. The manager in-charge noticed this, so spoke to me.

"Colin, the lads can eat whatever they want for breakfast, but please tell them, food is not to be taken out of the restaurant."

After cooped up in the hotel for several months, Ray and I decided it would be good to go to the Caspian Sea for a long weekend break. When we asked the lads who fancied going with us, to our surprise, only four said yes. In fairness, the prospect of sitting jammed up in a minibus for six hours put them off.

Paul, one of our foremen who agreed to come, asked our hotel assistant manager about somewhere to stay there. He proved most helpful and phoned his counterpart at the Caspian Hyatt Hotel. As a result, they booked us in to stay there.

After trying without success to hire a minibus to take us, I asked Jim, our admin guy, if he could arrange transport. To my relief, he later said he had managed to do so.

To extend our trip, we would depart after ending work on a Thursday evening.

Come the evening of our departure, when we left work and stepped out into the courtyard , we were shocked. Our transport was not a minibus as expected, but a 44-seater coach. On seeing this, several of the other lads decided they now wanted to go with us.

I grinned. "Sorry, but it's too late to change your minds. Plus, the hotel is full."

Laughing, the six of us carried a crate of beer that I had bought from the hotel bar on to the coach. After opening a bottle, we made ourselves comfortable for the long trip ahead. To pass the time, we sang songs while drinking the beer. Although the latter didn't last long, this was not a problem. We were happy just to be making the trip. After driving for a couple of hours up through the mountains, our driver stopped for dinner at a small, roadside cafe. Although the meal tasted okay, I felt sure the meat in the stew was a goat, not lamb or beef.

When we finally pulled into the car park of the Casspian Hyatt Hotel, it was around 11-45 pm. I thanked our driver and arranged for him to pick us up early Sunday morning. By leaving then, we would be back ready to start work on the Monday morning.

Despite feeling tired from our long trip, we were in high spirits when we entered the hotel. We were all looking forward to a relaxing weekend as we went to check-in. We had decided that after a quick shower, we would meet up for a drink in the lobby bar. Our plans were dramatically changed when the receptionist said, "I'm sorry, gentlemen, but we have no vacancies! We're fully booked."

Paul smiled and said, "That's all right, we have reservations in the name of Mr Paul Howard."

Her eyebrows shot up and she replied, "Oh! I am sorry, Mr Howard, but we have let your rooms to other guests." She then said, "When you did not arrive at 6 pm, as you said, we thought you had changed your mind about coming."

To say we were upset would be a colossal understatement. After working all day, traveling for almost six hours, we were now told we had no accommodation. In a tight voice, Paul said, "I did not say we were arriving at 6 pm, that's the time we were leaving Tehran. We didn't know what time we would arrive here."

The receptionist shook her head. "Well, I am sorry, sir, but we have no other rooms available! You will have to go back to Tehran."

"That's not possible," I interjected. "Our driver has gone and will not return until Sunday morning."

The receptionist said, "Well, I am sorry for the misunderstanding, but we still don't have any rooms." With that, she called for the manager. Our annoyance turned to anger when he arrived and repeated the receptionist's words: "Sorry, no rooms available."

I could not believe the situation we found ourselves in. "Right, Paul," I growled, "You made the booking, you sort it out while we go and have a drink, we need one."

We then stalked off to find a bar, muttering dire threats what we would do if our rooms problem were not resolved.

The five of us were sitting in the lobby bar, nursing a beer, when Paul and the manager came over to us.

Paul smiled. "Well, good news. I think we have a solution. I've explained to the manager that although we realise it was not his fault they let our rooms, it's his responsibility to sort things. Given this, he has offered us the use of the 'Royal Suite.' After looking at it, we could manage okay." Paul winked at us on the manager's blind side as he turned to him. "Of course, if we accept your offer, we will expect some perks for our inconvenience. Like some free drinks."

No doubt the manager was far from pleased with the prospect of having six men drinking free in his bar. Nevertheless, it would at least resolve his problem.

With apparent reluctance, he said, "As the chambermaids are now off duty, it will take a while to get the extra beds taken up and prepared." He shrugged, "Until they are, please have a drink on the hotel."

! What could we say? But thanks. After finding our way to the Cocktail Bar, we knocked back several Old Fashioned and Tom

Collins.' We were just getting into the swing of things when the manager returned to say the suite was ready.

On entering the Royal Suite, although cluttered with the extra beds, it still looked great. As Arnie was a snorer, we let him have the main bedroom, while George, being the oldest, we gave him the guest bedroom. The rest of us picked one of the army style cot beds that had been set up in the lounge.

Although a long tiring day and past 1 am, we decided to change and see what was going on downstairs. We found a casino, but they would only let in the three of us who was wearing ties. Luckily, I was one of them.

The interior of the casino was glitzy, with well-dressed men and women gambling at the various tables. My eyes widened, when I noticed the huge amounts of money being bet. It let me see how the other half lived.

After watching the action for a while, we returned to our suite. Before settling down for the night, I looked out from our balcony. Down below, I could see a fancy-shaped swimming pool. Next, to it, a wide terrace led down to a dimly lit sandy beach where numerous flags and buntings advertised Winston cigarettes. From signs I had seen in the lobby, they were promoting a Windsurfing competition this weekend.

From our balcony the next morning, I was surprised at the unusual shape of our hotel. Instead of being straight, the hotel curved in length and stood eight stories high. Each floor stepped back like a pyramid. As I watched, a pair of workers appeared. To my astonishment, they started to wash down the glass roof of the balcony they were standing on. My amazement rose, when on completing it, they dropped onto the one below. The glass must have been extremely strong to allow them to do this. The men engaged in activities that were highly risky, as they lacked any safety harnesses or ropes.

After a leisurely breakfast, we decided to show off our bodies by the pool. Ray, who had brought his video camera, filmed the lads playing around in the pool. After a while, he said, "This is no good, I've taken lots of films, but I'm not in any."

"No problem," I said. "I'll take some film of you with the boys?"

After he showed me how to operate the camera, Ray jumped into the pool. I filmed him and the boys for a few minutes then swung the camera around. I had noticed a group of bikini-clad girls sitting in deck chairs on the other side of the pool. Just as I started to film them, Ray looked up. When he saw where the camera was pointing, he yelled out. "Don't take them; my wife will see that film when I get home. She will kill me if she sees them on it."

At this, the girls burst out laughing at Ray's obvious discomfort.

Later, after a lazy day relaxing in and out of the pool, we enjoyed a few drinks with our dinner in the restaurant. It felt great being able to sit and relax without having to do anything.

That night in our suite we had a good laugh about the events since our arrival. Although things had not started well, everything had turned out okay.

The next morning, we made our way to the beach. The sea was rough, with a strong crosswind curling off the top of the waves, sending spray flying in all directions. As I had never seen live windsurfing before, I looked forward to seeing how the competitors would manage in such treacherous conditions.

Because of the adverse weather, only a few people were on the beach. Competitors wearing colorful wetsuits huddled around and talked. No doubt about if they could race or not.

As we watched, one guy decided to brave the conditions and made his way to the water's edge. No sooner had he climbed onto his board, when he shot off like a rocket. An instant later, because of the rough seas and strong winds, he became swept off his board and lost from sight. Fortunately, he re-appeared, after managing to get ashore, further down the beach, and someone brought him back to where we were. As a result, I, for one, was not surprised when the organisers wisely cancelled the event.

The following morning, after a relaxing weekend, we paid our bill and went outside we where our driver was waiting to take us back to Tehran. With it daytime, we could enjoy the fantastic views as we went up and over the mountains.

When they heard about our experiences, several of the lads said they regretted not having accepted our invitation.

In the meantime, due to the worsening problems downtown, as the Hyatt was way up out of town, people regarded it as safe. As a result, large numbers of people were booking in at our hotel. It became so busy that no sooner had we completed fitting out one of the guest floors; than the rooms became filled with waiting guests.

Unfortunately, as some of the electronic entrance door locks were faulty, we could not open ten rooms. I had expected a specialist from the lock company in England to arrive to sort out the problem. However, as time passed without his arrival, the assistant manager became desperate.

"Colin! Is there any way you can open the doors. We need as many rooms as we can get." He then accompanied me while I checked the make-up of the doors and frames. After looking, I grinned. "I could," I said, "but it will cause a certain amount of damage to the doorframe."

He gave a broad smile. "Colin, as long as you can repair whatever damage occurs, then it's okay with me."

Given his approval, I took a couple of men to the first room. "Okay, stand back," I said, and then gave the door a hard kick by the lock. The timber doorstop around the lock plate splintered, then broke apart, sending the door crashing open.

On inspection, I was pleased to find the solid timber door undamaged, with only minimal damage to the doorframes. After instructing the lads to repair the damage and change the lock, I then opened the rest of the locked doors using the same method. Although crude, it proved effective, with the Manager delighted when informed he could now use the rooms.

One incident that could have ended in disaster occurred when some of our guys became fed up with having to stay in our hotel. They decided to take a trip down to the town, which, given the present situation, was stupid to say the least.

On their return, one said, "All seemed okay as we walked around the shops, until a mob appeared around a corner, coming towards us. We turned and ran back the way we had come." He gave a grim smile. "It proved no help, for as we turned another corner, we found another mob approaching from that direction. In desperation, we tried to get into a shop for safety, but no shopkeepers would let us in. After managing to force our way into one shop, we ran out through the back door." He shrugged. "After a scare like that, we lost no time in finding a taxi to return here."

The story that they shared was frightening and left us all feeling uneasy.

# Part 5

During one of my leave trips home, my wife and some friends met me at Heathrow. While having a drink and a chat before going home, my friend's wife noticed I looked puzzled at something Jen had said.

She remarked on this to my wife, who asked, "Have you received any letters from me recently?"

I shrugged. "No! Since the troubles started in the country, no one has received any mail."

She smiled and said, "Oh! So you don't know that I've bought a house?"

"You're what!" I gasped.

She then explained. "You remember those houses being built near Sue and Mike's house in Plymouth? Well, I bought one of those. Or what I mean is, I've paid a deposit on one. I've planned for us to go down to Plymouth tomorrow to look at it."

To say her statement took me aback, would be a huge

understatement.

When we later went and looked at the house, I was not

Impressed. "I have bigger cupboards back home than the size of this third bedroom," I said to the saleswoman. "Can we look at a four-bedroom house?"

"I'm sorry, but we have no four-bedroom houses left." She shrugged. "Even if we did, the bedrooms are no larger than these."

After some discussion, despite my reservations, I decided a home was a better buy than a Mustang convertible, so we agreed to buy the house.

On my return to Iran, a group of us were enjoying a drink in the lobby area when a cheer went up. On looking, I noticed George and Frank, alias Fred and Ginger, were waltzing around together. Just then, the assistant hotel manager, who, as usual was wearing a big smile, walked in. On seeing the boys dancing, his smile changed to one of alarm. He turned, looked around, then on seeing me, he hurried over to our table.

"Colin! Colin! I understand that your guys are frustrated with having to stay in the hotel, but keep in mind that this is a luxury hotel. We cannot allow this sort of behaviour. Please remind your men that if they misbehave, they will not be allowed to drink here." He gave a grim smile. "That, as you well know, will mean them not being able to drink at all."

I gave him an apologetic smile. "Sorry, but its Ray's birthday next week. They are just getting in some practice."

His faced dropped, then brightened. "How would you like the use of one of the meeting rooms for the party?" he asked. "If so, I'll get Peter the chef to sort out some food." Before I could speak, he added, "What about roast beef and Yorkshire pudding?"

Although shocked by this unexpected offer, it was not one to turn down. "That's very kind, and of course, we are happy to accept your most generous offer."

"Now, what about drinks?" he asked, "Apart from beer, do you want any spirits?"

"No thanks, an ample supply of beer will be enough," I said. I knew that we would, of course, bring along some bottles of vodka.

On our later entering the meeting room, we found Peter the chef had done us proud. Two separate tables with a cook wearing a chef's hat stood in front of each, ready to carve a large joint of roast beef. Alongside were dishes of assorted vegetables and jugs of steaming hot gravy. The whole thing looked delicious.

Ray, Arnie, George, the German P.M., and his English girlfriend, (she being the only girl present) plus me, sat at one table. As the lads slowly drifted in, they sat at the various tables set up around the room.

I had given Ray a bottle of vodka as a birthday present, as did a couple of our other men. We were drinking this when the manager walked in. When he noticed the bottles of vodka on the table, his smile changed to a deep frown.

He strode across to our table and with a touch of annoyance said, "Colin! You told me you didn't want any spirits."

I looked up. "I did," I said, "because I knew Ray would receive some bottles of vodka as presents."

He then explained there was a problem. "Colin, we normally charge for opening bottles of spirit."

I chuckled. "That's alright," I said, "We'll pay it!"

He gave a grim smile. "I don't think so, Colin, the cost is 1200 Riyals per bottle."

My mouth dropped open. "How much?" I gasped. "We only pay 100 Riyals to buy a bottle." Before I could recover, he said, "Look, how many bottles do you think Ray will receive tonight?"

I shrugged. "About five, I guess."

"Okay! In that case, I won't charge you, but please, only five bottles."

I had thought we were going to have a big problem, so this came as a big relief. Before he left, I thanked him for making things right for the night.

Several of the men had made comical presents for Ray. It was funny watching and listening to them making their speeches as they handed them to him.

One lad gave Ray a life-size blow-up rubber doll, which caused amusement. He had brought two from the UK, but sold one. The one he brought was now wearing make-up supplied by one maid, with the lads doing a great job in making it look funny. During the evening, several of them used it as a dancing partner, which caused much laughter and several ribald comments.

The party was a great success. With plenty of beer, pleasant music, and excellent food. For sure, Ray's birthday was one to be remembered.

Only one incident spoilt our night's fun. It involved Jim, one of our younger men. I had warned everyone that the management had good at providing us with the meeting room. Therefore, I had assured them that no one who was drunk would go out into the main lobby. Jim, however, became drunk, and despite several warnings, kept going outside and had to be brought back in the lads. When I heard about this, I was furious, so I went to sort him out.

When Jim, our Admin guy, heard I was on the warpath, he bundled Jim into a bedroom. However, on being told where he was, I went and banged on the door. Jim, who was inside with him, refused to let me in.

"If you don't open the door," I yelled, "I'll break it open."

Realising I meant it; Jim opened the door. "Okay, if you want to hit him go ahead," he said, then stepped aside.

I went in and shut the door behind me. "What do you think you're doing, Jim? You've ruined the evening."

He shrugged. "Well, he's my mate. I thought they were going to beat him up, so I had to help him," he said.

I don't know what you're talking about," I snapped. "We're all mates here, and we don't go around beating up our mates." After talking to him for a while, I opened the door and went out, shutting the door behind me.

One lad who was waiting outside asked, "What happened?"

"Nothing," I said. "Leave him alone."

The next morning, I became shocked to hear Jim had resigned and asked for a ticket home.

"What!" I exploded. "He's not going anywhere. I need him to help finish the project." I then stormed off to find him. When I did, I said, "What the hell is all this about you, resigning?"

He looked downcast. "Well, after me being a problem last night, I thought it best I went," he replied.

"Forget it," I snapped. "You're not going! I need you here. I picked you as one guy to stay on. You're a good worker, so don't even think about leaving. Get back to work."

Jim looked both sheepish and relieved. "Thanks, Col, you won't regret my staying. I promise I won't cause you any more problems."

By now, we had completed a significant portion of the project, and I needed to reduce the size of our team. I had picked out a group of men to stay on, with the rest being sent back to the UK. To my surprise, one lad came and pleaded to be kept as one to remain.

"Col, I desperately need to stay on as long as I can," he said. It puzzled me until he explained. "On my last trip home, my doctor told me I'm going blind. As this will be my last job, I need to earn as much money as possible before I'm unable to work."

His news shocked and saddened me. However, as he was a good worker, I had no problem in saying he could stay on.


As all our return flight tickets to England included a stopover, a few of the lads decided to visit Moscow.

The night before they left, we had a farewell party for them, which resulted in them arriving at the airport, about two hours after stopping drinking. I later heard one was so drunk; he required help to both get on and off the plane.

I later met up with Geoff, one of the other lads who was part of the group. He said, "When I boarded the plane to Moscow, I never realised it would be so cold. I only wore a pair of trousers and a T-shirt." He shuddered on remembering. "I froze all the time I was there, and not sorry when I left to fly back to England."

In the meantime, the problems in town appeared to be getting worse. Every day, we heard the rattle of automatic gunfire and smoke rising from numerous fires. While looking across at the prison behind us one day, we saw what appeared to be piles of bodies lying on the parade ground. As I watched one day, a bulldozer pushed them into what we assumed were mass graves. Although only speculation, all who witnessed these scenes agreed this was what it looked like.

Because of the risk of attack on our hotel, a machine gun post was set up at the hotel entrance driveway. Given this, seeing armed soldiers standing around the driveway was nothing unusual.

One Friday morning, Ray and I had booked a taxi to take us where we could ride a cable car up into the snowy mountains. As we were about to go outside, an army truck pulled up at the top of our drive. We were shocked when a group of heavily armed soldiers emerged from the army truck. Then, as we watched, they took up defensive positions, blocking off the top of the drive. The events left me feeling disturbed and unsettled. We had never witnessed anything like this before.

"That's it then," Ray said, looked downcast. "No trip today."

I glanced back out the window. "No, it's okay, they're facing out, not in. Come on; it's time we went." With that, I walked out of the hotel and proceeded up the driveway towards the soldiers. On glancing behind, Ray hanging back, so beckoned him on. As I reached the line of soldiers holding sub-machine guns at the ready;

although short in stature, they seemed to be 10ft tall. I smiled as I casually walked through them towards the taxi rank. As I did, a waiting taxi driver came down to meet me.

On turning back to look for Ray. I noticed he had still not reached the line of soldiers.

"Come-on Ray," I called out. "It's okay; hurry up." On turning, I then noticed the taxi driver was not the one I had booked for our trip. On told him we had booked a driver to take us to the cableway, he said, "As he is not here, I will take you."

We watched as Ray reached the line of soldiers and hesitantly move between them. Suddenly, one soldier turned towards him, waving his gun and shouting. Ray stopped dead in his tracks, shot his hands up, then stood there, shaking like a leaf.

As the taxi driver ran towards them, he called out something to the soldier. After what must have seemed like a lifetime to Ray, the soldier turned away from him. When the driver reached Ray, who stood like a statue, he grabbed hold of his arm and pulled him up to where I stood.

Ray was still shaking with fright when our taxi pulled away and drove off up the road."I thought he was going to shoot me," Ray spluttered. "I thought I'd had it."

"You should have seen yourself," I said, laughs. "You looked terrified."

"Looked," he cried. "Believe me, I was."

After about a half-hour later, we reached the base of the cableway. Our driver told us that it was privately owned and had only recently opened.

As we went to board the cable car, I felt a wave of excitement to see the cables disappearing high into the clouds obscuring the top of the mountain. I thought it would be a trip to remember.

By now, Ray had calmed down, and although scared of heights, did his best to sit back and relax. Initially, the trip was smooth, as the cable car went up parallel to the mountain. However, on reaching and passing the top pylon, it then started to cut across a valley. As it did, our car dropped a few feet. Ray squealed. "I don't like this!"

I laughed at his discomfort. "Relax, you can't get off, so sit back and look at the view. It's fantastic."

It was a long trip to the top, with Ray relieved when we arrived there. As we climbed out of the cable car, it felt fantastic breathing in the crisp, fresh air.

We found many people walking around, with children laughing and playing in the snow. I thought it a typical scene, but then I had to look twice. Women in traditional long black robes were walking through the snow wearing sandals. It may not have been that cold, but to me, it was far too cold to be wearing sandals.

As we gazed around, admiring the scenery, I noticed another section of the cable car system that disappeared higher up in the mountains. However, to my disappointment, a man said this section would not be open for another six months.

On our return down to the base, we climbed into our waiting taxi. To Ray's relief, by the time we arrived back at the Hyatt, only a couple of soldiers who always stayed with the machine gunner were there.

To save the monotony of eating hotel food every day, Big Jess, so named because of being the tallest man among us, bought a slow pot roaster. Although I felt nervous when he went to a nearby village to buy meat and vegetables, Jeff thought nothing of it. After preparing them back in his room, he would leave them to cook during the day. As a result, Jeff had a hot meal waiting when he finished work. He was the only one of us who ever went out alone like that, which, given the circumstances, I thought dangerous.

Despite all the troubles in town, work on the site progressed well. We ended up with two fitting-out teams. One consisted of

Geordies from around the Newcastle area, with the other from different parts of the country. They were constantly racing each other to see who could complete fitting out a floor the quickest. As a result, they reduced the number of days taken from fourteen down to ten, with no loss of quality.

Unfortunately, because of the ever-worsening situation in the country, we could not get materials sent from the UK out of customs. As a result, we were running short of the items we needed. It was a pity, as by then we were working on completing the last floor, level 4, our old storage area.

About this time when the assistant manager informed me about a religious occasion that was coming up. He explained that it involved a procession, during which self-flagellation occurred. Given this, he said the present situation could get even worse. He then made me think, when he said, If the mobs decide to come up from town and attack the hotel, we could find ourselves in serious danger. As it was, they had already attacked all the other hotels except one up in the mountains near ours.

On hearing this unsettling news, I called the British Embassy for their advice. To my surprise and disbelief, an official, in an arrogant tone, said, "No need to worry old boy. The Shah will soon get things back to normal." I did not believe this for one minute, so I then phoned the American Embassy. Here, I received an entirely different reply. "Get the hell out of Iran, son; the shit is going to hit the fan."

# Part 6

Given this, I told John and Jim that I thought the time had come for us to call it a day and leave the country. They agreed, with Jim starting preparations for our departure. While checking what flights were available, he heard some unsettling news. One of the few remaining airlines still operating was going to close down. As he could not find out which one, Jim wisely booked flights for everyone on two different carriers.

Before leaving Iran, we had to clear out all of our hotel rooms and also get rid of our canteen benches and tables. The latter was no simple task, as the tabletops consisted of sheets of eight' x 4' plywood. On checking, I found the quickest and easiest way to get everything out of the building, would be to throw it out from a fire escape window. All being well, it would land on the wasteland behind the hotel.

After breaking down one table, we threw the top out. I watched with bated breath as the top floated down, then gasped in horror, as it turned back towards the hotel. Then to my relief, it turned away and crashed to the ground. We then threw out the remaining tables and benches in the same manner. Thankfully, all landed in a heap without hitting the side of the hotel.

Later, as I proceeded through the rooms, I was stunned There were mountains of abandoned clothing, numerous empty bottles, and a variety of rubbish. As we had no rubbish bags, we picked up armfuls, carried it to the fire escape window and threw it out.

On hearing the crash of the falling tables and benches, some locals came had come to investigate, and picked up whatever they wanted. When we started to throw out piles of clothing, this acted as a magnet, with more people arriving. They would dart in to pick up various items as soon as they hit the ground. Because of the possibility of empty bottles being mixed in among the clothing, we shouted out a warning before throwing anything down.

The night before leaving Iran, we had a leaving party, which, because of the excitement of leaving, everyone had a good drink.

Come the morning; because of the tense situation, I felt concerned about our getting downtown and through security at the airport.

Although we passed through several areas thronged with crowds, the trip proved uneventful.

After unloading our toolboxes and suitcases from the coach, we then pushed through the crowds waiting outside. Inside the terminal, we found it packed with people all desperate to get out of Iran. We then went through what seemed like endless security checks before reaching the check-in desk. Once checked- in, I felt relieved when handed my boarding pass.

While waiting to board, everyone was in high spirits. All around, the sound of crying and strained, shrill laughter could be heard above the chatter of hundreds of people all desperately waiting to escape. Everyone was anxious to get on board a plane and leave the country. Although things were bad, everyone knew they could quickly become far worse. It was the uncertainty of the unknown that made people so nervous.

As we waited, Arnie, who had bought a sizeable decorative knife as a souvenir, took it out and started to wave it around in his excitement. A stern-faced security guard came and took away the knife, and told Arnie to sit down. A few minutes, later, Ray took out a Swiss army pocket knife and started bragging-how they had taken away Arnie's knife, but he still had his. Seeing this, the same security guard who had taken Arnie's came and took Ray's knife. He then gave us all a sharp warning.

"If any of you causes any more trouble, the person involved won't be allowed to board the plane."

Funny, but all our guys became quiet. They either stood or sat on the floor until it was time to board their respective planes.

While Arnie, Ray, and I were going to take an extended stopover in Rome, several of our lads were also on our flight. They however, would only stay the night in Rome, and then fly on to England.

As the plane lifted off from the runway, an enormous cheer erupted, with people clapping and laughing. The relief of leaving Tehran was just too much. Shortly after take-off, Ray, who was drunk, got out of his seat and started to annoy everyone on-board. He would go up to people sat in their seats and put his arm around them. Then, in a drink-slurred voice, would said, "All right, sunshine, how are you doing? Don't worry; you're safe now; we have left Iran."

His actions became so bad, passengers complained to the flight attendant, who came and told Ray to sit back down. This he did for five minutes, then he would get up and repeating his previous actions. Despite both stewardesses and stewards repeating instructions, Ray continued to cause a nuisance. It only ended when the pilot came back from the flight deck. He warned Ray that unless he sat down and kept quiet, he would have him arrested when we landed at Rome. I felt sure, that had Ray continued being a nuisance; the pilot would have pushed him out of the plane without a parachute. For sure, there would have been no shortage of helpers.

Much to everyone's displeasure, including Arnie and me, not until we started our descent to Rome International Airport, did Ray fall asleep. We then had to wake him after we had landed.

After the three of us spent an enjoyable time in Rome seeing all the sights, we returned to England.

Peaceful Qatar

# Chapter Two

After Christmas, I went to our company's office . Here I learned that we had a contract to furnish the Ramada hotel in Doha, Qatar. My boss had anticipated the Shah's successful response to the rebellion, so had expected me to finish work on the Hyatt upon my return to Iran. As a result, he had given the contract to Arnie. Unfortunately, back in Iran, a major uprising led to the downfall of the Shah, and the end of the Peacock Throne. So, we could not return to Iran and complete the project. Nevertheless, I was pleased when my boss asked, "Colin, would you object to Arnie taking charge instead of you?"

I shrugged. "No, we get on well together."

"In that case, as you can't go back to Iran, you can go to Qatar with Arnie."

In 1979, Qatar consisted mainly of desert and sparsely occupied. To my delight, I learned that the project was in the capital city of Doha, on the edge of the Persian Gulf. Because of this, I knew working there would prove much different to Iran.

As we were going to fit out various sections of the hotel, we only needed a small team. This consisted of Arnie, Ray, Frank, Paul, Dick, Dave and me, plus Petroch and Nick, two French polishers. All of us had worked on the Hyatt in Iran.

A short time before flying out to Qatar, a colleague informed us, "You cannot buy alcohol there." To get over this, he suggested we take a bottle of spirits inside our suitcases. He chuckled. "*The Customs officials only check hand-carry bags.*"

However, on landing at Doha International airport, a surprise awaited us. After collecting our luggage from the carousel, we had expected to walk out of the airport. Instead, near the exit, an official instructed us to place our bags on a conveyor. I felt nervous when I saw them pass through an X-ray machine. As, one by one, our cases moved through, they instructed us to take them off and put them to one side. Once all had passed through, an official asked us to open them for inspection. On finding our bottles of spirits, he said, "It's illegal to bring alcohol into the country, so we will confiscate them. This I thought was not a good start to our stay in Qatar.

Outside, we found a man holding a sign with our company name written on it. After Arnie spoke to him, he led us to a waiting minibus.

Approximately twenty minutes later, he pulled up outside a villa. Arnie said, "Colin, you and the boys will be staying here. Frank, Ray and I will be staying at another villa." Ongoing inside, we were disgusted to find the villa infested with cockroaches. However, as it was late, we ignored them, picked out a bed each and turned in for the night.

Early the next morning, the wailing from a nearby mosque awoke us. It being something that up in the mountains in Iran, we had not heard.

Around 8 am, after a driver picked us up, he then collected Arnie, Frank, and Ray before driving us to the site. Unlike the 26 story Hyatt hotel in Iran, the Ramada was only five floors high. The hotel stood back from the edge of the main road, with a shopping centre named 'The Centre' located a short distance away.

As we drove up to the hotel, I noticed what looked like a container park, many of which seemed in a poor state. On commentating on this, our driver, said, "They contain materials for the hotel, once emptied, we will sell them off."

The driver then introduced us to Rodger, an English Project Manager, and Art, his American assistant. He explained that an English company was in charge of the initial construction, and an American company would handle the mechanical installations.

As we waited with Art for the lift to take us upstairs for a look around, instead of stopping, it went straight past.

Art shouted out, "That lift's overloaded. I'll have words with you lot later." When it came back up again, we went upstairs. As expected, the rooms were smaller than in the Hyatt, and not as luxurious.

Arnie put me in charge of the 'Gourmet Restaurant.' Although it had a drinks license, Qatar was not like back home, with the sale of alcohol restricted. It forbid premises holding a drinks license to have access from street level, so you could not just stroll in for a pint. Instead, you had to take an elevator or climb the stairs to gain entrance. Only then could you go in and enjoy an ice-cold glass of lager, all legal and legitimate.

To my surprise, I found the 'Gourmet Restaurants' lift, only elevated you about a foot and a half up from street level. However, as the said goes, 'Where there's a will, there's a way!'

I complained to Arnie that conditions in our villa were terrible. He said, "As originally you were not coming, they made no allowance for your accommodation. But, as you're a senior foreman, you will move into my villa."

Although good news for me, it did not go down well with the lads, who had to remain in what they had named, 'Cockroach Villa.'

A few days after our arrival, we all had to go to the police station to have our fingerprints taken, as part of the process of getting our work permits. Although packed, instead of having to wait, we were taken into a side room. Here we were told to line up and hold out our hands. I, for one was shocked, when a man then inked them using a paint roller. With our fingers covered in ink, one by one, we then pressed them onto a printed sheet of paper. An official gave us a piece of paper to clean our hands. This of course did nothing to remove the ink. However, on leaving the police station, we picked up some sandy gravel that removed most of the ink.

On our first weekend in Qatar, to our surprise, there was a party held on-site. Due to plenty of drinks available, it proved a noisy and boisterous affair. On talking to Rodger about the quantity of drinks, he explained. "The respective companies working on the project supply drinks for a party once a month." He grinned. "It's a sort of bonus." As alcohol was supposed to be illegal in the country, it puzzled me how they could buy it.

Rodger chuckled. "You can get a drink permit," he said. "Once you have one, you can then buy drinks from the government registered supplier." He then went on to said, "Alcoholic drinks are also available in specific hotels and bars.

During one of the party nights on the site, Ray and I ended up worse for wear, and did not feel up to walking back to our villa. As we staggered through the hotel grounds, I spotted a bicycle leaning up against a wall.

"That's it," I said with glee. "We will borrow this bike and ride home."

I sat on the bike with Ray climbing up behind, but no matter how hard I tried, I could not get the bike moving without Ray falling off. After several unsuccessful attempts, Ray gave in. "That's it," he said in disgust. "I'm walking."

I shook my head. "Well, I'm not; I'm determined to ride home." Then, without Ray unbalancing me, I somehow managed to ride the bike home.

After breakfast the next morning, I had to return the bicycle to where I had taken it. This proved much harder than riding it home the night before. Whereas it had been late with little traffic, now with it rush hour, the roads were full of fast-moving traffic. On reaching the hotel, only after putting the bicycle back where I had taken it, did I breathe a big sigh of relief.

When I later met Ray, I said, "Bringing the bike back was no joke. Next time I'll walk home."

At the time of my being there, Qatar was a mixture of old and new buildings. The population consisted of more Indian and Pakistani immigrant workers than Qatari citizens.

Qatar was peaceful, but with little to do in our spare time, I explored the town and wandered through the Souk. Here the aroma of spices filled the air. It's narrow; twisting passageways lined with stalls sold a wide variety of good. These included an incredible variety of bright coloured fabrics, including rolls of silk. The colours of which were so vivid, you could not help but stare as you passed them by.

While wandering around, to my surprise, I found English musical cassettes on sale. Not only were they inexpensive, but included many of the present-day top hits, as well as those from the 60s. With them far less expensive than in England, I bought several. One by the 'Bee Gees' 'Night Fever,' contained a track called 'Tragedy. To those who don't know, this song is rather strident.

One morning while Arnie was still asleep, I decided to wake him up by playing 'Tragedy,' so warned the boys.

After turning the volume on my cassette player to maximum, I switched it on. The sudden blast woke Arnie, who jumped up in alarm. Then, on realising what the sound was, he relaxed and slumped back on his bed. H turned and looked at me through bleary eyes. "You frightened the life out of me," he said. "I wondered what on earth it was. Still, I should have known it was you that caused it."

Wearing a mischievous grin, I said, "Sorry, Arnie, I didn't mean to wake you."

He shrugged. "Yes, and I'm supposed to believe that, am I?"

We found Qatari people both friendly and helpful. If they noticed us walking along, someone would usually stop and offer us a ride. While on our way back to the Ramada from a trip to the other side of the bay, a car with two young men in it stopped beside us.

Lowering his window, the driver inquired, "Would you like a lift?"

"Yes, please," I answered. "It's rather hot today." As we climbed into the car, Arnie told the driver where we were going. However, about five minutes later, I realised we were going in the wrong direction.

"Excuse me, but we want to get to the Ramada Hotel. We're going the wrong way."

"Oh," the driver said, "That's on the other side of the bay."

"Yes, but don't worry if you're not going that way, we'll find someone who is."

To my surprise, he said, "It's not a problem. Although we were not going that way, we will take you."

Despite our protests, it was out of their way, they insisted on taking us back to the hotel.

Because of the lack of industry in Qatar, with no pollution, the air smelt clean and fresh. Also, the sea had little in the way of pollution. When standing on the rough causeway jutting out into the bay, you could see a variety of small fish swimming around.

Things in Qatar were excellent, with the extensive new highways leading out-of-town having little traffic. One thing I did not like, was young Qataris putting out fishing lines to catch seagulls. Once they caught and killed the seagulls, they stuffed them and lined them up on the edge of the road to be sold.

Art—who was both helpful and friendly took a few of us one night to a bar named 'Barney's Bar, where we found a live rock band playing. After a while, Paul, who was drunk, got up and started to dance by himself. I burst out laughing when he fell over backwards and landed amongst the drummers drum set. Fortunately, neither he nor the drums were damaged.

During another visit, it surprised us to find a group of young women there. They were, Barney said, nurses who worked at the local hospital. On talking with one, she informed us they were leaving Qatar, to work in a hospital in Dubai, where conditions were more relaxed than Qatar. Although the pay was not so good, they would live in a guarded complex, and allowed to be in at a specific time each night. However, during the day, while not working, they could come and go as they pleased.

Until an enforced ban on alcohol forced its closure, "Barney's Bar" was our regular haunt. Still, despite the ban, we would still go downtown and order a pint, with only one difference. Instead of drinking ice-cold beer, we drank fresh squeezed fruit juice. These not only tasted delicious but quenched our thirst far more than a pint of beer.

We found the construction men a hard bunch, so we're glad when they completed their work and left. Before going, many of them bought gold coins and jewellery to take back with them. When I asked one man why they bought them, he chuckled. "Each time I've gone home on leave I've taken back some to sell."

"But what if customs had stopped you?" I asked.

The smile on his face faded. "I was once! The fine I had to pay wiped out all the profit I had expected to make on that trip."

Large It might well have been a coincidence, but the morning after they left, as I entered the Banquet Hall, I stopped dead in my tracks. I noticed that several of the large fabric-covered wall panels had been slashed. When told of this, the Sheik who owned the hotel offered a $50,000 reward for information about who did this. However, despite this huge amount, the person responsible was not found.

Once all the construction men had gone, Art also left, then started work on the construction of a bank a short distance from the hotel.

After meeting him one evening, he told us about a funny incident on his site.

"I had gone to check on how my local workers were getting on pouring concrete. To my amazement, I found them working barefoot. I felt sorry for them, so I bought them welly boots that I gave to their supervisor to hand out." He chuckled. "The next day, I could not believe my eyes; when I found the men had cut the toes off their boots. On asking the supervisor why, I was left flabbergasted. He said, "*We use our toes to feel the rebar under the concrete, which makes it easier for us to walk around.*"Although astounded at hearing this, what could one say! The men were used to working this way.

One weekend they held a 'British Week' at 'The Centre, with several Rolls Royce cars parked outside. Inside, we found various stands displayed a great variety of items all marked, Made in the United Kingdom. As we passed by a fish counter, we burst out laughing to see a selection of crabs, all had small Union Jack flags stuck on them.

One night there was a violent thunderstorm with torrential rain that lasted for hours. The next day, as we entered the centre, we had to laugh. Buckets, baths, and other receptacles had been put down to catch the water dripping down through the roof. Although we thought this laughable, to solve the problem, the entire roof required coating with a special waterproof membrane.

After we completed some of the guest floors, Arnie informed us we would be moving from our villas into the hotel. This was great, as not only would we no longer have to travel back and forth to work each day, but would also have far better rooms.

When the American workers found our rooms contained the full range of furniture and fittings, while their rooms didn't, they were furious. They informed the management that unless their rooms were fitted out as ours, they would cut off the air-conditioning to our rooms. After various talks and meetings, the administration agreed they would receive the same standard rooms like ours. To me, I thought this the only right thing to do.

While in Rodger's office one day, I glanced out of the window. To my amazement, I saw around thirty men stood in a line armed with picks and shovels, digging a trench. I turned in puzzlement to Rodger. "Why don't you use a JCB to dig the trench.You would only need two men, and get the trench completed far quicker?"

Wearing a broad smile, Roger replies, "You're right, of course, but then, what would I do with the other twenty-eight men?"

I stood wondering what he meant for a minute and then understood. By digging the trench his way, thirty men had a job. Whereas by using a JCB, he would only need two men. Strange though it may sound, the idea was to employ as many of the local workforce as possible.

One Sunday, we were pleased to accept an invitation from one of the Americans to go to the beach. Until then, we had only been around town.

Our transport turned out to be in the back of a large, open truck. Initially, all was fine as we travelled down a wide new highway. It felt good enjoying the rush of warm air blowing our hair everywhere. However, once we turned off and headed across the open desert; the ride became rough. Because of the uneven surface, we were bounced all over the place, and had to hold on tight to whatever we could. With not enough space for us all to hang on to the front of the truck, a few of us tried lying down on the floor. This was okay until we hit a significant bump. We experienced a sudden lift into the air before crashing painfully back down.

Our journey to the beach took about forty minutes, which ran as far as the eye could see. With soft, clean sand, clear blue sea, and massive dunes behind us, it looked fantastic. Also, because of its isolation, only a few people were sunbathing here and there.

We were relaxing on the beach when the sound of a struggling engine broke the peace and quiet. As I turned to see what it was, a jeep burst into view on one of the sand dunes. To my disbelief, it was trying to drive up its steep side. I thought the driver crazy to attempt such a feat, but on saying so, one of our American friends, he laughed. "It's what they call 'Dune Bashing," he said. "It's a regular pastime here during weekends."

As we watched the jeep struggling to reach the summit, more vehicles appeared. Some were on the same dune, while others were on different ones. To see them trying to reach the top of the dunes was an incredible sight. Then, as one managed to reach the top of a dune, we all cheered.

A short time later, we heard another high-pitched engine that came from the sea. A large, high-powered speedboat appeared, which in seconds had flashed by and disappeared from view. As the boat was close to shore and people out swimming, I thought the driver irresponsible.

After spending a while lying on the beach, Nick said, "I'm going for a walk. Does anyone want to join me?" Myself and a couple of other men and said we would. As we walked along the beach, we found a dead snake, about six feet long washed up on the shore. To my surprise, Nick bent and picked it up. "This will make a nice souvenir," he said. "I'll take it back to our hotel and skin it."

"Better you than me," someone remarked. "My wife would not be amused if I took that home."

Nick laughed. "As I'm single, that's not a problem," he said.

As we walked back to join the others, Nick held the snake slung over his shoulder. With him only around five foot four, the snake trailed down his back and onto the ground. On seeing this strange sight, several people gasped in astonishment.

On reaching the lads, I noticed Ray lying fast asleep, snorting and snoring. I had a great idea. "Nick, let me have the snake for a minute." After he handed it to me, I walked up to Ray. Then holding its head close to him, in a loud voice I said, "Wake up, Ray. I have a present for you."

On opening his eyes and seeing the snake in front of his face, Ray let out a horrified cry of alarm. Then, turning away, he leapt to his feet and ran off in terror.

I laughed, then called out, "It's okay, Ray, it's dead."

As on shaky legs, Ray walked back; "Never mind that," he said, "you almost scared the life out of me."

I grinned. "Yes," I said, "but at least it stopped you from snoring."

On our return to the hotel, after Nick cleaned and skinned the snake, he left it laid out on his bathroom floor to dry. He did not think this a problem.

The next morning, after he had gone to work, a maid entered his room to clean and make the bed. On opening the bathroom door and seeing what she thought was a live snake, she ran screaming in terror from the room.

Hotel management then went to investigate the situation. Although relieved to find the snake dead, they were far from pleased about it being in the hotel. As a result, The management instructed Nick in no uncertain words, to get rid of it.

To while away his days off work, Ray, a keen angler, decided to buy a fishing rod. I thought this an idea, so I went with him with our buying a rod each.

The morning , I still felt tired when Ray woke me up to go fishing. "Come—on," he said. "Arnie and I are leaving."

"You go on," I yawned. "I'll join you later." As they walked out, I turned over and went back to sleep.

Sometime later I became awakened when the door crashed open, and Ray stormed in. On looking, I could see he was in a foul mood, with his face red with temper. "What on earth happened?" I exclaimed.

Ray threw his fishing rod across the floor. "The bloody thing broke the first time I cast off," he said. "I then walked all over the place before finding the shop where we bought the rods. If that enough, " he snorted, "the man refused to change it for a new one."

I stifled a chortle. "All right, let me get dressed. We'll take my rod, then go and join Arnie on the beach." Once dressed, we made our way to where Arnie sat waiting. On seeing I had a rod in my hand, He laughed. "Well, here we go again," he said, "second time better luck."

I watched as Ray set my rod up, while Arnie held a hand in front of his face to stifle his laughter. Ray swung back the rod and cast off. I held my breath, hoping it wouldn't break. Nothing happened. Rays' cast was excellent, with the line splashing down quite a distance out.

"Ruddy typical," Ray snarls. "Unlike mine, your rod is okay."

Despite staying several hours, Ray did not catch anything. Nor did either of us during our later fishing trips. Still, we enjoyed the break.

Although while fishing Ray spent most of his time asleep, I guess he would have soon woken had a fish taken his bait.

When we learnt there was a cinema not far away from the hotel that showed films in English, we decided to check it out. As we had no car, and few taxis available, we tried thumbing a lift. We were fortunate as someone stopped to pick us up, then dropped us off outside the cinema.

To my surprise, inside we found it fitted with plush armchair-type seats. These being far more comfortable than those used in UK cinemas. Although we enjoyed the film, throughout , we could hear the crunching of nuts, and the disgusting sound of people spitting. When the lights went on, and we got up to walk out, we were shocked. In front of where people had been sitting, nutshells covered the carpet. It looked terrible.

Ongoing outside, we found it was like being at a racetrack. Cars were not waiting in a queue to pull out on to the road. Instead, they were going up and over the pavement. Then, once back on the road, with smoking tires, they shot off down the road like a bullet from a gun.

Although apprehensive about getting a lift back to the hotel, we were fortunate. The driver who took us drove much more slowly.

As we were not working a full week, we decided one of us should obtain a local driving license. It meant we could then hire a car to get out and about on our days off. I don't know how, but I ended up chosen to get one.

Ongoing to the police station to take a driving test, I found it consisted of an examiner holding up a selection of road signs. The person taking the test had to say what each one represented. All was going well until the examiner held up one, I did not recognise. Seeing my hesitation, he stabbed his finger at the sign. It was pointless; He told me to sit back down and go through the book of signs again. After a short time of studying, I stood up, retook the test and passed.

Unfortunately, by the time I obtained a driving license, we were working seven days a week, with no time to hire a car. Still, despite this setback, I later found it fortunate I had obtained a license when I did. On my return to Qatar several years later; I learned the driving test there was one of the hardest countries in which to obtain a driving license.

As time passed, we worked long hours and a seven-day week. Despite this, it was apparent we could not complete the project within the expected three-month contract period.

After we discussed the situation with Arnie, he agreed to inform the company we wanted a break. Either we would go back to the UK, or over to Bahrain. Because of the cost of flight tickets, we did not expect the company to agree with our returning to the UK. We would, however, be happy to fly over to Bahrain for a long weekend. As expected, the company only agreed to the latter. Arnie then told us he had arranged our flights and rooms at the Holiday Inn.

On the morning of our flight, no sooner had the plane lifted off than the stewards started serving alcoholic drinks. To our surprise, during the short trip, they were kept busy, serving mainly locals.

On arrival at Bahrain, a hotel taxi took us to the hotel. Once checked-in, we went and dropped our bags in our rooms, then went to the bar. Several hours later, I staggered to my room. Although I had intended going down for dinner, I didn't make it.

The next morning after breakfast, we all walked into town to look around the shops. After having lunch out, on our return to the hotel, we relaxed around the swimming pool. At the time, I smoked, using a slim green gas lighter I bought in Tehran. Our waiter had taken a fancy to it, for when we went to settle our bill, he offered to square it in exchange for my lighter. As I liked it, I refused his offer.

The next morning, after Ray and I took an early look around the shops, we returned to the hotel. To our surprise, the boys were not there. On their return a short time later, we noticed that Arnie had two large plasters stuck on his forehead.

"What on earth happened?" I exclaimed.

One boy laughed. "While sat around the pool watching one boy practising diving, Arnie called out, "*You don't know how to dive; watch this.*' He stood up and dived into the pool;.Unfortunately, he was at the shallow end, and crashed headfirst into the bottom. When he came up, blood was streaming from a severe gash in his forehead." He shook his head. "Despite his objection, we took Arnie to the hospital for treatment. Then, after waiting for some time without seeing a doctor, Arnie refused to wait any longer and walked out." He shrugged. "As we thought it best to cover the gash in his head, we called in at a pharmacy and bought the largest sticking plasters they had."

Arnie was fortunate. He did not suffer any side effects from the blow to his head, but it took months before the scar faded away.

When sat in one bar in our hotel, you could look through a window and into the swimming pool. On mentioning this to one of the waiters, he laughed as he recalled the sexual actions of a couple.

"While in the pool thinking no one could see them, they decided to make love." He chuckled. "Unfortunately, they did not know about the window, and only found out when they came into the bar for a drink. As they entered, they could not understand why some people stood up clapping and cheering. When the man asked why, someone pointed to the window. The girl took one look, burst into tears and fled embarrassed out of the bar. As for the man, he was unconcerned. He stayed in the bar, with various people toasting him all night."

"Crumbs," I said. "He certainly had some nerve."

On our last evening, before returning to Qatar, we decided to have dinner in the cocktail restaurant. Here we found a tank full of lobsters from which you could pick one to eat. It seemed a good idea, so we decided to have one each. On showing the waiter the ones, we fancied, he took the lobsters from the tank and into the kitchen. Once cooked and served, not only did the look good, they tasted delicious.

By the time we had drunk a couple bottles of wine and a few beers, we were all happy and relaxed. I am not sure how it started, but one lad took a lobster out of the tank. With it in hand, he then began chasing someone else around the restaurant. The waiters, of course, were far from pleased. I'm sure; they were relieved when it was returned to the tank, and we left.

After checking out of the hotel, a taxi took us to the airport for our return flight to Doha.

As we waited in the all but empty departure lounge, I noticed a man in Arab robes, sat alone on a bench seat. What made him so noticeable, he was drinking cans of beer and quietly singing. With our curiosity aroused, we went over and started to talk with him.

"Why are you drinking?" I asked. "I thought Moslems were not supposed to drink?"

The man explained. *The Koran does not forbid drinking, and like many Moslems, I enjoy a drink.* Given this, we joined him in drinking and singing until it was time for us to board the plane.

Before leaving Bahrain, we had drunk the bottles of wine we had bought. That is apart from Frank, who insisted on taking his bottle back to Doha. Although I warned him the customs would take it away, he was too drunk to take any notice.

After landing , ongoing through customs, as expected, an official found and confiscated Frank's bottle. He must have had a sudden brainstorm, as before our startled eyes, Frank reached out and snatched the bottle back from the customs officer. In a loud slurred voice, he said, "It's mine! You may have taken my last bottle, but you're not getting this one."

As the customs officer reached for the bottle, Frank lifted his arm holding the bottle. Then, before everyone's astonished eyes, he threw the bottle onto the floor, where it shattered into a thousand pieces. Someone stood next to me said, "Jeez, what a crazy thing to do, that's it for him."

"What do you mean?" I asked in puzzlement, as police appeared from everywhere. They converged on Frank, grabbed hold and took him away out of sight.

"They will keep him in a cell tonight, and then deport him tomorrow," the man said.

"But they can't do that," I exclaimed. "We need Frank to finish our project."

The man laughed. "Well, one thing's certain; he won't be around to help you," he said.

As we had no way to help Frank, we left, feeling downcast and concerned, and took a taxi to the hotel. We intended to get someone to go to the police station the next day to see if it was possible to get Frank out. However, when I entered the restaurant for breakfast, to my amazement I found Frank sat there.

"How on earth did you manage to get out of the police station?" I asked.

He grinned. "After the chief of customs had given me a real tough-talking to, he said I could go. When I told him, I had no transport to get to the hotel; he had a car bring me here."

I shook my head. "Well, you were more than lucky," I exclaimed. "A guy at the airport last night told me they would deport you. You can thank your lucky stars that the chief must have been in a good mood. If not, you'd now be on a flight back to England."

One night, the sudden banging and shouting in the corridor woke me. The next minute, I heard banging on my door and Arnie shouting. "Wake up, everyone! Get downstairs quick! We have a major flood on our hands."

I dressed as quick as I could and ran downstairs. Here I was shocked to find the ground floor under water. Fortunately, someone had managed to turn off the supply. Then, using sweeping brushes and pieces of plywood, we started to push the water out through an outside door. With it over four inches deep, this was hard work. It took about an hour before we managed to get rid of the water.

Later, ongoing to the Gourmet Restaurant to check on the carpet installation, I stood in shock. Even as I watched, the saturated carpet that had already started to shrink, shrank even more. To my amazement, a few hours later, the fitted sections had shrunk by over two feet. Had I not earlier seen the carpet well-fitted, I would have sworn it had been cut short. We were fortunate in that after re-ordering more carpet; it arrived within two weeks.

An investigation into the cause of the leak revealed someone had turned the temporary main water valve on full. As a result, the sudden increase in pressure caused a joint in the six-inch plastic water pipe to burst apart. Despite a thorough investigation, like the slashed wall panels, those responsible were not found.

Once the hotel swimming pool was filled, the lads used to make the most of it. Apart from swimming in it, they took delight in using it to play practical jokes. A favourite trick was to dive-bomb anyone who they managed to entice to the edge of the pool. By pretending to be pointing at something on the bottom, the unsuspecting victim would stand to look for something that wasn't there. One lad would run up behind them, jump into the air, huddle up, and then plunge into the pool. The resulting splash would soak anyone standing near the edge. They say little things please little minds, but whatever, the boys enjoyed their little jokes.

While in the pool one day trying to learn to swim, Ray called out, "Colin, you will learn easier if you swim underwater."

On seeing my puzzlement, he explained. "That way, your weight will not be a problem."

Although I thought his idea strange, I decided to give it a go. When I came up spluttering and spitting out water, I found Ray laughing his head off.

"You should have seen yourself," he said. "Your head was half underwater, while your bum was half out."

Still, as Ray insisted this would be a more natural way for me to learn, I tried it again. However, despite my best attempts, I never mastered this method. In the end, I decided it wasn't worth drinking any more water, so quit.

Once we had completed fitting out the restaurants, the hotel brought in their staff for training. To my surprise and delight, they then used us as guests for training the staff on cooking and serving meals. As a result, we could have a delicious English fried breakfast each morning. Plus, with a variety of tasty evening meals to choose from, it made for a glorious life..

Every day, we would listen to a local radio disc jockey who played requests sent in by listeners. This guy was incredible. If reading a request, he didn't like; he would stop. Then, in a dreary, monotonous voice, would said, "Well that's a load of rubbish. Let's see what's next." He would then begin reading the next request.

Sometime later, surprise, surprise, we heard the radio station was appealing for people to audition as a Disc Jockey.

"I'll go for that," Petrich said. "I cannot do any worse than the guy we've listened to each day." He then phoned the radio station and made an appointment for that evening.

The next morning, when asked how he had got on. He said in disgust, "When I arrived at the radio station and rang the doorbell, someone said, via the intercom, *to go away*. Despite explaining I had come for a booked audition, they refused to let me in." He gave a grim smile. "It did not amuse me," he said.

For some unknown reason, from the time we started to fit out the hotel, there was no mains electricity supply. Instead, the power we used came from the hotel's emergency generators. This strange situation became even more bizarre, for when we left the now fully functioning hotel, there was still no mains power supply.

# Chapter Three

A spoonful of danger in Saudi Arabia

My being in Saudi Arabia started when I lay helpless on my back on a mattress in my lounge at home. On hearing a knock on the front door, Jen, my wife, who like me had been anxiously waiting, went to open it. On her return, she led a man who we hoped would prove a solution to my dilemma.

Since putting my back out a few months ago, I had lost my job. As a result, it had left my family and me in a severe financial situation.

The man looked down and smiled. "Well, Mr Guest, tell me how you came to be here?"

Ater explaining how after I damaged my back at work, I went to see my doctor. I had just told him how while lying on the couch, and about to say what the doctor did when he stopped me. I felt puzzled when he said, "Right, now I will tell you what he did."

To my amazement, he then described what the doctor had done. To my immense relief, he went on to said, "I can cure you." Neither my wife nor I knew anything about Chiropractic treatment. It was thanks to our local postmistress that we heard about the Chiropractor. However, I was more than ready to try anything to help get me back on my feet.

To the annoyance of both doctor and surgeon who came to the house to examine me, within two months, he had cured me.

Shortly before I signed off from being ill, I said to Jen, "I'm going to try and obtain a job abroad. I can earn far more money there than in I can England.

Although it would mean my being away from home and the girls for long periods, Jen agreed. As I explained, it was our best chance to get ourselves out of debt and back on our feet.

I then sent my CV to a company I knew that carried out overseas contracts. To my delight, two weeks later, I received a reply, informing me that I had an interview with the Overseas Managing Director. This was great news, with my excited at learning the company required someone for a position in Saudi Arabia.

A few days later, my wife received a phone call from a man asking to speak to me. She later told me that when she explained I wasn't home, the man asked. "Is that you, Jen?"

"Yes, it is," I replied.

To my astonishment, he said, "Hi, Jen! It's Arnie."

My wife knew Arnie from years ago when he and I worked for the same company. "Oh, hi Arnie," she said, "how and where are you?"

"I am in Saudi Arabia," he replied.

"No, tell me the truth, Arnie, where are you?"

"Honestly, Jen, I'm in Saudi Arabia."

"That's a coincidence; Colin's just received a letter re an interview about a job in Saudi."

"Yes, and that's why I'm calling. The person Colin will be seeing is my boss. I would like to tell Colin what salary he should ask for when they meet."

When I later spoke with Arnie, it amazed me when he told me the figure. Never in my wildest dreams did I imagine I could earn that kind of money.

During my interview in London the following week, I met Ian, my future boss. He explained everything about the position, including the salary, which was as Arnie had suggested. After a discussion and a general chat, I accepted a one-year renewable contract, as a Projects Supervisor, based in Riyadh. Then, when Ian said I would be working on a palace for the Royal Family, my eyebrows shot up. I had never worked on one before, so I felt apprehensive when I later boarded a plane on my way to Riyadh.

By going to Saudi, I would earn far more money than I had ever made. It would also enable Jen and me to get back on a secure financial footing. On the downside, I would not see her or my two daughters for six months. After which, I would receive two weeks leave. Although not happy with this part of my contract, I had to grin and put up with it. In life, you can never have all you want. At times, one must make sacrifices on their journey.

On arrival at Riyadh airport, I found Arnie waiting to meet me. He looked the same as when I last saw him four years earlier. However, instead of wearing trousers and an open-necked shirt, he wore a suit and tie.

Arnie gave me a firm handshake and a warm embrace. His brown eyes twinkled as he said, "Hi Col, you're looking good. It great to see you after all these years."

"You to," I exclaimed. "You're looking very smart."

Arnie laughed. "Yes. In my job, I have to be," he said. Then, as we walked out to where he had parked his car, the heat hit me. Sweat broke out on my back. When I mentioned this to Arnie, he laughed. "You'll soon get used to it," he said. He then explained that he'd been in Saudi since leaving our old company four years earlier.

I shrugged. "Had I known you were here and earning a salary like I'm on now, I would have been here like a shot," I said.

Arnie shrugged. "Sorry Col, but after you left Benbow, I never knew where you lived, so I couldn't contact you."

Outside I found Arnie's car was a new-looking Toyota. As I climbed in, I chuckled. "Well," I said, "It's better than the old Morris you used to drive in England."

Arnie laughed. "You will find everything here is better than in England," Col.

As he drove out from the car park, Arnie said I would be sharing an apartment with him and another two of our guys. On the ride into town, I noticed the roads were wide, well surfaced, with modern buildings lining the streets.

From first impressions, I thought Riyadh looked a prosperous city. For sure, it was a significant improvement on either Iran or Qatar.

About thirty minutes later, Arnie turned off the road and parked in a large underground car park. After going up in an elevator to the company apartment, inside, he introduced me to Mike and Mac. They were the two colleagues I would be sharing with. Because of being tired from all my travelling, after a brief chat, I turned in for the night.

The next morning, a driver took me to the head office of our Saudi partner. Here, Ian, my new boss, disappointed me when he said there had been a change of plans. The Palace had informed him that as they didn't know me, they wanted Arnie Ian, my new boss, (who they did) to be the Project Manager. Ian shrugged. "Instead, you will be in-charge of re-fitting out works at the Hyatt Hotel."

Ian and Arnie then took me to the hotel, where Ian introduced me to Sa-ard, our Thai supervisor in charge of our Thai and Filipino workers. Ito my delight, in broken English, Sa-ard shook my hand and welcomed me to the site.

After Ian gave me a tour, he explained what works had to be performed in the various sections. One area, the main lobby, had a high ceiling. Ian pointed up. "Because of the hotel remaining open during our works, we need to install scaffolding," he said. "We can then work overhead, while the hotel guests walk safely underneath. I'll arrange for a specialist scaffolding company to come and install it."

A few days later, they came, erected the scaffold, and provided enough scaffolding boards for our men to install. These I instructed Sa-ard to deck out the scaffolding. However, on later checking, to my annoyance, I found only a few boards placed on top of the scaffold. Also, to my surprise, some of our Thais were walking around on them.

"What's going on, Sa ard?" I said, pointing up at the scaffolding. "Why have you not done as I asked?"

His big, round face lit up with a smile. "It's okay, Mr Colin, we Thais are used to working on scaffolding like this."

I gave a grim smile "You might be," I replied, "but I have to go up there as well. So, get it fully decked out, as I won't be going up there until it is."

After laughing at my obvious discomfort, Sa-ard gave orders for it to be done.

I had never worked with foreign workers before, so I felt dubious as to their capabilities. However, to my surprise, I soon found their work to be of high quality.

Once I knew my way around Riyadh, the company issued me with a Mazda 323. Although a small car, it had air-conditioning, which with the temperature around 40 degrees, made driving comfortable.

While travelling to the office one day, I noticed deep trenches dug out alongside the road. On mentioning this to Arnie, it surprised me when he informed me; they were storm drains. He said, "Although Riyadh is in the middle of the desert, there are periods of heavy rainfall that sometimes results in significant flooding."

Another thing I noticed were rows of empty high-rise apartment blocks. These Arnie said, "The King had built to accommodate Bedouins." He shrugged. "They had rejected living in them, as they much preferred their traditional nomad lifestyle."

Because of the roads in Riyadh being wide and in excellent condition, cars were driven at high speed. Despite this, I observed speeding vehicles slow to allow women wearing national dress to cross a busy dual carriageway. This Arnie said, was normal.

He then explained about a far uncommon situation that occurs in Saudi Arabia than in England. "If you're found guilty of causing the death of someone, you can pay what is known as blood money. If acceptable to the relatives of the deceased, you pay them a sum of money instead of going to prison."

I nodded. "Well, that would be a far better option than going to prison," I said.

On the way home to our apartment one night, a humorous incident occurred. Along with a couple of other guys, I was in Mac's Mazda and following Ian in his big American car. While waiting behind him for a set of traffic lights to change, Mac thought he would play a joke on Ian. He drove his car up against Ian's and nudged it forward. As quick as a flash, Ian responded. Putting his car in reverse, with screaming tires, he started to push our vehicle backwards. As Mac panicked and jumped out in alarm, Ian stopped pushing our vehicle. He got out and laughed, as Mac, embarrassed by his action, hung his head and climbed back behind the wheel of our car.

Ian stooped to Mac's open window. "Next time you decide to play a trick like that, make sure you're driving the bigger car," he said laughingly.

While walking around the shops one Friday, I noticed some men carrying large wooden sticks. Although puzzled as to why they had them, I soon discovered why, when the muezzin in the mosques called out at prayer time.

Where shopkeepers had not covered the goods outside their shops, the men used the sticks to turn everything upside down. It seems these men ensured that when the call to prayers went out, all shops closed. Additionally, the shopkeepers covered any goods displayed outside. Without a doubt, it was a fantastic experience to watch the men in action with their sticks.

At the office one day, it puzzled me when all the office staff, including the Managing Director, left the office. On following them, I found they had gone to pray. This Arnie informed me, was an everyday five times occurrence in Saudi Arabia.

One of our project managers got arrested and put in jail. When I heard about it, I felt disturbed. It seemed they caught him going through a set of traffic lights on red. When I asked Arnie about this severe punishment, his response shocked me, when he said this is normal. "If the police see anyone commit this offence, they stop the car and the driver gets taken straight to jail for three days." He grinned. "As the driver gets no opportunity to contact anyone to tell of their plight, make sure you don't get caught doing this."

Fortunately, I experienced no problems while driving in Saudi Arabia.

After working on the Hyatt project for several weeks, Ian asked me to call in at our head office. Ongoing there, he said a problem had arisen with Harold, one of our Project Managers. He was in charge of a Royal Villa project in Jeddah, and a palace type contract on the outside of the city. Because of this, he wanted me to take over running the Royal Villa project.

A few days later, Arnie and I flew down to Jeddah. As we were in business class, we were at the front of the plane when it landed. As the plane's door opened, an enormous blast of hot air hit me. It felt as though I had taken a shower with all my clothes on. To my amazement, although Arnie wore a suit and a tie, he seemed unaffected.

I exclaimed, "Boy! That sure is some heat." Arnie laughs. "Don't worry," he said, "although it's hotter here than in Riyadh, you'll soon get used to it."

To my surprise, we stepped from the aircraft into a special high-level bus. There being no direct walkways from the planes. Reaching the arrivals entrance, the body of the bus lowered itself on telescopic legs to ground level. To me, this was like a scene in a space film.

As I stepped out of the bus and entered the arrivals hall I found it enormous. To my amazement, Arnie informed me it was the second-largest airport in the world, with Riyadh the largest.

Neither of us had luggage, so we passed straight through customs. On stepping out into the bright sunshine, it felt as though the air had been being sucked out of my lungs. To my relief, we climbed straight into one of the waiting air-conditioned taxis. Arnie gave the driver directions to the villa, and we set off. On the way, I noticed Jeddah was much more western-oriented than Riyadh. There were numerous well-known branded shops lining the streets.

Twenty minutes later, we turned down on to what Arnie said was the Corniche. It consisted of a dual carriageway that ran alongside the Red Sea. To my astonishment, on various roundabouts we passed were massive monuments. One, an enormous bicycle, stood at least thirty foot tall. Another was a gigantic rocket-shaped structure, with yet another of a giant globe of the world. It was a fantastic sight; I had never seen anything as startling.

A short time later, we turned off and drove down a narrow road to the villa. This proved less than a hundred yards from the shore of the sparkling Red Sea. As we climbed out of the taxi, it surprised me at how salty the air was. Even had we arrived at night; I would have known we were next to the sea.

After we met up with Harold, Arnie and I attended a lengthy meeting with him and the chief engineer. During this, both men became angry. They were shouting and screaming at each other, with their noses just a few inches apart. Such a scene shocked me. I felt sure that both men would start fighting., but fortunately, Arnie managed to defuse the situation.

After calming Harold down, the three of us went for a walk around the site. After what I had witnessed, I now understood why Ian had to remove Harold from the project. It was apparent that he and the site engineer did not get on. Later, after a good chat with Harold, Arnie and I returned to the airport. Ongoing to enquire about flights, I was shocked when informed there were no available seats to Riyadh until the next day.

Seeing my discomfort, Arnie gave a knowing smile. "No problem," he said. 'I have a friend here who will sort this out."

As Arnie walked away, he left me wondering where we would stay the night. However, I need not have worried, for, on his return, Arnie wore a big smile.

"No problem; our plane leaves in one hour."

'Like the old saying. 'It's not what you know; it's the people you know.'

After our return to Riyadh, I arranged to take my car to Jeddah. I thought this successful. It meant I would pass through a large part of the country on the way. To my disappointment, because of my Ingmar (work permit) not yet issued and it being the end of Eid, my driver would drive the car down. I would fly down to Jeddah.

On my arrival back at Jeddah Airport the following week, Harold met me, then drove us to the site. With it lunchtime, Harold took me straight to the canteen. One of two English guys sat having lunch looked up and greeted me with a query. "Do you have my passport?"

"No," I replied, "my driver has it; he's driving my car down from Riyadh."

When the man said I should have brought it, I said, jokes, "Don't worry, he can only lose it!"

Without any warning, the man went crazy. He jumped up, sending his chair crashing to the floor. The next minute I felt the icy touch of the end of a spoon pressed tight against my throat.

With flared nostrils and eyes blazing with anger, he screamed, "Don't even joke about it."

I went icy cold with fright. I felt sure he would rip my throat out. However, after what seemed like a lifetime, he removed the spoon and stomped out of the canteen. I stood there in total shock, while from the surprised look on Harold's face, this incident shocked him as much as it did me.

When my driver arrived with the car, I asked if he had brought a passport with him. After taking it out of his pocket and handing it to me, I gave it to Harold to hand to the man.

During a walk around the site, I found Sa-ard and a couple of other Thai workers from the Hyatt in Riyadh were there. In the short time, I had known him; I had found Sa-ard both helpful and competent.

After Harold showed me the various areas of our work, he then drove me to a villa. Here he said I would live until they found me permanent accommodation.

The next day, the man who attacked me with the spoon came and apologised. "Sorry about the other day," he said, "but I've been here six months without a break. I need one before I go crazy."

I grinned and shook his hand. "No problem, I said.

Once Harold had left, I soon settled into a routine. The Thais were doing a great job, with my pleased about the progress.

For meals, I would buy food from a supermarket, where I could buy anything I wanted. That is of course, except for alcohol, which is forbidden in the country. However, as a foreigner, I could purchase pork that was kept in a separate section of the supermarket, and marked for foreigners only.

After living in the villa for a few weeks, along with our Thai workers, we all moved into 'Poon Camp.' With it only a five-minute drive across the sandy soil from the project, it was an ideal location. Here I lived in a Portakabin, with the camp providing breakfast and evening dinner. Our lunch came to site packed in stainless steel containers. Another bonus, they did my laundry free. Therefore, with no bills to pay. I thought this excellent. Unless I wanted to buy something for myself, I did not have to spend any of my money.

A few days after moving into the camp, one-lunchtime, Sa-ard came to see me. As he approached, I thought it strange to see his usually smiling face replaced with a frown. He looked unhappy.

In a severe tone, Sa-ard said, "Mr Colin, can you please help me?" As he spoke, he opened the food container he was carrying. In one section was a small leg of chicken that consisted mainly of bone. The other parts contained a tiny amount of rice and a few pieces of vegetables.

"This is all we get to eat all day," he said. "It is not enough for us to do a full day's work. Would you please try and get us more to eat?"

I became angry. "Leave it with me;" I said, "I will sort this out." On my return to camp in the evening, I carried the food container Sa-ard had given me. On finding the camp boss, I showed him the contents of the container. "This is disgusting," I said. "I get more to eat in my lunch container, and I'm only supervising. It's my men who are doing the work, not me. I expect them to be given far more to eat than this."

He apologised, saying he would instruct the kitchen staff to ensure our men received more substantial portions. From that day on, there were no more complaints about the lack of food for my men.

I later found my company treated its workers better than many from other companies. Unlike them, we never allowed more than four beds in one room. Also, the daily cost allowance for our workers was higher. In return for our company looking after our workers., they appreciated this, caused no problems, and turned out high-quality work.

I liked working with the Thais, and found them a great bunch of guys. They did excellent work without any complaints. As such; they deserved looking after. Thanks to my attitude, I got on well with them.

As I woke one morning, I detected a strong smell of fish, which on opening my door, became stronger. On investigating, I found it came from a 40-gallon drum set over a roaring gas fire. It puzzled me to see an assortment of large seashells beside the drum. A man was standing next to them, so I asked what they were doing.

"We're boiling up the seashell we collect while diving," he said. On seeing my puzzled expression, he explained further. "Once cleaned, we pack them into boxes and send them back to France. Our friends than sell them to souvenir shops."

It must have been a profitable side-line, as I later heard they had been doing this for some time. During the weekends, the Corniche became packed; it seemed as though everyone aspired to be there. Cars would park anywhere they could. It was common to see television sets plugged into the vehicles, with whole families sat on the ground watching TV.

While driving around one day, I spotted two Arabs sat on a rickety wooden table smoking Hubble Bubble pipes. I thought it would make a great photo, so stopped and took a picture.

When I later showed it to Mohammed the P.M., it puzzled me when he inquired, "Colin, did you ask for their permission?"

He then explained that in Saudi Arabia, it was against the law to take a person's photo without first obtaining their permission. If caught doing so, the person whose picture they took could demand the film. In extreme conditions, they could even confiscate the camera.

As I had not known this, I thought it best to reply I had requested their permission.

One Friday, our day off work, one of our Saudi colleagues took me to watch falcons being trained out in the desert. These he said were expensive, and only a hobby for the wealthy. I found it an enlightening experience to watch the different stages of their training. To my astonishment, my colleague informed me that the falcons get taken out into the desert in air-conditioned trailers. After hunting, they are put back in their containers and taken home.

In this respect, the care they received was better than that of many people.

# Part 2

I had no problem on site until Mohammed; the site Project manager came to see me one day. He complained that we had installed a row of door frames out of line. Mohammed, a Sudanese, was a big, powerful-looking man, standing around six feet, and weighing near 17stone. Despite his size, Mohammed was a soft-spoken, gentle giant. However, even after I explained that we had installed them to suit the position of his walls, Mohammed failed to understand. He kept saying we had fixed the frames in the wrong place.

After quietly explaining the situation, and his refusing to accept it was his walls that were the problem, I flipped. "It's your fault, not mine!" I shouted. "If you had built the walls in line, then we could have fixed the frames in line." I then stormed off, leaving him standing speechless.

A short time later, Ahmed, the construction manager, came to see me. He wore a big smile as he said, "Mohamed was shocked at my shouting at him. After he told me about your argument, I told him he was in the wrong. I said what you had been saying was correct."

Later, Mohamed came to see me. As he walked up, his face broke into a big grin. "Hello, Mr Colin, I'm sorry for making you shout at me. I now realise what you were saying was correct; I want us to be friends."

As I reached out and took his offered hand, I smiled. "We are friends."

To my surprise, he pulled me close and gave me a big hug and a kiss on each cheek. "Come," he said, holding my hand. "We will go and have a coffee."

As we walked off, I expected Mohamed to let go of my hand, but he did not. He must have sensed my discomfort, as his smiling face turned to a frown. "You don't mind me holding your hand, do you?" he asked, "It's a sign of friendship."

Although I thought it strange to be seen walking along holding a big guy like Mohamed's hand, I replied, "Of course not, it's not a problem for me."

"Good," he said, as we continued walking along hand in hand.

During a talk with Harold, we decided to obtain a Saudi driving license. As he worked way out of town, I agreed to take care of all the necessary paperwork. However, little did I know what was in store?

I later took the required papers to the police station dealing with driving license applications. Here I found long queues waiting in front of four booths. To my disappointment, none of the signs above them was in English. Therefore, I did not know which booth was for what. As I couldn't see anyone who looked foreign, I joined a queue.

When at last I reached the front, as I went to put forward my folder of papers, the man shut the booth window. To my annoyance, it was prayer time. I didn't know how long this would take, so left and returned to the site. The next day, I again found long queues at each booth. After joining one, I slowly inched my way forwards. I was next to be served when the booth window slammed shut. This time, not for prayers, but lunch. On my return to the site, I was far from happy at wasting yet more time.

The next time I returned to the police station early and joined one queue. It pleased me when the booth window remained open when I reached it. I smiled and gave my folder of papers to the man there.

To my disbelief, the man shouted something and threw my documents out of the window, leaving me shocked and confused. As I collected the scattered papers and put them back in my folder, I wondered what was going on. Then, to my astonishment, a man standing nearby informed me that my papers were in the wrong coloured folder.

On hearing this, I cried out in anger. This had been my third attempt at applying for a license. Until now, no one had mentioned the papers had to be in a specific coloured folder.

The next time I went to hand in our papers, I made sure they were in the correct coloured folder. This time, to my relief, the man in the booth accepted them.

As I had spent so much time handing in our applications, Harold said he would collect our licenses. On his return from going to collect them, he said he had to go to a different police station. Harold looked glum, so I asked, "What's up? Didn't you get our licenses?"

He shrugged. "Sorry, Col, I have mine, but they told me you have to collect your license yourself."

Although put out by this, I had no choice but to accept it. Harold then explained where I had to collect my license. "You shouldn't have a problem to collect it," he said.

The next day I followed Harold's directions and made my way to the police station. As I approached the counter where Harold had told me to collect my license. I found no one behind the counter. While I stood there, wondering what to do, a man in an air force uniform came in. On seeing no one was around, he went behind the counter and started rummaging around. As he stepped back out again, he noticed me. "Have you come for your license?" he inquired.

"Yes," I replied

"What's your name?"

I told him, and he went back behind the counter. On finding my license, he was smiling as he handed it to me. "Here you are, this will save you having to wait for the clerk to return."

Although I could not believe what he had done, he was right in what he said. I thanked him, left the building, and returned to the site.

When I later met up with Harold and told him how I obtained my license, he gave a broad grin. "See, I was right," he said. "I said you wouldn't have a problem with getting your license." What could I say? Nothing. We did, however, have a good laugh about it later.

I found it hard to believe Harold when he told me how the owner of the palace-like building he was in charge of, had an entire village relocated. It shocked me when on asking why? He shrugged and said, "It spoilt his view.Once the project gets completed, he will have thousands of trees planted in its place."

One can only imagine the cost of doing such a thing.

Cars driven at high speed caused two separate accidents, in which it left them impaled on the safety barrier. I shudder to think what had happened to the occupants.

Despite alcohol banned in Saudi Arabia, as with most things, where there's a will, there's a way. Some men staying at Poon Camp, like many others in Saudi, manufacture their own booze. The drink named Siddiqui that I never tried, reeked of aviation fuel. At one time, I witnessed a guy who had been drinking this fall out of his chair and slump unconscious to the floor.

After sent back to the UK, an examination revealed he was suffering from internal problems. No doubt caused by drinking Siddiqui.

On site, while unpacking sections of a large stained-glass dome, we found two broken. First, an insurance agent inspected the damage, and then a stained-glass specialist came from England the next week. It amazed me to watch him worked wonders on repairing the broken sections. In no time at all, they looked like new. Once they installed the dome over the atrium, it looked fantastic when they switched on the lights.

As I stepped outside the villa one day, I witnessed a barbaric sight. On an adjacent villa, as I watched, one of the Pakistani workers slit the throat of a sheep with a large knife. A few minutes later, I was further shocked when he started cutting the carcass into pieces.

On another occasion, I noticed the same man had just slaughtered a camel. Although of slight build, the man-made it look easy cutting the camel into pieces. I thought it would make a photo, so I went to my office and collected my camera. When the man saw me with it in hand, he bent and lifted the detached camel's head. Although shocked at such a gruesome sight, as he stood holding the head up wearing a big toothy smile, I took his photo.

Later, I discovered that Muslims use this method of slaughtering animals by slitting their throat while they are still alive. For those unaccustomed to such a sight, it can be horrific. Therefore, I would not recommend allowing young children to see this.

During a conversation with one of our building contractors, he asked if my company would be interested in obtaining a large painting contract. I said if offered such a deal, we would be. He then took me aback me when he informed his fee for arranging this, would be a BMW car. The specifications of the model he wanted, he would give me once talks were underway.

This was an unfamiliar experience for me. I had never heard of anyone being given a BMW in return for obtaining a contract. However, on informed my boss Ian, he said, "Colin if this man can get us the contract, I would be prepared to buy him the car he wants."

The man did not obtain the contract.

At one time we had a 40ft container arrive on site. 40ft containers from England delivered all items for the project to site. Inside this one was the carpet for the central living area. It turned out to be 44ft long, roughly cut to shape, and folded to get it inside the container. Getting it out proved a struggle. This, however, ended up the simple part. We then had to get it inside the villa. To do so, took all of our Thais, plus me and two carpet layers who had come out from England to lay it. With great difficulty, we put thick pieces of wood under the carpet. Then, with a man on each side, we lifted it and carried it inside.

The next day the carpet men started to lay the carpet. During this time, I received a visit from an official representing the villa's owners. To my surprise, he informed me that he wanted the carpet laid without any joints. I pointed out that because of the two columns in the room, this was impossible. To my amazement, the official said we should remove them. I am sure it disappointed him when I informed him these were concrete support columns, and what he wanted was impossible.

Part of the project involved the installation of a small fountain under the dome in the atrium. The builders having left a hole in the concrete foundations for it to be fitted in. Once we had installed the plumbing bits and pieces, a marble specialist came down from Riyadh. After fitting the marble sections, he then returned to Riyadh. We then completed the rest of the installation a short time before leaving the site one evening. I called Bob, the project coordinator, and informed him the fountain was ready for inspection. I said that I would return to the site after dinner. Bob, who had been eagerly anticipating this moment, said he would come and take a look.

On my return, I expected to meet Bob. To my surprise, not only was he not there, but the fountain was no longer working. Bob's response to my phone call left me shocked.

"On looking at the fountain, I was pleased," he said. "However, as I sat having a smoke and admiring it, the water stopped running. On investigating why, I found the bottom of the fountain had dropped, releasing all the water."

I thought he was joking, but on looking, to my astonishment, I found he was correct. One section of the bottom of the fountain had dropped, leaving a significant gap between it and the side. I returned to camp to seek Sa-ard, who like me, was shocked when I informed him what had happened.

Although most of our men had left camp for the evening, Sa-ard managed to find a few. After they removed the marble sections inside the fountain, to my amazement, we found a large hole underneath. Just how this occurred, I did not know. Still, on looking around, we found an old concrete post and bits of rebar. These we packed tight across the bottom of the hole, then poured a potent mix of concrete on top.

The next morning when I phoned Riyadh, I felt embarrassed when I informed them of the fountain problem . I said, "I need the marble man back A.S.A.P."

On his return, he laughed at hearing what had happened. After he replaced the broken pieces and re-fixed the entire sections, he again returned to Riyadh.

We then reinstalled the fountain after the marble had set solid. I can only think the problem was because of the main foundations not being connected under the fountain area. With the site close to the sea, when the tide came in, it washed away the ground under the base of the fountain.

Apart from that, on completion of the villa, both Bob and I were well pleased.

Shortly before going home on leave, I received a visit from Mick Weavis, the managing director of my company. One look at his face and although I knew something was wrong, I was unprepared for his news.

"I'm sorry, Colin, but I have bad news for you. The company has no available contracts for you after your leave period." He shrugged, "Given this, we have no choice but to make you redundant."

This came as a terrible shock; I had only been in Saudi Arabia for just over six months out of my one-year contract. My spirits then lifted when he continued. "Although it's not yet definite, the company might obtain a palace contract in Brunei. If it comes up, I would like you to work on it."

Despite hearing this, I felt downcast when a few days later, I flew back to the UK. Nevertheless, on the bright side, with it only a short time before Christmas, I would be home with my family for the celebrations.

On arriving home, although overjoyed at seeing me, my wife was concerned about my finding a job after Christmas. I forced a smile, saying we should forget about that until after the holidays.

Although my contract in Saudi had been a short one, it had solved our problem. Unbelievable as it sounds, I had saved enough money to get us back on a sound financial footing. Not only that, but I could also buy a brand-new car for cash. It being something we could never have afforded, had I not gone to work abroad. As it happened, during a recent M.O.T inspection, they found our old car too dangerous to drive, so a new car was essential.

While home enjoying Christmas, little did I know my next overseas contract would be far different from any of my previous contracts.

Hot times in Oman

# Chapter Four

Thanks to Harold, I obtained a contract in Oman shortly after Christmas. The Expat monthly magazine, with its usual overseas posts, advertised it. Although Expats no longer exists, there are other similar organisations. So, if you are seeking a foreign contract, I recommend you join Expat Network or a similar organisation.

The contract in Oman would be a bit of come down, for instead of being a project supervisor, I would be working back on my tools. Nevertheless, it was not a problem; the main thing was to get back working overseas.

A few weeks after accepting the contract, loaded up with my toolbox and suitcase, I flew out to Oman. My ticket was business class, so I felt like the cat's whiskers sat back and relaxing in comfort.

After clearing customs at Muscat Airport, I went outside. I had expected to be met and taken to the Al Falaj Hotel, where I would be staying. To my surprise, I found no one waiting for me. After an hour standing outside with little shelter from the blazing, scorching sun, I felt angry and sweating buckets.

I did not know how far it was in Muscat but decided it best to get a taxi there. The only problem was I never expected to have to spend money on my arrival, so only had a small amount with me. On looking around, I noticed a man who looked American, so went and asked if he knew how much the taxi fare was to the Al Falaj Hotel.

He shrugged. "Sorry, I don't know, but no problem, I'll go and ask a taxi driver."

When he came back and informed me of the cost, I had enough cash, so took the taxi. On the way, when I noticed numerous partially destroyed houses, I asked the driver what had happened.

I saw him smile in the mirror. "The Emir said they were too high, so had them reduced in height."

Later, as we pulled up outside the Al Falaj hotel, I found it looked much better than I had expected.

Entering the luxurious foyer, I crossed to the reception desk. "Good morning, my name is Mr Guest; I believe you have room for me?"

The receptionist eyebrows raised in surprise. "Mr Guest! They said you were not on the plane."

I gave a grim smile. "I was on the flight, but no one was there to meet me."

After checking me in, a porter took me up to my room. What with the flight and waiting out in the scorching sun, I felt tired? However, after a refreshing shower and a change of clothes, I felt much better. so went down to the restaurant for lunch. I hoped to find someone who worked for my company. I had received no contact details from my new company, so had no means of contacting anyone to say I had arrived.

After explaining to a waiter what I wanted, he told me one of the company's men had been in for lunch but since left. The waiter talked to the receptionist, who then phoned the man's room. After a few minutes, I heard him say there was a man in the lobby who would like to talk to him. A short time later, the man came down to reception. After explaining who I was and my situation, he gave me the office telephone number.

As we sat drinking coffee, he told me he was installing ceramic tiles on a mosque minaret. He said because of the extreme temperature; he couldn't work a typical working day. Therefore, he started work at 4 am and finished at 2 pm. Even then, I could only imagine the difficulty of working out under the blazing sun.

After he left to return to his room, I decided to have lunch before phoning the office. I later called and talked to someone. I said who I was and that I was in the hotel.

"What! When did you arrive?" a voice exclaimed. "They said you weren't on the plane this morning."

"I was on the plane, and not amused when I waited at the airport for over an hour before getting a taxi to the hotel."

"Oh! Sorry about that. I don't know what happened." He then surprised me. "It's late now, in the morning I'll send a car to take you to the airport. You will be working in Salahwa; down on the other side of the country."

The next morning, I flew down to Salahwa, where on arrival, I found two men waiting to meet me. They turned out to be Peter, my boss, and one of our supervisors.

As he shook my hand, Peter said, "Colin, I'm sorry about what happened yesterday. I can't understand what went wrong. Although we were told you were not on the plane, you were."

I grinned. "It's okay." I said, "But I'm glad I knew the name of the hotel where I would be staying."

After a brief chat, Peter left to fly up to Muscat. As we left the airport, to my surprise, the supervisor told me I would be staying at the Holiday Inn. I thought this a real treat. With my working on my tools, the last thing I expected was to be living in a hotel.

As we drove along, apart from a few palm trees scattered here and there, the landscape looked dry, barren and bleak.

Once checked in at the hotel, after changing into my working clothes, I was then driven to the villa where I would be working. As we pulled up outside, I noticed it was a large one.

Inside, the supervisor introduced me to the other lads working on the project. Besides myself, there were eight others joiners, as well as some specialized painters. It surprised me when told that these men usually worked on film sets. However, after later seeing the quality and fantastic effects they achieved, I could well believe this. After a few days, I found myself back in the routine of working on my tools. Still, I enjoyed it, as it made a change from supervising.

Living in the hotel was great; I had a comfortable room with all the usual trimmings. Plus, apart from lobster, I could have anything I fancied on the menu. Salahwa seemed a desolate place, so it did not surprise me to find only a few other guests staying in the hotel.

After a couple of weeks in Salahwa, one afternoon, a driver handed me a message. It read *You are required back in Muscat.* As no one had mentioned this, it came as a bit of a puzzle. The driver handed me a ticket for my flight in the evening, then drove me back to the hotel.

I had checked out and awaiting a driver to take me to the airport when the lads arrived back from work.

Seeing me sat there, one asked, "Why are you still here? You should be at the airport."

"Good question," I replied. "But no driver's come to take me."

To my relief, he said. "In that case, I will."

I was fortunate; they were about to close the check-in counter when I arrived at the airport.

Back in Muscat, I again found no driver waiting to meet me. This time, I only waited half an hour before taking a taxi to the Al Falaj Hotel.

As I walked up to the reception desk, I said. "Good evening. My name is Mr Guest; do you have a room reserved for me?"

On checking, the reception clerk said, "No! I am sorry, Mr Guest; we have no reservation for you."

I knew the company had an agreement with the hotel, so was not unduly worried. "Okay, never mind. Do you have a room I can have?"

T my relief, he said, "Yes! We do."

"Good! Would you please check me in?" Once done, I went to my room and took a refreshing shower. It was late and I hadn't eaten, so I ordered a snack from room service.

The next morning, I phoned the office. "Hi, its Colin Guest, I am back and calling to ask where I'll be working."

To my shock and surprise, a voice asked, "What are you doing here? You're supposed to be in Salahwa."

I said. "Because I received a message that you wanted me here, and given a ticket for last night's flight up."

The line went muted for a minute, then the voice said, "Well, I don't know who arranged that, but it's not a problem. You're here now, and we could use an extra body."

A driver then came and drove me to our office, where he introduced me to John and Terry, who I would be working with.

As John shook my hand, he said, "Hi Colin, I understand you were on the same flight as us when you first arrived here."

I shrugged, "Yes, I saw you at the airport but did not know we worked for the same company," I replied.

"Sorry about that," John said, "but we weren't informed about you."

I found John and Terry to be friendly, and always invited me to join them if they were going anywhere, including out to dinner. The way John and Terry treated me was a far cry from how I was treated down at Salahwa. There, the lads I was working with, just disappeared after we had dinner together.

Our first job together involved the fitting out of a large luxury villa. This John informed me; was the primary type of work we did. Although not challenging, getting used to the extreme heat was. Nevertheless, despite no air-conditioner working in any of the villas we worked on, I soon became used to it.

At one site, because of their company not supplying fresh drinking water, one of their men died after drinking contaminated water. As a result, all the building company workers went on strike. With this prohibited in Oman, the police went to where around 800 workers were having a meeting. They sorted the troublemakers by nationality and put them into coaches. With the temperature over 40 degrees, the heat inside them must have been unbearable. Approximately four hours later, the police asked the workers if they would return to work. They also informed them that the company had agreed to provide fresh drinking water every day. On hearing this, the men were only too happy to accept. However, for the workers, the police had classed as troublemakers; they were all deported.

The next morning, we found the company was as good as its word, with several fresh drinking water dispensers installed.

We were about to leave work one evening when I felt a sharp pain in my stomach. I almost doubled over in pain, which seemed to get worse by the minute. Mr Singh, one of our workers, must have noticed, as he came over. "What's wrong, Mr Colin?" he asked.

"I have this terrible pain in my stomach," I muttered, "it's killing me."

"Just a minute," he said, "wait here." He left and returns carrying a small bottle filled with what looked like a mixture of seeds. Opening the bottle, he shook some contents into his hand. "Here, take this," he said. From my expression, he could see I felt dubious. To quell my fears, he said, "Don't worry. Just take it; this will make you better."

Although unsure about taking this mixture, I had nothing to lose, so swallowed it down. To my amazement, a few minutes later, I felt much better. Just what Mr Singh gave me; I do not know, only it had solved my problem. Given this, I couldn't thank him enough for helping me in my time of need.

While out with John and Terry, we came across an accident. A large American car had ended up straddled across a deep irrigation ditch. How it had managed to do so without the front wheels dropping into it was a complete mystery. Seeing nobody stop to help the driver, we decided to see if we could be of assistance. After parking, we walked back to the stranded car.

John spoke to the driver, who stood beside the car, looking bewildered. "Hi, it looks like you could do with a hand," he said.

Although the man did not speak English, he must have understood what John had said, for he nodded.

Terry chuckled. "Well," he said, "this should be fun. Any suggestions on how to get the car back over the ditch? And don't say use a crane!"

While looking around, we found some scaffold planks on a nearby building site. These we carried back and laid them across the ditch behind the car wheels. Once done, John smiled as he glanced down into the depth of the trench. "Well, now it's the moment of truth," he said. "What do you think? Will they hold or not?"

"For the driver's sake," I said, crossing my fingers, "I hope so, but it's a heavy car, so who knows."

With much apprehension, the driver climbed back in the car. As he slowly reversed across the ditch on top of the planks, we held our breath. Although we thought they would hold, there was, of course, no guarantee. We were fortunate. Once back on the road, after climbing out of the car, the driver jumped for joy. He beamed a big smile of relief as he gave each of us a big hug, then said something we did not understand. No doubt thanking us for our help.

# Part 2

A few weeks after my arrival back in Muscat, Mike, and Bill, another two joiners, joined us. It pleased us when the company arranged an apartment for the three of us. It was a good-sized place, and not far from the centre of town. Given this, most nights, we would meet up with John and Terry and walk around the shops. During one of our walks, Terry decided to buy a video camera. Seeing one he fancied in a shop window, we all trooped inside the shop. The price the shopkeeper gave Terry was rather high, so he told him, then turned to walk out. Seeing he was about to lose a customer, the man called out. "I give you a discount." As Terry turned around, he asked, "How much?"

In the blink of an eye, the storekeeper replies, "40%." On hearing the fantastic discount offered, Terry walked out of the shop in disgust. It was apparent the shopkeeper had tried to cheat him from the start.

One day, Terry told us about an amusing incident that occurred when asked to take a package back to England for the Colonel. As he was the second most powerful man in Oman, one did not refuse such a request.

Terry said, "because of the late arrival of the package, I was late checking in for the flight. Then, after boarding the plane, the cabin staff were angry with me. It seems they had been instructed not to take off until I was on board the plane."

One asked, 'Who are you to make us delay take-off? Just who do you think you are?'

I replied, "Sorry, it's not my fault; I had to wait for a package the Colonel wants taken to England. If you have any complaints, I suggest you take them up with him." Terry smiles. "The change in attitude on hearing the Colonel's name was incredible," he said.

"Sorry, Sir, no one told us why we had to wait," the steward said.

Terry chuckled. "It was funny how well they then looked after me on the flight," he said." On disembarking at Heathrow, a steward wearing a forced smile, said, 'I hope you had a pleasant flight, sir?'

Terry shrugged. "In the circumstances, I could well understand their frustration at having to hold the plane until I was on board."

At work, Bill, Mike and I found ourselves getting rather tired, which we put down to the extreme heat. Terry must have noticed, for he asked. "Are you guys taking salt tablets?"

"Salt tablets! What are they?" I asked, "Nobody told us about them."

"Good grief," he exclaimed. "No wonder you're feeling knackered. You must take them."

After buying a supply, which we immediately started taking, we soon found ourselves feeling far less tired.

One evening, John said, "Tonight, you guys you are in for a treat." On asking what it was, he grinned. "We're going to have fish and chips," he said.

Although I had not seen a fish and chip shop before in Muscat, I thought this nothing unusual. However, to my surprise, instead of plaice, cod, or haddock, the fish was barracuda. I had never eaten this kind of fish before, but found it tasted okay.

With gold cheaper here than in England, I decided to buy myself a gold ring. However, this was not as easy as I expected, as I could not find one that fitted my index finger.

On speaking to one shopkeeper, wearing a confident smile, he said, "This is no problem; I can make one for you."

I explained I wanted an eagle design on it, like the one in his window. He nodded. "It will be ready in ten days."

On my return to the shop ten days later, sure enough, he had made my ring. I thought it looked great, so paid and took it home.

Later, while giving the ring a clean, I noticed what seemed to be small black marks on it. On closer inspection, to my annoyance, the scores were minor defects.

The next evening, I took the ring back to the shop and told the shopkeeper I was not happy with the quality.

He looked at me, then said, "It was my brother you spoke to about the ring, not me." He smiled. "Still, it's not a problem," he said. "Let me have a look at it." On taking a closer inspection, I was shocked when he said, "It's poorly made." I will make another one for you. It will be ready in two days."

Although I thought this impossible, two days later I returned to the shop. As expected, the ring was not ready, but when I again returned two days later, it was.

On inspection, I was not pleased. I pointed to the ring. "This is not good," I said, "why are these gaps here?"

He smiles. "That's because the ring is hollow," he said.

I almost choked in a fury. "Hollow! I don't want it hollow," I exclaimed. "It should be solid. I want the ring looking so good; people will want to know where I bought it." I shook my head. "As it is, you wouldn't get many new clients if they saw this."

He expressed shock at my outburst and stated that it would be more expensive to make the ring solid. I gave him a friendly pat on the shoulder, and told him this was not a problem. In total, they remade the ring three times before I was satisfied.

At work, I was well pleased when informed the three of us could have a company car. As I already had obtained an Omani driving license, this was great news. It meant I could take Mike and Bill out and about on our day off work.

This worked out well until driving in town one day I took a wrong turn. As a result, I found myself driving the wrong way down a one-way street. If that was not bad enough, as I drove past a police station, two police officers came out and climbed into a police car.

"That's it," I cried in panic. "They will put me in jail." To my horror, the police car started up, then followed us down the road. Just before the main junction, the police car shot in front of us and stopped. I broke out in a sweat, expecting to be arrested on the spot. To my surprise, after getting out of their car, one police officer went and stopped the traffic coming around the corner. The other beckoned me to turn the car around, which I did as quickly as possible. I could not believe my luck when instead of arresting me, the police officer waved me on my way. To say I felt relieved, would be a grave understatement of the facts.

While on the way to the beach, we had a puncture. With the temperature in the forties, changing the wheel was no joke. As a result, we were all exhausted by the time it was.

On our arrival, after I parked, while walking across the sand towards the sea, a young boy holding a small shark up by its tail gave us a big smile. "You like to buy fish?"

"No thanks," I replied, as we carried on down to the sea. Although none of us had swimming trunks, we were wearing shorts, so took our tops off and had a paddle. As I could not swim, this was fine by me.

On looking around, an enormous building under construction caught our eyes. Even with the camera lens set at wide-angle, and my standing in the sea, I found it impossible to get all the building in the frame.

After no more than half an hour of paddling around in the sea, I said, "Sorry, boys, but it's far too hot for me, I want to leave."

"You're right," Bill said, "Let's go."

Once back at our apartment, I took a refreshing shower. I felt good as I walked into the lounge wearing just a pair of shorts. The next minute it shocked me when Bill cried. "Jesus! Look at the state of you."

I did not know of what he was talking about, so asked in puzzlement, "What's wrong? What's the matter?"

"Wrong! You're redder than a tomato," Bill exclaimed.

On looking in a mirror, it horrified me to see Bill was right. From being sunburnt before, I knew that I had to get treatment right away. Once dressed, I rushed to a Pharmacy in town where the pharmacist gave me some special cream. Fortunately, it worked, and I didn't suffer like in the past.

On Friday evenings, the official day off work in Oman, the streets of Muscat were always jam-packed. The majority of people walking around being Indian and Pakistani workers. Terry informed me that many of them were looking to buy gold. This he said, "Is not only a means of saving, but used as a dowry for when they married." With thousands of Indian and Pakistani workers in Oman, the gold shops must have been doing fantastic business.

As we walked around the town one night, we burst out laughing. Painted in big red letters on a wall next to a parking area, was a sign that read, 'Piss Here.' We were so shocked; we had to look twice.

For the first month of working in Muscat, I believed the country to be flat. Even when we drove out of town to the various villas we worked on; the roads were mainly flat. However, one day, as we drove out of town, I was amazed to see that mountains surrounded Muscat. Until then, because of the extreme heat haze, they were impossible to see. This day the wind must have changed direction and blown away the mist, revealing the mountains.

It's because of them, why Muscat is so hot at night. The heat from the sun during the day gets absorbed by the rocks, then at night, releases the heat back out again. It explained why the water in the swimming pools was still too hot to enjoy a swim at nine o'clock at night.

One Sunday, the three of us went to a different beach than our usual one. To our surprise, we found it packed with Indians and Pakistanis. As we wanted peace and quiet, we walked along the sandy beach until on our own.

A short time after we had sat down, we saw four people coming towards us. Pointing to one wearing a large cowboy type hat and a long coat.

I said, "What does he look like? Does he think he's Clint Eastwood?" I soon discovered I was mistaken, when the person wearing the hat and coat stripped off to reveal an attractive woman wearing a bikini. A few minutes, later a group of Pakistanis came up and sat, forming a semi-circle behind them. From the way they were staring, it was apparent they were looking at the woman in the bikini.

The man sat with the women became angry and shouted, "Go away, and leave us alone." Despite his calls, the men took no notice. For us, English, there was nothing unusual about seeing a woman wearing a bikini, but not for them. For us, it was far from ordinary to see Indian and Pakistani women paddling and swimming while wearing their sari dresses.

On one of our trips out of town, we found road widening ongoing. Usually, this would be no big deal, except this road ran through the mountains. To do so, entailed cutting back one whole side of the granite rock face. At over 100 feet high, it was a mammoth task to blast and cut away the rock face. Plus, apart from a few hours each day, they kept the road open, which made the task even more complicated. To our amazement, when we passed by a month later, they had completed the road widening.

One thing I found surprising about working in Muscat was the generous food allowance I received. I could afford to buy anything I wanted from the supermarkets. These were like those in England and selling everything, including pork. This they kept in a separate section of the supermarket, and marked, 'Only for sale to foreigners.'

For us English, life was good, whereas, for our Pakistani and Indian fellow workers, conditions were far less so. After accepting an invitation to visit Mr Singh, I was shocked to find that he and the other men were living in tents. They had few facilities and no hot water.

I found these guys were incredibly skilful and able to make up a variety of their tools from many things. For instance, they made an old saw blade into a plane iron; while they turned an old file into a chisel. I found it fascinating to watch them making these tools whenever they had the chance, and also found them to be hard workers. As such, I enjoyed working with them. To me, they were always polite and helpful.

At one time, John, Terry and I went to join Bill and Mike who were working on a Mosque opposite the Emir of Oman's palace. With the mosque still in use, we could not wear shoes inside. So, with no shoes, there was not much point wearing socks, so we worked in bare feet. The temperature inside the mosque was over 40 degrees, and even working in only a pair of shorts, I still sweated buckets. I had never worked in such hot conditions before, or since.

Our works in the Mosque involved installing new windows and doors. We also applied decorative plaster mouldings, to both walls and ceiling.

Although delighted at having all this work carried out, the Mullah was far from happy when informed air-conditioning was not part of the plan.

One morning, Ahmed, one of our men, climbed up the scaffold to start painting the ceiling. Unfortunately, he didn't look up as he stepped onto the top of the platform. By misfortune, it was right under a large operating ceiling fan.

As Ahmed stood up, we heard a sickening thud as the moving fan blades struck his head. On seeing him drop like a stone onto the top of the scaffolding, I thought he must be dead. However, to my relief, before anyone could go to help, he stood up, with blood pouring down his face.

I called up to him to come down. By the time he reached the floor, he was shaking like a leaf. To our amazement, on examination, apart from a large gash on his head, he seemed okay. Nevertheless, a driver took him to the hospital, where after receiving stitches, he returned to work with a large plaster on his head. Given the force of the blow, I thought it a miracle he survived.

On completion of our works on the mosque, we moved across the road to perform a variety of tasked in the Emir's palace. I felt excited about entering, as I had never worked on a palace before.

To get inside, we required a special pass that allowed us through a security check at the gate. While walking through the courtyard towards the entrance to the palace one morning, we heard a sudden commotion. On looking, we noticed a soldier amongst a group on parade had collapsed. From what I could see, the poor man was thrashing around on the floor, no doubt having a fit.

Several of his comrades dropped to the floor to restrain him. As he still held his automatic rifle, it was a dangerous situation. Fortunately, without any mishap occurring, his comrades wrestled it out of his hand. They then picked him up and carried him away.

Our work on the Palace consisted of updating and renovating various areas. Here I found it an incredible experience to watch our specialist painters, who were, as we in the trade would say, the business. The number of different textures and finishes they applied to plaster, and wooden items was a sight not to be forgotten. Once they had completed their work, the results proved nothing short of amazing.

During a walk around the palace with John, he stopped. "Just a minute," he said, "I have to check in here." He opened a door and walked through, with me following. I felt puzzled at the strange sight in front of me. Sat on the floor in a line, were a group of our Indian and Pakistani workers holding on to a thick rope. I then noticed that one end wrapped around the base of a short column, while the other end disappeared up into the ceiling, some fifty feet above. It looked like the men were doing an Indian rope trick.

I turned to John in bewilderment. "What on earth are they doing?"

He grinned. "They're lowering the chandelier so that we can change it for a new one."

As I looked up at the massive chandelier, I yelled out in alarm, "Stop! Look at the rope; it's fraying. No doubt caused by rubbing against the edge of the ceiling."

As John turned towards me wearing a puzzled expression, I stabbed my finger upwards. On seeing the frayed rope, John yells to the men, "Stop! Just sit tight and keep hold of the rope." With the chandelier directly above their heads, the men were in great danger. Had they let go of the rope, the chandelier would have crashed down on them before they had a chance to get out of the way.

John alerted the Palace maintenance men to the problem, who rushed up into the roof space. In a matter of minutes, they had connected a new rope to the chandelier.

I breathed a sigh of relief when the men then lowered the chandelier down to the floor. I shudder to think what could have happened had I not walked in and noticed the fraying rope

On waking one morning, I found a lump had appeared on my leg above my knee. Still, as a similar one had appeared while working in Saudi Arabia, I was not too concerned. That one had burst open one day, and after cleaning it up, was okay. Therefore, I thought this one would go the same way.

When John, our supervisor, noticed my leg, he recommended I go to the hospital and have it treated.

I shrugged. "It's nothing to worry about, I've had this problem once before."

John did not agree. "Maybe, but it looks infected. You should go and get it seen to A.S.A.P.."

"Thanks, but as I say it's okay," I replied.

Late evening, my leg became so painful; I called John. When I explained how bad my leg was, he was far from sympathetic.

"Serves you right," he said. "I told you to go and get it seen to; now it's too late. You'll have to wait until the morning."

The next morning, one of my workmates took me to the hospital. The scene at the hospital shocked me. We found the corridors crowded with people, both standing and sitting on the floor. My first impression was, I would be there all day.

On telling my workmate of my concern, he smiled. "No problem," he said. "The head doctor is a good friend of our partner. You won't have to wait long."

He was right. A doctor came to see me shortly after I entered his room. After examining the lump, he said. "It's not a problem." He then instructed a nurse how to treat it, who took me into a cubicle.

After asking me to lie down on the couch, he then used a sterilised needle to burst the lump. I thought that bad enough, but what followed was far worse. After screwing up a piece of gauze, he pushed it into the raw open hole in my leg. To my shock and horror, he then twisted it around to clean it out. I winced and gritted my teeth. until satisfied it was clean.

The next day I returned to the hospital to have the hole cleaned out again. Once done, and the doctor had checked it, he informed there was no need for me to return.

After what I had been through, it made me realise I had to take more care of my health. If not seen at an early stage, little things can develop into something much more severe.

Part of our work in the palace involved installing gold-plated door furniture. Every night, we locked all the uninstalled sets inside a large kit box. One morning, when as usual, we counted the door sets, we found one set missing. Despite everyone looking, we could not find it.

When informed of the loss, John, our supervisor, became angry and questioned the Pakistani carpenter in charge of locking up the kit box at night. When the worker admitted he had forgotten to lock it the previous evening, John went mad.

He kept shouted, "Why did you not lock the box? It's your fault the handles are missing. You lost it, so you will have to pay for them."

The boy started sobbed, said, "I'm sorry, I'm sorry. It was an accident. I never intended to leave the box unlocked."

Despite his sobbing apologies, John kept yelling at the boy. In the end, the boy could take no more and ran away sobbing.

I felt sorry for the boy, and ongoing to look for him, found him sobbing his heart out behind a pile of wood.

"It's okay," I said. "Calm down; Mr John will get over it. It was an accident; you never left the box open on purpose."

"No," the boy sobbed. "He will not forget it. First, he will make me pay for them, and then send me home. I will lose everything."

I could well understand his concern. If sacked and sent home, it would be a big disgrace. Moreover, it would mean his unable to send money back home to help support his family. After staying a while and calming the boy down, I returned to my work.

Despite several days of looking, we never found the handles. However, the boy was not dismissed, which pleased me.

After several weeks working in the Palace, I had completed my three-month contract, so I returned to the UK.

About a week later, I went to the company's office to collect my retention money. I had not been happy about this part of my contract, but it had proved to be a good way of saving money. To my extreme delight, along with my money, they also handed me a ticket to return to Oman for another three months.

Little did I know about a phone call. I would receive a few days later. It would result in a complete change of plans. My future would involve some incredible incidents, and a new adventures.

Incredible experiences in Brunei

# Chapter Five

While packing for my flight back to Oman, I received a phone call. As I answered it, a woman's voice asked, "Is that Colin Guest?"

I felt puzzled as I replied, "Yes, it is."

To my surprise, the woman said, "I have a message from Mick Weavis. He would like you to go out to Brunei and work on the palace contract!"

Usually, this would have been fantastic news, but I had a flight booked back to Oman in the afternoon. I felt gutted as through gritted teeth. I replied, "I'm sorry, but I can't go to Brunei. I'm because I'm flying back to Oman later today. I've been working there for the past three months."

"Oh! She said, Mick will be disappointed to hear that you can't make it. He particularly asked for you to go there."

"Thanks for the call," I said. As I put down the phone, I swore out loud, cursing like a lunatic.

"What on the earth's the matter?" Jen called out. "There's no need to swear like that."

"There most certainly is," I snapped back. "That was Mick Weavis secretary. She's just told me that Mick wants me to work in Brunei on the palace contract."

"So! What's the problem?"

"What's the problem?" I snapped. "In case you've forgotten, I'm flying back to Oman this afternoon."

"You haven't signed a contract, have you?" she said.

I glanced at her. "No, but I should go back to Oman," I replied.

"If you would rather go out to Brunei, then go there instead," she said. "You can always phone up and give some excuse for why you can't return to Oman."

After a brief talk about the situation, I phoned and spoke to Mick's secretary. "Hi, its Colin Guest, can I speak to Mick, please? I've decided I will go to Brunei."

"He is not here," she said, but I will give him your message."

I was feeling sorry for myself as I put the phone down, then ten minutes later, it rang again.

As I picked it up, a familiar voice said, "Hi, Colin, it's Mick. What's all this about you going to Oman? Don't go there; stay on the plane and come on over here."

Waring a beaming smile, I replied, "Hi, Mick, its good to hear from you. I've decided I will go to Brunei."

"Good! This contract will be really something," he said. "Once we arrange your visa, I'll get the office to arrange tickets for you."

As I put down the phone, it took me back when Jen asked, "Are you going to Brunei?"

I did not understand and felt confused as I replied. "Of course," I asked you what you thought about the idea, and you said OK."

"Yes, I but never thought you would go."

"Well, it's too late now to change your mind; I've said I am going." I then called my old company and said that because of a family emergency, I could not returned to Oman. I had not liked doing this, but the opportunity of working on the Sultan of Brunei's palace was too good to turn down.

On checking, I found Brunei a small country, mostly covered in a dense forest. However, because of abundant offshore deposits of oil and gas, was immensely wealthy. The Sultan of Brunei ruled the country, and was the wealthiest man in the world. The country was split into two parts. In one-half was the capital city of Darussalam, where most of the population lived, and in the other half was Muri. This was where the major oil and gas facilities were located. In between the two, there was nothing, with it sparsely populated.

After leaving Heathrow early one morning, I arrived in Brunei late the following afternoon. It had been the longest flight I had ever taken.

As I trudged into the arrival hall, I found my old friend Harold from Saudi Arabia waiting. He wore a big smile. "Hi, Colin, it good to see you again," he said.

"Likewise," I replied, "but boy, am I glad that the trip is over. It seemed like it would never end."

Harold laughed. "Yes, it's much longer than the flight to Saudi. Anyway, once we get your luggage, I'll take you to the hotel where we're all staying. Until we sort out permanent accommodation, we will stay there." I was well pleased when he added, "Once checked in, you can then rest for the day." At my look of puzzlement, he said, "because of the time difference, this happens here. That way, you'll start work tomorrow, feeling refreshed." He chuckled. "Or at least a bit."

When my luggage came out on the conveyor belt, the briefcase I had checked in did not appear. It was not a good start to being in Brunei. After making enquiries, an official told me to return the following morning. After Harold drove us to our hotel, I checked in, then crashed out in bed.

Because of jet lag, I still felt tired when I woke up early the next morning. However, Harold gave me time for a lay-in, and a late breakfast, before coming to take me to site.

Harold said, "The project is a twenty-minute drive from town." As we set off, I felt eager at the prospect of seeing where I would be working for the foreseeable future. The road wound its way past houses with corrugated tin roofs, set on the edge of the jungle. Everywhere was green, a stark contrast to the desert of Oman.

On stopping at a police checkpoint, Harold said it was the security entrance leading up to the Palace. After he showed his security pass and my passport to the police, they allowed us through. We then drove up a steep, narrow, mud-rutted track to the top of a hill where the Palace was located.

It surprised me when Harold informed me that this was for the Sultans second wife. I found the palace consisted of several individual buildings, all of which were at various stages of construction. As I looked around, I could look out over the jungle spread all around, and see the nearby China Sea. Without a doubt, the palace was in a fabulous location.

On entering our site office, Harold introduced me to Martin, our Project Manager, Peter, our admin guy, and Mike, one of our designers out from our UK office. There was also a young guy named Mick, who Harold said was a supervisor like him and me. As we were talking, a man came in, who Martin said was Ian, our Q.S.

After introductions, Martin informed us that we three supervisors would each have sections of the Palace to control and supervise. As I knew and got on well with Harold, I suggested we all worked together.

Harold agreed, but Mick exclaimed, "You look after your sections, and I'll look after mine."

His statement did not impress Harold or me, but we felt it was his loss, not ours, so said nothing.

When Harold later returned from a trip to the airport, I felt relieved to see him carrying my briefcase.

"You're lucky to get this back," he said. "There's no name on it, and it's locked!" He grinned. "The airport staff were worried that it might have been a bomb. They were considering whether to blow it up when I arrived." He shook his head. "In future, always take your briefcase on the plane with you. Oh, by the way, Sa-ard and several of the other Thais from Saudi will be working with us."

I had found them not only hard workers, but also friendly and helpful.

A few days after my arrival, Harold took me to a small cafe for a beer. Once seated, a server took our order. On his return, I noticed he carried a tray loaded with a large teapot and cups and saucers.

"Excuse me," I said, "We didn't order tea."

Harold, grinning ear to ear, said, "It's all right, Colin, you'll enjoy this tea."

Although puzzled by his statement, when he poured what I thought was tea, it made sense. It was, in fact, beer.

Harold then explained. "Due to not having an alcohol license, the cafe serves beer this way. Then, if the police call in, they would only see a teapot, cups, and saucers on the table."

The following week, Harold flew to Thailand to interview a bunch of carpenters. On his return, he said out of forty-five, only one was not suitable. Once their visas were processed, the rest would arrive.

While wandering around town, I stumbled upon a few well-stocked supermarkets. Here, despite the absence of large size shops or stores, from these, it appeared one could buy most things. I also found a fish market, which with a wide variety of fish on sale, was well worth visiting.

At the fruit market, I discovered a fruit called a 'Durian.' When I asked Harold about it, he said, "Its smell is so strong; it's banned on planes, most restaurants and shops," He chuckled. "You either love it, or hate it."

Besides our hotel, there were several other small hotels, plus the Sheraton Hotel. As it had full business facilities, it enabled one to keep in touch with the outside world. Also, there were only a few taxis, but these stopped operating at 9 pm.

As I made my way down to the sea-front, I stopped in astonishment. There in front of me was a large village ,out on the water. All the wooden houses, shops, and a small mosque, were built on wooden stilts, with wooden walkways connecting them all.

I watched in fascination as numerous long narrow boats, powered by large outboard motors were darting here and there. These boats acted as water-taxis, taking people and goods between the shore and the village. On talking with Harold about this strange sight, he said the village was where the early settlers in Brunei first lived.

Apart from the village, a nearby large mosque with a gold-coloured dome caught my eye. Its reflection in the water made it a beautiful photo.

After a few weeks of living in the hotel, we moved into a government camp on the outside of town. It was isolated and set on a sizeable flat-grassed area and surrounded by jungle. The only way in and out, was a mile-long narrow road that wound its way up and down through the jungle. As for our living accommodation, it was in Portakabins, like I lived in Qatar.

Apart from us English and our Thai workers (when they arrived), on the camp were many Filipino workers. These Harold said were working on the Istana, the Sultans main palace.

The Filipinos lived in one section of the camp, with our Thais going to live in a different part. "It was necessary," Harold said, as when in large numbers, Filipino, and Thais do not get on well together."

I found life in the camp excellent; the meals were tasty, plus, a small cinema showed English films once a week. Although out of town, I thought the camp well set-up.

Among the first Thais to arrive, were Sa-ard and several other workers I knew from Saudi. Sa-ard soon got things organised, with priority given to erecting a workshop next to our site offices. We also had a block of toilets built for our company's use. Unfortunately, to our disgust, we always found the seats covered in muddy footprints. It seems because of their religion, Thais don't sit, they stand on the toilet. To get over this problem, we had one fitted with a lock, and the key hung in our office.

After a torrent one night, the road outside our office became swamped. When Martin drove up and into the water, he didn't realise how deep it was. He soon found out, however, when his engine cut out, leaving him stuck in the middle of it. As he couldn't get out of his car, we had a crane come to lift it free.

As it started to raise the vehicle, we gasped in horror when it slipped in the supporting straps. Fortunately, they caught under the front wheels, leaving the car hanging downwards. Although a dangerous situation, I thought the panic-stricken look on Martin's face funny. Then, a few minutes later, the crane lowered the car down on its wheels, out of the water.

As he stepped out of the car, Martin remarked, "I guess you lot thought that rather funny?"

Our burst of laughter gave him his answer.

At the time of going to Brunei, I had thought no more about spending Christmas with Jen and the girls in Spain. This being something we had booked up for several months earlier. With my going to Brunei, I had told her to cancel me from our booking. I was therefore stunned and unprepared when one-day Martin pulled me aside. "Colin, as we won't be busy until the New Year, you can have Christmas at home."

I shrugged. "That's a pity. Before Mick offered me the contract, I had booked to spend Christmas with my family in Spain. After accepting his offer, I cancelled myself out. My wife is going to take our two girls by herself."

Martin gave a wry grin. "Well, call her and see if she can book you back in again. If she can, we'll arrange your flight to Spain instead of England."

This was fantastic news. I was full of anxious anticipation when I called Jen. "If, I can join you and the girls in Spain," I said. I heard the excitement in her voice as she said, "Oh, that would be fantastic if you could. I'll phone the company and do my best to get you booked back in."

After a sleepless night, the next day, after she contacted the tour company, Jen called. "Successful news! If you can get there, you're back in the holiday."

Although successful news, because of being Christmas, this proved not as easy as I expected. Nevertheless, to my delight, a few days later, our Admin guy said, "Colin, I have booked your flights as far as Alicante in Spain." He shrugged. "From there, I've arranged for you to pick up a car to drive on down to Benidorm."

I thought he was joking about the car, so I laughed. "Thanks a bunch," I said, "but I'd rather fly than drive."

To my surprise, he shook his head. "Sorry, Colin, but it's the best I could arrange at such short notice."

This part of my trip proved interesting, to say the least. Still, thanks to my company, I spent a fabulous Christmas with my family in Benidorm. I then dropped the car back off at Alicante, and flew back to Brunei.

In addition to enjoying myself, I also had the chance to travel to another country at no cost, which was a great advantage of being an expat worker.

Once back in Brunei, on the way to work in my company jeep, I glimpsed a snake curled up in the road just before I drove over it. I stopped, got out and walked back to where it lay. With bright black and yellow stripes, it looked beautiful. I decided there and then it would make a successful decoration at home. As I did not know if the snake was alive or not, I approached the snake from behind. I crouched down, and as the snake never moved, as quick as a flash, I grabbed hold of it behind the head. This I had heard this was the safest way to collect a snake. It shocked me when I later learned it was a sixteen banded Krait, an extremely dangerous snake.

Still, when I collected the snake, I must admit I thought it was dead. But, just in case it wasn't, I held it tight when I threw it into the back of my jeep. Then, as I drove on to work, I kept one eye on the rear-view mirror.

On my arrival, I stopped alongside Wonchai, Sa-ard's brother-in-law. "I have a snake in the back," I said, "Can you get someone to clean it out for me? I would like to stuff it."

To my disappointment, on my return a few hours, Wonchai said, "Mr Colin, snake smelt so bad no one would clean it. I threw it away."

"What! Where did you throw it?" I asked.

He pointed up the bank. "Up there."

I scrambled up, to find the snake lying on top of some fallen branches. I had not noticed the length until then, but I was pleased to find it about four feet long. Although it did smell terrible, I did not intend for a little thing like that to put me off. I found a bucket and filled it with water mixed with disinfectant. Then, after curling the snake up inside, I put a large stone on top of it to keep it under the water.

Several hours later, as the snake smelt okay, I took it back to Wonchai.

I grinned. "Here," I said, "it no longer smells."

Late afternoon, I asked Wonchai how my snake was. When he came back holding it up, I was furious. Whoever had cleaned it, had cut off its head.

"It's ruined!" I exclaimed, "I can't stuff a snake with no head." After thinking for a minute, I said, "Right, as I can't stuff it; you had better get it skinned."

Once done and dried out, I hung the skin on my office wall. Unfortunately, the disinfectant had taken away its original bright colours; it now looked dull and nothing special.

While driving to camp, as I turned a corner, I ran over a snake as it crossed the road. As you never knew what you would see while driving in Brunei, I always carried my camera with me. I stopped and jumped out to take a picture of the snake. To my amazement, the snake was not dead. Instead, it curled up and thrashed around in circles in the middle of the road. As I watched in fascination, the snake straightened up, then slithered down the bank and into a small stream. After it swam a short distance, it came out of the water and climbed the bank on the other side. In a flash, crazy as it may seem, I jumped over the stream and took its photo before it disappeared into the dense undergrowth.

Another incident re snakes occurred, when our Thais were driving back to camp in their van. It amazed me when Harold told me what happened.

He said, "After they felt a large bump, when they stopped to investigate, they found a large python stretched across the road." He grinned. "As Thais eat snakes, this was too good an opportunity to miss. Although large, there were seven Thais in the van, who then jumped on the snake." Harold chuckles. "The snake bit one man while they were struggling to catch it." He shrugged. "He was fortunate," he said, as Pythons are not poisonous, they rely on crushing their victims to death."

My eyes lit upon hearing this. It sounded as though there were possibilities of obtaining a large snakeskin.

That evening, I went to see Sa-ard, who I found sat talking with some of his men.

"Welcome, Mr Colin. Sit down and have a beer."

"Thanks, I will," I replied. Once he had given me a can of beer, I said, "I heard you caught a large snake last night."

He beamed a smile. "You like to see it?"

My eyes lit up. "Yes, please," I replied.

To my surprise, he took me to a refrigerator and opened it "Here it is Mr Colin; we are going to eat it tomorrow. You must come and join us."

On looking inside, I found they had cut the snake up into steak size pieces that filled the fridge.

He grinned. "We have just cooked a sample," he said, "would you like a piece?"

Although apprehensive about what it would taste like, I nodded, "Yes, please."

He then offered me a small piece on the end of a fork. To my surprise, it tasted like chicken.

"Hey, its good," I said. "But, if possible, I would like to see the snakeskin."

He grinned. "You want it, Mr Colin?" he asked.

I tried not to let my enthusiasm show. "Yes, please. I'll pay you for it."

"No," Sa-ard said, "You can have it, but you no pay for it."

"I will pay you for it," I exclaimed.

He shook his head. "If you pay for it, you not have it," he said. "You are my friend, for you, it's a gift."

He must have told of one the men to fetch the snakeskin, as one walked off. As I followed behind, he stopped to collect a long branch. Reaching a section of the perimeter fence, he stopped. After a few unsuccessful attempts poking around in the long grass, he located the snake. When I noticed the stick bending under strain, I realised the remains must be substantial.

As the man lifted it out of the grass, I almost choked with delight. The snake looked about 12 feet long.

With it hanging draped over the stick, we returned to where Sa-ard and the boys were sitting.

As we approached, Sa-ard looked up. "You want snakeskin?" he asked.

"Yes please," "I replied. "It will look fabulous back in my house in England."

With that, Sa-ard gave instructions to have the skin cleaned. Four days later, full of anticipation, I asked Sa-ard how my snakeskin was coming on

He left me puzzled and dismayed when he said, "No sun today, snake finished."

In the evening, I went with Sa-ard to look at the snakeskin. When I saw it, I cried in disappointment. The men had laid it stretched out to dry on pieces of plywood, placed on a patch of short grass. Unfortunately, ants and other insects had eaten away large sections of it. All that remained were a few short pieces here and there.

One weekend, Mick, John and I decided to take a walk into the jungle. As it would be our first time, we felt apprehensive about what we might encounter. Given this, we decided to take a baseball bat for protection.

After arriving at the spot where I had been told was the entrance into the jungle, I parked the jeep. Then, carrying the cold box and baseball bat, we set off along the track. We followed it as it wound its way through the jungle, alongside and over several small streams. The locals had built bridges over them, consisting of a log straddling the stream, with a branch supported above acting as a handrail. Had any of us been at all nervous, the first bridge would have been as far as we went. Still, we thought nothing of them and crossed with no problem.

To my surprise, despite walking through the hot and humid jungle for an hour, we never saw, nor heard any animals or birds.

As we went deeper into the forest, we found a group of young children. They were having a great time, jumping off the bank and into a small pond. We thought their actions would make a wonderful photo, but as we took out our cameras, some children ran away. Those who remained held their hands in front of their faces. It was apparent they didn't want us to take their photos, so with reluctance, we put away our cameras. The children laughed with the ones who had run away reappearing. They then carried on, enjoying themselves in the water.

A short time after leaving the children, the track started to wind its way through the trees and up a small hill. What with the combination of high humidity and the weight of the cold box, we were all sweating buckets?

At one stage, the track wound its way around and over some massive tree roots. Although in places someone had chopped away sections to allow the path to continue, the trees appeared healthy and unaffected.

After several tiring hours, we came to a clearing. At one end, a waterfall, about 18ft high cascaded down into a large pool. It looked so enticing, we stripped down to our underwear and waded into the crystal-clear water. It felt so crisp and refreshing; you could almost see the steam rising from our feet.

Mick and John swam out and dived in under the waterfall, then swam around under the falling water. As I couldn't swim, I had to settle for a paddle to cool down. I felt envious as I then sat watching them swimming around.

The boys eventually decided it was time for lunch, which thanks to being in the cold box, the salad was fresh and tasty. Once eaten, we washed it down with a couple of cans of ice-cold beer. Just tasting the cool refreshing food and drink, made the effort of carrying the cold-box worthwhile.

As I threw the remnants of my lunch into the pool, something grabbed and ate it. This was unsettling, as we were unaware of anything lurking in the water. On an investigation, we discovered it was some freshwater shrimps.

After relaxing and enjoying the view of the waterfall, we decided to push on further into the jungle. Because of its weight, we agreed not to take a cold box on future walks..

We then made our way up the track behind the waterfall and continued on our way. In places, small pools of water stretched across the trail, which to our disgust, we found infested with leeches. If you brushed against them, they would cling on and work their way into one's skin. Then, once they had sucked out blood until they were full, they'd let go and fall off.

To my amazement, one leach managed to climb into my trainers through an empty lace hole. They were such a nuisance, every so often we had to stop and pick them off our exposed skin. We found the best way to do so, was to apply the lighted end of a cigarette to them.

After we'd followed the narrow, twisting track for another hour, we decide to head back. By the time we reached the car, my legs were aching and I felt as though I had completed a marathon. Despite all our walking, we were disappointment at not seeing a single bird or animal. However, our first jungle walk had proved an experience.

One Sunday morning, along with Mick and John, we took a walk down by the river. As we did, an elderly man sat in a small boat tied up at the river's edge called up to us.

"Hello," he called out. "Would you like to visit a place called Skull house? If you do, I can take you."

This sounded interesting, so we said yes. After climbing down a ladder and into the boat, the man started the engine. He swung the boat around and we then began to travel slowly up the river. As we did, the man told us he used to be a guide, taking people on river trips. He sighed. "Now, since I retired, I only do so part-time."

For the next two hours, we wound our way along the major river, then turned off up one of the numerous side tributaries. On each side of us, tall grasses lined the edges of the river banks.

As we turned yet another bend in the river, the man pointed towards the left bank. "Look over there," he said.

Initially, I could not see what he was pointing at; then, through the tall grass, I could see what looked like a large dog kennel. As we approached the bank, through the mesh sides of the structure, we could see several skulls. Disappointment coursed through me and I couldn't help but feel let down. It was not at all what I imagined.

Our guide explained that headhunting, once practised in Brunei, had been abolished. Our guide explained that disposing of the heads that belonged to old enemies, would anger their spirits. Therefore, they remained in this small structure as a memento.

After taking a few photos, we continued up the river to see a friend of our guide. Ten minutes later, I spotted a hut near the edge of the river. On a small rough-looking wooden jetty nearby, was what I thought could be a toilet? As we approached the bank, a man appeared and called out what I took to be a greeting to our guide. After he tied up the boat, we clambered out and followed him up the bank. The two men greeted each other with a warm handshake; then the man shook hands with each of us.

Our guide said as his friend did not speak English, he would translate questions we might have. He explained that his friend earned a living making Sago, and would show us how he made it. The two men led us to a place where an old circular saw with sharp spikes sticking out on one side of the blade was set up. The man switched on the saw, which once running at full speed, he picked up a log that our guide said was from a Sago tree.

As the man pushed the end of it against the spinning spikes, to our amazement, it reduced it to a pile of rough-looking sawdust. He then switched off the machine and led us to where two large hollowed-out logs lay on the ground. On seeing our puzzled expressions, our guide explained that the man placed the sawdust into these logs and covered them with water. The mixture ferments and turns into a paste that once dried, it becomes Sago."

I thought it amazing that something as primitive as this setup could create Sago. The two men spoke to each other; then our guide turned back to us. "My friend is barbecuing a fish, and invites us to join him eating it."

We had not eaten since breakfast, so accepted his offer.

As we stood around talking, John started to fidget. "I have to go to the toilet," he said.

Our guide pointed to the little hut out on the floating jetty. "There," he said.

I thought this could be interesting, as every time a boat passed by; its wash sent the jetty bobbing. John was in the toilet when another boat passed. He was fortunate; as it only caused the toilet to rock a little. When John came out, he grinned. "Well, that was an experience I won't forget," he said.

I laughed. "If that boat had been moving faster as it passed, you would have had an even bigger experience."

After eating some of the tasty fish, we thanked the man and then said our goodbyes. Our guide then took us back to where we first met him. Although he had requested no money, we were more than happy to give him some. Thanks to him, we had enjoyed a pleasant and enjoyable trip.

I found work on the Palace fascinating. Many of the elaborate designs in wood and fibrous plaster required gold leaf applied to them. This required so much gold leaf, an armoured car with armed soldiers was at the airport to collect a shipment when it arrived from Thailand.

To apply all this gold, about forty guilders, both male and females, came over from Thailand. The women lived in a large villa with security guards posted outside every evening. With only ten male guilders, they lived in Martin's house.

I found it an incredible experience to watch the gilders at work. At one time, I observed six of them working on a single door. Had I not seen it with my own eyes, I would have said it was impossible.

Apart from our carpenters, we also had six Thai woodcarvers. Their work was intricate and time-consuming, but these guys were professionals and made things look easy. I found it fascinating to watch them carving out various patterns on lengths of hardwood. Some of the decorative pieces they carved for the doors, were something to behold.

To my surprise and delight, one day, Charit, the supervisor carver, presented me with an elephant he had carved. He later gave me a painting of a Thai war canoe he had painted, with both on display in my home in Turkey.

One morning, Andy, the head of the project management team, came to see me. "Colin, I'm going on the hash Friday evening, would you like to come?"

"Hash, what's the Hash?" I asked in puzzlement..

He explained. "The hash is a run through the jungle where you follow a paper trail laid by two guys called 'the Hares.' The run can take one to two hours, depending on how fast you run." He chuckled. "After the run, we have what we call a down-down. It's a laugh, and involves drinking a lot of beer."

I grinned. "That sounds good to me, count me in."

That afternoon was the start of my going on a hash. I enjoyed the experience so much; I joined the club. Details of all the crazy things that occurred over the years of my running on a hash, I shall include in a separate book.

One Sunday, a near tragedy occurred while our three ceiling fixers were relaxing on the beach. I felt shocked when I later heard what had happened.

It seems that while Alan lazed on the beach, John, and Dave went for a swim. They were later standing in water chest deep, when Dave said to John, "I'll race you back to the beach."

On hearing John answer what he thought was okay, Dave started swimming. When he reached the beach, he ran up to lie down beside Alan. When a minute later he realised, John had not joined him, he sat up. "Where's John?" he said.

When he and Alan looked out to the sea, they were shocked to see John floating motionless. They sprinted down and swam out to where he was bobbing up and down. With difficulty, they dragged John back to the beach, laid his unconscious body down, then tried to revive him.

While doing so, some Thais who had witnessed the incident came over. One said they should put John over their shoulder and run. The motion would bring up any water he had swallowed.

When this failed, Dave and Alan carried John's limp body to their truck, then sped back to camp. Unfortunately, the camp doctor was not there. By the time they had driven to the hospital in town, over thirty minutes had passed since they dragged John out of the sea. On explaining what had happened, nurses rushed John to the emergency unit. Fortunately, after being in a coma for several days, John woke up.

When asked what had happened, John explained. "When Dave said about racing back to the beach, I never said okay. I was saying I was in trouble. Because of the powerful undercurrent, I could feel the sand under my feet being washed away. As a result, I was getting out of my depth. I'm not a strong swimmer, so I always try and stay where I can touch the bottom. Anyway, despite doing my best to swim back to shore, I found myself being taken further out to sea. In the end, I felt so exhausted I gave up trying." He shrugged. "I remember no more until waking up in the hospital."

It was a miracle that after drowning and being in a coma for several days, John suffered no ill side effects.

Work on the palace was going well, with the fibrous plaster men starting their part of the contract. These men were experts in installing ornate plaster ceilings and cornices. However, they were also what we called "Prima Donna." They seemed to think themselves better than anyone else on the project.

These men lived in a group of Portakabins at the bottom of the camp, where they formed the 'Sundowners' Club. This got its name because of its members starting to drink at sundown, and continuing until the early hours of the next morning. Because of their heavy drinking, various traffic accidents happened. These usually occurred when they were driving in or out of camp in their rented jeeps.

On my way into town one morning, I noticed one of their jeeps had crashed off the road. Harold later informed me that when the jeep crashed, it had broken the water pipe leading to the village above the camp. This only became known after the headman came down to complain his village had no water. Fortunately, a plumber quickly repaired the broken pipe and restored their supply.

An investigation revealed the jeep driver had been drinking for several hours on camp before he crashed his jeep.

On another occasion, one of their men was driving back to camp being chased by one of his colleagues in another jeep. On entering, one vehicle went the right way, with the other one taking the way-out road. The jeep driving the right way hit a government coach, ripping off the rear side-wheel panel. It then crashed into the back of a parked car, before coming to a stop on the grass verge.

Witnesses said when the man staggered out of his wrecked jeep, he declared he wasn't drunk. As he could hardly stand, stinking of drink, and empty beer bottles inside the remains of his vehicle, it was apparent; he was.

This was yet another accident involving damage to both jeeps and property caused by the fibrous plaster men. Martin, our project manager, decided he had had enough.

After a meeting with their company, they agreed to ban.

the driver from the camp. His company then put him in a hotel in town until they sorted his future out. The man had inflicted immense damage to both government and private property. Despite this, he asked a lawyer to help get him reinstated. Martin outright refused when the man's lawyer suggested that he should be allowed to return to camp.

We later heard the man went back to the lawyer's office where he not only slagged off Martin but Brunei as well. In this, he made a big mistake. A government official was in the office and far from pleased on hearing what the man said. He informed the man that because of his unacceptable and offensive attitude; he would be deported. The official called the police, who came and escorted the man back to his hotel. After packing his case, they took him to the airport and put him on a plane to Singapore. As the man had no money, he had to get help from the British Consulate to fly back to the UK.

On hearing this, everyone agreed it was his fault; and he got what he deserved.

Although the fibrous plaster men were heavy drinkers, they did excellent work. Unfortunately, their attitude to our Thai workers and local drivers was poor. As I went to leave work one evening, Sa-ard came to see me. He informed me these men were causing trouble on their coach. After being sworn at and threatened, the driver had refused to take them back to their hotel.

I went straight to their parked coach and climbed on board. "What are you guys playing at?" I snapped.

"It's nothing," one replies. "These black bastards don't speak English or understand what we're saying."

I was furious. "No, they don't speak English," I said, "but your driver understood very well what you're saying. Anyway, you guys have a choice, either you apologise to him, or he won't take you to the hotel."

As I left them to decide what they were going to do, a chorus of offensive language broke out. Nevertheless, after thinking about what I said; the men apologised to the driver, who then drove them back to camp.

While at the helicopter club one night with Ron, we were invited to go on a helicopter trip with the Flying Doctor. As neither of us had been in a helicopter before, it sounded too good an opportunity to miss. The following Sunday morning, we met Peter, who worked at the main airport, who then took us to the flying doctor's helicopter. Shortly afterwards, the doctor and his assistant arrived in a van. Once they had transferred the contents into the helicopter, we took off. The deafening noise took me by surprise; I never realised how noisy a helicopter was. While the pilot and co-pilot wore headphones so they could communicate with each other, Ron and I did not. We had to shout or point at whatever we wanted the other to notice.

After a half-hour flight over the dense jungle, we started our descent. As we came into land in a small clearing, I noticed a group of people standing nearby. No doubt they were waiting to see the doctor.

Once the helicopter rotor blades had come to a stop, we all climbed out. The doctor and nurse carried the various bits and pieces they had brought, while Ron and I followed behind. After walking a short distance along a well-worn path, we came to a shack-like building. It consisted of a basic timber made roof, covered in corrugated metal sheets, and supported on tree trunks.

Underneath, were some roughly made timber benches that soon filled with the people I had seen as we came into land.

Once the doctor had established the table and chair he had brought, he called the first person. On looking around, I noticed a small hut to one side of the waiting area, where the doctor made more personal examinations. Without a doubt, this was a very basic doctor's surgery.

While the doctor was seeing his patients, Ron and I went off exploring. We hadn't gone far when we came to a small clearing where hidden by tall bushy trees, was an old timber house. Outside, a young boy aged around seven was playing with a homemade catapult. To my surprise, he was not at all nervous as Ron, and I approached. He even gave his slingshot to Ron, who after a few shots with it handed it back.

By the time we returned to the doctor's waiting room, he had just finished seeing his last patient. As he packed up his bits and pieces, I heard the sound of our helicopter returning. I thought it would make a pleasant picture, so went and stood on the edge of the clearing. To my surprise, as it came into touch-down, the downwash from the rotor blades blew me off my feet. I had not realised how intense it would be. Fortunately, I landed unhurt in some bushes, so picking myself up, I took a photograph of the helicopter as the blades were stopping.

Once all were aboard, the helicopter took off, and before I realised, we had touched back down at the airport. Our trip had made me aware of the difficulties people living in the jungle face when they need to see a doctor.

As I arrived at the site one morning, the sight of a big hole in the wall where my office air-conditioning unit used to be shocked me. We had had various items stolen from our premises, but none as significant as an A/C unit.

When Martin arrived, and I informed him, he made an official complaint to our local representative. A few days later, the police came and searched a worker's camp in the jungle at the bottom of the hill. It resulted in a lot of stolen items recovered, including my A/C unit.

While about to drive up the hill to the site one day, Ron, the fibrous plaster project manager w ho was on his way out, stopped me. "Hi, Colin, this guy crashed his jeep this morning. He got out okay but left his briefcase behind. We're going to look for it. Do you want to come?"

"Sure, why not? I replied. "What happened?"

Ron grinned. "He was driving down the shortcut, lost control, and went over the edge."

The shortcut he referred to was one we sometimes used. It entailed driving up and then back down a steep, winding, rugged surfaced hill. On one side, there was a sheer drop down into the jungle. With no safety barriers, it made it a dangerous drive. I shook my head in disbelief. For the Thai to survive going over the edge, he had been extremely fortunate.

I parked my jeep, climbed into Ron's, and then we set off. On arriving at the turn off junction to the shortcut, we turned off the main road. We then had to drive between two large concrete sections of pipe that were filled with earth. Someone had placed these there to prevent trucks from using this side road. With the remaining gap narrow, only the brave and stupid did not slow down to pass between them.

Once through, we then drove slowly up the hill. As we did, we kept a sharp lookout for signs of where the jeep had gone off the road. Despite going up and down the hill twice, none of us saw any sign of where the accident had happened. The Thai was of no help, as he did not know where he had gone over. As we inched along on our third attempt, Ron spotted faint tire marks. These were right on the edge of the gravel bordering the steep drop. We stopped, got out and looked over the edge.

Initially, we could see any sign of the jeep. Then, through the bushes some distance down, Ron spotted part of a number plate. He and I then set about climbing down the steep bank, which with the surface loose and slippery, was far from easy. Sliding and grabbing hold of small plants to slow our descent, we made our way down.

We found the jeep upside down with the roof caved in, but soon found the briefcase. We were fortunate to complete the task swiftly, as hundreds of ants were climbing all over us. Then, with difficulty and briefcase in hand, we scrambled back up the bank.

As I handed the architect his briefcase, I said, "You are fortunate that you did not get knocked out during the crash." If so, the ants would have eaten you alive." I shrugged. "No one would have ever found your body, as no one would have known where to look for you."

While driving along in my jeep one day, I felt something was wrong. After stopping and finding nothing, I remained unconvinced that all was well, so I drove on slower than usual. As I drove along a section of the road by the sea, I gasped in shock and alarm. A wheel had appeared flying through the air in front of me. I wondered as to where it had come from, then when the front of my truck crashed down, I realised it was mine. With the w heel missing, I had no control over the jeep. As I glanced in the mirror to see if there was any traffic near me, I saw a terrified face. I clenched my teeth, braked hard and locked my hands tight my hands on the steering wheel. As the front hub ground along through the surface of the road, bits of gravel and sparks were flying everywhere.

Then, like a bomb falling from the sky, my wheel crashed down onto the road ahead of me. It bounced twice, then disappeared off down towards the sea. After what seemed like a lifetime, I breathed a sigh of relief when my jeep came to a stop. I had been fortunate. If I had been driving at my usual speed, I would have crashed down onto the rocky beach.

A few minutes later, I had relaxed enough to get out of the jeep and go in search of my wheel. I found it a short distance down from the road, wedged between rocks that had stopped it from bouncing down into the sea. After a struggle, I wrenched it free, then half carried it back on to the road. Unfortunately, with all the wheel nuts gone, there was no way I could replace the wheel.

While stood wondering what to do, a car coming towards me stopped. On hearing my problem and where I was working, the driver drove me back to the Palace security checkpoint. I thanked the man, walked up to my office, then called our mechanic. Once he had collected some wheel nuts, he then drove me back to my jeep.

He jacked it up, checked the hub for any damage, then to my surprise, he said, "It looks okay. Once I replace the wheel, you can drive the jeep back to camp."

I never discovered who did it, but I'm sure someone tampered with my jeep, causing the wheel to come off.

Yet another terrifying incident involving my jeep happened while on my way into town. Just before a sharp left turn, my front offside tire blew out. To my horror, I found myself crossing to the other side of the road right on the bend. Lucky for me; as I did, no traffic came the other way, and the jeep ended up on the grass verge. After getting my breath back, I changed the wheel, then continued on my way.

While about to leave work one evening, Ian asked Mike, Mick and I if we fancied a drink in the yacht club. With it on our way home, and none of us had been there before, we said yes. We then met up there a short time later. On mentioning it strange to find a yacht club in the middle of the jungle, Ian agreed. "There are plans to build a new clubhouse at a bay near the town," he said.

We ordered dinner, and while waiting, had a few rounds of beer. With a wry grin, Ian asked, "Does anyone fancy going through the top shelf?"

"What you mean?" I asked

Ian explained. "We start at one end and have a drink from each bottle on the shelf."

Before I could answered, Mike interjected, "Count me out," he said. "I've done this before, and it's no joke."

"Come on; I'll give it a go," Mick said.

"It sounds like this could be fun," I said, "so count me in."

The barman smiled when Ian asked him to pour us a drink from the first bottle on the top shelf. We had drunk about five different drinks when a server informed us our meals were ready. Once finished, we returned to resume drinking our way through the top shelf. We only had two more drinks when Mick said he had to go to the toilet. After waiting over five minutes for his return, his wife, who had accompanied us, went to find him. On her return, we had to laugh when she said that Mick was being ill out in the car park. At this, Ian and I decided to call it a day.

The next morning, because of a hangover, I was late getting into work. On asking Ian who I had to thank for driving me home last night, it shocked me when he said. "No one, you drove yourself."

"What! I don't remember leaving the club," I said, "never mind driving home. By the way, how's Mick?"

To my surprise, Ian said, "He's in hospital."

"Why? What happened to him?"

"It seems Mick suffers from bleeding piles. He knew he shouldn't have been drinking like we were," he said.

On his wife's return from visiting him in the hospital the next day, she said, "Mick is getting better. He's now complaining the food."

A few days later, Mick was more than happy when released from the hospital. On talking with him, he vowed never to get involved again in heavy drinking.

One night, while a couple of us were having a drink in a local restaurant, Mark, a guy we knew, came in. "Does anyone want to buy a blowpipe?" he asked. As this seemed unusual, I asked if I could see them.

"Sure, they are out in my car," he replied.

When we went outside, to my surprise, I found the blowpipes were about six feet long, with a foot-long metal spear at one end. Although they looked dangerous, I thought one would look great on the wall back home, so bought one.

With the blowpipe came a bamboo quiver full of darts. As Mark handed it over, he said, "I could have bought quivers with poison on top of them, but decided not to. It would have been far too dangerous to use them."

Mark told me he had been in Brunei for some time and had set himself up with a couple of profitable schemes. One involved going into the jungle and visiting villages. From these, he would buy various handmade items, including blowpipes and machetes. These he would sell to expats like me. Mark later took me to see another scheme of his. It turned out to be a collection of various species of pitcher plants. On seeing my puzzled expression, he said. "I pack them up and send them off to various nurseries in other countries." He grinned. "They sell them, then send me the money."

One evening a few of my hash friends and I went to our Hash Masters house for a drink. While playing darts in his sports room, someone noticed a couple of blowpipes stood in the corner of the room. That was it. From throwing darts at the board, we were soon blowing darts instead. Once we learnt how to hold the blowpipe steady, we found them very accurate.

At work, one-day Martin called me into his office. "Colin, you take a lot of photographs, how would you like to take site photographs for the company?"

"Sure, no problem," I replied. "What exactly would you like me to take?"

"Just go around each week and take photographs showing the progress of works."

I then did this that later enabled me to take photos of finished areas. Apart from an official photographer who came in later, I was the only one permitted to take photographs inside the palace.

On one occasion, while near one entrance to the Palace, a group of ladies walked in. Although wearing lounging style tracksuits, I realised they must be of importance to get inside the palace. Seeing me stood there, one lady came over and asked me a few questions about the ongoing works. She was friendly and relaxed as we spoke, then thanked me and left.

No sooner had she gone, when one of the Project Management team appeared. "Do you know who that was you were talking to?" he inquired.

"No, but she must have been someone important," I replied.

To my shock and surprise, he said, "That's the Sultans wife. This is her palace.

It was pouring down with rain one evening when I wanted to go to the camp cinema, so I drove there. After the film finished, with it pitch black and still raining I ran out and jumped into my jeep. As I started to reverse, I heard a loud crash. With the aid of a torch, I found I had backed into John, our decorator's car. My jeep had badly damaged the front of John's car.

On hearing the crash, a group of the lads, including John, came out to see what had happened.

"John," I said in exasperation. "Why on earth did you park right behind me?"

"Sorry, Col, it's my fault. With it pouring with rain, I didn't want to get too wet, so parked as close as possible to the door."

Although my jeep was unharmed, John's car was a mess.

On-site, we had a Quality Controller who inspected all our works. While I accompanied him one day, we went to the Billiard Room. As we walked inside, it shocked me when he yelled, "Get them down, get them out of here." When I looked, I found he was shouting at a woman. She was hanging curtains. The poor woman looked panic-stricken.

"What's wrong?" I asked in puzzlement.

"Look at the curtains," he cried. "They have dogs on them. You cannot hang something like this in the Sultans Palace, he exclaimed.

With trembling hands, the poor woman unhooked the offending curtains and took them away.

Later, once the installation of furniture started, a young woman came to assist the quality controller. She was attractive, and so acquired attention from our Thai workers — especially when walking around the site in flimsy long dresses.

Martin, our project manager, did not approve of her wearing such apparel, so asked that she wore something less revealing. Things, however, did not turn out as he wanted. For instead of wearing a dress, she turned up wearing tight-fitting jeans and a top.

One-day Martin informed us that he and his wife, Pam, were having a party, and they invited all our office staff. I had never met Pam before, so I felt apprehensive about going. However, I need not have worried, as she made me welcome.

There were a few people at the party, including some from work, plus a variety of Martin and Pam's friends. While having a conversation with a man named Peter and his wife, Mary, with an innocent look, she enquired, "Colin, why are you not dancing?"

I laughed. "I rarely dance until I've had a few drinks," I said. "My wife thinks I'm crazy when I dance. She calls me rubber legs and said everyone watching is laughing at me. I've told her I don't mind them laughing, as they're happy, and I'm happy."

It left me puzzled when Mary said, "So, you don't mind people laughing at you? Good! What are you doing Thursday night?"

I shook my head. "Nothing I know of, why?"

"Because that's when I'm holding an audition for people to act in a pantomime I've written. As you don't mind people laughing at you, you're ideal for a part."

I shrugged; it would be a fresh experience for me. "As this sounds like it could be interesting, count me in," I said.

The following Thursday evening, I drove to the hall where the audition was being held. As I walked inside, I found twelve people, some of whom I recognised from Martin's party.

When Mary noticed me enter, she came over. "Hi, Colin, I'm glad you made it." After introducing me to the others, she said, "I have already given a couple of people parts to play, but most parts are still up for an audition. By the way, the show is called, Emberella.

When it was my turn to recite words from the script Mary had handed me, despite feeling nervous, I managed okay. In total, I auditioned for four parts. Either I was better than I thought, or they were desperate. Either way, I ended up with three roles to play. Mary said the play would occur in the hall where we auditioned. As it would hold five hundred people, it was a daunting experience to look forward to.

For the next few weeks, I went to rehearsals several times a week, where I learned my words for the various parts. Although hard work, I enjoyed it, and we all had a lot of fun.

In one part, I had to wear women's black tights, which to save time, I put them on before leaving camp. I often wondered what anyone would have thought if I had an accident and found wearing them. Fortunately, I never had to find the answer.

During rehearsals one evening, Peter said Mary was in England, and if I wanted to stay the night at his house, I could.

"Thanks for the offer," I said. "I may take you up on it."

After rehearsals, Peter and I went to the bar to have a drink. About an hour later, Peter left, saying he was going home to bed.

Shortly after he had gone, I met a group of young Englishmen. It wasn't until after a few drinks that I realized they were from the S.A.S. Once they left, as I was tipsy, I decided to take up Peter's offer. On walking to his house and not receiving an answer to my knocking, I guessed Peter had gone to sleep. However, as I knew where the spare room was, I let myself in and crashed out in bed.

When I woke the next morning, I found I was late for work. I dressed, let myself out and walked to my jeep. Once out through the camp gates, I put my foot down and drove as fast as I could.

On my arrival at the site, I found Harold awaiting news of me. "What happened?" he said. "I thought you might have hit a lorry, so sent people out to look for you. But no one could find you."

I explained where I had been and whom I had been drinking with the previous night.

He grinned. "I'd heard the S.A.S. are always in and out of the country to assess the Sultan's security," he said.

That afternoon, we heard a guard had discovered a suspicious package under a plane on the camp where I had stayed the night before. They raised a general alarm and conducted detailed inspections of all buildings and aircraft. It revealed suspicious packages inside hangers, and underneath several planes and helicopters. On investigation, as all were dummy bombs, the authorities decided it was the work of the S.A.S. From what I learned, they planted them during an exercise to discover how good security was on the base. Given the discovery, it was far from good.

During one hash run, Jimmy, a Bruneian hasher, invited my friend Murphy and me to watch cock-fighting the next weekend. Although illegal in Brunei, it occurs in various isolated locations.

The following week, Jimmy drove us to a village way out in the jungle. It was so remote that without him taking us, we would never have found it. Even had we done so; we would never have had the grandstand view we did. Jimmy led us through the crowds and upstairs to the living room of a house, which he said belonged to the head of the village. The room was large, sparsely furnished and spotless. However, what was most noticeable was a litre bottle of whisky on top of a small table. Next, to it, a large glass container full of a strange-looking liquid caught my eye. It appeared to have various objects floating in it.

A man appeared who Jimmy introduced us to as the headman of the village. He grinned, then added, "he is a relative of mine."

This explained why we were permitted to enter his house, where we had an excellent view of the cockfighting arena.

On asking if it would be okay to take photographs, Jimmy said this was not possible. "Those at the scene would think you were a police officer getting evidence against them." To my delight, he said, "If you like, I can take photographs for you?" After showing Jimmy how my camera worked, he went downstairs. I watched as he pushed his way through the crowd until he was standing at the edge of a circle where the cockfighting would occur.

It started when two men, each holding a large cockerel, entered the circle. Another man, who was going to be the referee, also stepped in. The two men paraded around the ring, holding up their cockerels and showing them to the crowd. This caused a wave of excitement to erupt, with numerous people waving money and placing bets on whichever bird they fancied.

Once the birds had a set of steel spurs tied to the legs, they were ready for action. The two men came together at a line drawn in the dust, then held out their cockerel, showing them to each other. It seemed this was to get them angry and ready to fight. They put together the birds twice and then parted them. Next, the birds were brought back to the line and released. They immediately attacked one another, with both soon covered in blood, drawn by the sharp steel spurs. The fights came to an end when one bird could not keep fighting because of severe injuries or death. Although cockfighting is bloody and barbaric, I must admit I found it exciting.

When the last cockfight had finished, Jimmy came back upstairs. As he handed back my camera, he said, "I have some good shots there."

After the headman and Jimmy spoke, Jimmy asked if we would like a drink. I thought this strange; as we had already received several bottles of beer. However, Murphy and I soon found he meant something much different. The headman walked over and lifted up the large bottle with strange contents. As he brought it over, to my amazement, inside, I could see an assortment of small reptiles. A closer look revealed these included a snake, frog, and a lizard. This I thought an incredible sight.

Things became even more incredible when he opened the bottle and filled two small glasses. One he gave to Murphy, the other to me. I felt apprehensive about drinking whatever it was, so I watched Murphy. He first smelt the crystal-clear drink, then sipped it.

I was about to drink when he exclaimed, "Bejabbers! Sure, it tastes just like Porcine."

This made me even more apprehensive. I knew Porcine was similar to whisky, which I didn't like. However, with us honoured guests, I had to drink. Murphy was right; it did taste like whisky, a strong but smooth one. I could not believe such a delicate flavour could come from a bottle filled with such an assortment of reptiles. It was a day I will not forget in a hurry, that's for sure.

After rehearsals for the pantomime one night, I joined friends at the bar for a drink and a chat. By the time I headed home, it was pitch black, with the road deserted. Suddenly, out of the gloom, I saw what appeared to be a large dog crossing in front of me. As I swerved to avoid it, to my amazement, it was not a dog, but a huge monitor lizard. Despite breaking hard and almost going off the road, I could not avoid hitting it. I felt a bump and heard a sickening crunch as I went over its tail. I jerked to a stop and reversed to look for the lizard, but it had vanished into the night. I only hoped it was not too severely injured.

When I mentioned this incident at work, the lads laughed. They said I must have been dreaming. However, when I mentioned this incident at the next rehearsal, one of my friends said, "Someone spotted two huge monitor lizards near where you hit one."

On the site one day, as I walked over to see how things were going with Harold, it surprised me to find no one working. When I asked him why, he shocked me when he said, "My men are considering going on strike."

"What! Why? What's happened?" I asked.

Harold looked downcast, "As I walked past the gilding supervisor, I ruffled his hair."

My eyebrows rose and I asked, "So? What has that got to do with the men planning a strike?"

He shook his head. "Colin, it's regarded as an insult to ruffle the hair of a Thai person." On asking if he had known this before, I could not believe it when he said he did.

Then why on earth did you do it?" I asked.

He shrugged. "I don't know. It is because I felt tired. I would normally never have done such a stupid thing."

As I walked away, Harold went to apologise to the man. Thankfully, the man accepted his apology, and his men returned to work.

Apart from not ruffling a Thais hair, I also learnt of another insult to Thais. When sitting with one, you should never sit with your feet facing them.

After rehearsals one night, I accepted an offer from Peter, to join him and Mary, plus Peter and Sue at the beach on the Sunday.

When I later approached the meeting place, I spotted Peter waving for me to follow his jeep. As I did, I could not believe the condition of the track we drove down. The surface was a mass of deep, jagged channels, gouged out by rainwater pouring down on its way to the sea. It required all of my strength and concentration to prevent the jeep from slipping into one. When I reached the sandy beach without mishap, I let out a sigh of relief.

On getting out and looking around, apart from my friends, the beach was deserted. I chuckled. "I can see why there is no one else here," I said. "Only crazy people would risk driving down that track."

Peter laughed. You're right," he said, "that's why we come here; it's always like this."

As I couldn't swim, I stripped to my trunks and sunbathed while talking to the others. A short time later, Mary's, Peter, suggested skinny-dipping, which, to my surprise, Sue's Peter said, "Okay."

Mary's Peter pulled off his swimming trunks, ran down the beach, and dived into the sea. When he surfaced, he found Peter still sat on the beach talking.

After swimming for a while, Peter called out, "I want to get out!"

Sue laughed. "Okay," she said, "then do so."

"I don't want to get out with you sat there," he said.

Sue giggled. "That's alright, Peter, I've seen it all before."

"Not mine!" Peter exclaimed. "And I'd rather not start now."

Sue laughed. "But Peter," she said, "it was your suggestion. Anyway, I don't know what your problem is, but I'm just going to sit right here enjoying the view."

After standing in the water for a while, Peter waded out. He covered himself with his hands as he walked up to where his trunks lay. Turning away from the girls, he slipped them back on. The two girls curled up laughing, whereas Peter was red with embarrassment.

Although I thought the beach great, I soon discovered why there were so few people on it. No sooner had I awaked the next morning, when I started to scratch. On checking, I discovered that I was covered in large bumps, so I went to see a doctor. On his asking where I had been, I replied, to the beach.

He smirked. "Sandflies have bitten you, "he said. "These are a big problem on the beaches in Brunei." He then gave me a prescription for some cream and tablets.

From then on, anytime I went to the beach, I would light a fire to keep the sandflies away.

One evening, along with some fellow actors in the pantomime, we went for a barbecue on the beach. We were about to set it up when someone noticed dark storm clouds gathering out at sea. That was it; we decided to leave and have the barbecue at one of the group's house.

Without delay, we packed up and drove there. A short time later, the barbecue was lit, with a variety of delicious food odours wafting through the air. Along with meat, chicken, and prawns, someone had brought small live crabs. These had their claws tied, to prevent them from pinching whoever picked them up. The cook had just placed a few of them on the barbecue when one girl came to see how things were going.

On seeing the crabs, she looked horrified. "That's barbaric!" she cried out. "At least kill them before you cook them."

Without a word, the cook reached over. He picked up a long metal skewer, and in front of her shocked eyes, stabbed them. "There," he said, "now they are dead. Satisfied?"

As the girl turned and went back inside the house, we heard her said, 'Barbarian.'

One Sunday morning, along with a dozen men and women, we set off to meet a guide who would take us to see an Ilban longhouse. These are so named, due to them being around100ft long. To meet the guide, involved a half hour's drive along a narrow, twisting track through the jungle. When we arrived at the river meeting point, we found our guide waiting, with a long, narrow, open boat. It looked too small for us all to fit in, but after manoeuvring around, we all squeezed aboard.

Our guide started the outboard motor, and we began to move up the river. I don't think any of us knew how long this trip would take, but it took much longer than I expected.

On the way, our guide informed us we would be going out of Brunei and into Sarawak. Our guide's information shocked me. This would be illegal.

Our boat only had a small canopy over the centre portion. Therefore, the people sitting at the bow and stern sections experienced exposure to the blazing blistering sun. Approximately three hours later, we pulled over and tied up at the riverbank. By then, those not wearing a hat were looking sun-burnt. With much relief and aching bodies, we climbed off the boat.

After we scrambled up the muddy bank, we followed our guide along a narrow path through the jungle. A few minutes later, there in front of us was the 'Longhouse.' Running the full length of the timber building, was an open veranda with children playing on it. Some adults sat on the floor, engaged in conversation.

The children must have known we were coming, as they wore what appeared to be their best outfits. With the girls' dresses a multitude of bright colours, it made a beautiful picture. On approaching the building, many of them came to greet us. All were happy and laughing as they ran up, waving and pointing at us.

As we stepped onto the verandah, our guide introduced us to the Headman, who then introduced us to the other adults. To my surprise, all spoke English. One told me he was an English teacher at a school in town, and only came home on weekends to visit his parents.

Once introductions were over, we took packets of balloons from our backpacks and handed them to the waiting children. The air became filled with the sound of them shrieking with delight as they ran around holding them. For the adults, we had brought packets of cigarettes and tobacco, which were gratefully received.

As I took a walk around outside the Longhouse, a man wearing a pair of shorts that exposed an array of tattoos from the waist up caught my eye. However, even more noticeable, he was sharpening an old bayonet on a whetstone.

I walked over and asked him where he got the bayonet. Without stopping, he replied, "I took it from a Japanese."

It seemed pretty obvious what he meant by that remark, so I said nothing more.

After spending hours at the Longhouse, we then returned to our boat for the long trip home. Although it had been a long, hot and exhausting day, it was also one of great pleasure.

To my surprise, one day Sa-ard invited me to a party to celebrate Wonchai getting engaged. In the evening, all the Thais dressed in their best clothes were ready and eager to go to the restaurant for the party. As they only had their old truck to get everyone there, I offered my jeep. Although only sitting eight, it was cleaner and more comfortable than their vehicle. Also, by using both, everyone was soon at the restaurant.

Wonchai and his intended fiancé were there waiting, and after a brief ceremony were engaged.

Later, I became shocked to learn that Wonchai had a wife home in Thailand. Sa-ard laughed as he explained that being engaged while having a wife was not a problem. It seems once engaged; the couple could then live together. I am sure this idea would not go down too well if one's wife were English.

The evening was a great success. Everyone was drinking and eating spicy Thai food, with a lot of dancing going on. It was late by the time I returned to our camp feeling drunk. I fell into bed and went straight to sleep.

The next morning, it shocked me when Harold informed me what had later happened. They found Wonchai badly beaten, lying in a pool of blood on the floor in the camp toilet. He told his friends who found him that some Filipinos had attacked and beaten him up."

"That's terrible, what a way to finish the evening," I said.

Harold shook his head. "You think that bad," he said grimly. "Much worse happened. I'm surprised you never heard anything. Anyway, on hearing about Wonchai, the Thais immediately woke and told everyone what had happened. As Thais and Filipinos don't normally get on too well together, this incident was like waving a red rag to a bull." He paused, then continued. "From what I gather, after the Thais picked up various items to use as weapons, they looked for any Filipinos who might be around. However, it seems the word had already gone around the Filipinos section of the camp, as they found none."

My eyes lit up in horror at what he said next. "Finding no one to fight, the Thais then manufactured a variety of deadly weapons, including knives and nail-studded coshes. Once made, they decided to ambush any unwary Filipinos they could find." Harold gave a grim smile. "The Filipinos must have known what was going on, so wisely stayed in their rooms. When this action failed, the Thais decided to confront the Filipinos head-on in a pitched battle to avenge Wonchai."

"Wow! This is unbelievable," I said. "I can't think how I missed all this."

Harold chuckled. "Yes, well," he said. "It was the sound of drumming that woke me and the camp management. Ongoing to investigate, we found all the Thais walking down the road heavily armed, and following a drummer. We realised it meant something extraordinary must have happened.

When Martin was called and informed of the situation, he came to camp and told Sa-ard to get the men off the street. After Sa-ard ignored the warning, Martin warned him that unless the men gave up their arms and dispersed, they would face deportation. Only then, with reluctance, did Sa-ard agree and instruct the men to return to their rooms. They were far from pleased about having to give up their weapons. Only when Martin said the police would be called in to find who had attacked Wonchai, did they agree.

"Christ! What a night," I said. "I must have been dead not to have heard all the noise."

Ongoing to see Wonchai, it horrified me to see his bottom lip split wide open into two parts. It looked like a letter-box. I had never seen such a gruesome sight. It was no wonder the Thais wanted to take their revenge on the Filipinos. When I asked why Wonchai was not in the hospital, Sa-ard said, "We have no money to pay for a doctor."

After I said the company would pay all costs, they took Wonchai to the hospital and his split lip sewn back together. It then took several months before it healed, and Wonchai looked normal again.

As for who attacked Wonchai, the police never found who was responsible. This, of course, did not go down well with the Thais.

Harold later told me that one of our Thais— a champion kickboxer—had challenged any four Filipinos to a fight. Although he offered to take them all on at the same time, there were no takers. Had there been, for sure there would have been more work for the hospital.

Sometime later, Sa-ard invited Peter and me to celebrate the Thai New Year with them. As we walked to where a group were standing, I noticed that although wearing their best clothes, they appeared wet. We discovered why, when after they asked us to sit on two chairs, wearing a big smile, Sa-ard poured a bowl of water over our heads.

Peter and I were shocked. "What's the big idea?" I spluttered.

Sa-ard, who was standing with several of the men laughing, explained. "To celebrate our New Year, it is the custom to throw water over everyone."

It was the first time I had heard about this type of celebration. We were about to get up when Peter and I were each handed a present. However, after putting our gifts to one side, they then took great delight in pouring more water over our heads. This time, they had mixed it with red dye. This not only soaked us from head to foot, but also stained our shorts and T-shirts. Although this had come as a bit of a shock, we both had to laugh at seeing the state we were in.

When I unwrapped my present, I found it was a beautiful watercolour painting of a Thai war canoe. Each time I look at it, I smile on remembering my first Thai, New Year.

Martin informed us one day there would be a Wiltshier Hash Run, and all company staff and workers had to attend and run. Harold tried to get out of this by saying he was too fat to run, but Martin told him if he couldn't run, he had to walk. When we drove out to the start of the run, a surprise awaited us. The camp cooks were there busy preparing a large barbecue. As we awaited the run to start, the Sultan—who as usual was driving himself—drove past. On recognising who we were, he gave us a royal wave, which I thought a friendly gesture.

A short time later, a horn blasted, and we were off. Those who were fit and able ran off following the trail, while the rest of us followed along as best we could. It was comical to hear a group of the Thais, who stayed back with Harold shouts, "Come on, Mr Harold, run, don't give up." Thankfully, despite his bulk, Harold managed to complete the course without having a heart attack.

The Thais enjoyed themselves, with the cooks doing us proud, producing a variety of excellent barbecued food. This in itself, made the run worthwhile.

While down in the basement of the Istana (main palace), I discovered the Sultan's collection of cars. These ranged from small Fiats and Minis to stretched Mercedes and Rolls-Royce. There was also a 1950s pink Cadillac with huge rear fins and massive chrome bumpers, plus an old London taxi. Both of which used to belong to the Sultan's father.

To my surprise, I learned that apart from ceremonial circumstances, the Sultan drove himself, in whichever car he fancied on the day. Without a doubt, this was something few, if any other monarchs would dare do. He did, however, always have a carload of bodyguards following behind.

Work on the Palace was going well, with various sections receiving final touches. During this stage that I nearly caused an accident involving the Sultan. It occurred while on my way to the Sultan's Study, carrying a large mirror that partially obstructed my view. I was about to walk around a corner in the corridor when a pair of hands grabbed me, and a sharp stern voice said. "Stop!"

I almost dropped the mirror in shock, but somehow managed to keep hold of it. After resting it on my foot, I turned to the grabber and snaps, "Why did you that?"

Just then, the Sultan walked past. That's why!" he replied. "If I hadn't stopped you, you would have walked straight into the Sultan."

I realised just how fortunate I was. The man had prevented what could have been a nasty accident. Given this, I calmed down and thanked him profusely.

While driving through the camp, I spotted a group of Filipinos washing a puppy. I thought this good of them until I mentioned it to the camp boss. Wearing a grim smile, he said, "They always wash the dogs before they cook them. By now, they have killed and are cooking it. His words horrified me, but I was even more shocked when he continued with a grim smile, "They always wash the dogs before they cook them." He then shocked me when he said, "As Filipinos eat dogs back home in the Philippines, this is normal."

While on my way back to camp one evening, as I turned a corner, I found the road blocked by a jeep lying on its side. I slammed on the brakes and screeched to a stop. I ran up to the jeep to see if anyone was injured. To my surprise, the driver was nowhere to be found. My surprise then turned to anger when I realised it was my jeep blocking the road. The last time I had seen it was when I left it with our mechanic for servicing.

As I stood wondering where the driver was, a jeep pulled up on the other side, and John, our decorator, appeared. He ran over, cries out in alarm, "Are you okay? Are you hurt?"

"I'm okay, thanks. Although it's my jeep, I was not driving it." Just then our Thais' truck pulled up and out jumped Sa-ard and five of his men. They walked up to us and said, "Good evening, Mr Colin, how are you?"

"Never mind how I am," I snapped, "why is my jeep upside down in the middle of the road with no one in it?"

Sa ard beamed me a smile. "I am sorry, Mr Colin. Tonchai was driving it when a dog jumped out in front of him. He swerved to avoid it, but went into a spin and landed upside down. After climbing out, he ran to the camp to fetch help and get the jeep back on its wheels."

I shook my head. "No doubt, he was driving too fast as usual?" I said. "Still, is he okay?"

"Yes, but I told him to stay in camp because it shook him up."

"Okay. Now let's try and get the jeep back on its wheels." With all of us pushing and pulling, we eventually managed. However, it was off the road and down one side of the bank. With the roof smashed in, the jeep looked a right mess.

"Mr Colin," Sa-ard said. "I will drive it back on the road."

"No!" I replied. "It's my jeep; I will." With the roof smashed down, I had difficulty climbing in. I started the engine, then drove slowly up the bank onto the road. To my disbelief, before I could stop, the jeep shot across and down the other side. In total, it took three attempts before I managed to stop on top of the road.

In the meantime, the Thais were laughing and giggling at my efforts.

"There are no brakes," I called out. "The fluid must have run out when the jeep was upside down." After a struggle to get out of the jeep, I said, "Okay, Sa-ard, you drive the jeep back to camp. If you keep behind your van, it will act as a brake."

It took a week before they repaired the jeep in good enough condition for me to drive. However, one look at the dented roof showed it had been in an accident.

In the meantime, before I knew it, the opening night of the Pantomime was upon us. I learned I would be the first person to walk on stage. However, to my relief, as I walked out, I found Emberella sat awaiting my appearance. The show went down well, with the audience clapping and cheering at every opportunity. It proved such a success; we had to make at least three curtain calls. Each of the following three nights' performances also went well, with the last night a resounding success.

A few months later, I played a part in another stage production, which unlike the last play, was a drama. Although I enjoyed acting in it, I much preferred the comedy show. Both shows were held in front of packed audiences, which to our delight, went down well on each of the three nights we performed.

The experience of acting in both Marys' 'Emberella,' and Sue's play, was an incredible experience. It being one of the leading highlights during my stay in Brunei, and something I will always remember.

Right before the completion of our works on the Palace, Martin planned a works party at the Yacht Club. On the evening of the party, all the Thais wore their best outfits. Once everyone sat down, Martin stood up and used a microphone to give a brief speech.

"First, I would like to thank you all for coming. Tonight's party is in appreciation of all the hard work you have done. The finishing works in the Palace are of the highest possible standard. Therefore, on behalf of Wiltshier International, I congratulate you on the fabulous Palace. He gave a broad grin, and then said, "Oh! One last thing. Tonight, the drinks are on the company, so go and enjoy yourselves."

On hearing this, a big burst of applause broke out. While stood at the bar when the first group of Thais came up, the first one or two requested a gin and tonic and a vodka tonic. To my astonishment, Tonchai requested a bottle of Johnny Walker Black Label whisky. I thought this much, however, the bar staff must have been instructed to give whatever drinks people requested. The barman smiled, and handed over a bottle.

Tonchai, grinning ear to ear, then returned to where Sa-ard and a group of his close friends were sitting. Their faces lit up when they saw the bottle he held. Seeing Tonchai given a bottle of spirits, several other Thais asked and also received bottles. The evening was a successful success, and although I don't know what the evening's bill came to, it must have been rather expensive.

I had such a successful life in Brunei, I didn't want to leave when my contract was over. What with the experience of acting on stage, running on the hash, and talking with the Sultan's wife, it's something I will always remember?

In appreciation of my work on the project, the company arranged my return flight back to the UK to be via Thailand and Hong Kong. I was going to Thailand as Sa-ard had invited me to visit him and his family. As for Hong Kong, like Thailand, I had not been there before. Also, with it close to Thailand, it was too good an opportunity to be missed.

So as not to be loaded down with luggage; I decided to send the blowpipe, along with a suitcase of clothing back to England by cargo. Ongoing to the customs office, our company liaison man explained to a customs officer what I was sending back to the UK. He made clear; it included a blowpipe in a box I had made for it. The official wrote this down on the list of items to be shipped.

Then, on going to inspect what I was sending, the customs officer inquired, "What's in the long, narrow box?"

His causal appearance turned to one of shock when I replied, "That's the blowpipe."

"What! You cannot take that out of the country," he exclaimed. "It's a dangerous weapon."

I chuckled. "It is in your country, but in mine, it's just a decoration to be hung on a wall."

To my relief, after a bit of talking, he agreed I could send the blowpipe back to England.

On leaving Brunei with the last of our Thai workers, we flew over to Bangkok. Unfortunately, due to receiving incorrect information, Sa-ard was not there to meet me. To my relief, my Thai friends found me a small hotel for the night.

The next morning, Sa-ard and several other Thais I had worked with came to collect me.

On seeing me, Sa-ard's face lit up. He gave me a big hug and said, "Welcome to Thailand, Mr Colin. I am happy to see you."

"Thanks, Sa-ard; it's a pleasure to be here," I replied.

Sa ard's transport turned out to be a pickup truck, fitted with seats extending to the end of the open tailgate. This I soon found was a regular mode of transport in Thailand. After about an hour drive, we arrived at Sa-ard's village. As we pulled up outside his house, I was pleased to see more of the Thais I had worked with. Although everyone greeted me as though I was an honoured guest, I felt privileged to be there.

To my surprise, Sa-ard had arranged a dinner party for me. It went off well, with my happy and relaxed among such friendly people. I felt proud when Sa-ard told me that by visiting him in his village; I had made him a cheerful man.

After dinner, Sa-ard took me to see the new house that he was building. From here, we went to meet other Thai work colleagues and their wives. It felt good seeing them, with them happy to see me.

During the two days of my stay, Sa-ard, his wife, and some of the other Thais took me to various places of interest. This included a snake farm where I had my photo taken with a full-grown tiger.

We also visited the "Summer Palace," which I thought fantastic. Even on its own, it would have been reason enough to visit Thailand.

When Sa-ard and the others dropped me at the airport for my flight to Hong Kong, I felt sad. They were such friendly and happy people; I felt sorry to leave them. I had enjoyed both working and spending time with them.

The two days I spent in Hong Kong was incredible. It was so colourful and bustling with life; I wished I had longer to see more of the city. Still, thanks to my company, I felt fortunate to be there.

After flying back to Heathrow, I then took a local flight down to Plymouth. Here I was pleased to find Jen and my two daughters waiting to greet me.

Several months later, I received a surprise call from my old boss, Mick. He informed me the Sultan had invited him and Mr Wiltshier (the owner of the company) to attend a meeting in London. During this, he said The Sultan and his wife had thanked the company for achieving such a high standard of work on the Palace. It made me feel proud to have been on the project. The following week, I received a letter from the company thanking me for my participation. This was much appreciated, and numerous years later, I still have the letter.

The experience of working on the Sultan's Palace was incredible. Without doubt, I did the right thing by not returning to Oman. All the recent activities and adventures I experienced in Brunei are a highlight in my working life. However, it made me wonder if I could ever obtain such a contract again. Unknown to me, this would not happen until years later. In the meantime, I would experience near-drowning and the thrill and adventure of working in a variety of other countries.

Lucky escape in Qatar

# Chapter Six

While at Expats International office in London, I found an overseas contract advertised that sounded right up my street. I sent them my CV, then followed it up with a phone call to Robert, the contact name at the company. After he found and read my CV, it delighted me when he asked if I could attend an interview. During this talk, Robert explained the contract was a palace in Doha, Qatar. At the end of our talk, he invited me to attend a meeting at the company's head office in London. After doing so, I felt over the moon when he offered me a one-year contract.

The following week I flew to Qatar. On arrival at Doha airport, awaiting driver met and drove me to a camp on the edge of town. I found my accommodation was in a Portakabin, furnished and split into two sections. One section would be mine, with the other half occupied by someone else.

After dropping off my luggage, the driver took me to the site and introduced me to Bill, the project manager. He informed me my stay in the Portakabin would be temporary. As soon as one became available, I would move into a room at the villa where he and the other company personnel lived.

No sooner had I returned to my Portakabin when there was a knock on my door. As I opened it, a man with an Irish accent said, "Hi, I'm John; I live in the other half of the Portakabin." He grinned. "I'm an architect, and like you working on the palace project."

John explained the camp provided all meals, (which he said great) and also did our laundry free. This sounded much better deal than living in the villa. Bill had informed me that the food allowance money the company paid me would go towards funding meals at the villa. Also, although a houseboy would do my laundry, I would have to pay him.

The next morning, after a tasty breakfast in the camp canteen, a driver drove John and me to the site. Here John introduced me to various people working in our site office. Philip, I had met in the London office, was there, along with a man called Russell, another site supervisor. There was also an architect named Hussein, who John said worked with him on designing the interior joinery works. A Frenchman named Andre, informed me he had two French teams. One created joinery works, while the other drew up plans for plaster ceilings. A German named Helmut was in charge of a team of Portuguese marble fixers. I had never worked on a project with such a variety of nationalities.

> John had a friendly temperament, with our becoming friends, both in and out of work. On two separate occasions, I found him, making what to me were simple mistakes in his drawings. When I informed him why he could not do what he had drawn, he shrugged. "I'm a chancer." He then explained, "As I have never taken the final exam, I am not a qualified architect. Therefore, I'm more than happy for any advice you can give me."

John's honesty made me appreciate his friendship.

I considered the location of the Palace excellent, being only a short distance to both the sea and the palace the Emir used. When I first walked inside the new palace, my eyes lit up. The massive atrium where most of the marble installation works were ongoing, stood over 80 feet high. It surprised me to learn that the palace project team used feeler gauges and an eight-foot straight-edge for their examinations. I had never seen this method of testing used on any of my previous contracts.

Helmut seemed a typical German. He was abrupt in his manner of talking and sounded like Adolf Hitler addressing a meeting. However, he turned out to be both friendly and helpful.

At the time of my arrival, no joinery works had received final sign-off, so, there were no joinery items for me to inspect. Bill said given this; he wanted me to look after the fibrous plaster installation works. I had no problem with this, but because of a lack of this type of work ongoing, I became bored doing next to nothing. A short time after my arrival, someone told me that Phillip had returned to the UK without notifying anyone of his intention. As we had had no problems, I can only think he was as bored as me.

The weather in Qatar was hot and humid. Walking the short distance to the site, checking ongoing works and then back to my office, left me soaked. The first time this happened, after returning to the office I shared with Russell, I switched on our A/C unit. On finding it not working, I contacted our electrician to come and fix it. When he arrived, it shocked me when he said, "I can fix it, but Mr Russell will just break it again." I turned to Russell, who had just arrived and asked what he meant. To my astonishment, he said, "What he said is correct. If he repairs it, I will break it." Before I could commented, he said, "Let me tell you why. As you know, it's sweltering outside. If you were to use the A/C in the office, you would feel the heat much more outside than if you had not used the A/C. Given this, I find it best not to use it. Instead, I always have a spare shirt to change into after I've been on-site for a while."

Although I did not agree with what he said, I had no choice but to accept. From then on, I always kept a spare shirt in the office and would change into another shirt after having lunch back at the camp.

After lunch, I used to strip off and sunbathe outside my Portakabin for twenty minutes. I did, until after one session when I went inside to have a shower, I collapsed. With the temperature around 100+, I must have had a touch of sunstroke. Whatever the cause, I never sunbathed again, nor on the beach.

During the installation of the Atrium ceiling, the French workers captured two large owls they found there. As a nature lover, I was pleased to hear that they released them back into the wild.

While talking with Russell, it shocked me when he informed me of an incident involving a German tourist. He said the man had parked outside the Emir's old palace, as he wanted to take some photos of it. However, the guards asked the man to move his car, it being forbidden to parking outside the palace. After the guards warned him several times to move his car, which he refused to do, the guards opened fire on his car." Russel gave a grim smile. "This action no doubt horrified the man, but he could do nothing," he said. "He should have moved his car when first told by the guards."

While driving around town one day, it puzzled me to see army scout cars blocking several roads leading off the main highway. Then, as I neared the site, a convoy of fast-moving vehicles appeared. To my amazement, without slowing down, they shot up the ramp and into the Emir's Palace.

I later heard these were the usual security precautions when the Emir went anywhere. It being far different from when the Sultan of Brunei drove around in Brunei.

A few weeks after my arrival, the company gave me an old twin cab pickup truck for my use. This I then used it on our day off work to take John, and Ian (our quantity surveyor) out and about. Strange, but although we used to set off in different directions, we always ended up at our favourite beach.

Although ideal for swimming, snorkelling, and lying out on the beautiful sandy beach, there was no shelter from the blazing sunshine. Given this, we searched the beach and adjacent reed-covered dunes for items to make up a canopy. When I found a piece of canvas protruding from the sand, I managed to dig it out. Although quite big, with the help of the two guys, we dragged it back to where we had been sitting. I said, "Now all we want are sticks to hold it up to form a canopy."

After finding a few branches and bits of wood, we made up a rough canopy. As it proved ideal, we took it with us when we left the beach. Back at the site, we collected pieces of old packing crates to make stronger supports for the canopy. From then on, each time we returned to the beach; the canopy enabled us to stay all day without getting burnt.

As we thought Arabs wore robes to keep cool, John and I bought one each that we used to wear on the beach.

Not only did these prove ideal, but also made us look the part. At one time, while wearing my robe, John and I called in at a supermarket. After getting back in the truck, John told me about an English family who were entering the supermarket as we left.

They had remarked on my wearing the robe, which showed that all I wore underneath was a thong. It being what I wore whenever we were going to the beach.

While driving back from the beach one evening, the exhaust started making a lot of noise. I pulled over and stopped the truck on the edge of the highway. Then, while John and Ian kept an eye out for passing traffic, I slid underneath to investigate. I found the exhaust pipe had broken in half. To make a temporary repair, I called out that I needed an empty coke can or similar. By the time I scrambled out, John had found a can. Using my sheaf knife, I cut off the bottom and top, and then went back under the truck. After I jammed the two broken bits of pipe inside the can, I tied it in place with some of our shoelaces. In the circumstances, it was the best I could do.

While under the truck, I heard trucks and cars blasting their horns as they passed. I thought little it, but when I finished repairing the exhaust and stood up, I found John and Ian laughing.

"What's so funny," I asked?

John, who could hardly contain himself, said, "You. When the passing headlights picked you up under the truck, all they could see was what looked like a naked body."

While out another one day, I noticed that we were approaching the border to Saudi Arabia. As we didn't want to go to Saudi, on seeing a narrow side turning, I swung the pickup off the road and up the trail. As we drove up a sizeable sandy hill, it shocked me to see on a rusting barbed wire fence, signs showing the skull and crossbones. Underneath was a warning, danger minefield.

Ian called out, "Hey, Colin," "Do you think we'll be okay going up here?"

I forced a grin. "We have no choice," I said. "If I stop now, we'll not be able to turn around or pull away again. This is not a four-wheel drive, and the sand is too deep. Anyway, I'm sure the minefields are the other side of the fence. If they were this side, there would be a warning not to use this trail."

A few minutes later on cresting the hill, we all breathed an enormous sigh of relief. The trail turned away from the fence and the minefield warnings.

We only had a rough map that didn't show where we were, but I thought we were going in the general direction of our beach.

After about an hour driving along a faint trail across the open desert, I stopped in amazement. Crossing in front of us was a dual carriageway. I thought this peculiar; as there were no signs of any road on our map. The road was brand new. Although t it had roundabouts and streetlights in position, it was unsurfaced. After a discussion as to which way we should go, we decided to turn left.

A short time later, we found the road blocked by a massive pair of metal gates. Next to them were a number of Portakabins, which as we drove up, men appeared from them. I got out to ask where we were, but no one spoke English. One man went to one of the Portakabins, and then returned with another man. He was a supervisor and could speak English. I showed him our map and asked him to show me where we were. To my astonishment, we were on the opposite side of the coast from where I thought we were. On asking, he said the road led to a large building at the edge of the sea. One thing for sure, the owner must have been extremely wealthy to have it built the road.

We thanked the man, turned around, and drove back down the dual carriageway. Approximately thirty minutes later, we came to the main road. Then, after another thirty minutes, we found the road that led to our favourite beach.

By the time we parked at the beach, it was 3 pm. Our journey had taken over five hot and tiring hours. Once stripped off, after a refreshing swim, we spent the next two hours relaxing on the beach.

On the drive back to camp, although the light was fading, I put my foot down. It resulted in some hairy moments when the truck became airborne as we shot over the top of small hills. Overall, by the time we reached the camp, it had been an exciting day out.

During another trip out, while driving across the desert following a faint trail, I spotted someone ahead walking. As we got closer, the figure turned to reveal an elderly man dressed in Arab robes. Where he had come from we did not know, as there were no houses or a sign of life anywhere. I stopped alongside him and asked if he would like a lift. Although he couldn't speak English, he gestured yes, and pointed down the trail. After climbing up into the open truck bed, the man sat with his back against the rear window of the cab.

We then continued driving for the best part of an hour before a village appeared. As we drove into it, the man in the back banged on the roof; he wanted to get off. On stopping, he climbed down, bowed his head in thanks, and then walked away. I thought it unbelievable that he had been prepared to walk to the village. It would have taken him at least two hours.

One weekend, Helmut asked if John, Hussein and I would like to go on a trip with him and his wife. They were going to an inland lake where he said were large groups of Flamingos. It sounded like it could prove an adventure, so we were happy to accept.

Helmut drove his Toyota Land Cruiser accompanied by his wife and baby son. John, Hussein, and I followed, with my driving a car John had borrowed from a friend. About half an hour later, Helmut turned off the road and started to cross the desert. Initially, the trail was firm, but as we went further into the desert, the going softened. Helmut must have realised, as he pulled to a stop near a rocky outcrop.

As we pulled up alongside, Helmut said, "I think its best you all get in my truck. I have special sand tires fitted that will prevent us from sinking in the sand."

I had wondered why the wheels on his truck were more substantial than standard, now I knew. After squeezing into the back of Helmut's truck, we continued across the desert. About an hour and a half later, on cresting a rise, there stretched out below was a large lake.

Helmut weaved his way down the rocky hillside, then parked near the edge of the lake. With sighs of relief, we eased our cramped and aching bodies out of the truck.

Our long trip became worthwhile when we spotted large numbers of Flamingos standing out in shallow water. As we walked down to the water's edge, we were all looking forward to taking off our shoes and cooling our feet.

To our utter disappointment, the ground at the edge of the water was soft and spongy. So much so, we didn't want to stand on it in case it was quicksand. Although unhappy about not being able to go in the water, it was not worth the risk. Because of this, after lunch, we only spent a short time watching the flamingos before starting our return to Doha.

On the way, we stopped to collect my car, then followed behind Helmut.

At one point, the trail passed near the sea. Helmut drove down towards the shore while I parked further back. The next minute, after driving too near the water's edge, Helmets truck became stuck in the soft sand. Initially, we thought it funny to see water shooting up from his wheels as he tried in vain to get out. As he couldn't do so, we went down to help push the truck out. This proved impossible, as the more we tried, the deeper the truck sank into the sand. Even using an empty forty-gallon oil drum and a large branch we collected, we still could not get the truck out of the sand.

As we struggled in vain, a passing pickup-truck stopped. Two Arabs wearing long white robes got out and came to help us. Unfortunately, it only resulted in them sprayed with wet sand, thrown up by the spinning wheels of Helmut's truck.

We were still struggling when we heard the sound of engines approaching. As we looked, a convoy of five jeeps appeared. One of our two Arabs ran towards them, waving his arms, and they stopped nearby. We were fortunate; as one jeep had a winch fitted. The driver drove down and parked a short distance away on the dry sand. After attaching the winch-cable to Helmut's truck, with bated breath, we watched as the cable tightened. Although now down to the running boards, to our immense relief, they pulled the jeep out of the sand.

We could not thank our Arab friends enough for helping us. Had they not, at high tide, the truck would have ended up underwater. After all this excitement, we said our grateful goodbyes to our rescuers and returned to Doha.

A few days later, when we told friends about our trip to the lake, one enquired, "How many jeeps did you take?" When he heard we only went with one, his inquisitive look turned to one of shock and disbelief.

"You must be mad," he exclaimed. "No one ever goes there without taking at least three jeeps. If you had broken down out there, you would have had it. No one usually goes there, and you could not walk back to the road."

On this sombre news, it made us realise how fortunate we had been.

One Sunday, friends drove John and me out across the desert in a Pajero jeep. It was a fantastic experience. I had never been in a car or truck where the driver's seat moved in tune with the rough surface of the road. In comparison, our seats in the back were bouncing up and down. John and I were so impressed with the ride, we thought about buying a Pajero between us.

After a talk, we thought that at the end of our contract, we would buy a Pajero and drive it back to England. However, while John was checking potential routes back to England, he received news. We couldn't drive back to England, because John's colleague said we couldn't cross Saudi Arabia. We were both disappointment and it dashed all thoughts about enjoying a different mode of transport home. As it happened, neither of us completed our contracts, so this was no longer a problem.

Despite having a time on my days off work, on the site, I found myself with little work to do. Some people would have been happy to have little to do while getting well paid. Whereas I did not like wasting my time. I enjoyed working and keeping busy.

We then found there were problems re-finances on the site. As a result, numerous project management employees became redundant. To my disappointment, the company also made John, my architect friend, redundant.

One Sunday after John returned to England, Ian and I drove to our usual beach. Ian walked down to the sea and in a few minutes, had swum out over the sandbar. Meanwhile, after putting on my flippers and snorkel, I entered the water and started to swim out towards the sandbar. Although a strong wind was making the sea choppy, I thought little about it. Nevertheless, I had only gone a short distance, when my snorkel (the old type, just a curved tube) filled with water. I turned over on my back, cleared the water from it, then turned over and continued out towards the sandbar.

Unfortunately, because of my inexperience, I found myself unable to prevent water from going down the snorkel. Given this, I decided it best not to go on. I turned around and started swimming on my back to the beach. Although I couldn't swim without using flippers, I could float and could swim on my back. However, despite this, because of the strong wind, even this proved difficult.

I realised I had a choice, either I would either swim back to shore, or drown. Then, after making a supreme effort, I managed to get back to the beach.

When Ian returned sometime later, it horrified him to hear of my

near death. "Good grief, Colin! Why didn't you call out?" he said.

I shrugged. "There was no point. Even had I been able, you wouldn't have heard me. By then, you were way out past the reef."

Because of my near-miss with death, I never attempted snorkelling again. Also, not until years later did, I tell Jen about my fortunate escape.

About a month later, I received a letter from my wife, Jen. In, she told me she had a severe health problem that required hospital treatment. Given this, I resigned from my contract. I had been unhappy with my lack of work, so this news made my mind up.

My company did not want me to leave, but after explaining why, they understood. To my surprise, they even paid for my flight back to the UK. This good of them, as if you break an overseas contract, you usually have to pay for your flight home.

Shortly after my return home, Jen went into the hospital for treatment. This proved both a shocking and painful experience, made worse by the fact her treatment was only partially successful.

Once she had recovered from her ordeal, I started to seek another overseas contract. Although I never knew, it would end with my having the longest paid holiday ever.

Abu Dhabi, my shortest contract

# Chapter Seven

My next contract, a position as a joiner in Abu Dhabi, again came via Expat's International. With it not the kind of job I wanted; I called the company. I explained to the manager that I was seeking a supervisory position, not one on my tools. He said at present, he could only offer me a short-term contract as a joiner. However, my spirits lifted when he said the company expected to receive a contract for a Palace. If successful, he could then offer me a long supervisory contract. As there was nothing else on offer, I accepted the contract.

I found the project involved installing a variety of timber ceilings in an office for the Abu Dhabi Oil Minister. Although it meant working in the Middle East again, this was not a problem. I looked at it as an adventure in a country I had not visited before.

On arrival in Abu Dhabi late evening, a young Pakistani met me. When he smiled, even in the pale light, his dazzling white teeth made me jealous.

After he took to a company apartment, and showed me my room, he left. I went to bed and fell asleep.

The next morning, as I walked in for breakfast, I stopped dead in my tracks. There, sat at the breakfast table were two familiar persons. "Hi, Ron, Jeff," I exclaimed, "what are you guys doing here?" The last time I had seen them was in Brunei, working on the Sultan's Palace. When they stood up, smiling, it was apparent my arrival was no surprise to them.

"Hi, Colin, glad to see you arrived okay," Ron said, as first he then Jeff shook my hand. "Although we're working for the same company, we are on two different projects." He grinned. "We knew you were coming, but your expected arrival was too late for us to stay up and meet you."

Ron then explained the apartment set-up. "We have two Pakistani houseboys, Mehmet, and Fahri. They cook our meals, do our washing, and in general look after us."

I thought this successful news, and better accommodation than I had expected.

As we were talking, one boy came in and served me a full English breakfast. This I thought a great way to start the day.

I had just finished eating when the driver from last night arrived to drive me to the site. It turned out to be thirty minutes from the apartment. I found I would be working with an English guy named George, while the rest of the workers were Thais. From previous experience, not only were they able to turn out quality finishes, but were also friendly and helpful people.

In a brief space of time, George and I became friends. He told me he had been working in Abu Dhabi for some time, and lived in a rented apartment he shared with two friends. Apart from that, as George said little about himself, I knew nothing else.

At lunchtime, to my surprise, Mehmet, and Fahri turned up to serve us a three-course meal. On mentioning this to George, he chuckled and said, "This is normal." I soon found that a full English breakfast, a three-course lunch, plus another one for dinner, was too much to eat in one day. On mentioning this to George, he agreed, so from then on, we only had a snack for lunch.

During a visit to the site, John, our project manager, asked if I would like to look inside the Oil Minister's villa that was next to where we were working.

George had told me there were problems with the interior, so I wanted to see what was what. I had learnt that one of my old companies had installed the interior finishings.

"Yes, please," I replied. "From what I've heard, it sounds it could be interesting."

I found the villa massive. In some rooms, the ceilings were over forty feet high. The villa contained a great variety of luxurious features, including highly decorated and ornate ceilings. As we walked into one room, a display of guns fixed on one wall caught my eye. To my amazement, on closer examination, one appeared to be a gold-plated Uzi sub-machine gun.

As we entered one room, John said, "This is the main dining room." He pointed upwards and said, "because of the gilded ceiling flaking, the Minister refuses to dine in here."

How to rectify the ceiling that was so ornate; I did not know. Only that it would cost the company that had carried out the works, an immense sum of money.

To my further astonishment, John told me of another problem. Because of beetle infestation, all the timber work inside the villa had been replaced by a second interior company. I had never heard of this type of problem, and could only wonder at the enormous cost of replacing all the timber. On leaving the villa, I thanked John for showing me.

Because of the complicated and intricate shapes of our project ceilings, I found the work interesting. As a result, we were so busy installing them; the days passed in no time at all.

I found Abu Dhabi to be a modern city, with wide, tree-lined streets and a variety of shops. There were also bars, with English singers and dancers supplying the entertainment. Some evenings, Ron, Jeff and I would go to one of these bars to listen to live music while enjoying a drink.

The bars were fitted out in an English flair, dark-coloured timber beams and wall panelling. Hanging on the walls were pictures of English country scenes. As such, you would think you were back in England. There was, however, one big difference; the prices. If going out for a drink more than twice a week, it meant having to change money at an exchange office. This, of course, was not the idea behind my working away from home and family. I was here to make money, not spend it.

One Saturday night, Ron and I went for a drink at the International Hotel. We found it busy with a live band playing slow dance music, and a few people out dancing on the floor.

As we looked around, a tall, attractive coloured girl standing on the other side of the room caught our eye. She noticed us, as she smiled across at us.

Ron grinned. "I think I've just scored," he said.

I laughed. "Go for it," I replied. Ron made his way across to where the girl stood. I saw her give Ron a beaming smile as he spoke to her. The next minute, it did not surprise me when they were out dancing cheek to cheek. Given this, I didn't expect to see him again that night. After finishing my drink and seeing them still out on the dance floor, I left and caught a taxi back to our apartment.

During breakfast the next morning with Ron and Jeff, I asked Ron how he had got on last night.

He laughed. "While we were dancing, I asked if she would like to come back to my apartment for a drink. It puzzled me when she gave me a knowing smile and said, " You know you will have to buy me a little gift." At first, I wondered what she meant! Then the penny dropped, she was a prostitute."

I curled up laughing. "So! What happened?"

He shrugged. "I said sorry, but I don't pay for it." She smiled. "It's not a problem. At the end of the dance, I thanked her and said goodnight. On not seeing you anywhere, I guessed you had left, so I left as well. I must have arrived back here not long after you did."

I grinned. "Well, if nothing more, I'm sure you enjoyed dancing with her," I said.

Ron gave a wistful smile. "Of course, I did! It's a long time since I held an attractive woman that close." His smile widened. "Who knows, I might meet another beauty before leaving here." He shook his head. "Only one who is not a prostitute," he said.

One Sunday morning, Ron, Jeff, and I took a walk down by the creek. Tied up on both sides were a variety of different-sized Arab Dhows. What caught my eye, however, were two luxurious motor yachts moored on the opposite side of the creek. Their gleaming white superstructure sparkled in the bright sunshine. Compared to the dull-looking dhows, they made an eye-catching sight.

The whole place bustled with activity, with dhows being loaded with all sorts of things. On one, different sized crates were being stacked around a large Mercedes. Although I thought this an unusual sight, no doubt for the locals, it was normal.

As we wandered further along the embankment, we came to the Gold Souk. It was a fantastic place, with shop windows packed with gold jewellery of all shapes, sizes and designs. One could only imagine the value in one of the shop windows. After walking through the Souk, we returned to our apartment. It had been an experience to see all the activity at the creek, plus wandering through the Gold Souk.

On our return to our villa, as we walked inside, we stopped on hearing the sound of Tina Turner belting out. On entering the lounge, we found Ahmet and Fahri standing mesmerised. They were watching our VCD of Tina Turner performing live on stage. As per usual, she was wearing little in the way of clothing. For us, this was normal, but from their enraptured looks, the boys had never seen a half-naked women before. When they realised we were watching, they were shocked and embarrassed. We laughed when with their heads down in shame; they ran out of the room.

While talking with some of our Thai workers, one informed me they had paid an agent in Thailand a large sum of money to obtain this contract. He said unless they worked a minimum of six months, they would not earn any money. I knew what he said about the payment to an agent to be correct, as Sa-ard had once told me the same thing. Because of my contract being only for three months, I felt concerned for them.

A short time later, on a visit to the site, I noticed John, my boss, looked glum. I discovered why when he said, "I'm sorry, Colin, but I have both good and news for you. We didn't get the palace project. It means that after this contract, we have no more work for you. However, as you have completed all the works on the office, you can fly back to the UK on Friday."

He smiled. "That was not the good news. Although you've not completed your three-month contract, the company will pay you for the full contract period."

He then looked downcast. "By the way, if it's any consolation, my contract is also finished." "Like you, I was hoping the company would have obtained the palace contract."

The palace news was not good, but that they would pay me for nearly another six weeks certainly was. It meant I would be paid while searching for a new contract.

After talking with me, John went to talk to George. I later found him far from happy. Although like me his contract finished on Friday, his salary also stopped then. Nevertheless, it was our Thai workers I felt sorry for. As they too were finishing on Friday, it would leave them in a serious situation. A short time later, it did not surprise me when one of the Thais came to talk with me.

"Mr Colin, can you help us, please? Mr John has told us there is no more work for us. We cannot go back to Thailand as we haven't earned enough money to pay our agent."

I said, "I am sorry, I wish I could help you, but I'm also out of work. All I can suggest is to talk to Mr John. Ask him if he knows of another company looking for workers."

Unfortunately, when I left Abu Dhabi a few days later, none of the Thais had found another job. Unless they managed to do so, they would be deported, which would leave them in debt to their agent.

As this had been my shortest contract ever, I decided not to include it on my CV. Nevertheless, I had visited another country at no expense to myself. Plus, thanks to the generosity of the company, I would have the longest paid holiday I had ever had. I only hoped that during this time, I would find another contract.

Little did I know I would soon be enjoying another thrilling adventure, which would prove crazy in the extreme.

More crazy adventures in Brunei

# Chapter Eight

While seeking another contract, Wiltshier, my old company, contacted me. They asked if I would return to Brunei, to help supervise alterations to the Sultan's palace. As I had enjoyed my last time in Brunei, I was only too happy to agree.

My arrival in Brunei did not start well. Because of the late arrival of my flight at Singapore, I missed my connecting flight on to Brunei. Fortunately, the airline gave me a hotel room for the night.

Upon arriving the next day, I found Harold waiting to meet me. At the site office, I found my old boss David Smith from Saudi, and Mike, one of our designers from our UK office were there. After exchanging greetings, David informed me a supervisor named Bill would be arriving the following week. "The three of you will supervise various sections of the Palace." Then he mentioned, "Two men from the original UK team of fibrous plasters are on-site." Before I could speak, he shook his head. "Unlike last time, they will work with a group of Thai plasterers."

On hearing this, I breathed a sigh of relief. When they were all English, they had caused numerous problems.

To my delight, Sa-ard and a couple of our old team of Thai carpenters would also be working with us. Another bonus, Jamlong, a Thai decorator I had worked with in Saudi would arrive shortly. To my surprise, David said part of our work involved alterations to the Banquet Hall ceiling. This I remembered as having intricate designs covered in gold leaf.

A few days later, David attended a meeting with the Sultan in the main Istana. Upon his return, David's announcement delighted Harold and me. We were going to perform various works in the

Istana. David must have known this, as part of the work involved redecorating the young princesses' bedrooms. No doubt this was why Jamlong would be joining us.

As I had never been inside the Istana before, I looked forward to seeing it. All I knew, the Guinness Book of Records listed it as having the greatest amount of rooms in a single residence.

On my first visit to the Istana, I felt disappointed. I thought it like a massive five-star hotel, and far less opulent than the palace I had worked on for wife number two.

After Jamlong arrived, I took him to the Istana to see the wallpaper for the princesses' bedrooms. It pleased me when he said he had hung a similar paper in Saudi. Once he had all the equipment set up, Jamlong started work on the first bedroom. On completion, I found he had done an excellent job.

During this time, the King, and Queen of Malaysia made an official visit to the Sultan.

At the time of their arrival, Jamlong had almost finished work in one princesses' rooms. Given this, I led him along the external corridor to our storeroom, where we kept the wallpaper for the next bedroom.

As I walked through the door and out into the lift area, to my horror and embarrassment, I found myself stepping out between the Sultan and the Queen of Malaysia. The Sultan's wife and the King of Malaysia were walking close behind. I am sure; they were as shocked I was by my sudden appearance. In a flash, I turned and pushed Jamlong back through the door, with my close behind.

I thought it showed a complete lack of security. However, on reflection, I realised it would have been impossible for an outsider to get through the top security into the Istana.

Shortly afterwards, Derek, a decorator from the UK, arrived to help Jamlong decorate the bedrooms. Between them, and the unique room furniture, the finished bedrooms looked fantastic.

In the meantime, works were ongoing in the Banquet Hall, with my pleased to hear the English and Thai fibrous plasterers were getting on well.

One morning, while on our way with a group of Thai workers into the Istana, security stopped and refused us entry. As we had been in and out often, I asked what the problem was. To my astonishment, a guard said, "The Thais have black eyes We don't trust them."

Despite my explaining about our previous entries, he refused to let us enter. He said we should use another entrance on the other side of the palace. After a ten-minute walk, we reached it, and with no problem, allowed into the Istana.

During a visit by Mick Weavis, our M.D, he said the company could not offer me full employment, but were finalising a contract in Monte Carlo. If they obtained it, he asked if I would be interested in working on it. I, of course, said, "Yes." The only possible drawback Mick could foresee was my lack of speaking French. However, this proved not a problem as the company did not obtain the contract.

While looking out a window in the Istana, I noticed a helicopter land outside. After switching off the engines, the crew climbed out, then lined up on the edge of a turnoff into the Palace. As I wondered why, a Rolls Royce appeared from the underground garage. Afer it drove the short distance to the helicopter, the Sultan climbed out of the car. He walked a few paces, then climbed inside the helicopter. Once the crew had boarded, it took off. I later heard the Sultan, a qualified pilot, frequently commutes between the palaces by helicopter. For sure, it's a far quicker way than driving.

How it came about, I don't know, but while in the Istana, I had been on the roof terrace talking to the Sultan's wife. She had been showing and informing me about a variety of exotic caged birds kept there. After a while, she left and walked away. I then heard her speak. As I turned back towards her; I said: "Pardon, your Majesty?" But to my amazement, she was nowhere in sight. This puzzled me until I heard one of the Myna birds start talking. I had to laugh when I realised it imitated the Sultan's wife voice to perfection.

One evening, Harold, David and I went to a barbecue at the camp boss' house. After the meal, David asked me to join in a game of badminton. Although I had never played before, I said I would give it a go. Although my efforts in hitting the shuttlecock back over the net amused the others, my partner was not pleased. Because of my lack of skill, we lost each game we played.

As we were busy working in both the second palace and the 'Istana," time passed. Before I realised, it was time for my break back home in England.

The day before leaving, Sa-ard invited me to join him, and the other Thais celebrate the Thai New Year at the Thai Embassy. While there, Sa-ard handed me a yellow rosette. This he said, showed me to be a member of his security unit. Although I never had to do anything, I enjoyed a colourful and pleasant evening.

During my trip home, I had booked a two-day stopover in Singapore. After landing, I took a taxi to my hotel and checked in. While doing so, I noticed an advertised evening coach tour of the city, so booked a ticket.

Compared to Brunei, where there were few hotels and only one new shopping centre, the bright city lights made a spectacle. During the tour, we visited the 'Night Safari,' where the animals are in enclosures fitted with two-way glass.

I found it an amazing experience to watch a variety of animals pressing up against the toughened glass only inches away. If ever in Singapore, I recommend you visit the 'Night Safari.' Without a doubt, it's something not to be missed.

The next morning, I went on another city tour that covered more areas of interest, including 'Raffles Hotel.' Here I had one of their famous Gin Slings that not only looked good, but tasted delicious.

I enjoyed my stay in Singapore, which is said to be the safest city in Asia. For sure, it's the cleanest city I have ever visited.

The next morning, I checked out of my hotel and took a taxi to the airport. The driver was friendly, and proved to be an honest man. After he dropped me at the airport and wished me a pleasant flight, he drove off. As I went to walk into the airport, I stopped dead in my tracks. My mouth opened wide in shock. I had left my small bag containing tickets, passport, and money on the back seat of the cab. In a mad panic, I dashed outside to stop it from leaving, but to my dismay, it had gone.

While stood in a daze wondering what to do, a taxi drew up beside me, and the driver tooted his horn. When he tooted again, I looked to see what he wanted. To my immense relief, it was my taxi. I almost cried with joy. I had felt sure I would not see my bag again.

The driver climbed out and, wearing a mile-wide smile, said, "You're lucky. I always make sure passengers have not left anything in my cab. Then, as I drove down the road and glanced in the rear mirror, I noticed your bag." He shrugged. "As it's a one-way street, I had no choice but to go on until able to turn around."

I took my bag from his outstretched hand, and then embraced him. Thanks to his honesty, he had saved me from enormous problems. Although reluctant to take the money I offered him, I insisted he did.

Once checked in, a shop selling orchids caught my eye. They looked so beautiful; I bought a large bunch for my wife. These the assistant wrapped, then placed them inside a presentation box.

A couple of hours later, I caught my flight to Heathrow. Being a long flight, I was tired by the time the plane landed. However, I still had another flight to catch. After collecting my luggage, I went to domestic departures, where I took a flight down to Plymouth. Unlike the jumbo jet I arrived in from Singapore, this plane only seated fifty people. On boarding, due to all my hand luggage, the lack of overhead storage proved a problem.

On my arrival at Plymouth airport late morning, I found Jen and my two daughters waiting to greet me. After a warm embrace and kissing my two daughters, with my luggage in the back of our car, Jen drove us home.

Once there, I handed Jen the orchids, who eyes lit up in delight. She thought them beautiful. We had been talking for a while when I remembered I had bought presents for the girls. I rose to my feet. "Sorry girls, I forgot I have something for you."

On going out in the hallway to fetch them, It shocked me to find my briefcase not there. I immediately went into a state of sheer panic. Inside were my return plane tickets, passport, and money, along with my camera and Walkman.

As I rushed out of the door to drive back to the airport, I yelled, "Jen, phone the airport. Ask if anyone has handed in my briefcase."

I jumped into our car and drove like a maniac back to the airport that was only a short drive. Upon arrival, I screeched to a stop, rushed inside, then looked around for my briefcase. My heart sank on not finding it anywhere.

On asking, I was fortunate to find the supervisor Jen had spoken to on the phone. He said, "I'm sorry, Mr Guest, but despite making enquiries, no one has seen your briefcase." His words mortified me.

He raised his eyebrows and asked. "Are you sure you took it off the plane when you landed?"

Thinking back, I remembered it had been impossible to put all hand-carry in the locker above my seat. Given this, I had put my briefcase in one further down.

You're right!" I exclaimed, "I never took it off the plane." After explaining where my briefcase was, he nodded. "Okay, we will contact the plane. A steward will check to see if the briefcase is still in the overhead locker."

On his return, I was relieved to see him smiling. "Well, news, Mr Guest. A flight attendant found your briefcase." Before I could speak, he continued. "Unfortunately, the plane has already left Newquay, where it went from here. It is now on its way back to Heathrow." When he noticed my downcast look, he said, "If you give me your phone number, we will contact you the minute the plane arrives tonight. You can then pick up your briefcase."

I could not believe my good fortune. Since leaving Brunei, I had twice misplaced my briefcase. I caught hold and shook his hand. "Many thanks for all your help, it is much appreciated. I'll be here to collect my briefcase five minutes after I receive your call."

As I headed home, I drove slower than on my way to the airport.

For the rest of the day, I could not relax, with my like a cat on a hot tin roof. When the phone rang in the evening, I grabbed it before it could ring twice. It was as I had hoped, the supervisor.

"Mr Guest, I'm pleased to say your briefcase has arrived." With a quick thank you, I was out the door in a flash and accelerated to the airport. As I walked inside, I observed the supervisor standing with my my briefcase in-hand. As he handed it to me, in a severe tone, he said. "I suggest you be more careful in future, Mr Guest. You could well have lost your briefcase."

"I will be," I said. "These past hours have been a nightmare."

# Part 2

During my time at home, Jen and I looked at several houses for sale in Hartley, an area where we had always wanted to live. On finding one, which we fell in love with; we made an offer. Unfortunately, the owner's rejection left us disappointed. I thought for a minute, and although Jen did not agree, I said I would now offer the full asking price.

"Look!" I said, "The house is exactly what we want. Not only that, we both know it's worth the asking price." With that, I called the agent and made a full offer. The next day, we were over the moon when he called to say the owner had accepted.

When I left to fly back to Brunei two days later, I wore a deep glow of satisfaction on my face. I looked forward to our moving into our dream home.

On arrival back in Brunei, Harold met me. To my surprise, after saying. "Did you have a pleasant holiday?" He shrugged. "By the way, I hope you're in a mood!" Before I could respond, he said, "The Thais have rolled your car."

This was a disaster, as without a car in Brunei, with no public transport and few taxis, it was difficult to get around. To my relief, the following week, David issued me with a Jeep hired from a local company. It meant I no longer had to rely on getting a lift to go anywhere. Plus, I could attend a hash run.

The following week, two specialist decorators arrived from England to install three large murals in the Istana. Because of their size, they arrived in sections, but once hung and the joints painted over, you would have sworn they were in one piece.

In the meantime, Harold and I found that Bill, our fellow supervisor's attitude, was not to our liking. Either he was not used to working with TCN workers (Third County Nationals) or, did not like people of colour. To our displeasure, he always referred to the Thais as Black Bas.... This, as far as Harold and I were concerned was way out of order. We liked and appreciated the Thais for all the hard work they did.

Some evenings Harold and I used to go to the World Wide Club at Berakas, the chief Army camp in Brunei. The World Wide Club at Berakas, the chief Army camp in Brunei, was the venue for the amateur dramatic shows. While there one night, a friend introduced us to a man called Eric. He turned out to be a supplier of darts and accessories to the many darts teams based in Brunei. The news about darts clubs in Brunei came as a big surprise. It was not a game I thought played here.

As I enjoyed a game of darts, I formed the 'Wiltshier' darts team. We then played one match a week. One at the WWC, the next an away match.

While at the RBA club, (Royal Brunei Airlines) one night, we won our game. Our celebrations ended up short-lived, when some of the RBA team blamed their fellow players for losing. Things escalated when some of them collected chairs and started throwing them around. One of our team, a Bruneian, advised we should leave. As this seemed a good idea, we left without delay.

Despite all the games we played in Brunei, this was the only time we experienced problems.

One team we enjoyed playing against the most was the 'Double Tops,' the only women's team in Brunei. Unlike other teams, we treated them as equals; so they liked playing us. In our last match, before I left Brunei, they presented me with a small shield. The inscription read, 'In appreciation of all the fun we had playing darts together.' This I thought was a friendly gesture.

In early March, with their works completed, Mike, Bill, and Derek returned to the UK. As a show of appreciation on their completion of the princes' bedrooms, I took Sa-ard, Jamlong, and a few other Thais out for dinner.

The following month, David informed me I would be required until at least the end of the month. I thought this great, as the longer he needed me, the better. However, along with the good, there always comes bad news.

Harold had been suffering with back pains for several weeks. Therefore, it did not surprise me when he said, "I need to return to the UK to see a specialist. The pain in my back is getting worse each day."

Although a pity about Harold leaving in these circumstances, from experience, I knew only too well what it was like to have back problems. David felt concerned about Harold going, whereas I didn't think it too big a problem. We had completed a large portion of our works

The next piece of news came when Jen phoned to say she had two buyers for our house. When she next phoned me, she had more good news. She had received two phone calls regarding a contract in Algeria for me. The first came from an agency, I had contacted, the second from Baxter Fell, the contractor.

"I contacted and informed the company I had already received a call re this contract. In response, they said as I had contacted them directly, I would be dealing with them, not the agent."

It surprised me to hear from Baxter Fell, as since contacting them a year earlier re this contract, I had heard nothing. Still, with luck, Algeria would start after my completing work in Brunei.

That same evening, David informed me there could be enough work for me for another four-six-week. This was fantastic news.

On checking, I found my airline flight ticket was non-extendable and expired on 27th July. Therefore, it meant the two would work out well.

During the following weeks, I went on the Hash and enjoyed myself. But, with many of my hasher friends from my previous time in Brunei gone, things were not the same. Also, because of the pressure of work, I could not attend as frequent as I would have preferred. Still, I was in Brunei to work, not play, so was grateful to go whenever I could.

> During one hash run, one of my friends introduced me to a man named Peter. While talking with him, he asked if I would like to join him on a Jash the following week. I had never heard of a Jash, so asked what it was.

He flashed a smile. "Instead of running through the jungle, we drive through in modified Jeeps."

As this sounded interesting, I arranged to meet him at 7 am the following Sunday.

On my arrival at the meeting point, I found one of the Jashers already there. As I climbed out of my jeep, he greeted me. "Hi, you must be Colin? I'm Dave." He grinned. "Although you've not been on a Jash before, I'm sure you will enjoy the experience. It's a lot of fun." To my surprise, he then said, "Anyway, let's start the day right and have a beer."

I thought it rather early to start drinking, but when in Rome, do as the Romans do. As I sipped my can of beer, I asked, "By the way, where are we going today?"

He turned, pointed up the hillside behind us, and said. "Up there."

> It looked quite a climb to the top of the hill, so I thought he was joking.

"How do we get there?" I asked.

He chuckled. "No problem, we drive most of the way." Little did I know his statement would prove somewhat of an understatement!

On finishing his drink, he said, "Come on, we just as well drive up to the main meeting point."

With Dave sat beside me, we set off. Initially, driving up the rocky tree-lined track was okay, but the higher we went, the narrower and steeper it became. Eventually, we had to lean out of the jeep and push branches out of the way to allow us to carry on. Although concerned about damaging my jeep, there was nowhere to turn around. Also, with it impossible to reverse down the track, there was no choice but to continue.

As we turned yet another corner, I breathed a sigh of relief. There a short distance ahead was a clearing.

"Here we are," Dave said, "Park over there."

As I did, I said, "Boy! Am I glad that's over? I didn't think we were going to make it."

He laughed. "Yes, it was rather difficult in places," he said.

After getting out of the jeep and looking back down the hillside, it surprised me to see how far up we were.

A short time after our arrival, we heard another jeep approaching. When it came up to us and stopped, I saw the driver was Peter. As he climbed out of his jeep, he pointed and said. "Who's the crazy bas....... who drove that up here?"

I shrugged, "I did. Dave said to."

Peter grinned. "Well, you're lucky you managed to get it here, that's for sure. Anyway, given your madness in driving a nigh on new jeep up here, you should fit in well with our lot."

When I studied Peter's jeep, I noticed it was a stripped-down Suzuki, with the exhaust sticking up in the air. No doubt necessary when driving through deep water. Another puzzling feature was the heavy steel girder sections fitted in place of standard bumpers.

About ten minutes later, another two Jeeps arrived. Although both were Suzukis, they were not stripped down like Peter's. After Peter introduced me to the drivers, Steve, and Mike, he said, "Right, now we're all here, let's get going. Colin, you come with me."

I climbed into Peter's jeep and we set off to drive even higher up the hillside. We followed a narrow track that I thought more suitable for goats than a vehicle. After bouncing our way up, working between trees and rocks, it became too steep to drive anymore. At least, that's what I thought. Peter, however, had other ideas. He stopped the jeep, with the others stopping behind us. Peter climbed out, and wearing a big grin, said, "Now the fun begins. First, I'll see how far up I can drive."

On peering up the rock-strewn steep hillside, I thought he must be joking, but to my amazement, he proved me wrong. Putting the jeep in gear, Peter revved the engine, released the clutch, then bounced his way up the hill. However, because of the steepness, he only managed a short distance before coming to a stop.

In the meantime, it puzzled me to see Steve, carrying a hand-winch, climb to the top of the hill. I understood the reason when after securing one end to a tree, he then dragged the cable down and fastened the other end to Peter's jeep. Then before my astonished eyes, they then did what I thought impossible.

# Part 3

Taking it in turns, Steve, Mike, and Dave slowly but surely, winched the jeep to the top of the hill. As it reached the top, we all cheered.

Once released from Peter's jeep, they lowered the cable down for the next vehicle. In a brief space of time, all the jeeps were on top of the hill. After a few minutes rest, we set off driving along a fairly flat surface with sparse trees. When Peter stopped, as I looked behind, Dave drove straight into a tall young tree. Although the crash didn't knock it over, the tree now leant over at an angle. I thought it an accident, but to my amazement, he reversed, then again crashed headlong into the tree. After doing this twice more, the tree toppled over. As it fell, Dave stopped his engine and climbed out of his jeep. With a mile-wide smile, he said: "That feels better, but I'll have to strengthen my bumper, it's rather bent."

This was an understatement. I now knew why Peter had girders fitted to his jeep instead of bumpers. We continued on a short distance until what seemed an impenetrable barrier blocked our way. Coming to a stop, Peter climbed out of the jeep. After taking a look, we saw him shake his head. When he returned, he sighed. "It's a pity, but we cannot go any further. There are too many large rocks, with no way around them. We'll have to turn around and go back down."

We then made our way back to where we had earlier winched up the jeeps. Peter stopped, and we climbed out to await the others to join us.

On their arrival, Peter shrugged and said, "I'll go down first."

I looked down the steep hillside and shuddered. To me, it was impossible. I thought Peter must be joked, but just in case, I said, "You drive, and I'll walk. It looks like a suicide mission to me."

Peter laughed as he climbed back in his jeep. "It's not a problem," he said, "just watch."

To my amazement, he then bounced and slide down the hill. I thought it a miracle that he got down in one piece. However, on seeing this, the others also thought it not too difficult. One by one, they drove over the top and down the rock-covered hillside.

I thought I had seen it all, but another surprise was in store. My day of crazy adventures was not yet over.

Once all the jeeps were down, I climbed back into Peter's. He laughed at my obvious discomfort at not sitting with him when he drove down the steep rock-covered hillside.

"Well, today I have witnessed the impossible," I said.

Peter laughed. "It did seem crazy to you," he said. "Still, after a few trips out, you'll think nothing of it."

We then drove down the trail to my jeep. I climbed inside, then followed the others down to the main road. I felt relieved to get there without incident. Nevertheless, to the cost of my nerves, I vowed never to drive off-road without a suitable vehicle.

Once back on the main road, we all followed Peter. To my surprise, a short time later, he turned off down a track towards the sea. On arriving on the beach, we sped in procession along the sun-baked sand. All went well until, without warning, Peter braked to a stop. We stopped behind him, then walked on to see why Peter had stopped.

In front of us was a fast running river that flowed out into the sea.

Oh well," I exclaimed, "that's that."

Peter, however, had other ideas. He turned to us and, wearing a big smile, said, "Oh, I don't know. Let me see how deep it is."

He then walked into the fast-flowing river and waded across to the other side. Once there, he turned and yelled, " it's okay; it's not too deep." I was shocked. In parts; the water had come up to Peter's thighs. I called over, "Do you mean we're going to drive across?"

"Of course," he called back. "You can drive my jeep."

I felt nervous as I climbed into his jeep and drove down into the water. Not used to driving across rivers, I drove too slowly, and the engine cut out a few meters from the edge of the bank.

Peter, who had returned to our side of the river, shook his head. "Not like that," he said.

Between us, we then managed to push the jeep back out of the water. Peter climbed in, reversed a short distance, and then drove at speed into the river. I stood amazed, as with water foaming up all around the jeep; he sped across and up the bank on the other side. He made it look easy.

Peter got out of the jeep and yelled in delight. "See, it's easy. Come on over."

The next jeep drove into the water and started across. However, about halfway across, it stopped. Apart from Peter's vehicle, none had the exhausts pointing up in the air. This feature prevented water seeping up into the engine and stopping it from working. One lad waded out to the stranded jeep. He attached one end of the winch cable to it, while another one carried the winch across to Peter's jeep. Once connected, Peter then pulled the vehicle across to the other side.

Despite their best efforts, the other two jeeps suffered the same fate and had to be pulled out of the river. This left me alone, with my shiny new jeep on the wrong side of the river. I called across. "I can't drive mine across the river"

When Peter waded back over, I said, "First, it's not mine, and second, it's a hired jeep."

He grinned. "No problem, I'll drive it across," he said. "First, though, we'll disconnect the fan belt. That should help prevent the engine from flooding."

Without further discussion, Peter disconnected the fan belt. He then drove my jeep into the river, which, as I expected, ended up stuck in the middle of the river. It was then winched out over the last part.

Once I had waded across after him, I shook my head. "If my boss had seen where my jeep had been today, he would have had a heart attack."

Peter laughs. "Never mind," he said, "the excitement is over now."

Once he had reconnected the fan belt, we all set off along the beach. To my relief, when I checked, only a little water had entered the jeep.

We continued driving across the sandy beach until Peter turned off and up a narrow path. To my surprise, it took us into the back of the Berakas Camp, and a few minutes later, we pulled into the WWC car park.

Over a few drinks, we discussed what to me had been a crazy day. To the others, however, this was just an average day out.

On another Jash, we set off with me sat in Peter's jeep, Dave in his, with Mark with Pat following behind in theirs. We had left the main road and started driving along a trail through sparse trees. Suddenly, Peter stopped dead. Cutting across in front of us was a narrow ravine. We climbed out and looked down. The chasm was about 30ft deep, with the muddy bottom around 14ft wide. A steep incline led to the top of the bank on the other side that was about 40ft higher than our side.

After a bit of thought, Peter calmly said, "I can manage that okay."

I took a second look and said in disbelief, "Are you mad? You can't drive down, and up the other side, it's far too steep. You'll most nose dive into the bottom or crash into the opposite bank."

Peter laughed while the others said nothing. "Well, we will soon find out," he said, then climbed back in his Jeep. He slowly drove up and over the edge. To my amazement, after sliding to the bottom of the ravine, he accelerated and fishtailed up the other side. I thought it unbelievable he had managed to do such a crazy thing. He stopped at an angle higher up than we were, then yelled, "There, see it's not so hard. Come on, if I can do it, so can you."

While Mark and John stood deep in thought, Pat and I climbed down the gully, then up to where Peter stood.

"I can't believe you did that," I said, "I would have put money on you failing."

Peter face lit with a broad smile. "It's a pity I hadn't known that," he said, "I would have taken your bet."

One after the other Mark and John drove their jeeps down into the gully. However, neither could follow Peter's example. Both became stuck while making the sharp turn up from the bottom of the ravine. After Peter attached one end of the winch cable to his jeep, Mark attached the other end to his jeep. Peter then pulled it up and then did the same with Dave's jeep.

Once done, we walked up to the top of the hill. We found it V-shaped, with the other side steep and littered with rocks. One look, and even Peter agreed he could not drive down. We then had a short hair-raising drive along the top of the ridge with two wheels on each side until we found a place to turn around. We then headed back.

After searching around, we found a way around the ravine. Once clear, we then made our way back down to the main road. Again, going on a Jash had proved an exciting and exhilarating experience.

Unfortunately, because of time restraints, I could not go on another one.

In early July, it shocked David when I asked him to book me a flight home later that month. To my surprise, he was unaware the company had purchased me a non-extendable flight ticket. I felt bad on hearing this, as I had assumed, he had known.

Although an unfortunate state of affairs, when the company booked my tickets, no one knew our works would take so long. My having to leave was a pity, as because of our tasked increasing each week, I could have been required for some time to come.

However, Jen had sold our house with our scheduled move into our new house a week after my impending departure,. Therefore, I could not have stayed on longer.

When David knew about my having to leave, he suggested getting Bill back. When I said, I did not recommend this, he asked why. On explaining Bill's attitude to our Thai workers, David didn't find it amusing. "In that case, I'll not bring him back. But, as neither you nor Harold will be here, I'll have to find someone else."

The weekend before my departure from Brunei, while at the beach with friends, one asked if I would like a trip out on his 'Hobie Cat.' Although I couldn't swim, it would be an unfamiliar experience, so I said yes. No sooner had I climbed aboard, when we shot off like a rocket. What followed was an incredible and thrilling experience. I never realised a Hobie Cat could move so fast. It turned so fast; at one point, it nearly bounced me out over the side. Only by sheer luck did I manage to hang on. Given this, I was not sorry when we returned to the safety of the beach.

Although I again felt sad at leaving Brunei, I had more unforgettable adventures. I had been on a Jash and now talked with both of the Sultan's wives. The latter I considered both an experience and honour.

On the flight back to Heathrow, my mind was on our impending move into our new home. I also wondered how I would get on at my interview for the contract in Algeria. This I had arranged to have after landing at Heathrow.

On arrival, I put my luggage into left luggage then set off for the interview. If offered a contract, it would mean working in North Africa, an area I had never been before. For sure, it would be a big difference from working in steamy Brunei.

Life in the Algerian desert.

# Chapter Nine
# Part 1

After my interview, it surprised me when they offered a one-year contract. My interviewer then asked when I could travel. "In two weeks," I replied. This I thought would give me enough time to help Jen get settled in our new house.

In mid-August, after I helped Jen get our new house set up, I flew up to London and collected my plane ticket from head office. I then flew out to Algeria. On arrival at Algeria International Airport, a man met and drove me to our main office in Reghaia. Here he introduced me to John, the General Manager, who informed me I would be based in the main camp, for now. I would later move to another location. I thought this, not a problem, as it would enable me to see more of the country.

When he said I had to surrender my passport and return ticket to the accounts department, I was not pleased. I always liked to keep my passport in case of emergency. Still, rules were rules, so I handed them over.

I found life in the camp excellent, with tasty meals, and my laundry done free. Therefore, I had no expenses other than if I wanted to buy something for myself.

To my surprise, I heard that we had twenty-two sites based in various locations throughout Algeria. It further surprised me when told the company had over five hundred English workers in the country. This was a vast amount of men for a company to have working in a single country.

While based at the main camp, I used to read the work lists posted each week. These gave details of men leaving and arriving each week at the various sites. I noticed the biggest group of men going were from a place called Constantine.

On mentioning this to some of the men I worked with, one laughed.

"That's Big Jim's site," he said. "It's because of him everyone jacks it in. No one works for him for long."

After completing outstanding works at Reghaia, John gave me a site in Bouzerah to look after.

I found no problem in working in Algeria, with the men I worked with friendly. I also found those who had been in the country for a while, would advise newcomers on various things. One was not to change money in the local exchange offices. To my amazement, while they offered the official rate, by using an unofficial person, you could get five times the amount. I found it general knowledge that our men were receiving sterling sent out from home, which they then changed on the black market.

One new arrival thought he had done well by changing several hundred pounds in England to Algerian Dinar. He was disappointed on finding he had made a big mistake.

Come the end of September, John said I would be transfer to Constantine. I shrugged. Oh well, now I'll discover why so numerous people kept leaving this site.

The next morning, a driver took me to the airport, where as soon as I entered, found I had a big problem. All the signs were either in French or Arabic, neither of which I understood. Despite this, on looking at the various departure gates, I managed to find mine.

However, come the time for boarding, when I produced my ticket at the gate, an official informed me I did not have a confirmed flight. He said I would have to await the next one, which was not for another three hours. Despite my arguing, I had a confirmed booking; no one took any notice. I was furious; my boarding pass showed that I should have been allowed on the flight.

I felt angry about this, so I called our office to request someone to help me. On explaining my problem, they informed me someone would come down and sort things out. After waiting another hour without anyone coming to help, I again phoned the office. This time I snapped at the person on the other end. "Unless someone comes to sort things out A.S.A.P., I'll not go to Constantine. I will return to head office."

About half an hour later, one of the office staff found me waiting in a foul mood.

"What's the problem, Colin?" he enquired.

"They would not let me board the flight," I snapped back. They said my ticket was not confirmed."

"Let me see your ticket, please." He checked, then frowned. "Your ticket is fine," he said, "You should have been allowed to board."

Although this was not unexpected, I felt angry about the treatment I had received.

"Right!" he said. "Just wait here while I go and sort things out." He returned a few minutes later. "It's okay; you'll be on the next flight, but you'll have to wait another hour."

I shrugged. "I'll wait, but I want you to stay until I board the plane."

He grinned, "Don't worry; I'll stay until you leave."

An hour later, I boarded the plane and set off. By the time I arrived at Constantine, it had taken me eight and a half hours.

On arrival, I found a driver waiting to take me to camp. Once there, he introduced me to John, the Project Manager, and Jim, the Site Manager. John ,"You will be in charge of a barrack site at El Kantara, about half an hour's drive from here."

I soon settled in with work on the barracks going well. One day we had a sudden sandstorm, with the visibility dropping to nigh on zero. Everyone took shelter as metal roofing sheets stacked on the roof were sent flying. Just how dangerous this situation became, was evident once the sandstorm finished. In places, it left roofing sheets embedded deep in wooden telegraph poles. One can only imagine the consequences had they had hit anyone.

After only a few weeks on the site, I fell afoul of Jim. It came about after he and I disagreed on how things on the site should be run. As a result, he took me off the project and put back to work on the main camp. Although I complained to John, the Project Manager, about this, he did nothing. Some lads told me they thought he was afraid of Jim, so did nothing to upset him.

It seemed all knew that Jim was abusive and aggressive to everyone. It confirmed why so many men jacked in from his site. However, despite his attitude, Jim and I got on okay. He realised I would neither bow nor scrape to him, nor resign.

It surprised me to find there was a bar on-site. Apparently, because of many of our sites being in remote locations, all major camps had bars. This was because there was nowhere for the men to go, and nothing for them to do after work.

At one time, the guys on our site drank eight crates of beer in one hour, which I thought an incredible amount. We were, I am sure, the best customer the brewery ever had. Sometimes, to save time awaiting delivery, we would send one of our trucks to collect the beer from the brewery. Although not too once you got used to it, the brewery had a problem, as during an inspection, some unopened bottles were found dirty inside.

Excess drinking in our camp became so severe; the company decided it would give any man found fighting the choice of resigning or being sacked. If sacked, you had to pay your own airfare home. Therefore, any men found fighting usually left of their own accord.

While talking to our camp doctor, he told me about his terrifying experience on the way back to camp the previous night.

He said, "It was pitch black as I drove back when a sheep dashed out in front of me. Although I did my best to avoid it, the car hit and sent it flying. On getting out and checking, I found the sheep dead. Although there did not appear to be any houses nearby, out of the darkness, several people appeared. They must have heard the noise and came to investigate. Seeing the dead sheep, someone shouted something at me, which brought, more, people to the scene. From their tones and gesticulating, I realised they wanted money for my killing the sheep. As I only had a little money with me, I knew it would not be enough to satisfy them. I started to panic and thought they might attack and even kill me when a van pulled up. To my relief, as the figure got out and came into the car's headlights, I found it was a Gendarme. The crowd became silent when he asked, 'What's going on?'

I explained about hitting the sheep and the people demanding money. On hearing this, he turned and shouted at them, with them immediately fading away into the darkness, leaving me gasping with relief.

The Gendarme said, 'It's okay. I told them that if anyone is to receive money, it's you to pay for repairing your car. I said if they had kept control of their sheep, the accident would not have happened.'

After I shook his hand and expressed my thanks, I lost no time in driving back to camp." He shuddered. I am not fond of thinking what might have happened had the Gendarme not appeared."

In my contract, the company paid for a return airfare home every three months. This great; as in Saudi, leave was every six months. The day before one trip home, because of a dust storm, no planes could take off from the local airport. To get over this problem, four of us drove overnight to Reghaia where visibility was not a problem there. Our trip turned out to be long and dangerous, with visibility in places only a few yards. Still, to my relief, we arrived without incident at the Reghaia camp early the next morning.

During another of my return trips home, I had to stay the night in the main camp in Reghaia. As most works in this area were complete, it was all but deserted except for two plumbers.

One informed me of a shocking discovery they had made. "When the main drain in the staff toilets became blocked, we had to clear it. While doing so, we found the blockage caused by letters and envelopes being flushed down the toilets." He shook his head. "They were all addressed to men who had been staying at the camp."

Further investigation revealed the local cleaning staff had been stealing the envelopes. Because of the black-market exchange rate, they knew our workers were receiving money sent from the UK." He shook his head, "The money theft was enough, but losing the accompanying letters was far worse. It meant our men were deprived of news from family and friends back home."

During my stay in Algeria, as I had the use of a company car, I used to take some of my workmates on trips into the desert on our day off. On one trip, we discovered a deep, long and winding canyon that appeared like a miniature Grand Canyon. After looking around, we found a steep, twisting goat track that led us to the bottom. As we walked along the dried-up river bed, I noticed what looked like seashells embedded in some rocks. Inspecting, it amazed me to find they were a variety of fossil'd seashells. I thought it incredible to find them so many miles inland. It seems that at one time in the past, the river had been connected to the sea.

On the opposite side of the canyon, cut into the cliff about eighty feet down, were the remains of a building. I later heard it was the remains of a hotel that had been under construction years ago, but then abandoned. It was a mystery how people were supposed to reach the hotel. As far as we could see, there was no way down to it.

During one day out, we were driving along a dusty, winding road. The scenery was just desert, with rocky hummocks and sparse vegetation here and there. Suddenly, someone noticed a couple of camels had appeared on the hills above us. As these were the first, we had seen in Algeria; I stopped the car. We climbed out and stood to await the camels to get closer. As we prepared to take photos, a man appeared behind them, who seeing our cameras, shouted, "Money, money! If you take photos of my camels, I want money." Given this, we decided not to take any.

On yet another day out, we were again driving along deserted roads without seeing either traffic or people. Then, as we turned a bend in the road, I noticed a man sat at the side of the road. I thought he wanted a lift, so slowed down. As I stopped alongside him, we noticed he had stones lined up on the edge of the road. It puzzled us as to why he appeared to be selling them, so we got out to investigate. As we approached, the man, lifted one to show that someone had broken it in two. To our amazement, the inside was full of crystal globules. After haggling, I bought a couple of stones, which I later found are called Geodes.

We then drove off and had only driven another few miles when we found another man selling stones. These we found were larger and filled with brilliant blue crystals. They looked fantastic. The man said if we wanted to buy any of his stones; he would accept items of clothing in exchange. Plus, he would also take cameras, radios, and watches. On seeing our puzzled expressions, he explained., "Because of many items in short supply and expensive in Algeria, this barter is normal," he said.

However, even after haggling, the man still wanted a lot of money for his stones. So, although we would have liked to buy some, did not.

# Part 2

At one time, I drove a few of my colleagues to visit 'King Herald the Great Hot Springs,' down near the Dead Sea. After driving for several hours through a barren wasteland, we started a steep descent down through the mountains. Near the bottom, we passed a large hotel nestled back off the edge of the road. Then, a short distance on, a sign informed us we were now below sea level. I knew we had descended a long way but hadn't realised it was that far.

A few minutes later, we came to the hot springs. They looked great. The top section of the rock-face, high above the base of the springs was stained bright green. One could only imagine how many years it had taken to become this colour. With spring water crystal-clear, it made a startling contrast to the various shades of green on the upper rocks. Although unusual, there was nothing else to see, so we drove back up to the hotel for a well-deserved drink. It being the only building we had seen for several hours.

By the time we arrived back at camp, it had been a long, hot and tiring day.

On yet another trip out, we visited the ancient remains of Timgad. Once an important Roman city, in the largest wheat-growing area in the country. As we walked up to the main entrance to the ruins, some children approached. They were selling what they claimed were genuine old Roman coins. Because of our not sure if they were real or not, we declined to buy any.

After paying a small entrance fee, we started to walk through the ruins of the city. It covered a vast area and spread out around a prominent hillside. There were numerous large standing columns, with some over thirty feet high, making a spectacular sight. The intricate details to the ornate capitals on top of the columns were mind-boggling. The highly skilled masons who had carved them must have spent many long, painstaking days to complete their work.

At one point, alongside an ancient stone-laid road was another marvel. This consisted of covered drainage channels and showed how advanced the technology was in those long-ago times. In places, chariot wheels had left deep cuts in the flagstones. One can only imagine the amount of chariots that must have driven along the road to cause this.

After two hours of exploring the ruins, we returned to the entrance, where next to it was a small museum. Inside, dominating the central area, were two huge and beautiful coloured mosaic wall panels. These were in fabulous condition, with details so outstanding, they made a fantastic display.

At one project I worked on, I discovered that our camp had been built on top of an old Roman ruin. There were pieces of ancient pottery scattered everywhere. From looking at the shape of some stone fragments, it looked as though they might once have been part of a wall. It seemed a shame that the future was covering up the past, as there was plenty of space to relocate it away from the ruins.

In November, about twelve of my colleagues and I had to renew our visas, which meant our having to leave the country. Because of the border with Tunisia being the closest, we would go there. The intention being that once we had passed out of the country, we would then return straight back into Algeria. By doing so, it would automatically enable us to obtain visas for another three months.

On going into our office, I found John, our admin guy, rubbing one page in my passport that to him. I felt sure it was the page with my entry date into Algeria, so yelled, "What are you doing? You'll get me deported if they see you've altered the date."

He grinned. "Relax!" he said. "I am not altering it. I'm only making it difficult to read. As your visa has already expired, I don't want them to know this when we pass through customs."

Still, on checking, I felt relieved to see no visible sign of his trying to obscure the date.

The day before we were due to leave for Tunisia, I flew to Reghaia to collect the money necessary to pay for all our new visas. After staying on the camp for the night, I then flew back to Constantine. Around 11 pm that evening, the coach taking us to Tunisia pulled out of camp.

Because of our all being illegal in the country, John, our admin guy who spoke French, accompanied us. Also, to prevent potential problems, he had arranged for us to enter Tunisia at a remote border crossing. The idea being to pass through early morning when the customs officials were unlikely to take much of a look at our passports.

For the first hour, there were no problems, and we made good progress. However, when we entered the mountains and came to an unmarked road junction, our driver was unsure of which road to take. Fortunately, despite the hour, he found someone who gave him instructions on the right one.

After driving all night, we arrived at the Algerian border post at 6 am. Here we wearily trooped off the coach and followed John into the office. As we stood to wait for our passports to be processed, I noticed a notice reading, 'Welcome to all Tourists.' I thought this a friendly welcome. Then, as I stood looking around, through an open door, I noticed an Arabic squat-style toilet. This was nothing unusual, but the colossal termite mound that filled the toilet pan stood at least two feet high. It was not exactly a welcoming sight for tourists entering Tunisia.

John explained to the officer in charge why we were entering Tunisia. He informed him that after crossing into Tunisia, we would then return straight back into Algeria.

For some strange reason, the customs officer seemed to think we were a bunch of mercenaries up to no good. This seemed so funny I choked. However, a bunch of English guys arriving early morning at a remote border crossing did seem suspicious.

It took John a lot of explaining until approximately three hours later they allowed us to pass out of Algeria. As we left, the officer informed John, it would not take so long to cross back into Algeria. This however, proved incorrect.

Once through, a short drive down the road brought us to the Tunisian border post. Unbelievably, it then took another three hours before they allowed us into Tunisia. Thirty minutes later, we drove into a small town. Apart from the border posts and one small village, we had seen few buildings since leaving camp.

We intended to stop only for fuel and then return to Algeria. However, while refuelling (with a guy smoking as he filled the tank), our driver dropped a bombshell.

What John told me he said, meant a complete change of plans. It had taken over 12 hrs to drive into Tunisia, so our driver had run out of legal driving time. Therefore, he could not drive us back until after having an official break.

I shrugged. " In that case, we might as well find a hotel and spend the rest of the day here. We can then leave early tomorrow morning." As our driver had to have an eight-hour break, John agreed this was our best solution. After asking the petrol attendant for directions to a hotel, our driver drove us there.

We were fortunate; the hotel had enough vacant rooms for all of us. After checking in, we went for a walk around the shops. As we found little in the way of souvenirs, we returned to the hotel.

Then, after being awake for most of the trip, most of us decided to catch up on a few hours' sleep.

In the evening, we met in the hotel's restaurant where we ordered dinner and some bottles of local beer. To our surprise, after only a couple of rounds, we were told the hotel had run out of beer. It was apparent they got little demand for people ordering large quantities. With no beer, we then drank several bottles of wine. I am sure this pleased the hotel manager, who stood watching the proceedings. Several hours later, despite no heating in my room, I managed to get a night's sleep.

After breakfast, we checked out, climbed back into our coach, and set off up the road. At the border post, the procedure with the paperwork was taking forever. I asked John what the problem was. He told me that all had been going well until the officer noticed the sum of money, he had put on his declaration form. It being less than he declared when he entered Tunisia.

John said, "I explained that as our driver had run out of time., we had spent the night in a hotel, which accounted for the difference." He shrugged. "The officer then asked how much Tunisian lira I had. When I told him, he said it was illegal to take this amount of local currency out of the country. He has given me a choice. I can either leave the excess money at the customs office or return to town and deposit the money in a bank." He shrugged. "I thought it best to deposit the money in a bank."

I grinned and agreed that the latter was the wisest thing to do.

John turned to the others. "Sorry lads, but we have to return to town." This, of course, did not please anybody. However, with it lunchtime; I suggested we might as well have an early lunch. "After all," I said, "on the way here, we didn't pass anywhere we could get something to eat or drink."

On hearing this, the lads gave out a call of approval. Our driver then drove back into town and dropped us off outside a restaurant

While we went inside, John left to deposit the money in a bank. We were in no hurry to get back to camp, so took our time having our meal. We were still eating when John returned.

As he walked up to me wearing a big smile, he said, "Right, that's that problem solved. I've deposited the excess money in a bank."

"Good! In that case," I said, "we shouldn't have any more problems leaving the country." Boy was I wrong.

Once John had eaten, we went outside to get back on our coach. As we were doing so, I thought it strange when I noticed several customs officers stood nearby.

On arriving back at the customs office, the officer in charge stood, waiting at the door. From the look on his face, there was something wrong.

John inquired, "Is there a problem?"

The officer gave a grim smile. "Yes, a big problem for me. He then explained that he had stamped our passports with an exit stamp, before noticing the problem with John's declaration form. Therefore, we were all in the country illegally. Because of our being so long in town, he had sent his men to find us. Unbelievable, even then, it still took another two hours before they allowed us to pass through the customs post. Could you tell me why on earth it had taken so long was a complete mystery.

As we reached the Algerian customs post, we were all feeling fed up with the delays. To our dismay, despite what the officer had said, it still took two hours before they allowed us back into Algeria.

By the time we arrived back in camp, it was late evening. Everyone, including our driver, was relieved to get off the coach and stretch their legs. Our trip had proved nothing short of a nightmare. I hate to think how long it would take for a coach-load of tourists to pass through these border crossings.

Although our journey had been successful, it had been a long, tedious, and tiring experience. One I hoped; I would not have to go through again.

# Part 2

Outside the site office one day, I noticed all the windows in Jim's Land Rover smashed. Ongoing inside, I found Jim sitting in his office wearing his usual scowl.

"What on earth happened to your truck?" I asked.

"One of our Algerian workers did it," he grunted.

"How do you know that?" I asked.

Through gritted teeth, he said, "Because I stood and watched him do it."

I shook my head in puzzlement. "But why didn't you stop him?"

"Because he had a bloody great stick in his hands, that's why," Jim snarls.

I couldn't understand this, so asked, "But why did he smash up your truck?"

"Because he'd been reported as being asleep on the job, and I sacked him, that's why."

I nodded. "So, what's going to happen now?" I enquired.

"The Gendarme are on their way here to arrest him." Suddenly, the man who had been standing nearby ran off. On looking to see why, I spotted two Gendarmes had entered the camp. What followed was a complete comedy. On seeing the man run off, one gendarme shouted for a passing truck to stop. As we watched in amazement, both men jumped onto the running boards and yelled at the driver to follow the man.

What followed was like a scene from the 'The Keystone Cops,' an old comedy film. In the meantime, two of our English workers were chasing after the man. On seeing he could not get away, the man stopped and picked up a large rock. He then threatened to throw it at the two men if they approached. As one man pretended to move toward him, the man turned his way. Seeing his chance, the other worker dived at him and brought the man crashing to the floor. The two men overpowered him and held him tight until the truck with the two Gendarmes clinging to the sides reached them.

One Gendarme told the workers holding the man to hit him.

"Not me," one said. "He's one of yours. You hit him. If I do, I could end up in big trouble."

The Gendarmes then grabbed hold of the man and frog-marched him out of the camp to their parked van.

A few days later, I was in the site office when one of our guys burst in. His face showed sheer panic, as he shouted to Jim, "Quick, get me on a plane, he's out again."

It was the man who had reported the Algerian for sleeping. The one who had smashed up Jim's truck. The man cried out, "I've just heard the Gendarme has released him pending a trial. He's also been spotted with a gun. I'm afraid he'll come and shoot me. He knows I'm the one who got him the sack."

Given a possible act of retaliation, the man was on a plane back to England the next morning.

On one site, we had a big problem with our local workers, who were stealing all kinds of items. In most places, this would have been quickly dealt with. However, our site, like all the others in the country, came under strict local trade union rules.

Although we had John; a security man based at the entrance to the site, under union rules, it did not allow him to search the men when they left each night. It meant he could not check the men bags when they boarded a coach to take them home in the evening. The men used their bags to bring their lunches with them. It was also a means of hiding things when they left the site in the evening.

For a joke, one evening, John stood at the coach door and announced he was going to make an inspection. What followed was hilarious, for as John made the announcement, people started throwing all sorts of items out of the coach windows. As a result,

John recovered several electric drills and other tools from around the coach.

The theft problem became so severe that even live wired electrical items were stolen. To my surprise, it turned out it was not only the locals who were stealing from the site.

A month before Christmas, our company offered all men the choice of going home on leave for Christmas or the New Year. I chose to go back at Christmas.

On arrival at Annabel Airport for our flight back to the UK, hundreds of men who had made the same choice joined us. While in a long queue waiting to check in, I noticed that all luggage was being searched. It explained why there was such a queue. As I stood there, John, our security man, turned up, bringing our site maintenance man with him. When the man saw the line, he looked puzzled. "What's going on?" he asked.

I shrugged. "The company announced that they will check everyone's luggage for stolen goods."

A few moments later, the man turned to John. In a casual voice, he said, "John, could you take one of my cases back to camp for me. I've decided I don't need it this time."

"No problem," John replied. "I'm not going home until the New Year' flight."

On my return from holiday, John, our security man, told me what had happened after I left. He said, "On my return to camp, I spoke to Jim. I told him about bringing back the maintenance man's case." I said, "Because it's so heavy, I have suspicions about what was inside. Also, he only decided not to take it after hearing everyone's luggage was being searched at the airport. Jim said, Right, that enough for me, open the case. When I forced it open, we found Hilti drills, screw guns, and various other items. Given this, Jim said they would sack the man, with a notice re this placed on the camp's notice board."

John chuckled. "However, the office slipped up, as they did not contact the man and inform him he'd been sacked. As a result, he returned to the site after his Christmas leave. When Jim informed him, he had sacked him for theft, he was shocked. Also, apart from the discovery of stolen items in his suitcase, they found a large case of other items hidden in his workshop."

After being in Algeria for eight months, I received a message from our head office. They were asking if I would work on a new hospital contract. I had no problem working in Algeria, so was pleased to accept.

Jim called me to his office a few weeks after my good news and shattered it with his message. In his office, he informed me the Gendarme had demanded the passports of all the companies expats working in the country.

On asking why, he said, "Because of the large turnover of our workforce, the company have used up more than its allocated amount of work permits. As a result, the Gendarme has refused to let any of our expat workers leave the country until they completed their enquiries."

This news did not go down well with anyone, especially one guy who had been because of go on leave a few days later. He was furious, as he had a holiday booked in Spain with his family. Although informed of this, the authorities would not permit him to leave Algeria. Given this, the man informed Jim he would stop working. He was fortunate, as a few days later, the Gendarme returned all our passports.

Jim then called all our workers to a meeting. He informed us that because of the Gendarmes' investigation, anyone due to go on leave could do so. However, only those who had a valid work permit could come back. This caused an uproar from a number of the men. It meant some, could only work for three months out of their one-year contracts.

Despite this news, I was one of the fortunate ones. Although I could not return after my next leave, I would have completed nine months out of my one-year contract. Unfortunately, it meant I could not work on the hospital contract.

The following month I left Algeria. It being another country to add to the ever-growing list of countries I had visited at no cost to myself. While in Algeria I had visited several interesting places, and also made new friends.

My next priority was to enjoy life back home with my family in our new house. However, I would also be seeking a new overseas contract. I just hoped one day to obtain a married status contract, so my wife Jen, could experience life in another country. Although I didn't know, this would happen a short time later.

An unforgettable visit to Petra

# Chapter Ten

After unable to find another overseas contract, with reluctance, I accepted an offer from my old company to work for them in London. I hated travelling to and from work on the underground, and did not like this job. However, I needed the money, so I had to grin and put up with it.

Two weeks after starting the job, I received a call from Jen, my wife. She said a man had called about a contract in Jordan. This was great news, as it could result in my escaping from working in England.

I was in a buoyant mood when I later met the man at a hotel in London. During a chat, he said he was the owner of a construction company in Jordan, who were performing refurbishments to the King of Jordan's 1948 Raghadan Palace. He explained that he had seen my CV via Expats International, and wanted me to control quality issues on the project.

In a normal situation, I would have jumped at such an offer. However, due to him informing me not to take any notice of the English, Site Manager, I had doubts about this contract. As I would be working with this man, it seemed a strange thing to say. I was also unhappy with the salary offered that I thought low for this position.

When I told him this, he smiled? "Maybe, but at the end of your contract, you will receive a good bonus."

I laughed. I said, laughing, "I've been offered excellent bonuses before, but I never received them."

To my surprise, he said, "Okay! In that case, if you prefer, instead of a bonus, I will add it to your salary."

Although I still had a gut feeling something was incorrect with this contract, I accepted his offer. After all, it was the only overseas contract I'd been offered in more than three months. Also, I would be earning more money than I presently received.

After shaking hands on the deal, I noticed my new boss wore a quizzical expression. "There is only one problem," he said, "What should I call you?" It puzzled me for a minute until he explained. "We already have a Project Manager and a Site Manager." After a few minutes, he face broke into a beaming smile. "I know," he said, "We will call you 'Luxury Interior Finishing Manager'."

I laughed to myself, not caring what he called me, so long as he paid me.

A few weeks later, in early June, I arrived late evening at Amman International Airport. A driver met and took me to a large, well-furnished apartment. It was, he said, above the company's office.

The next morning, I went down and met my new boss. After greetings, he said, "Your first job will be to look through all the project drawings."

As I knew there would be many, it would keep me busy for some time. He then explained why. "Until you have done so, you will not know what or which part of the palace is what."

I nodded this made sense. A few minutes later, we set off to the Palace, which turned out to be a thirty-minute drive away.

Before allowed into the Palace grounds, we had to stop at a checkpoint guarded by armed soldiers. Once out of the car, the soldiers made a detailed inspection of the car. This included looking underneath with a mirror on a shaft, then under the bonnet and inside the boot.

While they were doing this, we had to go inside the building, show our passports, and then walk through a metal detector. Only then, were we allowed to drive into the palace grounds.

At the site office, my boss introduced to Ahmed, the Jordanian Project Manager, and Chris, the English, Site Manager.

After a brief chat, Chris pointed out my desk and the location of the project drawings. Once my employer left, Chris then took me into the Palace for a look around. I found things were not as I had been told. I quickly realized that the project was nowhere near as advanced as I had been led to believe.

After spending the day poring over the project drawings, a driver took me back to my apartment. I then did this for the next two days. On the third day, as per my contract, I received a company car. I was pleased, but not amused when told I had to pay for the petrol. As the company expected me to take three Italian marble workers (who lived in the same building as me) to work and back, I thought this a joke.

I told the admin manager, "Either the company pays for the petrol, which is normal, or I won't accept the car. You can then continue taking all of us to work and back."

Although the company agreed to my demand, it was not a good start to the project.

While on the way to work with the marble men, as usual, we stopped at the security guardhouse. We were inside when the two guards started joking around with their Uzi submachine pistols. Initially, watching them draw on each other was funny. Then, when one cocked his gun and pointed his weapon at his colleague, everything changed. I could not believe he had done such a stupid and dangerous thing. His colleague facing the cocked weapon shot up his hands and unleashed a torrent of words at his colleague. Then, after what seemed like a lifetime, the soldier uncocked and lowered his gun. Only then did I breathe a sigh of relief. Had the gun gone off in the enclosed room, it could have proved fatal. Not only for the soldier but for us men as well.

Because of spending days pouring over the project drawings, I made infrequent visits inside the Palace. When I did, it surprised me by how few workers were on-site. In general, l found little work ongoing in various areas.

As I was about to leave one evening, Chris came over to my desk. "Hi, Colin, can I offer a word of warning?"

I felt puzzled at his question. "Of course," I said. "What's up"

He told me he had heard Ahmed, the project manager, informing our employer that I spent most of my time in the office.

I shrugged. "He's right. That's what the boss instructed me to do."

Chris nodded. "Yes, that's as may be. However, you have to be careful of this man. He is always causing trouble; none of his men like him."

This came as no surprise, as a few of our Jordanian workers had already told me the same thing.

When I met Ahmed on site the next morning, I said, "Ahmed, next time you have something to say about me, say it to my face."

He blustered and tried to pretend he knew nothing about what I meant, but I ignored his protest and warned him not to do it again.

I thought this yet another omen; I had been right to doubt accepting this contract.

Apart from this incident, I was also concerned about materials delivered to the site. To me, the quality was far below what I considered acceptable for a Palace. It was not only the quality of materials, I unhappy about. The skill level of some of our workers was also unacceptable. In one instance, I watched as a man fixed plaster mouldings on a ceiling. On telling him, they were not satisfactory; without any argument, he removed them. He then installed new sections, but with the same result.

When I informed my boss of this, his reply did not amuse me. He said he would have to take them down and refix them until I was satisfied.

I shrugged. "I'm sorry, but that's not possible. Although he's doing the best he can, he cannot produce the quality expected for a Palace." He then turned and without said any more on the subject, walked away. I decided this was enough. I did not feel comfortable working on a project where the quality was unacceptable to me. The next day, I sent a letter home to my wife. In it, I said if anyone contacted her about a contract for me, I would be interested.

A few days later, when Chris asked if I fancied a trip to Petra, I eagerly accepted. To visit, Petra was one of my lifelong ambitions. I said, "Count me in; I've always wanted to visit Petra."

"Right, in that case, we will take two cars," Chris said. He then explained. "Apart from my wife and two daughters, I also have one of the girls' boyfriends staying with us."

As we intended to visit an old Crusader castle on the way, it meant having to stop the night somewhere. After we studied a map, as Chris had an ample supply of sleeping bags, we decided to sleep in the castle grounds. It would save us from having to pay for accommodation. Plus, with the castle only a short distance from Petra, we would arrive there early the next morning. It would then give us plenty of time for exploring Petra.

We later departed, with Chris leading and my following behind. All was going well until suddenly, Chris braked hard. I wondered what was up, then saw a parked police car with an officer waving us down to stop. By the time I had, Chris was out and talking to one of the two officers. When I noticed a radar gun established on a tripod next to their car, I realised we must have been speeding.

As I approached Chris and the officers, Chris informed me that they wanted to book us both for speeding. He said, "I've told them we were driving close together, so it was impossible for them to clock both of us."

Despite this, the police officer insisted we were both speeding. As a result, we were each fined the equivalent of £40 each. Although Chris wanted to continue arguing, I told him it was no use. They were the law, and we had no chance. We paid the fine, then continued on our way. This time, we drove slower than before. By the time I spotted a sign showing the Crusader castle up ahead, the light was fading fast. A few minutes later, Chris turned off the main road, with my following him up a narrow track.

By the time we parked at the base of the small hill on which the castle had stood, the light had all but gone. We took the sleeping bags from the cars, then carefully made our way up a well-worn path.

To my disappointment, I could see nothing left of the castle, but thousands of stars lighting up the sky made a fantastic sight.

With nothing left of the castle, we laid out our sleeping bags on the ground. We were all tired from the long drive and with it not a cold night, in a matter of minutes, we were all fast asleep.

I awoke early the next morning and finding the others still sleeping, I got up to take a look around. To my surprise, I saw a small section of the castle still standing. Because of the darkness when we arrived, we had not seen it.

With camera in hand, I found my way into what used to be part of a tower. As I looked out through one of the narrow-slit window openings, I could see a beautiful sunrise, so I took a photo. A ray of sunshine coming through another window lit up the interior of the tower, and stone steps covered with earth. I could only imagine how it must have looked once upon a time.

From another window slit, I could see Chris and the others still asleep in their bags. They looked so peaceful; I took a photo, then made my way back out to where they lay. I found some awake, so I told them about my exploring inside the remains of the tower. Once all were up, they took a look inside, then a short time later, we made our way back down the hill to the cars. On arrival at Petra, we found guides were offering rides on horses to go down through the narrow gorge and see the various sites. However, we decided to walk, which turned out a decision. By walking, we could see everything . On our way down towards the gorge, we stopped to look at a number of openings cut out of the solid rock. These were so straight, level, and plumb, you would have thought a laser had cut them out. A short distance on, after turning a sharp bend in the gorge, we gasped. There in front of us stood the 'Treasury.'

With bright sunshine highlighting the red sandstone, it was an impressive sight. As we approached, the door opening looked to be around seventy-five feet high. Ongoing inside, we found the ceiling even higher. Like the openings we had looked at, the walls and ceiling were straight and smooth.

Apart from the Al-Khazneh building known worldwide as 'The Treasury' there is another remarkable sight. This is the Al-Doir, widely known as the 'Monastery.'

On passing the Treasury, and out of the gorge, we came to a wide valley. With the blazing blistering sun and little shade, it made walking uncomfortable. However, with so much to see, we soon forgot about the heat.

From looking, it appeared as though several generations had left their mark in Petra before disappearing. On the right-hand side of the valley, cut into the hillside were some monumental structures. Unfortunately, they were under restoration, so we could not explore them. After we had walked a way past an old Roman Amphitheatre, I noticed a sign pointing up the steep hillside; it read, 'The Monastery.

By the time we started climbing the steep steps leading up the hill, the kids had called it a day. I couldn't blame them; we had already been walking for several hours. As Chris and his wife followed me, we started up the hillside. The path seemed to go on forever. Every time I thought I reached the top, it continued higher. At one point, I turned to say it wasn't in sight. I then gasped, as to my astonishment, there before my eyes was the Monastery.

With it hidden away around the side of the hill, I had passed it by without seeing it. Like the Treasury, the Monastery is an enormous building. From where I stood looking down, the people in the enormous doorway looked like insects. It was an incredible sight. Ongoing down to look, like the Treasury, there was nothing inside the building. It was, however, a unique design, and without a doubt, well worth the long trek up the hill.

Once back down to where the others were waiting, as we had bought no bottles of drink, we were all hot and thirsty.

We were fortunate, as on our way back towards the entrance, we found a stall selling bottles of water and soft drinks. Without even querying the price, we bought a few and guzzled the contents. We then bought more to quench our thirst on the long walk back to the entrance. By the time we reached it, I, for one was exhausted.

With our walking for over six hours, it had been a long, tiring day. Nevertheless, the fantastic sights of Petra made the effort well worthwhile.

We had taken the long route to Petra so we could visit the old Crusader castle, but on our return to Amman, we took the Devil's

Highway. This winding road passed through the mountains and made for a shorter way home.

A few days later, I received a phone call from Jen. She informed me that a man named Jamie from a recruitment company wanted to talk to me. She said, "When he first contacted me, I told him you were working on a contract. He then explained that he usually handled engineers. Therefore, he did not know of what person he needed for the position in question. When he asked if I would send him a copy of your CV, I thought it not a problem, so sent him one. After he received it, he phoned me. 'Your husband is just what I need,' he said, 'he is perfect for the job.'

I then asked if she had received a letter from me. When she said, "No," I said, "If you had, you would have known I would be more than interested." After a chat, Jen told me she would get Jamie to call me direct.

As I would be in our head office when he called, I knew I had to be careful what I said. The next morning, I received a message saying my brother would be calling me at 3 pm. As he did not know where I was, I guessed it was Jamie. It was, with him doing most of the talking. He explained the contract was with Lossinger, a Swiss company, with the project a five-star hotel complex in Turkey. The position, an Interiors Finishing Advisor, sounded great. Then when he said it was a married status contract, I almost yelled in delight. It was something I had been hoping to obtain for a long time.

Although a successful contract, with salary and conditions excellent, there were a few minor things I wanted sorted out. After informing Jamie what they were, he said he would attend to this A.S.A.P.

I said as he was, in fact, working for me, if he was satisfied with the contract offered, then it was fine by me.

The following day, Jamie called again. He told me the client had agreed to the changes I requested. They did, however, want me to fly straight from Jordan to Turkey. This I said was impossible. I had to return to the UK to arrange things with my wife, who I knew she would want to join me in Turkey. Jamie also said that once he received my contract, he would sign it on my behalf. By now, I didn't care if the office knew about my leaving. Still, with all the phone calls I had received, they must have suspected something.

When Jen called to say she had received a copy of my contract, I handed in my letter of resignation. Although my employer was away, his secretary informed me he would be back in a few days time.

The next day, I received a letter from the office, stating that I would have to pay for my flight home. Because of my breaking my contract, I had no problem in accepting this. However, I felt shocked the next day when the company accountant informed me I would not receive any payment for my first week's work.

"What!" I said, "For what reason?"

He looked downcast. "Sorry, Colin, but during this time, it seems you were on an unpaid trial period."

I was furious. There had been no mention of this when offered the contract. "Right, that's it," I snapped. "Would you please inform the boss I want to talk to him? This is a bad joke at my expense."

A short time after going in to see him, he returned. He looked even more downcast.

"Sorry, Colin, but he doesn't want to talk to you."

I thought this a terrible way to treat me. "No, well we will see about that." I went to my apartment and wrote a report of all the things going on at the site. Once finished, I took it downstairs and handed it to the accountant.

I gave a grim smile. "After reading that, you'll find he will talk to me."

Although puzzled, he took the letter into the boss' office. On his return a few minutes later, he wore a quizzical expression. "You're right, he will see you."

Ongoing in to see him, despite saying he was sorry I was leaving; he omitted to mention about the contents of my letter. Given this, I said nothing. I felt sure it would have been a waste of time.

I left Jordan in August and returned to the UK. I didn't make any money because I paid for my flight and didn't get paid for my first week of work. The primary reason was acceptable; the second was not. However, on the plus side, I had been and explored Petra. It had made a dream come true, so I thought it worth the cost.

Little did I know the contract in Turkey would result in a complete change of life for my family and me? For sure, I did not know the incredible things it would bring.

The start of a new life in Turkey

# Chapter Eleven

By the time I arrived home from Jordan, Jamie, had finalised my travel arrangements to Turkey. Although neither Jen nor I knew anything about the country, she had agreed to come with me. Both her family and friends said she should, as it was an opportunity too good to miss.

Despite only buying our house a few months earlier, we decided to rent it out. The money gained would help us update it. After checking around, we chose a house rental agency. However, had we but only known of the horrors ahead, we would never have chosen this one.

As for our two daughters, Kim, our eldest, had moved into an apartment she'd bought a short time earlier. She was also enjoying her job with a real-estate company. Anita had also decided not to come with us, so we had set her up in a well-furnished bedsit, and also paid the first two months' rent. With Anita working, she said she could pay the rent herself.

I flew from Plymouth to Heathrow Airport in early September. Here I would meet Jamie, before flying on out to Istanbul. Turkey would become a new and interesting part of my expat life, as for the first time, my wife would join me.

At Heathrow, I found Jamie and his wife waiting to meet me. After introductions, he drove us to a hotel nearby. During our conversation, he mentioned that a representative from Lossinger, the company I worked for, would meet me in Zurich. I would then fly on to Istanbul

I was well pleased with Jamie who had done an excellent job arranging everything related to my contract. After our talk, Jamie handed me my flight tickets to Istanbul, then drove me back to the airport.

On disembarking in Zurich, I found no one waiting to meet me. Still, as I thought I knew everything about my contract, I was not concerned when I later boarded my flight to Istanbul.

It was late afternoon when the plane descended through the clouds towards the runway. For the first time, I viewed the ancient city of Istanbul that appeared immense. Istanbul is unique, as the winding Bosphorus Sea makes it the only city in the world to straddle two continents. One part is in Asia, the other in Europe.

From high above, I could see mosques everywhere. Some were so large they soared high above nearby buildings. Also, a vast variety of domes and minarets showed up between masses of apartment blocks. I thought the entire scene amazing.

After landing, I clearing customs, collected my luggage and walked out into the arrivals area. Here I found a man holding a sign with my name on it. After introducing myself, he led me out to his parked car. The ride that followed was an incredible experience. Both cars and trucks weaved in and out around us with no regard to lane discipline. After an hour of driving in dense traffic, we pulled up outside a large office building. The sign, "Ucgen Insaat," puzzled me. I had not heard of them.

Upon entering, a secretary introduced me to Haluk, Omer, and Orhan, they I found, were the owners of Ucgen Insaat. Haluk then introduced me to a man named Esref, the Project Director for the hotel contract. This seemed rather strange, as I did not know why I was in Ucgen's office. However, I guessed I would soon find out. No doubt Jamie had expected the man in Zurich to have informed me about Ucgen.

During a talk with Haluk, I discovered that Lossinger had seconded me to work for Ucgen Insaat. They were the construction company building the hotel complex.

After a meeting that lasted several hours, a driver took me to a hotel on the edge of the Bosphorus, where I would stay the night.

An hour later, Esref came and took me out to dinner at a nearby fish restaurant. With no idea of what to choose from a wide range of fish on the menu, I let Esref decide. During dinner, I found him friendly and informative. He told me that the Bosphorus area was famous for its many fish restaurants. After finishing what had proved a delicious meal, I could understand why.

When Esref informed me, he would be driving us to the construction site; I did not know how distant it was from Istanbul. To my surprise, he said it was down on the Mediterranean coast, the opposite side of the country.

The next morning, Esref came to collect me, and we set off. Because there being no motorways, and only a few sections of dual carriageways, it proved a long drive. The verdant countryside we passed through amazed me. I had imagined Turkey more arid and desolate. The closer we came to Kemer, which Esref said was the nearest place to the site, the more trees there were. These were mainly pine that Esref said, were in the extensive national forests that the road passed through.

By the time we arrived at the construction site, it was late afternoon. To my delight, I found the hotel complex set out on a beautiful, wide and long sandy beach. It extended back to the bottom of a pine-forested hillside. My first impression was! I knew right away that I would enjoy working in such a fantastic location.

Esref took me to the main construction offices where he introduced me to my two colleagues from Lossinger. One named Joe was a Project Manager; while Graham, was a Quantity Surveyor.

Esref then took me to another office where I met Erol, Ucgen's Project Manager, and Bekir, the Construction Manager. From there, we went to the Hotel Project Management office. I found that everyone I met, to be friendly and greeted me with warm handshakes. Their words of greeting made me feel relaxed and welcome.

After a brief chat, Esref took me for a look around the site. I found the main hotel building most unusual. Unlike other hotels I had worked on, it did not have any bedrooms. These Esref explained, were in buildings both on the beach, and set at the base of the steep pine-forested hillside.

After passing around a small headland, we came to a secluded bay. Here I found a large, ornately shaped swimming pool under construction. To my surprise, Esref mentioned that they would build a disco and dive centre on yet another beach around the adjacent rocky headland. Overall, I thought the location fantastic, with the layout perfect for that of a five-star complex.

By the time we returned to the office, it was the end of the workday. Joe was waiting to drive me into Kemer, where he and Graham lived. On the way, he said I would stay in a pension (small hotel) until the company found me a suitable apartment.

After a short drive, we arrived in Kemer. As Joe pulled up outside the pension, he pointed out his company apartment; on the opposite side of the road.

On walking into my new home, the owner, and his wife welcomed me. Although not large, my room was bright and well furnished.

A short time later, Joe took me to dinner at a small restaurant. During our meal, he told me his wife and family were on holiday in the UK. With our meal finished, Joe took and introduced me to the owner of the Mandalina Bar that he said, was his and Graham's local.

While enjoying a drink of Efes, the local beer, Joe explained the situation on-site.

"As advisors, our job is to point out any problems we see and advise Ucgen on how to rectify them." He shrugged. "Unfortunately, as they don't always agree with our suggestions, it makes our task frustrating. Still, apart from that, things good, with both our wives enjoy living here, as I am sure yours will when she arrives."

In this, it later proved right. But I did not know how Jen would react to living in a strange country.

After a tasty continental breakfast, the next morning, Joe drove us to the site. He explained that both he and Graham had company cars, and I would also have one. This was great, as it meant I could go out and explore the area on my day off work.

To my surprise, Joe said the labour force on the site comprised over three hundred Turkish workers. He then added, "Graham, you and I are the only English on the project."

A few days later, Haluk arrived and took me on a tour of the site. As we walked, he asked if I could see anything that needed improving to a better standard. If I did, I was to notify him or Esref.

I emphasized that with only concrete works ongoing at present, there was little I could suggest, but would certainly do as he asked.

As Joe had said, shortly after my arrival, I received a company car. Although old, it enabled me to get about on my day off work. While waiting for Jen to join me, I visited various ancient historic ruins, including Olympos, Phaselis, Perge, and Termessos. After visiting Termessos, I learned it was the only place in Turkey that Alexander the successful, never conquered. History said he took one look at the steep, narrow, twisting path leading up through the pine trees to the city, and decided not to attack. As it happened, the city later surrendered itself.

While living at the pension, the loud calling out of a cockerel used to wake me early mornings. When I mentioned it to the pension owner, he laughed. "That's the pet of the little girl who lives next door," he said. "If you're here when she comes home from school, you will see a sight to remember."

I knew the girl was the daughter of the employer of our electrical division, but did not know what he was talking about. However, a few days later, I witnessed what he had meant. When the girl came home from school and opened the gate to her front garden, she called out. The next minute, the cockerel appeared and ran towards her. As it approached her, before my astonished eyes, it launched itself up into her outstretched arms. To my astonishment, she then wrapped her arms around it and kiss it. Never had I seen or even heard of anyone kissing a cockerel. It was a sight I will always remember.

One morning, as I went to unlock the door of my car parked in the street, I felt puzzled. A pair of pliers were lying on the front seat. On getting inside, I found the ignition wires pulled down and twisted together. Someone had broken in and tried to hot-wire my car.

When I informed Joe, he burst out laughing. "What kind of thieves do they have here? Your car is a wreck, while mine is newer and parked just up from yours with the doors unlocked." He chuckled. "If whoever had tried to steal your car had only looked, they could have taken mine."

During my first month in Kemer, I lived in the pension. Then, on the day my wife was due to arrive, Haluk appeared on-site. When he asked how I was, I said, "I'm not happy."

He frowned. "What's the problem?" he asked.

I said, "Although the office knows my wife arrives this evening, there's no accommodation arranged for her."

His eyebrows shot up. "What! Do you mean you still don't have an apartment? What on earth is going on?" Then to my relief, Haluk said, "Don't worry, Mr Guest, I will deal with this immediately. There are several hotels in Kemer; I will have you put in one until they arrange suitable accommodation for you and your wife."

Given this, I told him the Frog Hotel, a small hotel and only a short walk from the centre of the village, would be okay. I chose it as from the front-facing rooms; there were beautiful mountain views.

"Right, if that's alright with you, I will arrange for you and your wife to move in today."

True to his word, I moved in late afternoon.

When I drove to the airport to meet Jen, I had a satisfied look on my face. I knew Jen would enjoy living in a hotel, even if only for a short time. However, I never realised the impact Turkey would have on her.

It was with successful excitement that I met Jen with a warm embrace as she came through arrivals. On the drive back to Kemer, I told her about our staying in the Frog Hotel.

"Oh! That's a lovely surprise," she said. "I had wondered where we would be living." I gave a short laugh. "Until late this morning, there was nowhere for you to stay." I shrugged. "Don't ask why, but the office had arranged nothing. It was only when my big boss Haluk arrived, and I explained this that he sorted things out."

"Well, give him my heartfelt thanks. From what you say, the hotel sounds nice."

After checking in and going to our room, Jen squealed with delight at finding our room faced the nearby mountains. Unfortunately, over the next few weeks, our beautiful view slowly disappeared. A block of shops and apartments replaced what had been a street of old tin roof shacks. It was a pity, as they had given a touch of character to the village. However, little did we know; this was a sign of things to come.

Kemer impressed Jen, and despite being small, it was a perfect place to relax and chill out. With warm sun and clear blue skies, life was far different from in England. Also, we found Turkish people to be both helpful and friendly.

The main street of Kemer started at a roundabout and ran straight down to a small, but well-sheltered yacht marina.

When looking back up the main street, a beautiful view of a range of mountains covered with pine trees faced you. On one side of the road, were a few restaurants and cafes that served tasty Turkish dishes. One café set among orange trees became our favourite meeting place. Although basic, with old wooden tables and chairs, we enjoyed sitting there and people-watching.

Kemer was a small village with few modern buildings. However, the construction of apartment blocks with shops beneath them changed things beyond belief. Given what was happening, I took photos of different views of Kemer. The difference now is incredible.

When I mentioned to some of my Turkish friends who had shops that the changes would bring in more business, their replies surprised me.

"We don't need more business. We liked Kemer as it was," one said. "Now, all we see is more and more concrete everywhere."

"You're right," I said, "The old Kemer had loads of character, whereas the new had no soul." I shrugged. "Unfortunately, this is what they call progress."

# Part 2

Only five weeks after Jen arrived in Turkey she shocked me one day. "I think after completing your contract, we should buy a piece of land and have a house built on it."

I nearly choked on the beer I was drinking. "What! I thought we had decided to move to Spain?"

Jens' face lit up in a wide mile smile. "We did, but Turkey is much better than Spain."

"You're right," I said. "That sounds a good idea to me."

This then started our search for a suitable piece of land. Mehmet, a Turkish friend, later took us to see what he thought was a suitable plot. The location was great, with beautiful views of the nearby mountains. Given this, we both felt excited when we went to see the owner of the land. We found him at home, and during a chat, he informed Mehmet the price he wanted for the land. When he told us, we thought it fair?

On our way back to Kemer, some Turkish men who had given Mehmet instructions where the landowner lived, stopped us. After one of them spoke to Mehmet, we were left disappointed. There were problems between the owner and his brother about the land. Given this, we decided against buying it.

Two months after moving into the Frog Hotel, because of a health problem, Joe returned to the UK. As a result, Jen and I moved into his apartment that we found bright and comfortable.

Most nights, Jen and I would meet up with Graham, his wife Caroline and several other English friends at the Mandalina Bar. Among them, Harry, a Project Manager, was working on a hotel project further down the coast. Harry was about my age, and like me employed as an advisor. His wife and two young children came out to join him about the same time as Jen arrived, with our becoming close friends.

In mid-December, a group of us went for Christmas dinner at the Erendiz Ranch. Apart from being a horse ranch on the outskirts of Kemer, its restaurant served excellent meals. Unfortunately, it turned out they were not used to serving Christmas dinners. Despite their best efforts, the meal was poor, which left us feeling hungry and disappointed come to the end of the evening.

The following week, Jen and I returned to the UK to stay with friends over the Christmas period. During this time, we met up with our two daughters. We were pleased to find Kim enjoying life in her apartment. However, things with Anita were much different. After a long talk, she decided to come and live with us in Turkey.

In the meantime, while we were checking through our bank statement, we were shocked. Despite having tenants living in our house for the past months, our house rental company had made no payments into our account. There was an obvious problem. The next morning, we called in at their office. Initially, they tried to say they had paid all money due into our account. In response, I informed them that our bank statement showed this incorrect. Later that day, the office manager phoned to apologise. He said there had been an internal mix-up, but all money due was now in our bank account. He also guaranteed this problem would not happen again.

Unfortunately, the lack of receiving our rent was minor compared to the enormous problem he later caused us.

The day after Boxing Day, along with Anita, we flew back to Turkey. With no direct flights from England to Antalya, our nearest airport, we had to wait nearly eight hours in Istanbul before boarding a flight to Antalya. Then, whereas our trip to Istanbul had been uneventful, the flight to Antalya proved nothing short of horrific. The weather changed not long after leaving Istanbul, and our plane ran into a major electrical storm. A steward announced that because of turbulence, all passengers had to fasten their seat belts. One would have had to be mad not to have done so. The plane was bouncing violently up and down and twisting side to side. Without a doubt, it was the most terrifying flight I had ever taken.

Anita, who sat next to me, looked as though she was about to burst into tears. "I'm frightened," she said. "are we going to be okay? Are we going to crash?"

Although apprehensive about this possibility, I said with false sincerity, "Don't worry; it's just a bit of turbulence. We'll be landing soon."

I am sure that everyone, including myself, were relieved when after what seemed like a lifetime, we landed safely at Antalya. As the wheels touched down on the runway, many of the passengers cheered and clapped.

Back at our apartment, Anita soon settled into living in Turkey and seemed happy with her new life. Unfortunately, for all of us, this would change beyond belief.

One evening, while having dinner in a hotel with Harry and his family, his big boss walked in. When asked if he could join us, we said yes. This turned out to be a huge mistake, as throughout dinner, Harry complained to his employer about both management and materials used on his site. Ultimately, I am sure this is why they sacked him a short time later.

While Jen and I were shopping in the local pazaar, an American man stopped to ask where he could buy stamps. While explaining where the PTT (Post Office) was, his wife came and joined us. As most tourists in Kemer at the time were Germans, we enjoyed talking to them. After walking around the pazaar together, we took them back to our hotel for coffee.

Ed and Evie, who were in their late sixties, informed us they were travelling around by car. To our surprise, they lived in a caravan they pulled along behind them. Due to them being friendly and sociable, we soon became friends. Although they only intended to stay for a few weeks in Kemer, they liked the area so much; they ended up staying for six months.

One day, they invited us back to their caravan. As we entered, a photograph on the wall showed a six-man raft shooting a foaming set of rapids. On closer examination, I found both Ed and Evie were on it. Ed was sitting in the front of the raft, wearing a successful big smile. When I mentioned this, Ed gave a wistful smile. "We were the oldest people to have made that ride," he said.

Ed told us one day that he had once been a Hollywood film director. He said years before, along with his sister and their parents, they lived in a large mansion.

> One amusing story Ed told us was about his sister, who had a pet boa constrictor snake. "One evening, my sister was playing her piano when our mother entered her room. When she found the boa draped around one post of her four-poster bed, she was far from pleased. She told my sister to take it outside to its cage where it belonged, then left the room." He chuckled. My sister was so engrossed with her playing that she forgot what her mother had said. When she later remembered and sought the snake, she couldn't find it. Not until making her bed the following day did she find it curled up underneath the mattress."

On another occasion, Ed told us about one of his father's birthdays when he didn't know what to get him. Wearing a broad grin, Ed said, "I then had a brainwave. It puzzled my father when I gave him a large case wrapped in fancy paper on his birthday. When he unwrapped it and found a baby alligator, he was not amused. Instead of thanking me, he told me to get rid of it. I felt disappointed at his rejection and didn't want to take it where I bought it. Fortunately for me, we had a large ornamental pond outside the house." He grinned. "I took the case outside and tipped the alligator into it. As no one ever saw or mentioned it again, I forgot all about it. Only years after my father died and the house was up for sale, did I remember the alligator?"

He shrugged. "I worried that had it survived, someone would have a nasty shock if they went for a dip in the pond. So, after picking up a friend, we drove to the house to see if it was still there. While prodding around in the pond with a large net, I felt something large struggling in the net. With difficulty, we managed to drag the net to the edge of the pond. To our amazement, trapped inside was the alligator that was around six feet long. After a struggle and dragging it out of the pond, with great care we picked it up and dumped it in the back of the truck. We then covered it up and took it to a reptile farm where we released it." He smiled, then added, "I hate to think of the consequences had I not remembered putting the alligator in the pond and the house sold to some unsuspecting family."

As I drove to my office one morning, I noticed a group of our workers standing around outside. Ongoing inside, I asked a colleague why the men were there.

"They are waiting to be paid their salaries," she said."

Because of knowing the company had a financial problem, I shook my head. "They need not wait, as they won't get paid," I said.

To my surprise, she said, "The men will receive their wages!"

I then informed her about the situation and repeated that the men would not get paid.

She gave a grim smile. "Colin, unless the men receive their salaries, they will kill one of the bosses. Then they will get paid."

"What!" I exclaimed. "You must be joking."

She shook her head. "No! In Turkey, if the workers do not receive their salary and cannot get paid, they will kill one of the bosss. She then added, "The other will then somehow find the money to pay them."

> I thought this unbelievable. Then, as I looked out at the group of men, I became nervous. Among them were several who were working as part of a small group under my control. I never discovered what happened re the men receiving their salaries, but thankfully, I had no trouble with the men working on the site.

At work one day, I heard a big commotion going on outside. Ongoing to investigate, I found many of our workers moving in a mass towards the main office block. I wondered what had happened when a man, gasping for breath, came running up to me.

"Please, Mr Colin. Could I have your car keys?"

On asked why, he said, "We found one worker lying unconscious inside the building. We want to take him to the hospital."

Not until sometime later did I learn the man was dead when inserted my car. He had somehow fallen from the roof down the lift shaft.

Apart from the bars in what was known as Bar Street, by the marina was the 'Porthole Bar.' Four young English girls managed it, and without a doubt, it was the most popular bar in Kemer. Although it played successful music and served a variety of tasty meals, the added attraction, were the girls who ran the bar.

In early April, Jen booked a flight back to the UK to see her parents. Chris, an Irish airline pilot friend of ours, drove us to the airport. After we watched Jen enter, Chris and I returned to Kemer. Shortly after Chris had dropped me off at home, I received a frantic phone call from Jen. She sounded close to tears.

# Part 3

"They won't let me leave the country!" Jen said. "They say I need that little black book." It was her residence permit that Chris had informed us we had to hand in at the Police station. Given this, Jen had left it with me to hand in.

"Okay. Don't panic; I will bring it to you," I said, then phoned Chris. Fortunately, he was at home. "Chris, sorry, but I have to go back to the airport right away."

He sounded far from pleased when he asked, "Why? What's wrong? We have only just returned."

"They would not let Jen on the plane," I said. "It seems she should have had her residence permit with her. I have to take it to her."

"Okay, wait outside; I'll be there in a minute." No sooner had I stood outside the front of my apartment when Chris arrived. As we set off at speed to the airport. he said, "I'm sorry, Colin, but I've never left the country since receiving my permit. I thought you had to take it to the police station."

As we walked into the airport, Jen's voice trembled as she said, "The plane has gone; what can I do?"

First, let's get the book problem sorted out," Chris said. Then, as he knew the airport layout, he took us straight to the customs office, where he explained our problem to an official.

"If you have a residence permit, you have to hand it in when you pass through customs," he said. "Do you have it now?"

"Yes, here it is." Chris handed it to him.

The officer checked through it, then nodded. "It is okay, but she will have to pay a fine for not having it when she tried to leave the country."

As it was our fault, we could do nothing except pay. So, after changing some Sterling into the Turkish lira, I paid the fine.

Then, to make matters worse, ongoing to inquire about flights to the UK, we learnt there were no seats available until the next day. Given this, we returned to Kemer.

The following day, Chris drove Jen and me back to the airport. This time, I stayed with Jen until she had passed through customs.

At one time, Chris bought an Irish setter puppy for his Turkish girlfriend. However, when he discovered dogs were not allowed in her apartment, he kept the dog that he named Brandy.

We found Chris, had an unusual way of house-training Brandy. While visiting him at home, he called him outside. "Come on, Brandy; let's do a pee on Turkey." Then, infront of our astonished eyes, Chris did a pee in the strange hope Brandy would do so as well. I had heard of some funny ways of training a dog, but nothing like that.

On another occasion, Jen noticed Brandy had done a poop on his lounge carpet. When she pointed this out to Chris, he shocked us by shrugging. "Yes, I know. He did it yesterday."

"But why don't you pick it up?" Jen asked.

"Oh, it's not a problem. My cleaner will be here tomorrow; she'll clean it up."

After leaving the Mandalina Bar one evening with Chris, Anita decided to walk Brandy back to Chris's house. As we were busy talking, Anita was not looking where she walked. Suddenly, she cried out in alarm. She had fallen into a deep hole in the pavement, and fortunate not to break any bones. However, this did not stop us from laughing at her misfortune. It was so funny. One-minute Anita was there, the next she wasn't. Although angry at us laughing at her misfortune, apart from having a few minor cuts and grazes on her legs, she was okay. It was her pride that damaged the most.

On our return to Chris's house the following evening, we had to laugh. Trees were now in all the holes, including the one Anita had fallen into.

At work, there were five young supervisors, the majority of whom spoke English. Despite one named Ugur speaking less English than the others, he proved both capable and helpful. I don't know how, but he always seemed to understand whatever I asked him to do and did it. He was also quick to learn and asked questions related to quality issues. Given this, we became good friends. When one day he asked, "Mr Colin, when you get your next contract, will you take me with you?" It didn't surprise me.

As it turned out, we later worked together on two more projects.

By my working with the Turkish supervisors, it helped improve their spoken English. However, despite buying books and cassettes, I found learning Turkish far from easy. Luckily for me, all the various site managers spoke English.

Shortly before Jen returned to the UK to see her family, I mentioned to Graham about wanting to buy a piece of land. To my surprise, he said he had a Turkish friend who also wanted to purchase land to build on. He suggested that with it easier to find larger plots than small ones, we should get together.

On Jen's return from England, we met Graham's friend Ahmed, who spoke excellent English. After a chat, we agreed to buy a plot of land between us.

The first plot Ahmed showed us was next to a river and full of large stones. One look was enough.

"Sorry, Ahmed, but this is not what we want," I said.

In was in early April when Ahmed called one lunchtime. He sounded excited. "Colin, I have found another plot of land that I think you will love. I want you to see before anyone else does."

After saying I could go now, Ahmed came and picked me up. On explaining Jen was in Kemer, we were fortunate to find her. As we set off, Jen and I were excited when Ahmed said he thought it an excellent piece of land.

We drove out of Kemer across the highway and crossed an old bridge spanning a dried-up riverbed. A short while later, Ahmed informed us we were now in a village named Kuzdere. After driving down and along narrow, twisting roads, Ahmed turned up a rough track. I was about to ask where we were going when he stopped. The track had finished where a narrow stream crossed it.

As we got out of the car, Ahmed said: "Come on, it's just a bit further." After jumping over the stream, a short distance on, as we passed through some trees, we came to a large, flat meadow. With a few orange trees on it. I thought the plot perfect. There were no houses in sight, with the plot surrounded on three sides by fruit trees. However, with Jen a city girl, I thought it a waste of time looking.

To my surprise and amazement, when Ahmed asked her what she thought, Jen said, "This is lovely, Ahmed, it's perfect."

My face lit with a wide smile. "Well, as Jen said, "It's an ideal location for a house."

When Ahmed informed us of the purchase cost, we agreed to buy it with him. Our idea was to build two houses, one for Ahmed and one for us. However, Ahmed had two brothers, so they wanted to build a house for each, plus one for Jen and me. Also, to our further disappointment, we found the houses would be joined together. Before we could comment, Ahmed announced, "I will position the two end houses forward from the middle two." I told Ahmed that if we could have one of the end houses, we would be happy to agree. He agreed, saying he would have whichever end house we didn't want. We chose the one nearest to where we entered the land, as it would have the best mountain views.

Ahmed said his brother, an architect in their family's construction company would design the houses. Once done and the house plans stamped and approved by the Belediye, (council) works could begin.

In the meantime, during a talk with Haluk, I mentioned our buying land and having a house built. To my surprise, he said, "Colin, if you like, we can build it for you? We have the men and equipment, it won't take long."

"Thanks', Haluk. I appreciate your kind offer. However, we have already agreed with Ahmed, who we bought the land with that his company will construct the houses."

During the construction, Jen and I were living in our company apartment in Kemer. One evening, while using a wood-burning stove to warm the room, we heard a loud crack. Getting up to investigate, it horrified me to hear a fire roaring inside the wall. I called and told our friend Osman about our problem, who a short time later, arrived with some firefighters. As they broke open the wall, we were shocked when flames shot out. As the firefighters doused the blaze, men from the Belediye, and Jandarma arrived to investigate. They determined the fire was most because of a bird's nest blocking the chimney. Whatever, it gave Jen and me a scare. Still, thanks to Osman and the quick response of the firefighters, only minor damage occurred.

With the hotel site near to our land, I used to go each day and see how construction works were going. To my delight, they had only cut down a few orange trees for the house's construction.

During the fitting out of the house, I complained to Ahmed several times about various things that were not correct. Not until much later did I discover his company had never built a house before. They only did the main concrete works. It explained why Ahmed became nervous each time I visited the site.

Once completed in March 1990, Jen and I were delighted. Not only was the house well finished, but we also had beautiful mountain views from most rooms.

About a month before the end of my ten-month contract, I woke with a severe pain in my back, and could hardly move. The last time I had back problems was six years earlier while working in the UK. At that time, a chiropractor cured me without my needing an operation.

After Jen contacted my office, they arranged for an ambulance to take me to a hospital in Antalya. There being only a small government hospital, and a few private doctors' surgeries in Kemer.

When some of our Turkish friends noticed an ambulance arrive outside our apartment, they came up with the driver to see what the problem was. On finding I could not walk, the men carried me down the narrow and steep stairs on a blanket type stretcher. I was worried they would slip and drop me, but they got me safely down and outside to the waiting vehicle. To my surprise, I found it was an estate car with a red cross painted on it. Ahmed, who Jen had called, explained. "Not only is there no major hospital in Kemer, there are no ambulances, either."

Once they laid me down in the back of the makeshift ambulance, Ahmed, and Jen climbed into the front. We then set off to Antalya, a one-hour drive. On arrival at a hospital, Ahmed went inside. He returned with two nurses who carried me inside on a stretcher.

After a doctor examined me, he said, "I want you to stay in the hospital for a few weeks." Although not what I expected, he then dropped a bombshell. "Unfortunately, we have no beds available for you."

We were all shocked at his unexpected statement. After thanking the doctor, Ahmed had the nurses put me back inside the waiting ambulance.

He shrugged.said, "Well, that was a waste of time. We'll go to another hospital to see if they can help you."

After a short drive, we stopped. I heard Ahmed tell Jen. "You stay here while I will go and talk to someone."

Fifteen minutes later he returned. "This hospital is worse than the previous one. No one seemed interested in knowing about your problem; you won't be going in there."

Because of being in the ambulance for nearly two hours, I did not feel too good. "Ahmed, I have to go somewhere," I said. "I cannot just keep riding around in this ambulance. I have full medical insurance, so money is not a problem."

After speaking with the ambulance driver, Ahmed turned back to me.

"Okay. We are now going to a private hospital. They should be able to help you."

A few minutes later, we pulled up outside a hospital, and Ahmed went inside. He returned with two nurses who carried me in to see a doctor. After examining me, he asked a few questions about what had happened. When I told him, he nodded and said, "I will now give you an injection." Though I thought this good, he then added. "I would like you to stay in bed for ten days to see if this helps."

I shook my head. "Thank you, doctor. I appreciate your help but think it best I to return to the UK for treatment. I have full medical insurance, and my company will pay for all costs involved in transport and treatment."

He nodded, "In these circumstances, it would be the best course of action." After he gave me an injection to help kill the pain, the nurses carried me back out to my waiting ambulance. Thanks to the infusion, during the journey back to Kemer, I felt much more comfortable.

On our arrival, some of my Turkish friends carried me upstairs to my apartment.

The next day, Esref came and we spoke about my problem. We decided I should wait a while to see if my back problem cleared up on its own. Given this, for the next few days, I slowly and painfully made my way downstairs. I then took a short walk up to the roundabout and back.

As this didn't help, I decided it best to rest in bed. While lying there, our friends Jim and Carole came out from the UK to stay with us for a week's holiday. This had been arranged before I had my back problem. Like Jen and I, they were disappointed to find I could not join them on their trips out.

During their stay, my company tried to arrange my flight back to the UK for treatment. It was a few hours after Jim and Carol left to return to the UK when Esref called.

"News, Colin. We have you booked on a flight to the UK tomorrow morning."

# Chapter 4

Although news, it came a day late. Our friends were going to Plymouth, where I intended to see my old chiropractor. As luck would have it, on their arrival at Heathrow Carol phoned to thank us for having them. While talking, Jen explained about my flight back to the UK the next day. To our delight, Carole said they would stay the night in London and meet my plane at Gatwick in the morning. They would then drive me down to their house in Plymouth in their Range Rover. What was even better, I could stay with them while having treatment for my back. This was an ideal solution, and we could not thank them enough.

As I could not walk, the company's insurance company agreed to pay for Ahmed to accompany me to the UK. For this, we were most grateful.

The next morning an ambulance came to take us to the airport. On arrival, they helped me from the ambulance and into a wheelchair. I then sat waiting until a member of staff wheeled me out to the plane. After being carried inside and laid on a stretcher bed, I noticed it had required the removal of three rows of seats. With no direct flights to the UK, it meant a change of planes in Istanbul. An airport staff member took me out of the plane and put me in a wheelchair. I then spent several uncomfortable hours while awaiting the flight to England. I felt relieved when at last they wheeled me out to the plane and placed me on a stretcher bed for the flight to Gatwick.

During the flight, Ahmed and I had a chat. Thanks to him accompanying me, it made the trip seem shorter. After Jim and Carol met us at Gatwick, Ahmed would go and stay with English friends of his. The flight went well, with my comfortable lying on the stretcher.

On arrival at Gatwick, a steward helped me off the plane, where, to my surprise, there was no wheelchair waiting. Fortunately, at the plane's doorway, were Jim, and Carole. In those days, this was possible, but now impossible because of security risks. Jim soon had a wheelchair brought for me.

After a brief chat, once Ahmed left, Jim wheeled me out to his Range Rover. Once inside and made comfortable, we set off for the drive down to Plymouth.

The next day, Carol took me to the same Chiropractic Surgery where I had received successful treatment six years ago. After an examination, one chiropractor gave me treatment. He also gave me an exercise machine to take home and use it between further treatments.

Although I returned every two days to the clinic for the next two weeks, unlike the last time I received treatment, I felt no improvement.

After a session, one day, Mr Walker, the chiropractor who had previously cured me, came and spoke to me. "Hello, Mr Guest. How are you?"

I forced a smile and told him I did not feel any better than when I first arrived.

He nodded. "Yes, I've been watching you over the past few weeks. As you say, I don't think you are responding to the treatment. Given your lack of progress, I will arrange to send you to a hospital for a different type of treatment."

I thought this good news, as I felt depressed about my lack of progress. However, little did I foresee the ordeal I was about to encounter.

Two days later, I went to a hospital where a doctor examined me. He then told me to lie down on my stomach, and explained he would be inserting a hollow needle into my spine. "Once it is in, I will inject a fluid into your spine via the needle." My concern about this only grew when he added, "Unfortunately, this will be painful."

Although I prepared myself, what followed was the worse than I expected. After a few seconds of the fluid pumped into my spine, an immense pain started to grow in my back. It was so bad I could not prevent myself from crying. During a brief break, I felt relieved when the doctor said he had finished. However, he then continued for what felt like a lifetime before completing the injection.

Despite being happy, my ordeal was over; I was not pleased when he said he wanted to see me again in ten days. He wanted to know how the injection had worked. During those next days, I told myself that even if the doctor said I needed another injection, I would refuse to have it. The pain had been so severe.

As a result, I felt nervous when I returned to see the doctor, so when he asked how much better I thought I was, I said around 85%. The doctor agreed and said I could either leave things as they were or receive another injection. The latter, he felt sure, would cure me.

As I intended to return to work in Turkey and needed to be 100% cured, with considerable apprehension, I agreed to have another injection. As I lay on the bed and felt the liquid slowly pumping into my spine, I grew tense. However, when I realised I could feel no pain, I relaxed. I told the doctor, who said, "That's because the first injection of fluid had to force the tissues apart in your spine. This second could pass through the gap."

Whatever the reason, I felt happy not to have felt any pain."

After the injection, I felt good. I could now stand up straight without any ache in my back. It meant I could return to Turkey without having to worry about my back playing up again.

While receiving my treatment, I received a fax from Ucgen. It informed me that Lossinger, my employer, was leaving the project. However, to my surprise, Ucgen were offering to take over my contract on the same terms and conditions. This was fantastic news. Without a doubt, it was the best contract I had ever had. I felt over the moon when I faxed back my acceptance. When I phoned Jen about my news, she said I know." Esref contacted and me of Ucgen's intention.

It was around the same time that I received a disturbing phone call from Jen. She informed me Anita was pregnant by her Turkish boyfriend, Levent. Although shocked, I was even more amazed when a few days later, she phoned to say Anita was getting married that weekend. Never in my wildest dreams did I think for one moment she would ever get married without my being present. As a result, Anita and Levent were married in mid-June without either my approval or being present.

Once back in Turkey, I spoke to Haluk about my concerns regarding salary payment. I told him I appreciated Ucgen's offer but knew there were problems related to finance. To my surprise and delight, he said, "If you want, Ucgen will pay you one months salary in advance." I of course accepted his offer.

During the time Ucgen employed me, I never had a problem in receiving my salary on time.

Now employed by Ucgen, things were far different from when employed by Lossinger. When I was an advisor, it was not necessary for Ucgen to take notice of my advice. Now, however, they had to.

During an inspection of painting works in one bungalow, I found the finish unacceptable. I had complained about this paint finish before, so I called in the painting supervisor.

With his face twisted into a scowl, he asked. "Who are you to say the paint finish is not acceptable?"

I shrugged. "No one, but until I am satisfied, you will not receive payment."

His attitude changed in a flash. Wearing a broad smile, he said. "Okay, I will ensure the finish is to your satisfaction."

While furnishing our new home, with no furniture shops in Kemer, we bought everything in Antalya. However, because of no road signs leading to our house, it was difficult to find. Therefore, I arranged to meet the truck bringing our furniture in Kemer.

While waiting with a friend, he asked, "Colin, is this your things coming down the street?"

On seeing a heavily loaded pickup truck approaching, I laughed. "No!" I said. "We have a lot of furniture coming; it will have to be in a lorry."

However, as the pickup truck grew nearer, to my utter disbelief, I found it was our furniture. Had I not seen it with my own eyes, I would never have believed it possible.

On the truck was our bedroom suite, including a double bed, a lounge suite consisting of a five and a three-seater sofa, plus two large armchairs. There was also a ten foot by six-foot wall unit. Given this, I found it hard to believe they had managed to get it all on the pickup.

My friend waved the truck to stop and explained to the driver he should follow me to the house. On reaching the narrow lane leading up to our house, I grew concerned. I wondered if the truck could pass under the overhanging tree branches, but to my relief, there were no problems.

At the house, the three men in the truck set to work. I was content with their progress until I found that the bedroom suite wasn't white as I had ordered but mahogany in color. However, after told it would take another three weeks to make a new suite, I decided to accept it.

Thanks to the men being quick and efficient, in no time at all, they had erected all the furniture. Everything looked fine, so I signed for the delivery, and the men drove off.

I was shocked as I went upstairs to our bedroom. The wardrobe was so long that it prevented the door from closing. Still, it was my mistake. I had given the shop the wrong sizes.

On calling Osman, who had taken us to choose the furniture, I explained the problem. He laughed. "It's not a problem," he said. "I will call the shop and ask them to take the wardrobe back and remake it shorter."

The next day the men returned to collect it. When they brought it back I was pleased to find it now fitted the room.

During a talk with Haluk, he said the company no longer needed my old company apartment. Therefore, if I wanted, I could have any of the items in it for our new house. I chose some pieces of furniture, and also paid a small sum of money for our old A/C unit and the wood-burning stove. Haluk had said I could have our large electric water heater, but because of a mix-up, someone else had it. On mentioning this to Bekir, he must have informed Haluk, for two days later, Bekir told me the company would buy me a new unit.

Ucgen proved very generous. They saved us a lot of money, and were helpful during our move into our new home.

Before moving to Turkey, as we only expected to be in Turkey for my ten-month contract, Jen arranged for our lassie dog, Ashley, to live with a family in Exmouth. For this, our bank would pay them a monthly fee. During the time they had him, the family asked if they could keep Ashley. Although neither of us was keen on this, we agreed, as we thought it best for Ashley. However, because of the husband being relocating to work in Liverpool, the family moved there. Here Ashley escaped, and it took two weeks before they found him. As a result, the family decided not to keep Ashley. On hearing this, Jen and I decided Ashley did not deserve being messed around. After a talk, we agreed he should come and live with us in Turkey.

While on a trip back to the UK, Jen found it would be best to bring Ashley over as excess baggage. He would then travel on the same plane as Jen on her return to Turkey. Plus, he would not have to wait at the airport for us to collect him.

> In mid-April, I met Jen and June, a friend of ours, at Antalya Airport. As we waited by the luggage carousel for their cases to come out, we heard a big commotion. Looking around, we found a large crate had come out on the carousel. To our astonishment, two men, with one walking along on each side, accompanied it. Everyone was staring and wondering what was inside the crate. Suddenly, we realised it was Ashley. On Jen indicating the crate was hers, the men lifted it and put it down beside us.

As Jen stooped to look at Ashley, she gasped in alarm. He had been given him a severe haircut. Before deciding to bring Ashley to Turkey, Jen had voiced her concerns to our vet about the hot temperature. He had said that because Ashley was a long-haired dog, it would not be a problem. Jen, nearly in tears cries, "Why have they cut off his fur? When I left him at the vets in London prior to them arranging his paperwork, he had long hair."

I shook my head. "Well, it's too late now, but don't worry, it will soon grow again."

On carrying his crate outside, we put it into the boot of our car, then drove home.

We were over the moon when Ashley soon settled into his new life in Turkey. With only a few dogs in our village, when out walking Ashley, we made quite a sight.

As I exited our driveway one day, with Ashley on the lead, I noticed a Turkish woman sat on a hummock of earth. Alongside her was a girl around six years old. As I passed by, I said, "Merhaba."

(A Turkish greeting). The woman looked shy and said something I did not understand. As I smiled at her, she rummaged in a bag beside her and pulled out a camera. I then realised she had been waiting to take a photo of Ashley. I held out Ashley's lead towards the girl "Yok Problem," I said, (No problem).

The woman nervously took the lead, then spoke to the girl, before giving it to her. After I told Ashley to sit, the women took a photo of her daughter holding Ashley close. Then, as I took the lead back from the woman, she gave me a big smile of satisfaction.

# Part 5

Taking Ashley to work with me always resulted in arguments. It was over who would take him for a lunchtime walk, which during the hot summer months was a three-hour break.

Some weekends I would drive up into the nearby canyon with Ashley. After parking the car, we would then go for a walk higher up the mountain.

After we decided to live in Turkey, we arranged for an international removal company to bring over various items from our house in England. Although they promised delivery within two weeks, it took over two months. For reasons unknown, customs in Istanbul held up our goods. Thanks to a Turkish friend, after many phone calls to the customs, they released them.

Come August; we had been living in our new house for four months. After giving it some thought, I said, "Look, Jen, I've been thinking. We cannot live in two countries. Where would you prefer to live?"

Without any hesitation, she replied. "Here in Turkey."

I nodded. "In that case, let's sell our house in England. At present, we have two mortgages. If we sell our house in England, we can pay off both mortgages and be debt-free."

Although we had a beautiful house that we had only bought six months before, we agreed to sell it. We had a lady renting it, who during several talks seemed nice. I called one day to inform her we would sell the house and were giving her a month's notice to move out.

To my relief, she said, "That's no problem, Colin, I can find somewhere else to live."

I put down the phone, happy to tell Jen what the lady had said.

"That good; now, all we have to do now is to find a buyer."

Oh boy, was she wrong, for the woman changed her mind and refused to leave. It then took the best part of a year of Jen going back and forth to England trying to resolve our tenant problem.

In mid-December, I accompanied Jen to court. This would be the third time she had attended. It shocked us when the Judge announced he was adjourning the case until the 29th December. It seemed our tenant's barrister was not available.

Thankfully, friends who had attended, let us stay with them. That Christmas was not a merry time, as we were worried about how we would get on when we returned to court. On the 29th, full of hopeful anticipation, we returned to court. While sat in an anteroom talking with our barrister, there came a knock on the door. Our barrister got up and went out to speak to whoever was there.

On his return, he was smiling. "Well, we may be in luck. They want to make a deal." He then explained that the deal involved our foregoing all the rent the lady owed, plus, we would pay all the costs of the case. Although far from happy about this, our barrister recommended we accept the deal. By doing so, it guaranteed we would get our house back. Given this, with reluctance, we accepted the offer.

When I first informed the tenant, we wanted to sell the house; prices were rocketing. Our house had doubled in value from when we first wanted to sell. However, by the time we got the house back a year later, there had been a crash in the housing market. As a result, we were selling the house in a falling market. Given this, I was relieved when Jen called to say she had sold the house. On paper, although we had lost around £40,000, we still made a substantial profit on what we had paid for the house. It enabled us to clear the mortgage on our house in Plymouth and our new home in Turkey.

How much it had cost to get our house back, I do not know, only that the stress to Jen was enormous.

The ordeal we went through re our renting out our house is one well worth remembering. We had thought we had picked an excellent agent. However, given our experience, I recommend using one recommended by someone who has used the agent in question. Also, the lawyer we used proved a waste of money. So again, a personal recommendation is without doubt, the best way to find a good one.

During the time we were sorting out our house problem, I received a letter from the Inland Revenue. They were querying about undeclared money I paid into a building society each month. This made little sense. We had no savings account with the named building society. Then the penny dropped. This was not our account, but that of the family looking after Ashley. As my bank handled all my tax affairs, I phoned and asked to speak to the manager. I enquired how the Inland Revenue knew about my payments to the building society. His reply left me shocked. He said they had sent copies of all my bank statements to the bank's tax division. I informed the manager in no uncertain tones that this was a complete intrusion of privacy. I had nothing to hide from the Inland Revenue, whereas many other expats who used the bank's tax division might well have. I said, "They would be unhappy if they knew the bank was doing this."

The manager tried explaining this was standard practice but soon realised it was unacceptable to me. From his tone, with reluctance he apologised. However, he then assured me they would not forward any further copies of my bank statements.

In late September, Jen took Anita and her husband, Levent over to England. Anita and her husband intended to live in Halifax, where Levent would work at a Turkish Doner Kebab restaurant. However, after the birth of their son (who they named

Levent junior), they moved down to Plymouth. Here, my friend Jim, who had his own building company gave Lee a job. Things went well until, because of lack of work; Lee became redundant. As a result, he then returned to Halifax, while Anita stayed in their Plymouth apartment.

When Jen and I flew over to England to see her and Leejay, we were in high spirits, but when Anita opened the door of her apartment, she appeared upset. Once inside and sat down, Anita, who was in tears, showed us a letter she had received. The letter stated that since Anita hadn't paid rent for two months, they would evict her. This news came as an immense shock to us.

Anita then explained things between her and Lee, were not good. Given her pending eviction, she and Leejay would have nowhere to live. After a long talk, Anita agreed to return to Turkey and live with us.

At the end of May, we all flew back to Turkey.

One weekend, I went to look at a revolving restaurant that was under construction on top of a hill near the Antalya marina. As I stood looking around, a young man came over to me. "Excuse me, but I noticed you drove up here in a car. Could you give me a lift back down to the main road when you leave? I came up by taxi, which has now left."

I told him this would not be a problem. While we stood chatting, the man said he was Swedish. He explained that he came to investigate the possibility of flying off the top in a hang glider. I thought he was mad when he said his idea was to land down on the beach. With it such a long way down; the idea sounded incredible. I thought he must be joking, but found out he was not, when he said. "If you like, we can jump together."

"What!" I gasped. "No thanks. You jump, and I'll meet you at the beach."

As he seemed a friendly young man, and I had time on my hands, I asked him. "Have you ever been to Termessos? It's about twelve miles on the other side of Antalya."

"No," he replied. "I have never even heard the name."

"I can take you there now if you like. It's the remains of an old city high up in the mountains, which I think will interest you."

His eyes lit. "If it's no trouble for you, then yes, please."

After driving to Termessos, we wandered around, exploring the ruins scattered about on the mountain. After leaving, I then dropped him off in Antalya where he was staying with his father.

Before Jen returned to Turkey, she had overseen the sale of our house. Given this, she said, "It's up to you to empty it of all furniture." As Jen had suffered such a stressful time dealing with the court and getting the house redecorated, I thought this only fair.

I later flew to England and set about excluding everything in the house. While doing so, Jen called. She asked if I would be interested in buying our friend Chris' jeep. It was a Dacia that he purchased from a dealer in Romania. As I thought it a suitable vehicle, and no longer had the use of a company car, I said yes.

Jen then called Chris in Ireland, who then called me. During a chat, as neither of us was working, we decided to drive his jeep back to Turkey.

On my last morning in what was by then an empty house, the phone rang. On picking it up, a woman asked, "Is Jenny there?"

"No," I said. There was a pause, then the voice asked, "Is that you, Col?"

"Yes," I said, wondering who I was talking with. I then realised it was Kay, one of our best friends. As I knew her husband, Tony, was not in health, I thought perhaps something bad had happened to him. However, to my surprise and shock, she informed me Oz, Tony's elder brother, who I had worked with for many years, had died. I had never known Ozz to be ill, and more surprising, although he had never smoked, he died from cancer.

When I called Jen, my news shocked her. Still, as Chris would not be arriving until after the funeral, I said I would also attend it.

On the day, I found the church packed with relatives, friends, and numerous of his work colleagues. Although an excellent service, I felt sad about losing my best friend.

A few days later, Chris later arrived at my mother's house where I was staying. Once he had sorted out car insurance, we took a ferry over to Roscoff in France.

I enjoyed our drive back to Turkey, with our stopping the night in several countries on the way.. As we were about to reach the Turkish border, I felt flabbergasted, when Chris said, "It would be best if we go back." I thought he joked and said so.

"No!" he said. it would be best if we turn around and go back to Turkey."

"What! Why on earth should we do that?" I asked. "We're at the border."

He shrugged. "Because I feel sure we will have a problem taking the jeep into Turkey."

"What makes you think that? We've not had a problem going through any of the other countries?"

He shook his head. "I sure there will be a problem." Anxious and silent, we continued to the border post. After parking, I accompanied Chris into the customs office. He then handed the jeep's papers to an official, who, after a quick look; got up and took them to into another office.

I went and spoke to Chris. "Is there a problem?" I asked.

He nodded. "Yes! Just as I knew, there would be. He's taken the papers to his manager. We now have to wait and see if he lets us into Turkey or not."

When the official returned to his desk, after stalking to Chris, he handed him some papers, then shook his hand. As Chris walked back to me, I stood up.

"Well, is it on or back?"

His face broke into a beaming smile. "Turkey, here we come."

We drove on down the coast, then caught a ferry over to Canakkale. After driving further down the Aegean coast, we checked in at a small pension for the night. The next day we drove on and arrived in Kemer late that evening. Driving from England to Turkey had been a fantastic experience. Unfortunately, my expectations of buying the jeep shattered when, because of legal issues, I could not purchase the vehicle from Chris.

I thought the jeep a good one, so enquired about buying a new one. To my dismay, because Chris had bought his tax-free in Romania, the price was twice what he had paid. Given this, it put paid to any ideas I had about purchasing a Dacia jeep.

At one time, Mehmet, a friend of ours, told Jen and me that he owned a plot of land in Kemer and intended to build a pension on it. To our surprise, he asked if we would be interested in running it for him. As we needed to earn a living in Turkey after my contract finished, we thought it a good idea. When Mehmet said we should pay for the construction, with land prices in Kemer being expensive, this sounded a reasonable arrangement.

He then explained his thoughts on how things should work. "You and Jenny run the pension for five years, during which we share the profits. Then you can leave, and I take over." This seemed ideal until I asked what we would receive on leaving. That's when Mehmet dropped a bombshell.

"Nothing!" he said.

"What! You are joking?"

"No, it's a good deal for you and Jenny."

We tried in vain to get him to understand it was not a good deal for us, but an excellent one for him. The three of us later talked with an English teacher friend of Mehmet's. After hearing both sides, his friend explained to Mehmet why it was not a good deal for us.

Mehmet looked down as he apologised. "I'm sorry, Colin. I had thought it a good deal for you and Jenny, but now I understand why you rejected my offer."

As we shook hands, I said. "Don't worry about it; it's not a problem."

Since then, we remained friends.

# Part 6

In May, during a dinner party Ucgen held at the Otem hotel, a belly dancer performed. While everyone was up dancing, Haluk had me join in. It being the first time I had tried Turkish dancing. As a result, I felt embarrassed while doing my best to copy what the others were doing. Nevertheless, it pleased me when Haluk told me I had done well. Of course, this might not have been true.

On the 1st of June, I had a shock when Haluk informed me my contract had finished the end of May. However, he said as I had not received notification, I could stay on until the end of June. This news surprised me, as there had been no talk about my contract ending.

The day after Haluk's surprise statement, along with many other people, Jen and I attended the grand opening of Kiris hotel. The hotel complex not only looked fantastic but soon became noted as the best hotel in the area. No doubt because of its popularity, the Turkish President visited the hotel two weeks after the opening.

My contract in Turkey had proved not only profitable but extremely enjoyable. We now lived in a new house in the country with fantastic views. But of even more importance, we were debt-free. Plus, despite only a few English people living in Kemer, we had made numerous Turkish friends.

After completing my contract with Ucgen, I set about finding a business to enable Jen and me to earn a living in Turkey. With our friend Chris, we tried to rent a place that we intended to use as a beach-side café. However, because of high rental costs, we could not do so. Not until a few years later that I found a suitable business venture.

Still, although the time spent in Turkey had proved a mix of challenging and disappointing events, life had been exciting and enjoyable. My initial back problem had been a blessing in disguise. None of this would have been possible had I not started to work as an expat. On the downside, we had spent a great deal of money, resolving our house problem in England. Therefore. I felt delighted when David, my old boss from Wiltshire, called and offered me a contract in Northern Cyprus. With it only a short flight from Antalya, I thought it could work out well.

Unfortunately, things in Cyprus would not go as expected.

Our house and Ashley in Kuzdere

The Karatas Rocks near our house.

Disappointment in Northern Cyprus

# Chapter Twelve

After receiving a call from David regarding a contract in Northern Cyprus, my wife and I decided to kill two birds with one stone. While having a holiday there, I could discover more about the job offer. The position, a supervisor on a five-star hotel project, sounded ideal. However, David had pre-warned me about various problems related to the contract. Despite this. I needed a job, so was interested.

On our arrival in Cyprus, a man from the hotel we had booked in Kyrenia met and drove us to the hotel. Although not large, our room was comfortable, with it only a short walk to the shops and beach.

Once settled in, we hired a car and went to see what the island had to offer. To our disappointment, apart from some impressive ruins and the Kyrenia seafront, there was nothing else. We had booked to stay one week, with an option of another. However, after our tour, we decided one was enough. No doubt our disappointment was because of living in a far more beautiful place.

> On the day I drove to the project to meet David, I found he was attending a meeting. To my surprise and delight, Harold, my old friend from Brunei, was there. He grabbed hold of my hand. "Hi, Colin, it good to see you." Harold chuckles. "Well, you're certainly nearer home here than when we were out in Brunei," he said.

"That's for sure," I replied. "It's only a forty-minute flight, plus a one-hour drive to my house. Nevertheless, I'm not stuck on this place. Where I live is a paradise compared to here."

Harold grinned. "Well, all I can say is your place must be something special. From what I've seen since I've been here, it's pretty good. Anyway, let me show you around."

I found the hotel site on a small peninsula jutting out into the sea, which formed a sheltered bay. Given this, it looked an ideal location for a five-star hotel. As we walked around, I mentioned that David had told me of various problems on the site.

Harold laughed and shook his head. "Yes, you could say that," he said. "The job is okay; the problems are mainly because of politics."

I shrugged. "I'm not too concerned about politics that's David's job to sort out. Besides, I need a job, so I'm interested in hearing what he has to offer."

Later that evening, David came to see me at our hotel. After a chat and hearing the salary on offer, I laughed. "If I still lived in England, I couldn't accept this salary," I said. "Nevertheless, thanks to living in Turkey, I can afford to accept your offer."

After agreeing to start work in two weeks, two days later, Jen and I flew back to Antalya.

On my later return to Northern Cyprus, David met me at the airport and drove me to an apartment. I would live here along with Harold and the other English supervisors on the project. After introductions, I found them all friendly.

As all our workers were Turkish, to ensure there were no language problems, each of us supervisors had an English-speaking Turk working with us.

While in the site office talking with David, his secretary informed him that a man named Ugur was asking to see him.

David seemed surprised. He turned to me. "When this man informed me, he had worked on the Kiris Hotel in Turkey; I remembered you saying you had worked on it." He shrugged. "Since applying for a job, I've not heard from him."

My eyes lit up."Ugur is a first-class worker and organiser," I said. "Without a doubt, he would be an asset if he works with us." I grinned, "The only drawback, he only speaks a little English."

When Ugur entered the room and saw me, his face lit up with a big smile. He came over and gave me a big hug and a kiss on each cheek (a typical Turkish greeting between close friends).

In broken English, he said, "Hi! Mr Colin. It's good to see you again."

"And to see you also," I replied. "It's been a long time since Kiris." After we had spoken for a while, David asked Ugur to wait outside for a minute. As he closed the door behind him, when David turned, he looked puzzled.

"Colin, Ugur doesn't speak English." He shook his head. "As you don't speak Turkish, how on earth do you communicate with each other?"

I chuckled. "Let's just say Ugur understands what I say, and gets on and does it. Despite his lack of English, I recommend you take him on. You won't regret it."

David looked at me in despair. He shrugged in resignation, then asked Ugur back in the room.

"Well, Mr Ugur, Colin said you're the man for the job, so it's yours."

We were both shocked when Ugur said, "Thank you, but money is not enough." He then mentioned a figure that from David's face, I knew was way above what he had offered him.

David shook his head. "I won't pay you that! But, as Colin speaks so highly of you, I'll give you forty % more than we offered you."

After thinking for a minute, Ugur accepted and agreed to start the following week.

I had hoped to have him work with me, but as I already had an assistant named Sultan, Ugur worked with Harold.

A few weeks later, Harold told me how pleased he was with Ugur. "It's amazing," he said. "I only have to tell him something once, and he gets it done." He shook his head. "How he does this without speaking English, I don't have a clue."

I laughed. "Don't ask me," I said, "I do not know either."

Over the next few months, work went well. We had an excellent team of workers, with the interior of the hotel soon starting to take shape. It looked great and had all the makings of a luxury hotel.

Our small team of supervisors got on well, both at work and in our apartments. Life good. The only problem we encountered was on paydays. Our salary was in Pounds Sterling, so we had to go to the bank to change money for ourselves, and to send home. Because of the local banking system, it usually meant spending the best part of an hour to complete our business.

Most evenings we would cook and eat in our apartments. We left going out for a meal and a drink until the weekend. I found the restaurants served excellent meals, with the portions large, tasty, and at reasonable prices. Additionally, dining at a restaurant on the seafront harbor with moored fishing boats, yachts, and motor cruisers was a delightful experience.

On the seafront, I had my first sip of 'Long Island Iced Tea', a blend of spirits, ice, and coca-cola. Although a potent mixture, I found the taste refreshing. On trying a sip, several colleagues liked it so much they switched to drinking it. However, because of its strength, it was not advisable to drink too many. Also, because of the number of spirits used, it was an expensive drink.

On the drive home from work one night, we called in at a supermarket. To avoid any problems with passing cars, I parked on the pavement. While inside we heard a loud crash, with one of our colleagues who had been waiting outside calling out in alarm. Ongoing to see what had happened, I was shocked when he said a car had hit mine. To my further disbelief, when I confronted the driver, he said, "It's your fault the accident happened."

"What?! How could it possibly be my fault? I said. "My car was on the pavement, and I was inside the shop?"

After the man insisted it was my fault, the shopkeeper called the police. On their arrival, they took statements from me and the other driver. To my relief, a few days later, they informed me that they would not take any action against me.

At work, the installation of ornate panelling was ongoing in several areas, with the decoration proceeds in the guest rooms. It impressed my colleagues and I with the look of the hotel. We could tell it would look fantastic once we had completed our works. However, it was around this time that we heard some disturbing news. The company doing the marble works were reducing its staff. On speaking to their supervisor, he told me it was because of non-payment of their account.

This was not good. The previous month, all the construction company's workers had attended a meeting of support for Asil Nadir. He was the employer of Polly Peck, the company we were working for. Although we did not know what it was about, something serious was going on. If he had problems, it would be a significant cause of alarm to Wiltshier.

During the bidding process for the project, Polly Peck had informed Wiltshier there could be another three hotels to be constructed. It would depend on how good the business was after the hotel had opened. With this latest news of non-payment, things did not sound good for the present, let alone the future.

Despite all this, I went and bought myself a fishing rod. I thought fishing would make a change from hanging around in Kyrenia on my day off work. Unfortunately, the fish decided not to accept the lunch I offered them. Although a pity, at least going fishing, meant a change of scenery.

As it happened, I need not have bought the rod, for a week after buying it, David called a meeting. We were all shocked when he informed us that all our contracts were being terminated. He then explained. "Polly Peck has gone bankrupt, with the company now under an official investigation. I'm sorry about this, but it is out of the company's hands. Nevertheless, you need not worry about your salaries. All staff and workers will receive their salaries up to this weekend, plus, a plane ticket home."

Although terrible news, we were fortunate. All the Turkish construction workers contracts were terminated, but unlike our workers, they did not receive plane tickets back to Turkey. Sad as it seems, the police later escorted them to the port and put them on a ferry over to Turkey.

I thought this a terrible way for their company to act. If I were one of those unfortunate workers, the way the company acted would have outraged me.

In total, I had only been on the project for three and a half months. Once back in Turkey, I set about finding another contract, preferably married status, so Jen could accompany me.

Although I never knew, this would take much longer than I anticipated. Also, when it did, a tragic incident would cause a major upset.

Death in Turkmenistan

# Chapter Thirteen

After being unsuccessful in obtaining a new overseas contract for more than a year; I received a phone from an old work colleague. He said that my former boss, Haluk Kaya, from Ucgen, wanted to talk to me. As a result, I later met Haluk, in Kemer, near where I lived. After exchanging greetings, he asked if I was working.

I shook my head. "No, not at present," I replied. I did not like to add I had been seeking some time. My heart skipped a beat at his next words..

"That's good, as Omer and I bought two villas that require modernisation. I need you A.S.A.P. in Istanbul, as we would like you to look after the quality of works." Before I could speak, he added. "Once I've sorted out an apartment and driver for you, I will contact you about moving to Istanbul."

I thought this great news, but to my further delight, he then said, "I also need your help on a hotel project in Turkmenistan. It's a one-year project, which, if you accept, the salary will be in US dollars."

The first bit he said good, but the latter part about the hotel project was fantastic news. I could not believe my luck. It was just the kind of contract I had been seeking.

Haluk then went on to say, "I will require you for the hotel project around the end of October. Haluk said, the villas should be completed by then, so things should work out well."

Although I had never heard of Turkmenistan or where it was, I nodded in delight. "If I can be of help to you and Ucgen, then I will go there," I said. I sincerely meant this, as Ucgen had looked after me well when I worked with them in Turkey.

After Haluk left to return to Istanbul, I had a spring in my step and wore a big smile on my return home.

All I knew about the contract Haluk mentioned was the country, the contract period, and the salary. However, I had an excellent relationship with Haluk and Ucgen. I knew I would have no problems working for them in Turkmenistan.

When I told Jen of my meeting with Haluk, she was thrilled. "Oh, that's successful news" She shrugged. "Where is Turkmenistan?"

I chuckled. "Don't ask me," I replied. "I do not know."

On looking at an atlas, I found Turkmenistan was once part of the Soviet Union. The Russians rebuilt Ashkhabad, the capital city, after a massive earthquake destroyed it in 1948. Since acquiring independence in 1991, President Niyazov ruled the country. However, apart from that, I did not know where I would be working in the country.

The news about earthquakes was not good, but as I lived in Turkey that also suffered earthquakes, I was not too concerned.

When Haluk later called to say he did not require my services in Istanbul, I felt disappointed. Nevertheless, I cheered up when he confirmed my contract in Turkmenistan would start the end of October.

I arrived late one evening in Ashkhabad, where from the time spent taxiing, I realised it must be a large airport. After disembarking, I followed my fellow passengers across the tarmac towards the arrivals hall. I thought it ominous when we made to stand in a queue outside a single door. When finally allowed to enter, we discovered a packed room with a large crowd. The room contained three desks, each surrounded by a frenzy of passengers thrusting their passports at the men seated behind them. Apart from shocked to see the men writing out the visas out by hand, I felt disturbed to see money being handed over. No one had warned me about this.

On asked one of my fellow passengers how much a visa cost, I panicked when he said "$40."

"I don't have any dollars," I said, "Only Turkish money."

"Then give the equivalent of $40," he said.

When at last I could offer my passport, I handed it over with my Turkish money. To my astonishment, the man behind the desk shouted something as he threw my Turkish lira back at me. Then saying nothing else, he took the next person's passport and money. I stood shocked. I didn't know what to do. Fortunately, on hearing my panic-stricken voice, a Turkish man exchanged my Turkish money for dollars.

After returning to the visa desk, I breathed a sigh of relief when the man took my dollars and wrote out a visa for me. On moving through into another room, I found the other passengers standing around, awaiting their luggage.

One man there asked, "Do you have a computer with you?"

"No," I replied.

"That's ok then, as customs are confiscating those that do."

Once my luggage appeared, I picked it up and walked outside. Among a crowd of people waiting to meet arrivals, I noticed a man I remembered as working with Ucgen.

He came over. "Hi, Colin, long time since Kiris. Is everything okay?"

I grinned. "It is now," I said, "but no one told me I needed dollars to pay for a visa. Thankfully; a stranger changed my Turkish Lira to dollars." I shrugged. "Had he not done so; I don't know how I would have got into the country."

He laughed. "Never mind," he said, "you're here now." On leaving the airport, he drove me to an apartment that he said belonged to SET, the electrical division of Ucgen.

It had been a long day, so after unpacking and taking a shower, I had an early night.

The next morning, a driver came and drove me to Ucgen's offices. Here I met Esref, the General Manager, who I worked with in Turkey. On talking with him, it did not surprise me to hear I was the only English person on the project. Still, as I knew the project management staff usually spoke English, it would not be a problem. After a chat, we went to the construction site, where he introduced me to a man named Emrah. As he only looked to be in his late twenties, it surprised me to find he was the site engineer. However, he appeared friendly and also spoke English.

On leaving the site, Esref then took me to a market shopping area that he said Ucgen had recently completed. From here, we went to the Parliament Building. It shocked me when Esref informed me, "All works have to be completed in six weeks." This seemed an impossible task. The place was a mess, with a mountain of work to be completed. Nevertheless, incredible as it appeared, six weeks later, it opened on schedule.

Returning to the head office and talking with Haluk, he explained that Ucgen worked primary on Government projects. "All of which," he said proudly, "we completed on time." He then informed me about an incident that occurred during works on the market project. "All the materials for the project were coming from Turkey by truck." He shook his head on remembering. "A war was raging in Georgia that our trucks had to pass through on the way here. Everything was going smoothly until one convoy of trucks got held up with some set on fire." He gave a grim smile. "The rest of the trucks managed to escape and return to Turkey. On hearing this disastrous news, I phoned the President of Turkmenistan. I explained that because of this unfortunate event, it would not be possible to complete the market project on schedule." He chuckled. "The President was far from pleased." He said, '*I have promised my people I will open the market on the date stated, so it must be open then.'*

"I informed him that because of the ongoing war in Georgia, we could not transport our materials by truck from Turkey. To my astonishment, he said, 'I will arrange air-transport for all your materials.' Incredible though it may sound, he was as good as his word. They arranged for all the materials we needed to complete the project to be flown in and delivered to the site. He shook his head. "This will gives you an idea of the cooperation we receive from the Turkmenistan government." He paused, then said, "Our men then worked many long hours to complete the market that opened on schedule."

It amazed me to hear such a story. To me, it was something one might read about in a fiction book, not in real life.

Esref said I would stay in the SET apartment until they found me a suitable apartment. To my surprise, he said he had assigned a young man named Noyan to work with me. Apart from acting as my interpreter, he would also learn about quality control. I thought this successful, as despite living in Turkey for several years, I could not speak Turkish. The next morning, he introduced me to Noyan, who I soon found both helpful and a quick learner. Given this, we became friends both on and off-site.

During my first week on-site, it rained nearly every day. As construction works had only started a few months earlier, it made it difficult to get any work done.

Despite phoning Jen on various occasions, I found it impossible to get through. On speaking with Emrah, he shrugged. "You have to go through the operator, but even then, it is not always possible." To overcome this problem, I used to send a fax to Expats International, who then contacted Jen for me.

On the same evening that Haluk and Esref returned to Istanbul, Enis, the site Project Manager, arrived back from holiday.

During a meeting the next morning, he seemed okay. A few days later, he informed me that a man named Ugur, who would be our Site Manager, would be arriving shortly,

To my disbelief, Enis told me we would be installing ready-made bathrooms. Train would transport these finished units that were being made in Finland to Turkmenistan. I had never heard of bathrooms manufactured off-site, delivered to site, and then slotted into position. The whole idea sounded amazing. Nevertheless, I knew using this technology would save an enormous amount of time. Given this, I looked forward to seeing how this system would work.

At our Main office compound, were blocks of living accommodation for our workers, plus a large canteen that supplied meals for them. On talking with Emrah, he said it was difficult to obtain much in the way of food in Turkmenistan. As a result, we truck in all the ingredients the cooks used to prepare our meals, from Turkey. I thought this unnecessary, but soon found what he said was correct. There was a general shortage of most things in the country. To my further surprise, Emrah said that when the shops received fresh supplies of stock; large queues would form outside. Once open, crowds would make a desperate bid to get in and buy whatever was on sale. I witnessed this one day when I saw police controlling crowds outside a shop.

I found Ashkhabad, a dreary-looking city. The major streets were wide, but poorly surfaced, with all the houses old and grey. Another thing I learned, there was virtually no public transport or taxis. Given this, people would stand in the hope someone would stop and take them in the direction they wanted to go. The drivers of cars that did, would receive a small sum of money for taking them.

Despite all this, there were several large open parks. From the one next to our hotel site, the nearby mountains that formed the border to Iran were visible. In this park, a large circular building called the circus held concerts and various other live shows during the year.

Because of the rapidly expanding oil industry, apart from ours, several other new hotels were under construction. There was also a new airport under construction by John Laing, a UK based construction company. Without a doubt, this was a city about to undergo a huge transformation.

Erdal, our administration manager, took me to look at an apartment, but I found it not good, so I refused to accept it.

The following week Erdal said I would move into a hotel. I thought this great, and better than an apartment. Early the next evening, Erdal drove us out of town to a street lined with a variety of different designed hotels. To my surprise, he said. "These all belong to various government ministries."

After parking outside one hotel, we went inside. It impressed me to find the entrance lobby large and well furnished, with a friendly and efficient receptionist. Once I had checked in and left my case, we returned to the site for dinner. On my later return, I made a closer examination of my room. Although large, the poor quality of the bathroom and bedroom doors appalled me. They appeared to be made from orange boxes.

The next morning, I found the breakfast consisted of two boiled eggs and some stale bread. Not exactly what one expects to receive in a hotel. However, I later heard this was the standard in many of the hotels in Turkmenistan.

One Sunday morning, Emrah drove a couple of lads and myself to an enormous outdoor bazaar. To my surprise he said, "You can buy many things here that are hard to find in the shops." These I found included basic food supplies, clothing, children's toys, and a wide variety of spare parts for cars. Where it all came from; I do not know.

While on our way to work in Emrah's car one morning, one minute we were happily talking, the next we were gripping our seats in terror. The nearside front axle had collapsed. With no control over the car, it swerved sideways towards the near side. To our horror, we were heading straight towards two men standing alongside a parked car. Emrah blasted the horn and waved frantically for the men to get out of the way. Seeing us sliding towards them, one man leapt to safety, while the other man remained, waving his arms for us to go away. Shortly before coming to a complete stop, our car clipped the man's leg and sent him flying.

As we exited the car, the man struggled to his feet. To our amazement, he shouted. "Why did you hit me? Are you mad?"

Emrah yelled back at him. "What! Why did you not get out of the way like your friend did? If anyone is mad, it's you. You could see we'd lost control of the car. It's your fault we hit you, not mine." Emrah shrugged. "You're lucky not to have suffered a serious injury, instead of only hurting your leg."

With the man still insisting it was our fault, Emrah used his radiophone to call our office. He informed them about the injured man and requested someone to come and take him to the hospital.

A short time later, Birol, one of our project managers, turned up. After Emrah said a few words of explanation, Birol took the man to the hospital. Then, soon afterwards, one of our breakdown trucks came, The truck lifted our car, then dropped us off at the site.

We later heard the man we hit had a fractured leg. Still, as Emrah had said, he was fortunate to have got away so lightly.

One morning Erdal took me to look at another apartment. It turned out to be a bungalow, in the grounds of a house owned by a man from Azerbaijan. Although he and his wife only spoke a little English, both were friendly. Ongoing inside the bungalow,

I found it had two bedrooms, a small kitchen, a bathroom, and a large lounge. I thought it ideal, so agreed to move in the next day.

The next morning, after another dismal breakfast at the hotel, one of our drivers drove me to my new home. Once I'd unpacked my things, I walked to the site. Given that it took less than ten minutes. the bungalow was in a perfect location.

In early December, the first twelve-bathrooms arrived on-site. I had never seen this type of unit before, so was interested in seeing what they looked like. To my astonishment, although the train had armed guards on the roof, we found that thieves had broken into several units. Fortunately, apart from some stolen showerheads, phones, and hairdryers, there was minor damage done.

On closer examination, to my amazement, I found the quality of the bathrooms far better than I had imagined.

The next day, one by one, our tower crane lifted the bathroom and placed them on the hotel roof. The following week, a supervisor from Finland arrived to oversee the bathrooms installed and tested. While we watched, the workers lowered one unit from the roof and brought it in through an opening left in the end wall of the hotel. Once inside and wheeled into position, they were connected to the plumbing and electrical supplies. To my disbelief, in only two days, ten-bathroom units were installed and completed.

During the first week of December, I received my first letter from Jen since arriving in Turkmenistan. It was good to read about what had been happening to my family and friends. To me, because of the difficulty of making or receiving telephone calls, receiving mail was crucial.

One Sunday, a couple of our workers invited me to join them for lunch on-site. It seemed that in appreciation of their work, Emrah had provided them with three sheep. With meat difficult to obtain, I accepted their offer. After one man slaughtered the sheep, they then barbecued it over an open fire. Not only did the meat prove tasty, but there was also plenty of it.

Because of Muslims not recognising Christmas, I worked over what would typically have been a holiday. Still, I could not complain. It was the first time since my beginning work as an expat.

On New Year's Eve, when I answered a knock on my door, I found my landlord standing there, who invited me to join him and his family for dinner. When I later went there, he greeted me, then led me inside where I met his wife, daughter- and son-in-law. Thanks to the son-in-law speaking English, I could have a conversation, via him, with his wife and in-laws. After a few glasses of wine, we went into the dining room. To my astonishment, there laid out on the table were dishes containing a variety of chocolates and fancy biscuits. With a general shortage of everything in the country, I thought it a big surprise. However, an even bigger one was in store.

When asked what I would like to drink, I requested vodka and lemonade. To my puzzlement, my host handed me two glasses. One of neat vodka, the other of lemonade. On my saying this was unusual, the son-in-law laughed. "Not here," he said. "This is how we drink spirits."

It felt strange to swallow a mouthful of neat vodka, followed by a quantity of lemonade. Still, as they said, 'When in Rome, do as the Romans do.'

The dinner proved excellent. As fine as you would get in a five-star hotel. For a start, they brought in a leg of lamb, a large roasted turkey, plus a roasted chicken. Next came dishes containing a variety of steaming vegetables, followed by jugs of gravy and other types of sauces. I thought it incredible to see so much food. My plate became piled so high; it only needed a flag on top to complete the picture.

After all had eaten and the dishes cleared away, the ladies brought in plates of fresh fruit, plus a variety of chocolate and cream topped cakes. Overall, I thought it a sumptuous meal, washed down by some excellent wine. Plus, I might add, several glasses of vodka/lemonade. It seemed no sooner had I emptied my glass; when someone refilled it.

I later left full and slightly drunk, but fortunately my bungalow was nearby. Once inside, I somehow undressed, before crashing out into bed. The following morning, I felt far from good, so thankful it was a holiday.

While out walking around with Emrah and several of our men, we discovered a supermarket we had not seen before. Inside, we were delighted to find a great variety of food items on sale. Until then, we could not find much in the way of food in the shops. After collecting a variety of items, we were laughing and smiling as we made our way to the cashier. Our smiles then turned to those of shock and disbelief, when the cashier made it clear we could not purchase anything. Despite our appeals and waving cash around, our words fell on deaf ears. We assumed it was because we were foreigners, and a severe shortage of all items in Turkmenistan.

However, despite this, I later bought a full-length anorak in one shop. This proved an excellent buy and kept me snug and warm during the freezing-cold winter months.

In mid-January, Anita called to say she had a baby boy that they had named. Levent, the same name as its father. Although I thought it strange, I knew Jen, who was with Anita at the birth, would be over the moon on becoming a grandmother.

While on the site one day, I heard a big commotion outside. Looking out a window, I saw a crowd of our workers gathered around a couple of cement trucks. The next minute, a car driven at high speed left the site and disappeared down the road in a cloud of dust. I realised something serious had happened, so I ran outside and asked one worker, "What's happened?" I then gasped in shock, when he said, "A truck knocked Emrah down; they have rushed him to the hospital."

Thirty minutes later, Esref walked into the office. One look and I could tell his news was not good.

On asking how Emrah was, in a choked whisper, he said. "He's gone."

Misunderstanding, I asked what he meant. In a breaking voice with tears in his eyes, he said. "Emrah's' dead!"

"How?" I gasped. "What on earth happened?" Emrah and I had been close friends. Only recently, he had asked me to join him on holiday.

In a choking voice, Esref said, "While Emrah guided a cement truck, he didn't see another one reversing behind him. The second truck backed into him, knocked him down, then ran over him. The doctor at the hospital said he died instantly."

"Christ, the truck driver, must be in a terrible state!" I said. At my suggestion, Esref gave instructions to close the site, with all our men taken back to their accommodation.

Ongoing out to where the men stood in silence, I found many crying. Emrah had been on the site since the project started, and popular with the men.

As Muslims should bury their deceased within 24 hours, after many phone calls, the company sent Emrah's body back to Turkey.

I still felt upset about Emrah's death the next day; so I asked Esref if I could go on holiday. He understood, and agreed.

When I arrived in Istanbul a few days later, I found it impossible to get a flight down to Antalya. Therefore, I stayed the night in a hotel, then flew down the next morning.

After a brief break at home, when I left Antalya for my return flight to Ashkhabad, it was bright and sunny. Therefore, on arrival in Istanbul, it surprised me to find it had been snowing. When our plane landed at Ashkhabad, I found everywhere blanketed in thick snow. To make things worse, we passengers then spent thirty minutes out in the cold, before able to enter the terminal.

On going outside, I found one of our drivers waiting to drive me to my bungalow. As I walked inside, I found the central heating on, with it nice and warm. On mentioning this to my landlord, he informed me all the houses in town had central heating. This he said, "Comes via a central system." He chuckled. "Although old, it still works efficiently."

The next morning, I tramped through the snow to the site. However, I need not have bothered, as because of the extremely low temperature, it was closed. That night, more snow fell, with the temperature dropping to minus five degrees. What with a bitterly icy wind blowing, the chill factor temperature must have been even lower. The site did not reopen until three days later, but even then, it was still snowing. With the temperature below freezing, working conditions for the men were challenging to say the least..

In an attempt to help keep warm while working as best they could, in some places the men had lit fires in oil drums. Under the circumstances, I thought it a good idea. However, when I mentioned this to Esref, he informed me that Enis had given instructions prohibiting this. I thought his decision incorrect. With only a few walls, giving minimum protection from the chilling wind, working conditions were appalling.

A few days later, although a slight thaw, with it still extremely cold on-site, wherever works were possible, they proceeded much slower than usual.

A few weeks before going on leave, I found two young dogs on-site. Both were thin, hungry, and searching for any scraps of food they could find. As I loved dogs and had an electric heater in my office, although not big enough for both dogs, I looked after one of them.

However, on my return from leave, I found both dogs were dead. Unfortunately, as Muslims dislike dogs, it did not surprise me to learn someone had poisoned them.

A short time later, I found an uproar going on over Emrah's death. An opened container revealed all kinds of safety equipment, including helmets and safety harnesses. This came as a big surprise, as far as anyone knew, there was no safety equipment on-site. Some men became angry about the discovery. They thought that had Emrah been wearing a hard hat; he might not have died. Things only calmed down, after Esref held a meeting. He informed the men that as a truck had run over Emrah, even if wearing a hard hat, he would have still died. Then, because of finding the safety equipment, Esref instructed me to ensure that they all safety measures were strictly adhered to.

The day before Emrah died, Enis had gone to Moscow to visit his brother who was working there. To my surprise, a week after Esref returned from leave, he informed me Enis had resigned and would not be returning. As Ugur, our site manager, was a close friend of Enis, Esref asked if I thought Ugur might leave to join him.

I nodded. "Given their friendship, yes."

Esref agreed. "When I return to Turkey next week, I will take Ugur with me."

I cocked an eyebrow. "Does he know about this?" I asked.

He shrugged. "No! I will inform him the day we leave."

Before he left with Ugur, to my delight, Esref put me in charge of the project. A few weeks after he returned to Istanbul, Orhan, one owner of Ucgen, visited the site. To my surprise, he asked, "Colin, could you run the site on your own."

"I can look after all the works related to the hotel building, which I have been doing since Ugur left," I said. "However, I cannot control the external works as well. This would be too much to handle." Then I said, "Seyfi, who has been managing the external works since Ugur left has done a good job."

He nodded. "In that case, I will inform Seyfi that you are in sole control of all works to the hotel, while he is to continue managing the external/landscaping works."

I appreciated his decision. It was a sign of trust by Ucgen of my abilities.

As I walked around the site one day, I noticed a couple of our men standing in a large steel bucket. Nothing unusual, except our tower crane was lifting it onto the roof of the hotel. As I shouted to ask what they were doing, the crane jerked to a stop. It left the two men suspended in mid-air, swinging in the bucket. That the crane had failed came as no surprise. It was an old Russian one, with the Russian operator about as old as the crane that he had operated for many years.

Seeing me looking up at them, one man called out. "How are we going to get down?"

I laughed, and called back, "You'll have to wait until we fix the crane. Still, it might take some time."

"Well, I hope it won't take too long; it's cold up here," one said.

I chuckled at their misfortune, "Serves you right for getting in the bucket. You know you shouldn't have done so."

When some workers came to investigate and found the bucket swinging in the breeze with the two men clinging to the edge, a chorus of laughing and yells broke out. It took some time to repair the crane and lower the bucket to the ground. By then, the men were freezing cold and feeling sorry for themselves. Wearing a satisfied smile, I said. "Next time you need to get on the roof, do the same as everyone else, take the stairs."

On another occasion, I found the same two men working on the formwork for an exterior staircase. Although pleased to find them wearing safety harnesses, I then became angry. The ends of their harnesses were hanging by their sides.

"What are you two playing at?" I yelled at them. "Get those harnesses clipped to something secure before you fall. If you don't, you'll be badly injured, if not killed. As I'm responsible for safety on-site, I don't want any accidents."

"Sorry," one man called out.

I then watched until they had clipped their harnesses to the scaffolding.

While on my way to work one day, as I passed an open gate, a small dog appeared. I smiled down at it and kept walking. My smile then turned to shock when it jumped up and bit my leg. When I yelled out in pain, it bit me again, then ran back inside the gate. Thankfully, with it a tiny dog, its teeth had not drawn blood, so I ignored it and carried on to work.

When later talking with our camp doctor, I mentioned this incident. To my surprise, he said, "Colin! This is serious; you must have an anti-rabies injection."

I had heard this involved having injections into the stomach, so said, "No thanks! I'll be OK." When he insisted, I had an injection; I told him the incident happened approximately two weeks earlier. I became speechless when he said, "Oh, in that case, you're okay. If the dog had rabies, you would be dead by now."

This came as a shock; I never knew rabies was a problem in Turkmenistan. In my ignorance, I had assumed that like in Turkey, the authorities inoculated all dogs in towns and cities against this. Therefore, I was fortunate the dog did not have rabies.

On the site stood a gnarled old tree. It looked so unique, Kasim, our architect, instructed we should save it. He wanted to include it in with the new landscaping works. However, a few days later, I found the tree had gone. When I asked one man what had happened to it, he said, "It was rotten inside and dying, so we removed it."

This would only have been revealed after the tree was uprooted, but it was too late to take any action about it. However, I did not doubt what he said was true. While on the way to work one day, a large branch of a tree broke and fell, just missed hitting me. For some unknown reason, quite a few trees near where I lived were dying.

On a visit to the local zoo, the terrible condition of the cages appalled me. They appeared not to have received any maintenance for years. As I stood in a crowd of people looking in a bears cage, we gasped with alarm. An enormous head had appeared in front of us. It happened so fast; it took a second before I realised it was a camel seeking scraps of food. The camel must have hoped some pieces had dropped from those thrown to the animals in front of us. With it only a camel, our cries of alarm, changed to laughter.

In one cage, a huge brown bear sat on the floor, shaking its head from side to side. I thought it pitiful to see its limited actions. From walking around and viewing the various animals, they all appeared starving. Several bears and monkeys had their paws outstretched through the bars of their cages, making a desperate bid to collect bits of food that had fallen short of their cages.

One weekend, Birol asked if I would accompany him to look at some Collie pups. At the owners' house, as we found both puppies and mother in excellent condition, Birol bought one the following week. Over the next few months, several of our men also bought dogs. These being inexpensive compared to those in Turkey. Unfortunately, none of those shipped to Turkey via the services of a local vet survived for long. Only the dog my friend Ugur took back to Turkey when he left Turkmenistan, lived for any length of time.

One evening, Orhan invited me, along with Birol, and another two of our project managers for dinner at a restaurant. On our arrival, apart from us and one table where four girls sat, we found it empty. We had finished eating and sat talking when the four girls leapt to their feet and the next minute were out dancing on the dance floor.

To my surprise, Birol stood up. "I am going to ask one of them for a dance," he said. The next minute he was dancing with one girl. When the music stopped, he came back to our table and sat back down.

"Well, that made a pleasant change," he said.

We all laughed. Then, when the music restarted, one of the other men got up and danced with another of the girls. The remaining project manager then danced with another girl. Given this, I decided to ask the girl no one had danced with for a dance. I approached the girls' table and asked if she would like to dance. She smiled, said yes, then stood up.

As we danced, I asked, "What's your name?" With a laugh, she said "It's "Natasha. My friends and I are all called Natasha."

When I asked what job she did, she looked surprised. Wearing a big smile, she asked, "What do you think?"

As I thought about a suitable reply, the music finished. I thanked her for the dance and returned to our table. By then, Orhan had left for home. I turned to the others. "That's strange. The girl I danced with told me they are all called Natasha."

Birol hooted. "Yes, and they're all prostitutes as well."

This shocked me. Although I had never been in the company of a prostitute before, I had to laugh at dancing with one.

On the project, all went well. Though pleased with myself, little did I know all this was about to change. Although not good for me, it would be worse for Ucgen. It all started when, while walking around the site, Esref approached with two men. "Colin, I want to introduce you to Ahmet," he pointed to one man. "He will be taking over as project manager on the site." Although I was not a project manager, I felt disappointed to hear this. I had not thought about anyone coming to take over the running of the project. Holding back my feelings, I shook Ahmet's hand and gave him a warm greeting.

In excellent English, he said, "Thank you Colin."

Esref then said, "and this is Ertan. He will be general manager of all our sites in Turkmenistan."

As Ertan shook hands with me, he said, in English, "It's nice to meet you, Colin. Esref, has told me how you have worked with Ucgen in the past. We will have a chat later."

"Thank you," I said. "Welcome to Turkmenistan."

After a brief chat, Ertan and Esref left the site. Ahmet, who Esref had already shown to his office, returned there to get himself set-up.

I later found Ahmet had brought his wife with him. However, this proved no deterrence to his later actions. A short time after his arrival, I found him trying to get himself fixed up with a girlfriend. Given the circumstances, I thought this rather strange. Apart from this, I soon found Ahmet expected everything done his way, right or wrong. As a result, I tried to avoid any conflict with him.

At one time, it surprised me to find a queue of women lined up the stairs leading to Ahmet's office. When I asked one man what was going on, he chuckled. 'Ahmet is interviewing them for a tea lady's position,' he said. I wondered what that was all about, then, realising what Ahmet was up to. I laughed. "It's not a tea lady he is looking for;" I said, "We already have one. It's just an excuse to find a bit on the side."

Before going home on leave, I had been sharing my bungalow with one of our engineers, but on my return, I found he had left. A few weeks later, Esref introduced me to a new project manager named Murat. "He will be in charge of the construction of a small airport terminal contract we have obtained." He then asked.

"Colin, would you mind if Murat moved in with you in your bungalow?"

I shrugged. "No problem. I'll be pleased to have some company." I found Murat, who was about my age and spoke excellent English, a quiet guy.

After dinner one evening, he said his men were working until 10 pm. I thought this strange, as he had earlier said he would not be returning to the site. Therefore, when Esref asked me to help Murat on his project, it did not come as a surprise. As it would make a change of scenery, I had no problem in saying yes.

On the site, I found several men who had worked on the hotel project. One, a foreperson I knew well, so as Esref had asked me to get things moving, I asked if he had enough men.

He shrugged, then replied. "No!"

On asking how many more men he needed? He looked glum, and said. "Twelve,"

He didn't think I could get this amount, then his face broke into a broad smile when I said. "Okay, you will have them."

After contacting Esref and telling him what I needed, a few hours later, the men arrived. Although it proved to a big help, a few days later I realised we needed even more men. I again called Esref. This time I said I needed another two dozen men. Esref knew that I must be pushed for time if I requested this amount of men. To my relief, Esref, said, "Colin, they will be with you tomorrow.

# Chapter 4

Sure enough, he was as good as his word. While at the terminal building, I stayed with the men until they left late at night, with Murat also staying. Besides supervising, I toiled doing various minor jobs.

Although a nice man, Murat seemed out of his depth in managing the project. Numerous activities were happening simultaneously;

The day before the official opening, we were working late when the quiet of the night became shattered by the sound of a jet engine starting up. On going outside to investigate, I found a lorry slowly driving around. This in itself was nothing unusual, but the jet engine fixed to one side of the truck was. The blast from the engine was directed downwards to dry up the water used to wash the new tarmac. I thought this unbelievable; then I noticed another amazing sight. Following behind the lorry was an old motorbike and sidecar. Where the tarmac was dry, a man in the sidecar was leaning out and painting markings on the road. It found this so astonishing; I had to blink twice to make sure I had seen these incredible sights.

A few days later, the President of Turkmenistan opened the terminal, with the President of Turkey in attendance.

The next day, I felt pleased when came and Haluk thanked me for helping on the project. In reply, I told him I had enjoyed the challenge and was glad to be of help. "However," I indicated that some items were not of the quality I would accept on one of my projects."

Haluk smiled. "Colin, we both know what you say is correct, but people will not take too much notice of the quality. What they will say is that we performed a miracle. We completed the project in just forty days that everyone said was impossible."

In this, I could only agree. After a few days more at the now open terminal building, I returned to work at the hotel.

While talking with Esref, I said we could do with Ugur to help out on the hotel. He looked at me and smiled. "Colin, as Ugur would not come and work for us in Istanbul; he certainly won't come to Turkmenistan," he said.

I grinned. "Well, if Ugur knows I'm here and need him, he will come."

He shrugged. "Well, if you think so, I will call him, I have his telephone number," Esref called Ugur, who was at home. After a brief talk, he handed me the phone. "Here, Colin, you talk to him."

"Hi, Mr Ugur, how are you?"

He answered with a cheery, "Hi, Baba, my best friend. It good to hear from you."

After a few pleasantries, I said, "Ugur, I want you here. I need someone I can trust to help me with this project."

To my surprise, he said, "Mr Colin, money not good." I cut him off. "Never mind the money," I said, "we can talk about that later. First, get yourself up here."

After a brief pause, he said, "Okay, Mr Colin, if you want me, I will come."

"Thank you, Ugur. I appreciate it, and look forward to seeing you soon." As I put down the phone, Esref could not contain himself. "Colin! I can't believe what you have just done." He shrugged. "I know he would not have come had I asked."

I gave a knowing smile. "Ugur and I have a special relationship. Although we cannot talk much, we understand and respect each other."

"Well, whatever it is, I'm happy Ugur has agreed to come. As you so rightly said, he will be a big help."

Shortly after the terminal opening, Esref asked me to accompany him to visit a house. On the way, he told me the house was part of what is called 'Special Projects.' He then explained what this was. "It involves updating some houses." It took me aback when he said. "The quality of work on this one is so bad; I'm afraid to visit the house. We have an architect/project manager on-site, but from what I've seen, he doesn't seem to know what he is doing."

I thought this strange, and it left me wondering what was going on. If the works were so bad, it was obvious what he should do, get rid of the project manager.

As we pulled up outside the house, I found it to be a large bungalow. As Esref went to get out of the car, wearing a grim expression, he said. "You go inside and see what you think. I'll stay outside and talk to the project manager."

As I walked inside, I found Esref was correct in his assumptions. It was obvious that the architect had no knowledge about quality or how to manage a site. It appalled me to see piles of rubbish and building materials lying everywhere. That, plus one look at the quality of wall marble was enough: it was terrible. After finishing my inspection, I went outside to find Esref waiting.

"Sorry, but you're right," I said. I then told him what I thought of the quality of works and the general state of the site.

Hearing my observations confirmed what he thought; Esref sacked the project manager on the spot. He then turned to me. In a half-pleading voice, he said, "Colin, I want you to take over the running of special projects. Whatever you feel is not up to scratch here, have it removed and replaced. I will provide whatever you require getting this house finished to a suitable standard."

This change of events took aback me. However, I felt elevated in being given the responsibility, which, in a way, would be a promotion for me. To my further surprise, Esref said, "By the way, Ugur arrives tonight, he will be working with you."

This was great news. Ugur was a top-notch worker and an efficient organizer. With his help, I knew we could get this project completed to the quality required.

After I met Ugur at our main office the next morning, I drove him to the house. As we walked around, I said, "Ugur, any of the installed marble you think is unacceptable, have it removed." I gave a grim smile, "Unfortunately, you will have to remove most of it."

After our tour, Ugur looked puzzled. "Mr Colin, has anyone been supervising this project?"

I smiled. "Yes! An architect. Esref sacked after I came with him and made a report on what I had seen."

I was still on-site late morning when Ahmet the hotel project manager visited. Apart from a curt morning, he said nothing. During the short time he stayed, he made what Ugur later told me were sarcastic remarks about the workers. Before returning to the hotel site, I told Ugur to ignore whatever Ahmed Said.

As expected, when I visited the next day, I found most of the wall marble removed. While discussing with Ugur what works I wanted him to concentrate on, Ahmet arrived. He walked around the site, said something to the men and then left. On asked Ugur what he had told the men, he said, "For them to get a move on."

I felt annoyed at his remarks. "Listen, Esref put me in charge of all special project works, so don't take any notice of what Ahmet, said."

When I called in at our head office the following morning, it shocked me when informed Ugur had resigned. I thought this unbelievable, so drove straight to the house where I found Ugur looking visibly upset.

"What's going on?" I asked in disbelief. "What's all this about you resigning?"

He shrugged. "Before leaving the site last night, I gave instructions to the plasterers to do some screeding. When I came in this morning, I found they had not done as I instructed. I was angry and asked why they had not done as I said. They told me that during dinner at the camp, Ahmet had asked what they were doing. When they told him, he said not to take any notice of what I say. He was a project manager, and the house came under his area of control.

Ugur looked downcast. "I am sorry, Mr Colin, but I cannot work like this. I will go back to Turkey."

I was furious. "You are not resigning! I will sort this." After speeding back to our head office, I found Esref in his office. As I walked in, I said, "Have you heard? Ugur has resigned."

Esref gave me a puzzled look. "Yes! What's going on?"

"Ahmet is what's going on. Since you put me in charge of work at the house, he has been on-site each day, causing problems. Last night, Ugur gave instructions for the plasterers to do some works ready for the marble to be laid today. Thanks to Ahmet telling the men not to, no floor marble can be laid." I was so angry, I said, "If Ugur leaves, I will leave the project and return to work at the hotel. If you want me to continue working on special projects, inform Ahmet he is not to go to the house, or any other special project."

Esref thought for a minute. "Colin, I want you to continue working on special projects. I will inform Ahmet he is not to visit any of your special projects."

I gave a broad smile. "Thank you. I will now go and inform Ugur, which I feel sure will result in his staying in Turkmenistan."

On my return to the minister's house, I found Ugur looking sad and miserable. I smiled and said, "Right, problem solved. Ahmet will no longer visit the site."

Ugur's face lit up with a big smile. "Thank you, Mr Colin. I didn't want to leave, but would have had Ahmet kept coming here."

From then on, works proceeded without any further disruptions. After finishing work on the house, Ugur and I worked on two more houses. In total, I looked after Special Projects until the end of May, when a new project manager came to take over. I then returned to work on the hotel project. Because of my previous problems with Ahmet, I felt dubious about doing so. However, when I mentioned this to Esref, he told me not to worry, and that all would be OK.

In late April, Ucgen dropped a bombshell. Without any warning, they announced that from now on, salaries would be paid in Turkish Lira. This came as an enormous shock. Until then, they paid us in US dollars. The company said that anyone who did not accept this situation would be sent back to Turkey. As a result, this news caused a virtual shutdown of all works. Everyone was discussing whether to accept or return to Turkey.

That evening, a supervisor in charge of a group of sub-contractors came to see me. He shrugged. "I'm sorry, Colin, but my men will not accept being paid in TL, we will return to Turkey."

On talking with Haluk, he said the change was because of a massive devaluation of the Turkish lira that resulted in Ucgen losing a considerable sum of money. Haluk said that as soon as the situation changed, the company would again pay us in US dollars. However, he warned this could take months. In total, it took three months before they again paid us in US dollars.

One morning I heard of a strange incident involving one of our managers. The day before going home on leave to Turkey, he had reported his car stolen. Like all our managers' cars, it had been imported it from Turkey. Therefore, it stood out from the other vehicles in the country that were mainly Russian-made Lada. After reporting it, the police began their investigations. They soon found the car had not been stolen. Unbelievable as it seems, the man had been trying to sell it that led to his immediate sacking. Just how he thought he could get away with selling his company car was a complete mystery.

During one of my leave breaks, I flew down to Istanbul on my way to the UK. Here I would meet up with Jen who had gone to visit Anita, her husband, and their new baby. Because of no connecting flight to England, I spent the night in a hotel. On my arrival at Heathrow the next day, I was delighted to find Jen and my grandson waiting. I felt happy and proud to see them. Levent junior (Leejay) was my first grandchild.

After spending a few days in London with Anita, Jen and I went to Plymouth and stayed with my mother for a week. Although a pleasant break, all too soon it was time for me to return to Ashkhabad.

Back on the site, I found all going well. Well, it was until Nihat, the manager in charge of the marble works came to see me wearing a worried expression. "Colin," he said, "we have a problem. Someone miscalculated how much marble we needed. As a result, we don't have enough to finish the flooring outside the hotel entrance."

With it impossible to obtain more within our scheduled completion date of the hotel, this was bad news. However, when Nihat told me, he had a surplus of travertine; I instructed him to use the marble as a border, with Travertine in between. Once finished, the result looked good, and solved what could have been a significant problem.

During a walk around the site with Haluk, he pointed up at some installed ventilation grilles. "They do not look in the correct position," he said. When I told him they were as per Kasim's architectural design, he smiled. "Colin, Kasim is just an architect, you know far more than he does about what looks right. In future, anything you see that you don't like, change it."

My eyes lit up. I had been unhappy with the position of various installed items in the entrance lobby ceiling. Although as per design, the fittings did not line up, which to me was unacceptable. Thanks to Haluk, it enabled me to give instructions to move everything into line. That is apart from the sprinklers. This would have been a major job to relocate them, so I decided to leave them where they were.

# Part 5

When Haluk next came to the site, I informed him of what I had done. He nodded, but as we walked into the main lobby, I stopped in shock. There were sizeable holes in the ceiling, with all the sprinkler positions being realigned.

Haluk frowned. "Colin, what's going on? You told me you had not asked for the sprinklers to be moved." Before I could speak, the mechanical manager who accompanied spoke. "Colin did not ask me to move them. When I saw what he had done, I decided it would look better if everything in the ceiling lined up."

I must admit that once finished, the revised ceiling layout looked much better than the planned one.

While working in my office one day, I head a commotion outside. Ongoing to investigate, I found a crowd of men gathered around the bottom of the stairs leading up to Ahmet's office. As I stood looking up, Noyan appeared, then Ahmet behind him shortly afterwards.

With his face red and glaring eyes, I could see Noyan was visibly upset. He turned to Ahmet, and in a loud voice said. "I will not allow it!"

Ahmet's eyes blazed as he shouted back. "You will do what I say!"

When they came down the stairs, I asked. "What's going on, Noyan?" It shocked me when he said. "Ahmet wants to put a woman in my house. He said I must not touch her, as she is for him. I've told him I would not allow it."

They were at ground level when Ahmet, whose eyes were bulging in anger, lunged at Noyan and yells at the top of his voice, "You will do as I say!"

As Ahmet went to pass in front of me, I grabbed hold, wrapped my arms around his torso and said, "Calm down, Ahmet."

However, he was in such a blind temper that even with my holding him, he still managed to advance towards Noyan.

I called out, "Noyan! Go home. I will sort this out."

Once he had left, I let go of Ahmet. With his face red with fury, he stalked off, calling his driver as he went.

As they drove away from the site, I thought that was the end of the matter. However, a few minutes later, I heard Noyan calling out in alarm. Then he re-appeared, running back toward me and yelling. "Help! He is after me!"

Apparently, Ahmet had told his driver to stop Noyan from reaching his house. Luckily, Noyan saw them, so turned and ran back to the site.

I could not believe what Ahmet had done. "That's it! That's the last straw," I snapped. "Noyan, you go on home, Ahmet will have gone by now. Tonight, you and I will make out a report of what happened today. In the morning, we will go to the head office and I will have this problem sorted out."

The next morning, I drove Noyan to our head office, where as we pulled into the carpark, I noticed Ahmet's car there. I didn't want any trouble, so said, "Noyan! You stay in the car while I go in and see Ertan."

"No!" He snapped at me. "I am not afraid of Ahmet; I will come with you." As we walked towards the main entrance door, it burst open, and Ahmet appeared. At the top of his voice, he yelled at Noyan. "I'll get you!"

Just then, Birol, Ertan, and a couple of other men came out behind Ahmet. "What's going on?" Ertan asked. As Ahmet stood yelling at Noyan, Birol, and another man grabbed hold of him.

"Ahmet's gone mad!" I said. "He attacked Noyan last night, and would have again now had you not stopped him."

After Ahmet had calmed down and taken to a side office, Noyan and I went into Ertan's office. I then handed him our written reports referencing Ahmet attacking Noyan.

Ertan read them, then looked up and said, "This is very serious. I must pass these reports on to Haluk."

"Ahmet should return to Turkey I exclaimed.He's only interested in women!"

Ertan looked puzzled, "What do you mean?"

I said, "At one time, Ahmet had a long queue of women lined up outside his office. On enquiring why they were there; I was told he was interviewing for a tea lady," I shrugged. "This was just an excuse for him to find a woman. We already have an efficient tea lady who is in her sixties, and is Noyan's landlady."

The following week when Haluk came on-site, I asked what would happen about Ahmet. He then explained, "Under Turkmenistan law, Ahmet is the official site, project manager. To remove him would cause a significant delay to the project. A new project manager would first have to be accepted by the authorities before allowed to take over the project." He shrugged. "Given this, Ahmet will have to remain as the official project manager." I was far from pleased at hearing this, but before I could said anything, he continued. "However, he will not have any say in future works on the site. I have brought in two project managers who will take over control of the project."

Although not what I expected, in the circumstances, it was the best the company could do.

During August, I didn't feel too good, and even worse in September. I must have looked ill, for Ahmed Said. "Colin, you need to go to a hospital."

I decided he was right, so after talking to Ertan, he had a driver take me to the American Hospital. Here, Noyan, who had accompanied me, explained to the receptionist that I needed to see a doctor. A few minutes later, a nurse took me to see one. She examined me, then put me on a drip. A couple of hours later, she returned and said I could go, but to return late afternoon to go on a drip again. I did so, and had the same treatment for the next two days. On the third day, the doctor gave me an ECG. It shocked me when she told me there was a problem with one of my lungs.

On seeing my concern, she said, "Don't worry, we will take an X-ray, to see if anything is wrong."

When I informed Ertan of this, he contacted the hospital to ask if they had a film to take my X-ray. Like the shops, the hospital also suffered shortages. The hospital said they had, but would appreciate it if Ucgen could replace it.

The next day, on my return to the hospital, they gave me an injection before being taken to have the X-ray. As we walked into where the machine was, I stopped in shock. It was enormous and took up a significant portion of the room.

After the x-ray, I returned to my room, where I waited anxiously for the . results. When the doctor arrived, much to my relief, she said my results showed no problems. However, she said to return the next day to have another injection. Only after doing so, and told there was no need for me to return did I relax.

At work the next day, Ertan called in to see how I was. He informed me the company had brought in some new X-ray film for the hospital. Ertan also told me that Ucgen had provided both the medicine and injections used while I was in the hospital. Given this, I asked him to pass on my thanks to Haluk, and Orhan.

On a later trip to England, I showed the X-ray to my doctor, who on checking, said the X-ray were too blurred to be of any use. After having another X-ray taken, I was relieved when told I had no problems.

One Sunday back in Turkmenistan, along with Ugur and a few of the men, we went to the bazaar. As they were not expensive,

I bought myself a real fur Russian style hat. Although it felt and looked strange, I knew it would keep my head warm during the winter.

In the meantime, works went well at the hotel. However, because of the late delivery of the carpet, installation only began a week before the opening date of the hotel. Still, because of the carpet layers working long hours, they completed laying it the night before the official opening.

This was a big ceremony, with both the President of Turkmenistan and the President of Turkey attending.

Despite the hotel now officially open, there was still some works to be completed. Unbelievably, it included the main kitchen units that had not arrived in time for the opening. Given this, the hotel chefs had used the kitchen equipment installed in one of the smaller restaurants for the opening. Therefore, I thought it a miracle they had provided such a high-class meal for the post-ceremony party.

A few days later, both Ucgen management and the hotel manager requested that I stay on until all the works were completed. However, because of my illness a few months earlier, I declined their kind offer and flew back to Turkey the following week.

Despite problems with Ahmet and my illness, I had enjoyed working in Turkmenistan. I had also assisted Ucgen in their time of need, which they appreciated. One way they did, I only discovered during a conversation with Esref months earlier.

On mentioning I never had a contract; Esref gave me a sly smile. "I don't have a contract for you, but I have another piece of paper you can have." He rummaged through his desk, pulled it out and handed me a slip of paper.

As it was written in Turkish, I smiled. "Sorry, Esref, but as I neither read nor write Turkish, I do not know what I'm looking at."

He grinned, looked up and explained. "Do you remember when you first worked with us at Kiris? You had goods brought over from England?"

I nodded. "Yes, of course. After all the trouble we had in getting them out of customs, it's not something I am liable to forget."

Esref's smile widened. "Well, Ucgen stood as your guarantor."

I shook my head. "But what's this letter to do with that?"

He gave me another of his sly smiles and then explained. "The country only allowed your goods for five years." After that, you should have paid a sum of money that would have enabled you to keep them permanently here in Turkey. However, as no one told you, you never paid the money, but Ucgen did. In the circumstances, I'm sure you will agree this letter is worth more to you than a contract. Without the company paying the money, you would have ended up in big trouble."

As I knew nothing about having to pay any money regarding our transported goods into Turkey, this came as a big surprise.

I reached over and shook his hand. "Well, what can I say, except a big thanks for Ucgen paying the money? As for a contract, Haluk's word was enough for me. That's why I never asked for a contract."

Once settled back home in Turkey, I fell back into my usual standard of fitness. All I had to do then was find another contract. Little did I know it would take much longer to obtain than expected, and result in my travelling the furthest distance from home I had ever been.

An unexpected attack in Indonesia

# Chapter Fourteen

Finally, I found a contract in Indonesia as a Project Supervisor at the Majapahit Hotel in Surabaya. On checking, I discovered that the flag of independence hotel was established there during a war with the Dutch.

On landing at Surabaya airport, a man introduced himself as Peter. "Hi, I'm the Admin Manager on the Majapahit project," he said. As we walked outside, he gave a knowing smile. "It's the men's hash tonight, so we're going to the Lido Bar. All our guys will be there."

On our arrival, a group of men dancing around and singing their heads off caught my eye. Peter chuckled as he pointed, "That's Rodger, our Project Manager." On his seeing me standing with Peter, he stopped dancing and came over.

He grinned. "Hi, you must be Colin? Good to see you." He laughed. "I'll talk to you tomorrow when I am sober," he said. With that, he went back to join in the dancing and singing. I had to laugh. I'd never seen a project manager in such a state. Several hours later, Peter dropped me off at a hotel. "You'll stay here until a room is available at a company house," he said.

The next morning Peter drove me to the site where he introduced me to Rodger, who gave a broad smile. "Hi, Colin. Sorry about the way we met last night, but it's the norm after a men's hash run."

I laughed. "Yes, I know. I used to run on the hash when I worked in Brunei."

His eyes lit. "In that case, you'll enjoy your stay here. Right, let me introduce you to Ian, our Construction Manager." After shaking hands with him, Rodger showed me around the site. To my surprise, he informed me there were approx. 1,300 Indonesian workers on-site. I had never worked with so many workers on one project.

"The project," Rodger said, "Is a joint venture between a Japanese and an Indonesian company. The Project Manager and one supervisor are Japanese, with the rest of the staff Indonesian." He then continued. "The work involves both reconstruction and refurbishment of the hotel and grounds."

My first job was to prepare a finished works program. I was doing this when Steve, an Australian supervisor dropped by to see how I was doing. As he looked over my shoulder, it shocked me when he exclaimed. "That's a load of crap. There is no way they will meet the times you have stated in your program." He then carried on to said, "I've been working in Indonesia for some time, so know how long it takes to get things done." I couldn't believe it when he said, "Hotels in Indonesia never meet their scheduled completion dates." They usually run one year over."

"What!" I gasped. "That's unbelievable."

Steve laughed. "The delays are mainly because of the low level of work carried out in a working day," he said,

Thanks to his advice, I revised my schedule to show a more realistic works schedule. Later that day, Martin, our Mechanical Engineer, arrived from the UK. While talking, he told me he had never worked overseas; I replied that I hoped he would soon get used to it. The following week, Neil, our Quantity Surveyor, arrived. Then Ian, our Planner, accompanied by his wife, Cathy. With his arrival, it completed our project management team.

Peter said, "The Lido Bar is our local." He chuckled. "They have no objections about putting up with a bunch of noisy drunken hashers. For them, it good business."

At lunchtime, I joined the others to go to the local Wimpy bar that I found quite an experience. To get there, involved crossing four to five lanes of traffic. Not a problem, except there were no traffic lights or crossings. Given this, although I expected to be knocked down, we managed to weave our way safely across.

I found it strange that although motorcyclists had to wear a crash hat, they did not have to comply with standard safety regulations. Some were made from compressed cardboard. I found this to be true when a motorcyclist lost his helmet that was not tied on and a car behind drove over it, leaving it crushed flat.

At the end of my first week's work, I received a portion of my monthly food allowance that left me well pleased. Not only did it pay for any food/meals, but it also paid for my drinks.

That weekend, I went on a hash run with Rodger, Peter, Steve, Martin, and Neil. With it the first run, I had been on since leaving Brunei; I felt knackered come the end. Still, the hashers were a good crowd, and I enjoyed the run. As a result, before leaving, I joined the Surabaya Hash House Harriers. Details of this and the numerous runs I attended, I will insert a later book.

While walking around the site one day, I noticed several labourers loading a lorry with rubbish. No big deal, except they were collecting bits and pieces by hand. To my disbelief, they put it into straw coolie hats that they carried outside and emptied into the back of the lorry. I shook my head in disbelief. No wonder works were so slow in Indonesia. I had never seen such a terrible state of affairs. Upon enquiring, I learned there were no shovels or wheel-barrows for the men to use. So much for modern times.

Steve, who could have acted as a stand-in for Patrick Swayze, was a real character. If on checking works he found them unacceptable, he would tear them down. Because of his physic from regular working out in the gym, this proved no problem.

During a talk with Steve, he informed me he was not on Expat's salary, but paid as a local worker. Given the difference in salary, I advised that when he finished his present contract, he should apply for another contract as an expat.

Steve showed me sketches he had drawn about some funny incidents that happened on-site. I told him if he could draw this well, he was wasting his time working on a building site. I suggested he try and get a job as a cartoonist. Therefore, it didn't surprise me when he later designed one of our hash T-shirts. As mine is now over twenty years old, it just goes to show the quality of both the fabric and printed design.

> In late May, I left the hotel and moved into a house that I shared with Ian and Cathy, Steve, his wife, and their little boy. Martin and Neil lived in another house, along with Greg, an Australian designer who also worked on our project.

After work one Friday evening, Ian drove several of us over to Madura where we stayed the night. The next morning, while driving along, I spotted a Bonsai stand on the side of the road. As I liked bonsai trees, I asked Ian to stop. While looking at the collection on sale, I noticed a man using a small axe to shape the base of a bonsai tree. This being something I had never seen done before. During a break from his work, I bought one of the man's trees.

Although our trip was a breakout, Madura, d not impress me, which I later heard is famous for 'Bull-Running.'

During one public holiday, Ian called around to the house to borrow some money. On seeing our puzzlement, he said someone had stolen his wallet the previous night. Although a nice place, we found Surabaya not a safe place to walk around. Also, with only a few areas having pavements, you had to be careful whenever you went out walking.

One evening, Steve, Martin and I went to the pictures. When the film finished, and we came out, we were shocked to find the road badly flooded. The water was so deep; we had to take off our shoes and socks and roll up our trousers to cross the road. Upon entering the Lido bar, our barefoot appearance took aback the staff. They did not know the flooding.

At work, because of the company having problems related to receiving payment from the prime contractor, things were not going well. Ian told us that Richard is organizing a task force to ensure everything is completed for the official opening of the International Meeting of Asian leaders. Because of the importance of the meeting, many people were expected to attend. Given this, the authorities informed several hotels under construction they had to be open in time.

The following month, Martin and I had to fly to Singapore to renew our visitor visas. (At the time, I didn't know we were breaking the law.) Once checked in at a hotel, we went to the embassy to put in our visa applications. To our surprise, an official informed us we were too late. The Embassy was about to close for the day. Fortunately, after a bit of talking, the man relented and accepted them.

The next afternoon we collected our new visas and then returned to our hotel. We checked out, then took a taxi to the airport for our flight back to Surabaya. On presenting our tickets at the check-in desk, we were shocked when informed we had missed our flight. We had mistakenly thought it took off at 6 pm, whereas it left at 16.00.

> Despite desperate attempts to get tickets with another airline, there were none available until the next day. This was not good, as our hotel was expensive, with neither of us having enough money to pay for another night stay. Given this, we decided to sleep in the airport. After spending an hour there, I suggested we go to Boat Quay, where we could have a drink and pass away a few hours.

On the way, we called in at the Raffles Hotel for a quick drink. By the time we returned to the airport, it was 1.30 am. Unfortunately, because of being unable to check-in, we couldn't access the departure area. There the chairs were comfortable. Given this, with the chairs in the main area uncomfortable, neither of us managed to get much sleep that night. Neither did we the next day while awaiting a flight back to Surabaya in the afternoon. As a result, we were more than happy when we arrived back there.

One evening, a crowd of hash members and friends went on an organised pub crawl that turned out to be a fantastic experience. For transport, we had a forty-five-seater coach plus two minibuses packed full of excited men and women. The evening proved far different from most pub crawls, as we had a police car leading us, with another one following behind. As our convoy approached a set of traffic lights, the leading police car sped on ahead. To my amazement, one police officer got out and stopped all the other traffic until our convoy had gone through the lights.

At the first pub on our list, it surprised me when our police escorts came in with us and had a drink. One of our guys said that in Indonesia, one could hire police for various events. This being something I had never heard of before.

On leaving one pub, instead of getting back into our coach, Steve climbed into the back of one police car. I laughed, thinking they would throw him out, but no. As it set off leading our convoy, Steve sat in the back wearing a big smile. On seeing this, when we left the next pub, Ian and I climbed into the back of one police car. To our delight, there was no problem, with our enjoyed the experience of being driven on to the next pub in the police car.

When we later went to leave the pub, there was a surprise announcement.

"Listen up. You will not be using our buses to get to the next pub. Instead, you will ride there in pedal-driven rickshaws."

I thought this would be fun. The voice then continued. "Oh, by the way, one of you will be pedalling each rickshaw."

At this, a great roar of laughter broke out. Then, as we all trooped out of the pub, we found a long line of waiting rickshaws. It was hilarious to see the rickshaws wobbling and weaving their way up the main road, with people singing and calling out. The whole evening was an incredible experience. I don't know how many pubs we visited that night, but for sure it was a night to remember.

When Peter asked one day for me to go to Singapore and check on the quality of bathtubs, I was delighted. I liked Singapore, where everything was clean and tidy, so was more than happy to go. However, had I but known the problems I would face, I would never have gone.

After flying first to Jakarta, I then flew on to Singapore, where I found Henry, the boss of the bathtub supply company, waiting to meet me. After introductions, he then drove us to his warehouse. To my surprise, instead of being lined up ready for inspection, the tubs were packed one on top of the other. When I told Henry what I needed, it disturbed me when he said this would take several hours. With my booked on a return flight to Surabaya late afternoon, this was not good. It meant I could not check all the bathtubs before having to leave for the airport. At my suggestion, Henry phoned Peter to explain the situation.

After doing so, Peter said, "Colin, you will have to stay the night. It's essential you check all the bathtubs before you return to Surabaya."

I told him I did not have enough money to pay for a night in a hotel. After Peter spoke to Henry, he said Henry would pay for my stay in a hotel. With this resolved, they laid out some bathtubs and I started to check them. A few hours later, Henry said the warehouse was ready to close for the night, so he took me to the hotel he had booked for me.

The next morning, after returning to the factory, I completed checking all the bathtubs. It was just as well I did, as because of various defects, I rejected quite a number. Although not pleased with my findings, Henry agreed with my report. A driver then took me to the airport for my return flight back to Surabaya.

At Jakarta airport, I noticed the customs man look through my passport twice. On asked what the problem was, he said, "You have no visa."

The news shocked me. "Yes, I do," I said, "I have a business visa."

He gave a half-smile. "You did, but the minute you left for Singapore, we automatically canceled it." Although shocked by this, much worse was to follow. I thought for a moment, then asked, "Is it possible for you to give me a tourist visa?" It would at least allow me to fly back to Surabaya.

His smile widened. "Of course. Do you have a return ticket from Surabaya?"

"Yes," I said.

"No problem, then. Please show it to me."

I shook my head. "I can't; it's in my house back in Surabaya."

To my horror and disbelief, the official became angry. He shouted, "Out! Out!" And that they would deport me. I couldn't believe it. Deported! To where? Singapore or the UK? Minutes later, a female airport official came to see me. The customs man must have told her I was illegal, as she asked me to accompany her to see the Chief of Customs. I felt nervous on hearing this. I did not know what he would say.

At his office, we found him talking on the telephone, so the woman asked me to sit and await him to finish. The call must have been about my situation, for when he finished, he looked up and stared at me. Could you tell me why do you not have a visa to enter Indonesia?" He asked.

"Sorry, but I thought I had a visa, a business visa. My company did not inform me it would expire once I left Indonesia."

His eyebrows shot up. "Your company! Are you working there?"

"Yes. I am." I felt nervous as I added, "On a hotel in Surabaya."

He shook his head in disbelief. "But you can't work there with a business visa. You must have a work permit."

"I'm sorry," I mumbled. "I never knew I needed a work permit. My company issued me with a business visa, so I thought it was OK."

"I see," he said, handing me a pen and paper. "Would you please write the name of your company and where you are working?"

I did and handed him the paper, I stood like a naughty schoolboy in front of his headmaster. All the time, he sat and stared at me. Finally, he shook his head. "Well, I don't know what to do with you," he said.

I felt myself beginning to sweat. "I'm sorry, but I never knew I was doing anything wrong. It's my company's fault. They should have obtained a work permit for me."

He sat in silence for a few minutes, then to my relief, said, "You are lucky. I am going to grant you a tourist visa so you can continue to Surabaya. However, I will forward your details to the authorities there. They will be visiting your company, so I advise you not to be found working without a work permit when they arrive."

His words were like a fresh bloom of spring. The weight on my shoulders since I had been in the Chief's office lifted and disappeared. I could not believe my good luck. "Many thanks for your help," I said. "It is much appreciated. I will make sure my company gets me a work permit A.S.A.P.."

After shaking his hand, as I walked out of his office, I vowed never to get into this kind of situation again.

The woman who had accompanied me to the office then escorted me to the flight check-in station. On glancing at my watch, I realised my plane had already left. I told the woman of this, who then made a quick phone call.

My heart sank when she said, "Yes. It's gone."

As I knew someone would meet me on my arrival in Surabaya, I asked, "Could I please make a phone call? A colleague will be waiting to meet me. As I won't be on the plane, I don't want him to wait for me."

It took me aback when she replied, "Yes, you can make a call from your hotel."

I turned in puzzlement and shook my head. "But I don't have a hotel."

"You do," she said. "Although it's not our fault you missed your flight, we are giving you a hotel room for the night. You can call from there."

I breathed a sigh of relief. "I'm sorry for causing you trouble," I said.

Then I realised I had another problem. "Sorry, but how do I get through check-in tomorrow morning? I checked in for both flights in Singapore."

"Show your boarding pass at the gate. If there is any problem, tell them to phone the chief of customs."

After she took me to a transfer desk, a courtesy bus took me to a nearby hotel. They must have been expecting me, for on showing my passport at reception, they gave me a room. Although basic, I was grateful to have any room.

After I managed to contact one of my guys in Surabaya, I said, "I won't be back until tomorrow morning."

I was still wondering if I could get on the plane in the morning when I fell asleep. The next morning, a courtesy coach took me back to the airport. I felt relieved when after showing my old boarding pass at the gate, they let me board the flight to Surabaya. Only then did I relax. On arrival, a driver met and drove me to the office.

When I told Peter what had happened in Jakarta, he grinned. "Sorry about that, Colin. We'll have to get you a work permit A.S.A.P."

"That's for sure," I replied. "I never want to go through another situation like yesterday. The customs man was so angry; I thought he would deport me."

Peter laughs. "I know it was not funny for you," he said, "But what more can I say other than sorry?"

I gave a grim smile. "Just remember the chief said he would report my working here to the authorities."

Peter nodded. "Don't worry; we will sort out your work permit."

That weekend I went to stay with my hash friends Paul and Bebe at Pigman's house. Like me, he was a hasher, and resided in the hills where the American hash run was scheduled for the next day. It turned out to be a day I will never forget; I thought I was going to die from a heart attack. (Details of this and other hash incidents will be in my next book.)

In mid-July, Rodger informed me I would be required on-site until November. This was good news. We had all been impatiently waiting to know if we would be needed on-site for another month. However, shortly after, I received a letter that confirmed I would only be required until the end of August. Then, a week later, Rodger said the company were still awaiting confirmation from our client regarding my stay until November. It was an unbelievable situation. I had never before been in such a crazy position.

It was about this time I received an invitation from Steve, the American Project Manager at the Westin Hotel. It was for me to attend the topping-out ceremony of the twenty-four-story hotel. As I had never been to one of these before, I accepted. On my arrival, I found there were no lifts in operation, so everyone had to go up in an Alimak (workers elevator). It being merely a wire cage hoisted up on the outside of the hotel. If one were anxious of heights, it would not be something to look forward to.

The ceremony involved a small section of the concrete roof slab being filled by several city officials and the building owner. This Steve said this was the usual procedure for a topping off ceremony.

Later, during a talk with Ian and Cathy, they asked if I would like to join them on a trip to Yogajarkarta. As it would be to somewhere, I had never been, I happily accepted. Cathy said we would catch a train there, and a plane back. On seeing my puzzlement, she explained that we would not have enough time to return by train. Although flying would be quicker, the train would be much cheaper and enable us to see more of the country,. This I thought could prove interesting.

After buying our tickets, Cathy said the journey would take about eight hours. Given this, on asking the cost, it amazed me at how inexpensive the tickets were.

Early one Friday morning, we went to the railway station and boarded our train. With the seats wooden, and no covering or cushions, they were uncomfortable. It explained why those in the know had turned up carrying cushions.

Whenever the train stopped at a station, a group of hawkers would board, selling all kinds of things. To my amazement, at one stop, a man got on selling what looked like a type of Kalawao bear. For sure, it was an eye-opening journey.

After sitting for approximately eight hours, we were glad to get off when the train arrived at Yogajarkarta. When we asked a taxi driver about the fare to our hotel, we were shocked. He wanted more money than we had paid for a train ticket. Despite haggling, the driver insisted, so we agreed to pay. In fairness, our hotel turned out to quite a distance from the train station. Nevertheless, in comparison to the distance travelled by train, it was an expensive ride.

We found the hotel well-furnished and comfortable, plus, there was a large outside swimming pool. Once freshened up, we took a taxi into town, where I bought a large wooden mask. On our return to the hotel, we enjoyed a refreshing swim. This, our long journey and walks around the town, was a great way to relax.

The next morning, we meet up with our tour guide for a half-day tour that Cathy had booked. Our guide turned out to be both knowledgeable and friendly, and took us to various sites, including several old temples, plus a Batik, and a Silver factory. I found both factories fascinating, with our shown all aspects of making Batik and silver jewellery.

In the afternoon, we visited 'Borobudur Temple' that we found an enormous building. Without a doubt, it was the largest temple I had ever seen. It was only found after a big storm caused the side of a hill to collapse, revealing part of the temple. Since its discovery, it had been wholly uncovered and restored. We found the temple covered with a vast number of stone carvings of all descriptions. At the top level of the temple were some large stone carved bells that stood over six feet high, and are called Cupolas.

The next morning, while looking around the shops, I bought a beautiful Batik with a dragon design. Then, during a talk with Rudi, the owner, he offered to show us some sights. After accepting his offer, Rudi took us to see the remains of the Winter Palace and the Bird market. The latter being huge, with hundreds of various types of caged birds for sale.

On querying the large number for sale, Rudi explained. "To an Indonesian, it is a good sign if you own a singing bird."

At the end of our tour, we thanked Rudi for showing us around. Although he had requested no money, we were happy to give him some.

After returning to our hotel, we had a last swim, then took a taxi to the airport, where a short time later, we flew back to Surabaya. Although quicker and more comfortable, our train trip had been much more interesting.

Once back in our house, I thanked Cathy and Ian for inviting me to join them. It had been a fantastic weekend.

At work, someone informed us the company were still experiencing difficulties in obtaining payment from our client. It meant until resolved; we would not know how much longer we would be required. Still, there was nothing any of us could do about it. We either accepted the situation or resigned; the choice was ours.

In the meantime, one weekend, I flew down to Bali to meet up with some of my hash friends. They had driven down from Surabaya for Mike, one of our hash guys, stag night. On arrival, I took a taxi to the Hard Rock Cafe, where we had arranged to meet. I found the boys there, plus Steve's wife, and a girl named Karyn, who lived in Bali. We had a great night in the HRC, plenty to eat and drink while listening to some fabulous music.

The next morning, I went to join an organised tour of the island. To my surprise, I found only three of us going on it. Still, this was good, as it meant we had plenty of room to spread out in our minibus.

As well as our driver, we had a friendly guide, who explained all about the places we visited. While approaching one destination way up in the hills, he warned us to be careful. He said, "The people would try and cheat us." It was the first time he had mentioned about any problems.

As we pulled up at a restaurant for lunch, I saw a crowd of people waiting outside. I wondered what was going on, then noticed some were holding up a variety of items. These our guide said, 'Are what they want people to buy." Apart from articles of clothing, I noticed that some held a variety of carved items. However, on instructions from our guide, we ignored them and followed him through the crowd and upstairs into the restaurant.

As I sat looking out, among several people holding up items, one was a carved wooden dragon. As I liked dragons, I decided that on finishing my lunch, I would take a closer look. When I went down and out to the crowd, the man holding the dragon came and thrust it towards me.

"You want?" he said. "I give you a good price." After haggling, we agreed on a price. However, on closer examination, I found the quality of carving was not as good as I had thought. On telling the man I had changed my mind, he muttered something and walked away. I later realised what I had done was not good. Once you have agreed on a price, you should pay the money.

Among the items thrust at me was a large carving of a fisherman sat on a log. It was far better quality than anything else I had seen. "How much?" I asked

"$200," the man replies.

I laughed. "Forget it," I said. "It's not worth $200, and I pay in Rupiahs, not dollars." Nevertheless, I was interested in the carving that on a close examination, I could see an expert had carved it. The details were excellent and well finished. After a lot of haggling, and no agreement on my ultimate offer of six hundred Rupiahs, I turned away. I had only taken a few steps when the man called out, "Okay! It's a deal."

I turned back towards him. "Six hundred Rupiahs, agreed?"
"Yes," he said.

I slowly counted out the money, placing each note in his
hand "There," I said, "okay."

To my annoyance, he said, "No! We agreed on six hundred and
fifty."
"Forget it," I snapped. "We said six hundred." As I went to take
back the money, the man thrust the carving into my hands and
took my money. "Okay! It's yours," he said.

When I felt the weight of the carving drag my arm down, I
knew it was not the one I had agreed to buy. When I looked up,
I was furious; the man had disappeared into the crowd. Despite
searching for him, he was nowhere to be seen. I then looked at the
carving. Although the same design as the one I had agreed to buy,
the quality was much inferior. Not only that, it weighed twice as
much.

As I kept an eye out for the man, I noticed our guide. He was
staring at me and shaking his head. As I walked towards him, he
said, "I did warn you to be careful, Colin."

"I know," I snapped, "but I thought you meant they would
overcharge us, not switch things." I was so angry about being
cheated. I felt like throwing the carving down over the hillside.
However, with numerous huts below, I did not.

We had only travelled a short distance back down the hill in
our minibus when our driver stopped at a stall selling souvenirs. No
sooner had we got out of the bus; the lady stall owner greeted us. "I
make you a good price," she said.

Before I could say anything, our guide pointed to me.
"Someone cheated him further just up the hill, so don't expect him
to buy anything."

"I am sorry," she said sadly. "There are many bad people up there. They are always cheating someone."

After looking at what she had for sale, we thanked her and drove off.

I still felt sorry for myself when we arrived back in town. As I walked into my hotel, I came across a few of the boys.

"Hi, Colin," one said. "Did you have a tour?"

I forced a smile. " Yes, it was great except from getting ripped off."

"Why? What happened?" he asked.

On explaining about the man switching the carving on me, they all laughed at my misfortune.

"Sorry, Col, but it does sound funny," Peter said. "Anyway, let's have a look at what you ended up with."

As I handed him the carving, I warned how heavy it was.

He took hold of it. "You're right;" he said, "it is heavy." After a closer look at the carving, he said, "Still, it's not bad. In fact, I would say it's quite good!"

I nodded agreement. "Yes, it is, but not half as good as the one I was supposed to have bought." I had to smiled. "It's so heavy; it's a good job I'm going back with you lot in the truck. If I were returning on a plane, I would have to pay for excess luggage."

That evening we all attended Mike's wedding and had such a successful time; it helped make up for my cheated over the carving.

The next morning, Karyn came in a jeep to take me to look at some temples up in the hills. We stopped at various villages that Karyn explained, specialised in one particular activity. One did wood carvings, one oil painting, one gold jewellery, with another silver jewellery. This I thought to be an excellent set-up.

At one place where we stopped, we found three men sat on the ground outside a store, carving wood. I found it fascinating watching them, as they were holding it between their feet. Also, although their tools were basic, the quality of their artistry was excellent.

Apart from visiting a couple of temples, we also stopped at a shop selling large wooden carved Garudas. These are said to be based on a bird creature of Buddhist mythology. It combines the features of gods and animals. It's also the name of the national Indonesian Airlines company. The carvings were fantastic, with some over six feet tall. They were well made and painted beautifully in various bright colors. However, although I liked them, it would have cost a fortune to ship one back home, so there was no point in buying one. Karyn, on the other hand, who lived in Bali, purchased a two-foot tall one that the man said would be delivered to her home the next day. After a great and enjoyable day out, we drove back to town.

The next morning, with Peter driving, we set off on our long journey back to Surabaya. On the way, we stopped to look at Tanalot Temple. It is set on a small hillock that when the tide comes in, becomes an island. The temple is off-limits to everyone except the temple guardians, and people say a giant snake protects it.

After driving from one side of Bali to the other, we caught a ferry back to the mainland, then drove on to Surabaya. Although it had been my first trip to Bali, I was so impressed; I knew I would return.

As stated in travel destinations, Bali is a must-visit place. It's beautiful, having long, fabulous sandy beaches, with a kaleidoscope of green vegetation. The people are friendly, and unlike the mainland, that is mainly populated by Muslims, they are mostly Hindus. This is why there are so many small, but incredible temples and shrines established in peoples gardens. It 's these that give the island a feeling of such peace and tranquillity.

In August, Rodger informed they would extend my contract until the end of October. It delighted me when he said, "If you want, your wife could come out to join you. The company, of course, will pay for her flight."

When I phoned and told Jen to get prepared to fly out and join me, her squeals of delight told me how pleased she was. I said, "Once you know when you want to come, contact our office in London. They will arrange your flight."

I thought it would be simple for her to come, but, as they say, things don't always go to plan.

In the meantime, things at work were changing all the time. They kept extending my contract at one point, but then suddenly informed me that I would not be required in two weeks time. As Jen was due to arrive shortly for a holiday, I found this most disturbing.

When Jen called from Singapore airport one Friday afternoon, it sounded as though she was in a bit of a state. On asking what the problem was, it shocked me when she said the company had not provided her with a ticket on to Indonesia. To make matters worse, nor had they booked her a room at the airport hotel. Just what had been going through the mind of whoever booked her flight, I did not know. Thankfully, after speaking with our office secretary, she resolved the problem. Jen stayed the night at the transit hotel in the airport, then flew on to Surabaya the next morning.

After I met her at the airport, she became excited on hearing we were going to the Hash Ball that evening. Later, at the apartment, after giving me all the news from back home, Jen fell asleep.

The Hash Ball turned out to be a great success. I introduced Jen to a number of my hash friends, including my boss, Rodger, who apologised for the trouble with her flight.

Jen also enjoyed watching the various sketches put on by members of the hash, and especially the one with me in that she thought hilarious.

During the first week of September, Steve Brooke, the Project Manager at the Westin Hotel, asked me to attend an interview. It was about a contract on the Westin. Steve later informed me it was pretty definite I would receive one. In fairness, because of expecting my contract to be extended with E C Harris until October, I told him I could not leave them at present.

A week later, I received a fax from Richard. My contract was being extended until the end of October. When I called to informed Steve about this, he said, "That's not a problem. Once you complete your contract, you are to start work here at the Westin Hotel."

This was great news. Not only was the Westin a luxury hotel, but Steve said I would receive a long-term -married status contract.

A few days later, with a long public holiday the coming weekend, I decided to take Jen to Bali. She was bubbling with excitement when we flew down on a Thursday evening. Upon our arrival, we took a taxi to the Simpang Hotel, where I had made a reservation. Although basic, the hotel was in an excellent location. Also, with our room air-conditioned, Jen was happy to be there.

The next morning, during an island tour, we visited the Royal Water Temple, the Monkey Forest, and Tanalot. All of which Jen thought fantastic. We also went to a lake high up in the mountains, where Jen had her photo taken with a 20kg python wrapped around her shoulders. This was no easy task for her, as apart from its weight, Jen feared snakes. After the man took the snake from her shoulders, he put it on mine. I wasn't too happy when, wearing a beaming smile, he said, "You're a big man so you can have two snakes."

Although I felt concerned, the man bent and picked up another python lying on the ground. As he wrapped it around me, he told me to hold their heads tight. As I did, I could feel the rippling of their muscles as they slowly breathed. Jen, who stood nervously watching, then took a photo of the pythons wrapped around my shoulders. When the man removed them, although he said they weighed approximately 45kg, to me, it felt like a ton.

After a great and enjoyable day out, we returned to our hotel. In the evening, we enjoyed a tasty fish dinner, washed down with a bottle of delicious white wine. We then sat and relaxed sipping cocktails — a perfect way to end what had been a wonderful day.

Shortly before going to bed, there was a torrential downpour of rain. It became so heavy; it caused a power cut that lasted until the morning. As a result, without A/C, sleep was hard, but in the end, tiredness won.

The next morning, we awoke to find it a bright and sunny day. Only a few puddles remained here and there when we went out looking at souvenirs. With the prices low, we bought several gifts for ourselves, and some for friends back home.

Ongoing to the nearby beach, we found it had beautifully soft, clean sand. Although the bright blue sea was too rough for swimming, it was ideal for surfers. A number of them were out among the curling white waves. The total scene was beautiful; it showed why Bali is so popular with tourists.

In the evening, we listened to live music and enjoyed another mouth-watering seafood dinner. Unfortunately, like all things, our stay had come to an end. The next morning after an enjoyable time in Bali, we flew back to Surabaya. However, as we had such a great time there; we agreed to return.

During her stay in Surabaya, Jen enjoyed going out with some girls she had met on the hash. Although Jen didn't run, she liked coming to the hash runs with me. She found them incredibly hilarious and enjoyed talking to everyone during the down-downs.

However, all too soon, it was time for her flight back to Turkey. When she left, neither of us knew her next visit would not end so well.

In the late afternoon, I moved into Bintang Delango, a housing complex where I would stay until the end of my contract.

Although I expected to move to the Westin on completion of my contract with E.C Harris, I still sent off my CV to various companies. I did so, in case I could obtain a definite commitment from another company.

Most evenings I would go to the Lido Bar to have dinner and a drink with some of the boys. However, it was the weekends I enjoyed the most. Then, I would go to the hash where I enjoyed both the runs and the down-downs.

In early September, there was another Surabaya Pub Crawl. On the due date, a large excited crowd moved off in a big coach, followed by two minibuses. As before, we had two police cars escorting our convoy. Those who had not been on the previous pub crawl thought it a great success. However, those like me who had, did not think it was. Our police escorts were not as friendly, plus, they would let none of us ride in the police cars. I guess we were spoiled during the first event, and so expected too much. Still, despite this, we had a great evening, with more than enough to eat and drink.

After one evening's men's hash run, I had quite a bit to drink before returning to the Lido Bar. I remember being the first of my fellow hashers to enter the bar. This was not good. for me, as I walked—or, rather, staggered—in through the doors, I noticed a guy sat at the bar smoking. I don't know why, but I approached him and said, "No Smoking in here," then took his cigarette from his mouth and stubbed it out in an ashtray. The next thing I remember was picking myself up off the floor, holding my jaw. The man had punched me, knocking me unconscious.

Although drunk when I arrived, his punch immediately sobered me up. I felt shocked, as no one had punched me since leaving school.

With the help of one of the boys, I got to my feet, and in a shaky voice, I said, "You hit me."

Some of my friends were in the bar, with the rest of my group coming in just after the guy hit me. None were pleased about the guy punching me, so gave him a hard time. One of them accidentally-on-purpose pushed the man off his barstool and onto the floor. Then, before he could move, several of the other guys fell on top of him, and a struggle broke out. One of my Indonesian hash friends whispered in my ear. "I have a knife in my car; I will get it and kill him." At first I thought he joked, but then realised he was serious.

"No!" I said in a sharp voice. "It's not a problem; it was my fault for taking his cigarette away."

For the next two weeks, I suffered from a sore jaw. The man who hit me, received a warning to not enter the Lido Bar again. If so, he would not be welcome.

A few weeks later, Neil and I called in for a drink on the way home from work. When we entered the horseshoe-shaped bar, Neil spotted a friend on the opposite side. He waved and called to his friend, who was with another man, to come and join us. As they came around and we shook hands, I thought his friend looked familiar.

Then, I realised. "I know you!" I said, "You're the guy who punched me out the other week."

In a soft Scottish accent, he replied, "Aye, I did that. Do we have a problem?"

It was apparent the man was concerned there might be trouble. I shook my head. "No! I took your cigarette out of your mouth, and you punched me. I'm sorry about what happened. It was my fault; I was rather drunk."

"Aye, you were that." The man grinned. "I didn't mind you taking away my cigarette, as I could see you were drunk. But when you took away a second one, that was too much."

My eyebrows shot up. "Two! I never knew I took two. I only remember one. The next thing I remember was picking myself off the floor, holding my jaw."

After we shook hands, the man again asked if we had a problem, to which I assured him we didn't.

In October, Rodger left E.C Harris to return to the UK and get married. The next day, Richard informed they would extend my contract until the end of the year. It delighted me when he said, it could be longer, but would know more after a meeting with our client. Although this sounded great, I knew from previous experience that things had a habit of changing daily.

At the end of October, I received my contract extension, then a week later, I received a phone call from Steve Brooke. He said it was still possible for me to receive a contract at the Westin Hotel project. This came as a big surprise, as because of the lack of contact, I held out little hope of this happening.

In mid-November, I received a phone call from Steve, inviting me to meet the American designer of the project. Later, on walking around the site, I found the quality of finishes impressive. They were far better than those at the Majapahit Hotel.

At the end of the month, I phoned Steve to ask what news he had. To my delight, he said, "The owner of the Westin think it's not necessary to meet you. He will be drawing up a contract that I expect to get signed this weekend."

This was great news. After such a long time since my interview, I did not expect to receive a contract from the Westin.

On the Monday, Steve sent over a copy of my contract. On a side note, he said he expected to get it signed the next day. However, not until several weeks later did I receive a signed contract. I then sent a letter of resignation to Richard. It was a pity, but the company had messed me around for months. Although not all their fault, I felt a move to the Westin would prove a better deal for me.

After attending a party at a friend's house one evening, several of us went to Studio East. This was a massive club and always packed with people listening and dancing to loud, pulsating disco music. On our arrival, it surprised us to find it being raided by the police. Ongoing inside, we found many of them checking various people for drugs. It felt strange being there, with no music playing, as the DJ had closed down until the police completed their search.

During the weekends, I went on the hash with my running on the men's hash on the Saturday, and the main run on the Sunday. I enjoyed both the good company and of course the On Ons.

One evening, Matsuzaki, the Japanese Project manager at the Majapahit Hotel, invited Ian and myself out to dinner. I had never been to a Japanese restaurant before, so found it strange when seated at a low table. Although my first experience of eating Japanese food, I found it tasty. Then after dinner, Matsuzaki surprised me when he stood and presented me with a Parker pen and pencil set. This he said was in appreciation for all my help on the project. Although pleased with his gift, I had had big arguments with some members of his staff, so what he said surprised me.

In mid-December, I flew back to Turkey. A few days later, Jen and I flew to the UK to spend Christmas with my daughter Anita and her family. After a good Christmas, on New Year's Day, I took a flight back to Surabaya.

Because of the late arrival of my plane in Singapore, I missed my connecting flight. Still, this proved not a problem, as the airline company put me in the airport Transit Hotel for the night. It also broke up my long flight. The next morning, I continued on to Surabaya.

In the afternoon, I moved into my new companies apartment at the Grand Residence. Although not large, I found it comfortable. Plus, with a supermarket on the complex, it saved having to shop in town.

Steve had suggested that instead of applying for a new visa and work permit, I should obtain a business visa. However, after the problem I had before, I refused point-blank. The next week I went to Singapore and applied for a work permit. On my return to Surabaya, I did not have a problem when changing flights at Jakarta.

At the end of the month, I received my work permit. This was an enormous relief. I no longer had concerns about being deported for working illegally.

My first job at the Westin was to prepare snagging lists. However, because of continual arguments with the prime contractor over what I put on them, I soon felt I was wasting my time.

After receiving my work permit, Steve gave me the keys to a Kiang, a cross between a van and an SUV. To my further surprise, a few days later, the company provided me with a driver. Although he left a few weeks later, this was not a problem, as by then, I knew my way around town.

In mid-February, I attended the opening of Desperados, a new nightclub that became the most popular place in town. It had a great resident group, who played to packed audiences every night. However, little did I know about the terrible incident that would later occur there!

As Bali was close and the flight inexpensive, one weekend I flew down for a few days holiday. During a trip up to the tourist village of Ubud, I noticed some beautiful hand-painted quilts. They looked so good; I bought a few.

A few days after returning from Bali, Jen phoned. She informed me that Esref, my old boss from Ucgen, had a job for me. However, with it in Russia, and winter there, I told her I was not interested.

In early April, Kim called to say she was coming back to Surabaya. As she arrived on a Thursday and had never been to Bali, I decided to take her there for the weekend. I then booked flights and rooms for us at the Simpang Inn hotel, where Jen and I had stayed.

After picking Kim up from the airport, I told her about our trip to Bali the next morning. As expected, she was well pleased. In the evening, I took her to the Lido for dinner, then on to Desperados, where she enjoyed both the music and atmosphere.

During our stay in Bali, Kim and I visited Tanalot, the Donkey Sanctuary, and the Royal Temple. We also went to Kintamani, where a man had cheated me when buying a wood carving. On our last day in Bali, I bought a large carved wooden dragon. Not only did it look great, but I thought the the cost excellent. After enjoying the break with Kim, we flew back to Surabaya.

Over the next few days, I introduced Kim to various of my friends. On the Saturday, I ran on the men's hash, then took Kim to the main hash run on Sunday. She loved it, enjoying and getting on well with everyone she talked with.

While working at the Westin, I could not help but notice our accountant never used a briefcase. Strange as it seemed, he always carried a plastic carrier bag to work each day.

One time, I asked him why. He shrugged. "I used to carry a briefcase," he said, "but after having two stolen, I decided not to buy a third." He then explained how he had lost them..

He said, "A favourite trick of thieves is to wait at a set of traffic lights. There, one would puncture the tire of a stationary car that only had a driver. When the lights changed, and the vehicle crossed the road, an awaiting accomplice would attract the driver's attention. When he stopped to find out what they wanted, the accomplice would inform the driver they had a puncture. While he was out changing the wheel, his partner would steal the driver's briefcase, or whatever else was handy." He shrugged. "That was how I came to lose two briefcases."

While visiting a friend's house in a security-controlled village, I heard a shout from outside the gate. Ongoing to investigate, a street guard informed me he had seen someone breaking into my Kiang. On checking, although I had left it locked, the Kiang was now unlocked. Still, the guard's vigilance prevented anything from being stolen.

I later learned I had been fortunate. During a talk with one of my hash friends, he informed me about how robbers robbed him and his wife. "We had just parked outside a friend's house and exited the car when I felt what I thought was a mosquito land on my neck. As I turned to swat it off, I found it was not a mosquito, but a man trying to undo my gold chain. I was about to yell at him when I noticed two men standing next to him. As one held a large knife, I thought it best not to argue." He shrugged. "After we gave the men some jewellery, they ran away. As our friend lived in an excellent area with guards patrolling the streets, it surprised me to be robbed there.

With theft quite a problem in Surabaya, you always had to keep an eye open and be prepared for the unexpected. Also not to wear expensive jewellery when out shopping. Plus, one always had to keep the car doors locked when driving around town.

Because of this situation, various housing areas had guards on patrol to act as a deterrent.

In early May, our friend, Ann, phoned me from Turkey. I was surprised when she informed me Jen had been ill and now staying with her. Given this, I asked her to book Jen on a flight to Surabaya as soon as possible.

Two days before Jen was due to arrive, Kim went on a planned trip to visit Yogyakarta for a couple of days. She was also going to the summit of Mount Bromo, a volcano that had erupted several times in the past. It was a place I had always wanted to visit, but never managed to get there.

When Jen arrived, she appeared pale and tense, but after a few weeks, she looked and felt much better. The three of us later went to the annual Hash Ball. It proved a great success, with our having a good time.

The following week, Jen and I moved into another apartment in Grand Residence. Although it had only had one bedroom, friends living opposite had an extra room, so Kim moved in with them for the duration of her stay.

One evening, while Jen, Kim and I were in the Lido bar, we met John, Paul, and Ken, three of our hash friends. How it started I don't know, but Ken, Paul and I started knocking back a series of whiskey shots. I must have drunk quite a few, as come the morning; I could not remember leaving the bar.

On later talking with Jen, it stunned me when she informed me that I was so drunk, John refused to let Kim get in my car. I having refused all offers to drive us home. Jen said although she had been frightened when she got in the car with me, she didn't want me to drive on my own. To my surprise, she said I drove well all the way home. Just how this was possible, I do not know, but I realised, it had been both dangerous and stupid of me. I should have let someone else drive us home.

Jen and I later attended a dedication ceremony at the Westin Hotel, she was then over the moon when I told her we could move in there as trial guests.

We packed up some things, drove to the Westin, and checked in. When we entering our room, Jen was delighted to find it contained a desk. She gave a beaming smile as I took a photo of her sat at the desk pretending to be working.

After lunch in the hotel restaurant the next day, when I requested the bill, to my amazement, there wasn't one? Steve had not mentioned that all the meals and drinks were on the house.

On leaving the restaurant, we both wore smiles as we returned to our room. As we entered, the telephone rang. Jen answered, then looked puzzled when she hung up. When I asked what's the problem, she said, "The receptionist informed me that we are late checking out."

"What! You stay here while I'll go and see Steve to find out what's going on."

I had to laugh when he said, "They've only given you the room for the night." This was not what I had understood, and I knew it would disappoint Jen when I told her. Luckily, Steve managed to get us another free night's stay.

However, when I returned and informed Jen, she still did not find it amusing. Like me, she had expected us to be staying in the hotel until the completion of my contract.

Jen still felt disappointed when after lunch the next day, we returned to our apartment. Still, despite only being a two-day stay, Jen had to admit it had been an enjoyable experience.

At work, all was coming on well. The main lobby flooring consisting of gleaming black marble tiles with a large motive set in the centre looked fabulous. Once completed, when Steve handed me a golf ball, I asked, "What's it for?"

He gave me a quizzical look. "Don't you know?"

I grinned. "If you mean except for playing golf? Then no!" I said.

He laughed. "It's for you to check the lobby flooring. You bounce the ball on each tile," he said. "You'll be able to tell by the sound the ball makes if it's fixes solidly."

Steve then bounced the ball on a tile to show me what he meant. This method of detection surprised me. I had never heard, or seen it used before.

Once armed with a detailed plan showing the lobby tile layout, I went off to check the floor. Although pleased to find bouncing the ball on the tiles worked well, I was far from happy with what it revealed. A number of tiles required removing and re-fixing down solid.

Jen was enjoying her time in Indonesia when, without any warning, she felt ill. After taking her to see a Doctor, he gave her an examination and a blood test. It later shocked us to hear the results revealed some of her blood results were not good. The doctor also discovered Jen had a lump in one of her breasts. This was real bad news.

The next day during a meeting with Steve, I explained that, because of Jen's ill health, I had to offer my resignation. Although not pleased, in the circumstances, he agreed I had no other choice.

After Jen and I discussed her medical problem, we decided she should see a specialist A.S.A.P.. However, with it being a Friday evening, we had to wait until Monday morning to determine who best to see.

To try and forget about her problem, Jen and I went with three of our hash friends up to Pig Man's house at Travas for the weekend. Although we all had a good time, things were subdued, after informing them of Jen's health problem, and my consequent resignation.

On Monday, I phoned our office secretary. After I explained the problem, I asked if she could find a specialist doctor for Jen. She proved a successful help, and phoned back, giving me the number of a doctor in Jakarta. After calling and explaining about Jen's situation, he recommended she saw a Dr Morhan in Singapore. I then called and arranged for him to see Jen on the Thursday morning. With the help of our office, I booked our flight to Singapore and a hotel reservation.

On our arrival in Singapore, after checking in at our hotel, we went to Dr Mohan's surgery. He gave Jen a thorough examination, and also took X-rays of the lump. Once done, he then drew some fluid from it, explaining why and what he was doing. The results of the fluid test he said he would get on Saturday morning. When we returned to our hotel; we were apprehensive about what the consequences would show.

To cheer ourselves up, in the evening, I took Jen to Raffles Hotel. She was happy to be there, and thrilled to have a couple of Singapore Slings. It also benefited us by going there, as by the time we returned to our hotel, Jen felt much more relaxed.

The next morning, we went by cable car over to Sentosa Island. This turned out to be the best part of our trip, as after walking around the island, we thought it nothing special. On our way back to our hotel, we called in at Clark Key. Jen liked it so much; we returned there in the evening when it was livelier.

> On the Saturday morning, Jen and I felt nervous when we returned to see Dr Morhan. The moment he spoke, it became evident that the test outcomes were not satisfactory. When Dr Morhan said Jen needed an operation A.S.A.P. to remove the lump, I gripped her hand tight. This was terrible news.

However, Dr Morhan proved most helpful. "If you want," he said. "I can perform the operation, or you may decide to have it done in the UK. Either way, it is up to you to decide which is best for you."

After thanking him for his kindness, we left to discuss the options. During lunch, we discussed where Jen should have the operation. We had full confidence in Dr Morhan and could afford the cost of him performing the procedure. However, the costs of going to and fro to Singapore for further check-ups could prove considerable. After much discussion, we agreed it best Jen have the operation back in England.

On our return to Dr Morhan, I thanked him for all his help and said we decided that Jen should have the operation in England. He said he understood and wished Jen well.

Once back in the hotel, we were fortunate in getting a flight back to Surabaya in the afternoon. Although I usually enjoyed a trip to Singapore, this one was one I wished had not been necessary.

On the Monday morning, Jen phoned our old doctor in Plymouth, England. After explaining about the lump in her breast, he gave her the number of a specialist. Jen then called and discussed things with him. After he asked to see a copy of her test results, I faxed them to him. He then called back and asked Jen to call him again on Thursday. Her call on Thursday left us puzzled. The doctor had said *that at present, she did not require an operation.*

As Dr Morhan had said Jen needed an operation A.S.A.P, this was most strange. It meant we would have to wait until Jen went to see the doctor on our forthcoming trip to England.

On our last weekend in Surabaya, I went to the men's hash on Saturday afternoon, then after drinking several beers and still in my hash clothing, I called into the Lido Bar. I had gone there to meet Jen and various other friends for the On Ons. After a few more drinks, because of being somewhat drunk, I went home. About an hour later, Jen and Kim came in through the front door, followed by Bob, one of our hash friends, which surprised me.

My surprise turned to one of shock and horror when Bob told me that someone had slashed Jen with a razor. When I looked, I noticed that both her arms had bandages up to the elbows. Bob then explained what had happened. "Jen was in the toilet at Desperados when two girls came in behind her. While one stayed by the door, the other girl attacked her with a razor. Although Jen managed to protect her face, she received a lot of cuts on her arms. Fortunately, when someone tried to get into the toilet, the girls ran out, leaving Jen bleeding badly from her wounds. It was one of our girls who interrupted the attack, who immediately informed security. Jen received first aid from a member of staff, who bandaged up her arms."

This was terrible and shocking news. I was dumbstruck and could not comprehend what I was hearing. Desperados wasn't a sleazy nightclub, but part of a luxury hotel group.

After a rough night, the next morning, I took Jen to see a doctor. Even though I knew her arms had been slashed, I still recoiled in shock when the doctor removed the bandages. Both Jen's arms were a mess of cris-crossed cuts. Fortunately, on inspection, none were deep or infected. After having her wounds cleaned and re-bandaged, Jen accompanied me to our last hash in the afternoon. Everyone who was not in the club at the time of the incident could not believe what happened to Jen. Until then, apart from the odd fight that was soony stopped by security, there had never been any trouble at the club.

The next day, Jen and I flew home to Turkey. The departure was far from what we had anticipated. Later, despite police investigations, they did not find who was responsible for the attack on Jen. The hotel that owned the nightclub, later paid Jen the equivalent of a weekend stay in the hotel as compensation. This being nothing compared to the shocking effect the attack had left on Jen.

Working in Indonesia had proved far more challenging than any other country I had worked in. Plus, given what had happened there, I hoped my next contract would work out better for all concerned.

Running on the hash, was great fun, with the time spent on the beautiful Island of Bali with Jen something good to remember. All this, however, did nothing to overshadow Jen's terrifying experience.

Bad news in Malaysia

# Chapter Fifteen

After our return to Turkey, Jen then flew to England to see our doctor in Plymouth. After an examination, he told her she did not require an operation. The news that Jen did not require an operation delighted, but left us puzzled. Although it meant I had resigned my contract in Indonesia for nothing, Jen's health was far more important. Once the doctor had confirmed his initial examination report, I flew over to England in search of a new contract.

During my stay with Anita and family in Kent, over the next two weeks, I spent most days in Expats Int: office in London. It being where I had obtained many of my previous overseas contracts. This time, however, despite many phone calls and sending off faxes, I was unsuccessful. Then my luck changed. In one day, I received faxes regarding two contracts.

One in Vietnam was for three months. The other, a one year contract in Malaysia, made my eyes light up. Richmond International, an Interior Design Company, required a Project Supervisor. They needed someone to take over from a man who was leaving the company. Apart from an extended contract period, it was also married status. With the project, a five-star hotel, it was just the type of contract I had been seeking.

I replied to both companies, saying I was interested, then awaited an answer. A short time later, I received a phone call from Simon, re the project in Vietnam. To my delight, after he told me the job was mine, I then explained about the possibility of being offered a one-year contract in Malaysia. He said given this, he would understand if I did not accept his offer. I said I would inform him yes or no before the end of the following week.

Later, while about to fax Simon, I received a fax from Richmond's manager in Malaysia, offering me a long-term contract.

When I faxed back my acceptance, I wore a big smile. I then phoned Simon and told him I had accepted the contract in Malaysia. He said, *'I'm sorry you're not taking my offer, but I'm unable to match Richmond's contract period. Anyway, best of luck to you.'*

I returned home to Turkey on the next available flight, then two days later, I flew to Malaysia. On my arrival in Kuala Lumpur, known by many as KL, a man named Paul met me. It was he who I would be taking over from.

As we drove along, Paul told me about the project. He said it was in Subang Jaya, a suburb of KL. Once checked in at the hotel where I would be staying, we drove to Richmond's office. Here I met Graham, the Area Manager, who said I would stay in the hotel until I had found suitable accommodation. I had explained that my wife would join me. After a brief chat, Paul drove me back to my hotel. After my long flight I felt jet-lagged, so after a snack from room service, I had an early night.

The next morning, Paul collected me, then drove to the office. Here I gave my passport to our secretary, who would apply for my work permit. We were about to leave, when Graham invited me for dinner at his house that evening. This I thought an excellent start to being in Malaysia.

Paul then took us to the site where I met John, the contractor's P.M. During a tour, John explained there were two hotel sections. One old, the other new, where most of the works were being performed.

At lunchtime, Paul drove me to a nearby shopping centre where he usually had lunch, and was also the nearest place to the site.

As John had suggested, I might find a suitable apartment to rent in his complex; I went one evening to where he lived. At his home, John introduced me to his wife, Peggy, who was also an Australian. After a drink and a chat, John took me for a look around the area. I found it well laid out, and thought it ideal. Unfortunately, although I looked at a few suitable houses, the rents were above my allotted budget.

During my first week on-site, Paul drove us to and from work, which, took about half an hour. However, I found it complicated, as it involved driving down two different motorways.

On the evening of Paul's departure, he drove us to the airport. After he left, I then set off to drive home. Instead of a thirty-minute drive, I got lost, and the journey took one and a half hours. In total, it took four days before I could drive to and from the site without getting lost.

While talking with Graham's secretary at the office one day, she mentioned the rate of tax I would be paying.

I laughed. "There is some mistake," I said. "I don't pay tax."

She shook her head. "But you have to pay tax on your salary," she said.

I gave a grim smile. "In that case, we have a problem." Graham, who was in his office, must have heard us talking, for he came out. "Colin, if I told you your salary would be tax-free, then it will be. The company will pay your tax the same as they do for me."

I felt relieved on having sorted this out, but unknown to me, another significant problem lay ahead.

During the following week, I looked at various houses and apartments. Some were out of my price range or unacceptable. I then found an apartment in Subang Jaya. Although I thought it okay, the furniture and fittings were rather basic. However, with the price within my budget and walking distance of a shopping centre, I thought it okay. Plus, with a large new hospital was close by the apartment, I agreed to rent it.

With Malaysia the birthplace of the hash, there were many hash clubs scattered around the country. This pleased me, as I intended to run on a hash whenever I could. Details of the numerous incidents while running on the hash in Malaysia will be in another book.

Work on the project was going well, with my pleased to find the quality much better than in Indonesia.

While chatting with John one day, he got up and closed his office door. I thought this strange, as he always left it open. He then surprised me when he said. "Some of my guys don't like me very much!"

I had found him a rather strange guy, so not too surprised to hear this. "Well, you cannot please everyone," I said. "They have to remember that you're the boss."

He gave a grim smile. "That's true, but they're Malaysians, and I'm not."

Although this might have been a problem for him, I never had a problem with any of the local workers.

During one hash run, I heard about a long holiday weekend trip to the Kinir Dam. With so numerous holidays in Malaysia, it seemed as though there was one every week. Nevertheless, as I thought this trip could prove interesting, I phoned Bek, one of my hash friends. When he later called back, It pleased me to hear he had arranged for me to join the group.

Come the evening of the trip, I found it impossible to get a taxi to take me to the meeting point. It put me in panic mode, but after calling Bek, he came to pick me up.

At the meeting spot, we joined sixteen people, most of whom were hashers. As we set off, I don't think that any of us realised it would take as long as it did to reach our destination. With it being a holiday weekend, the roads were jam-packed. As our coach crawled up a long, steep hill, I noticed hundreds of cars parked on the hard shoulder. Then as we drove down the other side, we found it also jam-packed with slow-moving traffic. Because of the amount of traffic, we did not arrive at the dam until late the next morning.

When we climbed off the coach feeling tired and weary, I thought it the end of our journey. To my surprise, it wasn't. A man waiting in the car park led us down to the shore of the huge dam. After we boarded three small motorised boats, each with a crewman; we set off. Our trip involved weaving our way through hundreds of partly submerged trees. I later heard that they filled the dam without removing all the trees first. This I thought a terrible waste of timber.

An hour later, we came in sight of our final destination. A large building set on a jetty. By the time we tied up at the wooden dock, eleven long, tiring hours had passed since leaving KL.

As we climbed stiffly out of the boats, a man welcomed us, then led us to the reception area. Once checked in, he informed us where our respective chalets were located. While we walked up a path from the jetty, I noticed many wooden chalets built up on stilts scattered around the tree-clad hillside. Each of these were connected to each other by suspended wooden walkways, which left me impressed with the setup.

I shared a chalet with two men, while the other members of our group, mainly married couples with children, moved into family-sized chalets. Ongoing inside ours, I found it more substantial than it looked from outside. Plus, although basic, I found it clean, with a separate bathroom at the rear. Unfortunately, there was no air-conditioning, only a fan, which did nothing to cool the air inside. However, by opening the mosquito netted covered windows and using the fan, the room soon became more refreshing.

Once settled in, we all made our way down for breakfast, that we found served on the jetty outside the reception area. There were no set meals; and you helped yourself from a wide selection of dishes.

While sat eating breakfast, I noticed numerous fish swimming around the jetty. On pointing this out to our host, he said, "They came for any waste food scraps thrown in for them."

In the afternoon, we were taken for a trip on small boats along a shallow, winding river. This our guide said, "Is one of several feeding into the dam." After approximately twenty minutes, we came to another section of the river, which our guide said was ideal for swimming. With the water so refreshing; it proved most welcome. What with a swim and sat out in the fresh air, I felt relaxed and had a healthy appetite when we returned to camp.

After all had eaten a large, which I thought a tasty dinner, they took us to a large hall. With it set in a hollow, a short distance away from the chalets, our guide said they used it for entertainment. Here we then had an impromptu karaoke session that proved a great success.

During breakfast the next morning, several of us fed the eagerly waiting fish. As we did, our host indicated what he said was a Fish Eagle, perched high in a tree some distance away.

"Do they catch much fish?" someone inquired.

Our host smiled. "Watch this," he said. "One will usually come down to feed on command." His statement puzzled us. Then as we watched, he used a net to scoop a fish out of the water, which he then stunned by banging its head on the floor. Next, he waggled the dazed fish in the water, before throwing it out. The Fish Eagle swooped down and snatched the fish from the water, leaving us amazed. With it gripped tight between its talons, it flew back up to its perch in the tree. I nodded in satisfaction when I later found I had captured this split-second moment on my camera.

In the afternoon, our guide took us along the river to a spot where a series of small waterfalls awaited us. While several of our group swam in some of the deeper pools, I went exploring. Suddenly, a centipede about one and a half feet long appeared. Its appearance shocked me. I almost fell off the rock I was standing on, I never knew centipedes could grow so large.

# Part 2

In the evening we had our last dinner at the camp. With various dishes to choose from; it was hard to know what to eat. The camp might have been basic, but the amount, and quality of food provided were excellent.

The next morning, we said our goodbyes to our hosts and boarded the boats waiting to take us back across the dam. I felt sad about leaving, as I had enjoyed the peace and solitude of the camp. Plus, I did not need to cook for myself. Nevertheless, I couldn't complain, I was in Malaysia to work, not spending all my time enjoying myself on holiday.

Once back across the dam, we boarded our waiting coach and set off. Unfortunately, the journey back to KL took longer than what it did to reach the Dam. This not only because of heavy traffic. A group of the lads had stocked up with beer before leaving the camp. As a result, they were calling for a pit stop every half hour. Initially, it was a joke, with much cheering and laughter. However, after numerous stops, it ended with dire threats and angry muttering. I, for one, felt relieved when we arrived back in KL. Still, although a long and tiring trip, it had been a successful weekend.

When Jen arrived at the end of April, I meet her at the airport. As her flight was two hours late, both my wait and her journey were longer than expected. However, the tiredness in Jen's face vanished when she saw me waiting to greet her. After a warm embrace, I led her out to my car.

On the drive to Subang, I told Jen about our apartment. When we arrived, and Jen went inside, her smiling face dropped in disappointment.

"The furniture and fittings are poor compared to our apartment in Indonesia," she said.

I shrugged. "Sorry. But because of my allowance, there was nothing as close to town and the hotel site as this."

After later walking to the shopping centre that only took ten minutes, Jen cheered up. A smile replaced her previous glum look. "Sorry about moaning over the apartment," she said. It's okay. Plus, it's near the shopping centre, so I can walk there while you are at work."

The following week, I took Jen to Petaling Jaya for dinner. Here I introduced her to some of the group who went to the dam with me. During an enjoyable evening, several people told Jen all about our trip.

She gave a half-smile. "As there was no A/C in the chalet, I would not have enjoyed it."

On Saturday, Jen and I went with Loke, one of my hash friends who organised walks through the jungle. Six of us went on what turned out to be a two-hour hike. At one point, we all felt tired when we had to climb a steep hillside. However, when Loke said about a McDonald's at the summit, we all cheered up

Although it sounded far-fetched, two of the guys started to rush off up the hill. One called out, "We're going on ahead to get a burger and drink; we'll see you at the top." With that, they disappeared from view.

When the rest of us reached the summit, we laughed. There was no McDonald's, only an old timber observation post. The two who had rushed on ahead were sitting down. Their disappointment at not finding a McDonald's was evident on their faces.

I laughed, "In future, don't believe all you hear."

After descending the other side of the hill, we had to pass through waist-high grass, which, to my surprise, Jen did not seem to mind. Her smile then disappeared when we had to cross a ravine via a swaying timber suspension bridge. Jen looked scared as she made her way across. Only when her feet were back on the ground did she relax and smile.

As neither Jen nor I had a mobile telephone, we thought about buying one. On talking to our secretary, I asked if the company would pay anything towards the cost of calls. When informed they would, we went out and bought a phone. This made things easier for us to keep in touch when Jen was on her own. I could also phone her from John's office on the site.

We parked the car at the railway station on a Sunday and took a clean and comfortable train to KL, with inexpensive tickets. On our arrival at KL, we visited 101, a large shopping centre.

While walking around, a Chinese professor giving a painting exhibition outside an art shop caught our eye. To our amazement, he did not use any paintbrushes. Instead, he used his fingers, hands, and arms, and for the delicate details, he used a steel nail. We found it fascinating to watch the scene he was painting take shape. After speaking to an assistant, it delighted us when he returned to say the professor had agreed to paint us a picture. This again was an incredible experience. Before he finished, it pleased us when he added in bits of colour as we requested. The ones he had painted earlier were in black and white.

Only one thing spoiled our day out; I had left our car lights on when we parked. Given this, we had a flat battery. Still, although we had to get a taxi home, we had such a fantastic day; it was not a problem.

For a change, one weekend we decided to have Sunday lunch at the Sheraton Hotel. While we were talking to the bar manager, the noise coming from the restaurant area shocked us. On mentioning we were thinking of having lunch there, he frowned. "Colin, you don't want to eat here, especially on weekends. If you look down into the restaurant, you will see what I mean."

Ongoing to the edge of the lobby floor, we looked down to see the restaurant packed. As we watched, numerous young children were running around yelling and screaming. To our amazement, nobody made any attempt to muted or stop them. We thought it an unbelievable state of affairs, which could not have happened in England or Turkey.

When I returned to the bar, I asked the manager, "What's going on down there? I thought this was a five-star hotel?"

He gave a grim smile. "This happens every weekend. Neither the parents nor childminders make any attempt to control the children." He shrugged. "They simply ignore them and let them do what they want."

I shook my head in disbelief. "Well, thanks for the warning, we would not have enjoyed eating down there." After finishing our drinks, we left to find a quieter restaurant to have lunch.

While in KL one Sunday, we went to the Bull's Head for dinner. It being our favourite place where both the service and meals were always excellent. While eating, we noticed Wyn and Huw, a couple of our friends, sat nearby talking. Given it seemed a private talk, we decided not to join them.

We had finished our meal and awaiting the server to bring our bill, when out of the corner of my eye, I noticed a man walking towards us. When he stopped at our table, I thought he was going to push the chair next to Jen in out of his way. However, to my astonishment, he snatched up Jen's handbag from the chair next to her, then ran off at high speed.

I pushed back my chair, jumped to my feet and gave chase. As I did, I yelled out. "Stop thief!"

On hearing this, a couple of our servers also took up the chase. I was so angry; I didn't even think of the danger as I weaved and dodged through the traffic across the busy main road after him. However, despite running as fast as we could, we lost sight of the man when he turned a corner. By the time we reached it, he had disappeared. As I stood there panting, one server said, "I think its best you go back and look after your wife. We will continue to look for the man."

I later heard the man who snatched Jen's bag was Indian. As the staff and management of the Bull's Head were also Indian, they did not like theft by one of their own. After thanking the men for their help, I made my way back to the bar where I found Jen talking with Wyn and Huw. When Jen saw me approaching, she called out, "Any luck?"

"No. We lost him the other side of the highway." I gave a half-smile. "I thought I could run, but that guy could run even faster."

Huw nodded, "Colin, I've been asking Jenny if she had any details of your address in her handbag. She said yes, plus the keys to your apartment. Given this, it would be best to forget about reporting this incident to the police until later. The thief could go straight to your apartment and let himself in."

"What!" Alarmed, I asked. "Do you think this could happen?"

Huw nodded. "Yes. I'm afraid so."

"In that case, we had best get home A.S.A.P. The last thing we want is someone breaking into our apartment."

After bidding them a hasty goodbye, we set off back to our apartment. On the way, we discussed how we would get inside. Apart from having no keys, we lived on the 4th Floor. Our only chance would be if Kelly, our Canadian next-door neighbour, was at home.

On our arrival, I knocked on their door. To our relief, Kelly opened it, with his girlfriend Sandra stood behind him.

He gave a broad smile. "Hi guys, how's it going?"

Frustrated, I explained about Jen's stolen handbag and our not having a key to get into our apartment.

Kelly frowned. "That's not good. Anyway, come on in." As we did, he asked, "Is your balcony door open?" He grinned. "If so, it won't be too big a problem to get into your place."

"Yes, it is," I said. "We always leave it open to get some fresh air inside."

Kelly gave a knowing smile. "In that case, no problem. I'll climb around the balcony and let myself into your apartment."

As we walked through to their balcony, I realised that there was nothing for Kelly to catch hold of. Given this, Jen bit her lip, as Kelly climbed onto to his balcony balustrade. To our relief, he eased himself out and around onto our balustrade. We then heard him jump down onto the balcony. Kelly wore a big smile as he poked his head back around the wall. "There, I said it would be easy!" He then disappeared from view.

A few minutes later, the front door of our apartment opened, with Kelly stood there with a wide smile of satisfaction on his face.

"Thanks a bunch, Kelly." I said, "You've saved us a lot of problems with your daredevil walk on the balustrades."

He gave a mock bow. "No problem! Glad to be of help."

On Monday, I took Jen to the office and explained about her stolen handbag. We then went to Subang to report the theft at the police station. To our disappointment, an officer informed us that as the robbery occurred in KL, we would have to go there and make a report.

On arrival there, it took a while before we found the police station. A police officer's statement about our going to another police station did not amuse me. One he said that specialised in dealing with thefts such as ours. We were fortunate, as the police officer arranged for one of his men to take us there in a police van. Once there, he led us inside and spoke to a police officer sat at the main desk. They then took us upstairs to an office and asked to wait. As we sat there, my eyes lit upon seeing a note written in chalk on a large blackboard. It said about a handbag handed in at the Bull's Head.

"Look! Jen!" I said, pointing to the blackboard, "It's about your handbag." Just then, a detective came into the room. His tone was friendly as he asked, "Good morning. How can I help you?"

As we shook hands, I said, "A thief stole my wife's handbag last night. From the note on the blackboard, it's the one mentioned."

After explaining about the theft, he asked us to wait a minute. We sat in expectation while he left the room. On his return, we were delighted to see Jen's handbag in his hand. The detective explained that shortly after we had left the scene, a man walked into the Bull's Head with the bag. It seems after he found it in the car park and asking around, he heard about the theft from the pub. Given this, he had taken it there and handed it in. We could not believe our luck. It just showed there were some honest people around.

On checking the contents of the bag, Jen found the only missing items were her purse and an electronic diary. Despite this, we were relieved to find our apartment keys still in the bag. After thanking the detective for his help, we returned home.

# Part 3

The following month, I considered buying a computer, which, as I was always on the move, decided a laptop would be best. Jen only wanted a brand name computer, so after checking, we bought a Texas Instruments model. The Chinese man who owned the shop we bought it from had a computer training school above the store. This was ideal, as neither of us even knew how to switch on a computer. As I had no time, Jen signed up for lessons.

To our displeasure, our computer proved a poor choice. Only two weeks after we bought it, it failed. The shop sent it for repair, and it had a new hard drive fitted. Despite this, it then failed again. This time it came back with a new motherboard installed. Our laptop was proving a big problem, and not what we expected from such a well-known brand.

While Jen had computer lessons, I tried to teach myself how to use ours. On her return home, she would tell me what she had learned. It puzzled her when sometimes I said. "I know how to do that!"

"How did you find out how?" she asked.

"By reading the manual and playing around."

Once the computer was working okay, it proved a big help. I used it to prepare my weekly site reports, which I then printed out on the small portable printer I had also bought.

We found Malaysia a fabulous place, with numerous exciting places to visit. Plus, thanks to an excellent transport system, getting around to see them proved easy. On one trip out, Jen and I visited the Bird Park, Orchid Garden, and the Butterfly Park. At the latter, we found it unbelievable to see so hundreds of butterflies in one place. With so many flying around and lying on the ground, one had to be careful not to step on them.

While in Bird Park, we found a park ranger showing a group of people, two large cockatoos, and a Toucan. As we watched, he put one toucan on a visitor's arm. After the people left, I asked the man if he would put a Toucan on my arm. He did, and to my surprise, also put a large Cockatoo on my other arm. I felt shocked when my arm sagged under the bird's weight. It being much heavier than I expected.

On our way home, we bought train tickets for a trip to Singapore the following weekend; it being cheaper than going by plane. When we later arrived in Singapore, we found we had to pass through a customs post, it being something we had not known about. Once clear, we took a taxi to Chinatown and booked into a small hotel.

In the evening, we went to Clarke Quay, where we enjoyed a tasty seafood salad at one of the seafront restaurants. It felt good to sit and relax while enjoying a glass of wine.

Unfortunately, our evening ended up spoiled after we returned to our hotel and went to bed. Because of the proximity of the lift machinery room, it made our room noisy. The situation became unbearable, so I called reception to complain. Although 1.30 am, the staff proved helpful and had us moved to a quieter room.

The next morning, after a walk around Chinatown, we checked out of our hotel and took a taxi to the railway station.

To our surprise, we found a long queue of people waiting to go through passport control. Although unexpected, we had arrived early, so thought it not a problem. When at last it came to our turn, Jen passed through okay. However, according to the passport officer, I did not provide a satisfactory reason for traveling.

"I don't think you're a tourist as you claim to be," he said. "You're working in Malaysia."

This was not good, as unless I could catch the train, it would leave me stranded in Singapore.

I pretended to be indignant. "I am not, as you suggest, working in Malaysia. My wife and I are on an extended vacation."

To my relief, after what seemed like hours, the officer accepted my story and allowed me through to join Jen and board the train. I had said I was a tourist, as my work permit had not yet come through. If it had, I would have shown it at the customs control.

While looking through a local newspaper, I noticed an article about wood carvers at a place named Carey Island. As wood carving interested both Jen and me, we decided to drive there to see them.

After finding the junction to the island, I turned off and started driving along a narrow, wet, muddy and, slippery road. With it about four feet above ground level with no safety rails, it was dangerous. As far as we could see, the road ran straight through the middle of a palm plantation. Although I drove with extreme caution, because of the condition, Jen was worried and asked me to turn around.

I gave a grim smile "If we get stuck, we'll have serious problems getting help. We've seen neither traffic nor anyone since we came onto this road." However, I agreed with what Jen said. When I came to a clean section of road, with successful care, I turned the car around. Not until we arrived back at the junction to the main road did we relax. Although unfortunate we couldn't visit the wood carvers, continuing would have been too risky.

In early July, the Ringgit, the official Malaysian currency, started a sharp fall against Sterling. Because I had mistakenly agreed to be paid in the local currency, I felt concerned. I can only put my mistake down to the rush of signing the agreement and faxing it back to Graham. Typically, my salary would be paid in either dollars or Sterling.

Ongoing to the office, I raised my concerns about this situation with Graham. To my surprise, he told me that both he and Nick, our senior designer, were also paid in local currency. Given this, he would monitor the situation.

Meanwhile, during an inspection in one of the new hotel rooms, it puzzled me to see a line of dust on the carpet in front of the wardrobe. When I checked, I found insects had bored holes into the bottom edge of the wooden front panel. We later found the cause to be insects in the old adjacent hotel buildings that flew across and into the new building. To resolve this problem, management had a potent insecticide sprayed in both sections of the hotel. Then, they removed all the damaged wood and replaced it with new. It reminded me of what had happened to the Oil Minister's house in Abu Dhabi.

Another incident ended with what I thought a harsh punishment for the hotel. It occurred when the authorities fined the hotel for having open pots of standing water. These were plant pots delivered two days earlier that during a torrential downpour, had filled with rainwater. Given that mosquitoes lay their eggs in any stagnant water they find, the authorities take a firm stance to prevent them from breeding.

While Jen and I were up in KL shopping, she received a phone call from her brother Cyril. It shocked us to find her mother had died the previous day. As she had not been ill, this news came as a terrible shock.

Cyril explained. That Mum had collapsed while going downstairs at home. On hearing a loud noise, Dad went out into the hallway to ask what had happened. He found Mum lying at the bottom of the stairs. Despite his blindness, thanks to his particular type of phone, he phone me and I drove to the house where on checking, I found mum was dead."

Jen was in tears as she called a friend in England to request her daughter to let Anita, (our youngest daughter) know her Nan had died. Jen then called Kim and informed her of her Nan's death.

The next morning, I went to the office and explained what had happened. I asked them to get Jen a ticket home A.S.A.P. Regrettably, because of the situation at work, I couldn't accompany her. Still, thankfully, the office managed to get Jen a flight back to the UK a few days later.

Since raising my concerns about the depreciation of the Ringgit back in July, the situation had grown steadily worse. In early September, I received a message from Graham, he wanted to see me in the office. Ongoing there, it did not impress me when he said, "It's your choice to decide what you want to do about the situation. Given this, I decided it best to seek a new contract. I then faxed my CV to four or five companies I thought might require my services.

In the meantime, while Jen was in England, one of my friends invited me to join him and his employer for a night out. After an enjoyable evening with an excellent meal in the bosses' club, we accompanied him back to his hotel. We bade him thanks and watched him get in an the elevator up to his room. We were walking back towards the hotel entrance, when a pretty young woman entered. It shocked us when she lifted her dress to reveal she wore no underwear. She gave us a beaming smile and said, "Evening, boys, see anything you fancy?"

We both laughed. My friend said, "Not just now, thanks." With that, we left the hotel.

What with Mum's death, and losing a significant proportion of my salary, I thought things could not get worse. I then received a call from Jen, who was home in Turkey. She had news regarding our daughter Kim. The company she worked for had gone bankrupt, and to make matters worse, Kim discovered they had not paid her salary for the past three months. As she had earned little in the first place, to lose three months' salary was a severe blow.

Meanwhile, because of the currency problem, the situation at work was getting worse. A friend working for the Sheraton informed me that the prime contractors were about to put from site. Then, a few days later, I received more bad news. My company's proposed Indonesian hotel project had been postponed. If it had proceeded, there could well have been a position for me on the contract.

When Jen arrived back in mid-October, I met her at the airport. As we were driving home, I explained the situation about the falling Ringgit. "As I'm losing a serious amount of money each month, I've decided to look for another contract." However, as Jen was tired from her long flight, I don't think she took in what I had said.

At our apartment, Jen gasped with delight when I showed her a wood carving; I had been making. It stood two feet high and consisting of a double-sided face with a ball in its mouth. From the head, four twisted sections ran down to the base. Being a hardwood and only using hand tools, it made my task difficult. However, once completed, I felt well pleased. The carving looked great, with everyone who saw it impressed with the quality.

With not much happening at work, I decided to take Jen to Singapore for a brief holiday. Again, we travelled by train, and like last time were unlucky with our choice of hotel. After checking into a small hotel, we went out exploring. On our return late evening, we found the room smelt musty and damp. I phoned reception and informed the Duty manager, who then had us moved to another room.

The next day, we visited the Tang Dynasty City and the Chinese Garden. Although a day out, by the time we arrived back at our hotel, we were both tired out.

On our last morning in Singapore, we treated ourselves to breakfast at 'Raffles Hotel.' It being a wonderful experience to eat and relax in such a famous hotel.

On our return and later checking out of our hotel, we caught a train back to Subang Jaya. This time, I did not have any problems with passport control.

When we heard about a gold exhibition in KL, Jen and I decided to visit it. We discovered a variety of stands offering all kinds of beautifully crafted jewellery. At one, I bought Jen a beautiful 22ct gold bracelet. I thought it only fair, as while she was in the UK, I had bought myself the latest Minolta digital camera.

In mid-November, along with a group of our hash friends, Jen and I went to Pangkor Island for the weekend. After a tour around the island, we felt disappointed to find nothing of interest to see. Still, despite this, the sandy beach close to our hotel was clean, and the sparkling blue sea ideal for swimming. Also, a hash run arranged for us, turned out well laid. We all agreed that the hares had done an excellent job of laying the trail

Come early December; I decided enough was enough. Because of the worsening exchange rate, I was now losing approximately 50% of my monthly salary. When I told Jen, to my surprise, she said I was stupid to want to give in my notice. "Do you think 50% of your salary is better than nothing?"

I shook my head. "If the company offered me my present salary, I would have refused the contract." Despite Jen's statement that 50% was better than nothing, I was reluctant to work for such a low figure. My services were worth much more than the salary I now received. Despite this, I felt sad when I went to the office to hand in my letter of resignation. When I accepted the contract, I never thought I would end up in a situation like this.

# Part 4

When I handed Nick a copy, he said he knew how I felt and could understand my leaving. After shaking my hand, as Graham was not in the office, I gave my letter to his secretary. She shook my hand and wished me luck in finding another contract.

By now, with little work happening on-site, John had left to find another contract. Given the situation, I booked Jen and myself a week's holiday in Bali.

The following week, we checked into a hotel I had booked via the internet. To my amazement, the cost was lower than if we had gone and booked in at the reception. Also, with the exchange rate better than our last visit, everything we bought being less expensive.

Although listed as four stars, our hotel was better than many of the five-star hotels I had worked on. Our room was large, well-furnished and overlooked the hotel swimming pool. On going outside, we found swaying palm trees gave it shade from the blazing blistering sun. With that, plus white stone columns with carved lizards on them, the entire set-up looked fabulous. Although Jen couldn't swim, she was so impressed; she managed a few attempts at swimming. Thanks to the excellent exchange rate, we could afford more meals in our hotel. We could also drink cocktails whenever the fancy took us. It being something we could not experience before.

With our hotel backing onto a long, beautiful sandy beach on the edge of Kuta, the central shopping area, it was in a successful location.

On our first day out, Jen answered questions from a man who stopped us outside our hotel. To our amazement, he said she had won a holiday. Although this sounded too good to be true, we decided to see what was what.

After being driven to the 'Risata Resort Hotel, our guide indicated some individual suites. With each one sheltered from the next by a variety of shrubs, they looked rather exclusive. After going inside the main building, we then spent several hours talking to some people. To our surprise, Jen had won a holiday. Unfortunately, we would not be around at the time it was on offer, so unable to accept. We found this to be a scheme to get people to buy timeshares in the company. Although initially not interested, when shown the hotel suites on offer, we were stunned. They looked fabulous. Also, the overall setup of the hotel and the beautiful gardens were impressive.

Given our interest to know more, we returned two days later for another talk, with Michael, the sales manager. I said if I obtained a new contract before the end of January, we would buy a timeshare. On leaving Michael, I thought we had made our intentions clear, but to our disbelief, a few months later, I found we were badly mistaken.

The next day, Jen and I went on a trip up to Kintamani. It being where I had been ripped off on a previous visit. We also visited various villages and watched first-hand how a wide variety of handmade craft items were made. The next day, we took a half-day trip to Mas and Ubud. These being popular destinations for tourists, and known for selling a wide variety of oil and watercolour paintings. The wide range of pictures on sale at reasonable prices amazed us.

Once back in our hotel, after a relaxing dip in the pool, we enjoyed sipping a cocktail while relaxing on a couple of sun loungers.

On our last day in Bali, we spent a lazy day looking around the souvenir shops. In one, I bought a wood carving of a chariot complete with riders and horses. It was an incredible piece of work and finely carved from one piece of wood. Because of being so delicate, we had the shopkeeper take successful care wrapping it for our trip back to Malaysia.

On our last evening, we went out and enjoyed a large sea bass cooked on an open charcoal fire. Once back at our hotel, after one last cocktail, we retired for the night.

The next morning, with sad hearts, we flew back to K L.

Since handing in my resignation, despite contacting various recruitment companies, it led to nothing. Then, just before Christmas, I received a phone call from Rob Milford, the Philippines manager of John Laing International. He had received my CV from Eden Brown, one of the recruitment companies I had contacted. I felt eager when Rob asked me to attend an interview in KL. He had told me he wanted someone for a position on a project in the Philippines.

I felt on top of the world when I told Jen about the prospect of obtaining a new contract. She, however, warned me not to get too eager. It might not come to anything.

At the meeting with Rob, he explained the nature of the contract. To my surprise, apart from needing someone knowledgeable, they should also be able to be diplomatic. This requirement was novel to me. No one had ever asked me this question before. Still, come the end of my interview, I thought things had gone well, with the prospects of being offered a contract looking good.

When I informed Jen how things had gone, it took me back when on hearing the company needed someone diplomatic, she laughed out loud. "You! Diplomatic!" she exclaimed. "Never in a million years would I or anyone else who knows you say you could ever be diplomatic."

"Listen!" I snorted. "To get a two-year contract, I can be the most diplomatic person in the world. Anyway, first, we have to wait and see if Rob offers me the contract."

We spent Christmas Eve at the Sheraton Hotel in KL, along with our friends Tony and Dawn, and their son Phillip. It proved a choice, with both accommodation and dinner excellent. Although the actual evening was nothing special, we all had an enjoyable Christmas.

For New Year's Eve, we booked into the Dynasty Hotel in KL with our hash friends Colin and Josh. Although a muted affair like Christmas at the Sheraton, we had an excellent dinner, and a successful evening.

On waking New Year's Day, like most days in Malaysia, the sun was shining. Given this, we thought a dip in the rooftop swimming pool would be a great way to start the year. Unfortunately, there was no shelter from the sun, which, because of my delicate skin, was always necessary.

Just before deciding it time to leave, Josh said I appeared rather sunburned. As we had only been on the roof a short time, I thought nothing of it. However, after checking out of the hotel, Colin, and Josh drove us home.

As the evening approached, I discovered that Josh was right. Luckily, after putting on some special cream, I bought in a pharmacy, I felt okay.

In early January, when I phoned Rob Milford to see what news he had, I felt disappointed, things sounded doubtful. A week later, I received much worse news. It came in a phone call from my daughter, Kim, who informed me my mother was in the hospital. Kim, who was staying with mum, explained she had called an ambulance after finding her covered in blood. At the hospital, a doctor said she had suffered a haemorrhage.

I called the hospital to see how mum was, but there was no news. The next day, Kim called to say mum appeared a little better. I thought this good news. However, when Kim called a day later, I was shocked when she said my mother had died early that morning. Until taken to the hospital, mum had not been ill. Although in her eighties, she had been in health.

The next morning, I went to my office and informed them about my mother's death. I said that Jen, and I had to fly to the UK, A.S.A.P. Thankfully, the company managed to arrange our flights two days later.

By the time we arrived in Plymouth, thanks to Mums planning, Kim had arranged mum's funeral. It was a sad time, with several of mum's old friends and family present. Once over, Jen flew home to Turkey, while I returned to Malaysia.

As I had not received a formal contract offer from Rob, I phoned Michael in Bali to cancel the option to purchase a timeshare. Jen and I thought this was the best thing to do. After explaining the situation to Michael, I didn't expect to have any further dealings with him. However, a week later, to my surprise and delight, Rob called to invite me to meet the client in Manila. As I had not heard from him for some time, I thought my chances of being offered a contract had vanished. Therefore, I was more than happy to accept his invitation.

On arrival at Manila airport early one evening, I felt apprehensive about the next day's meeting. If all went well, Rob would offer me a contract, but, if the clients did not think me suitable, that would be it. After passing through passport control and going outside, I felt shocked. Stood behind a high fence on the other side of the road, was a solid mass of people. Later, I discovered that the airport only permitted ticket holders to enter inside. Among those waiting, I saw a man holding up a sign with my name. After going across and through a narrow gate, the man introduced himself as Rob Beastall.

On the drive to the site for a quick look around, Rob told me he was an advisor on the project. If all went well, we would be working together. Rob said at present, he dealt with quality issues regarding concrete works. However, once the external window cladding works started, he would also be dealing with this. With the project a fifty-two-story luxury apartment block, there would be plenty of work for both of us.

On leaving the site, Rob dropped me off at a hotel where he said I would stay the night. Shortly after checking in, Rob and his Chinese wife, Mary, came to take me out to dinner. During our meal, Rob explained they lived in a company apartment that was within walking distance of the project. From what I had seen of the traffic in Manila, I thought this an ideal situation.

The next morning, a driver came and drove me to John Laing's head

office, where I met Rob Milford. After a chat, we went to the site where he introduced to the Project Manager. To my disappointment, because of the client's representative being called to a meeting, he could not meet me. As I had flown over specially to meet him, I felt downcast when I flew back to KL in the evening.

The next day however, after receiving a fax from Rob Milford. I was over the moon to read that I would shortly receive a contract. I was then on tenterhooks until it arrived. In the meantime, I had to go to KL for a medical, a requirement before given the contract. As I had recently passed a medical for the Malaysian contract, I was not too worried about this. However, to my surprise, it revealed my blood pressure and cholesterol levels were a little high. Still, apart from this, I was in health.

The next day, I signed a two-year contract as an Interior Finishing Supervisor, with my contract beginning in March. This was a fabulous day; I had never before received such an extended one.

In early February, Jen, who was home in Turkey, called to say she had just received our bank statement. To my astonishment, the time share company in Bali had taken money from our credit card account. Michael had assured us the company would not take any money from my credit until we signed an agreement. Therefore, they should they have debited my card. I had only given them my card details in the event we wanted to proceed.

Despite numerous phone calls and faxes to Michael, it took several months before the company repaid our money. However, it was a lesson not to be forgotten. Never sign a credit card or debit form unless you are buying something at that moment.

The week before leaving Malaysia, I went to Richmond's office, where I handed in my passport to have my work permit cancelled. I then called in to see Chris at the Eden Browns local office. It was Chris who had arranged my initial interview for my new contract. Given this, I was most grateful to him.

Because of our considerable belongings that had to be packed, I phoned and asked Jen to come back and help me. She, of course, was more than happy to do so, and arrived two days later. We then sorted out the things we would take back to Turkey with us. Apart from these, I took several boxes to Eden Brown office, who would send them to Manila.

After completing our packing, a member of Richmond's staff came and checked the apartment. Once done, we went next door to say goodbye to Kelly and Sandra. They had become friends and more than helpful during our stay.

With mixed feelings, we then went to the airport for our long flight home. I felt sad about leaving Malaysia. It was a paradise for tourists, with the people both friendly and helpful. Had it not been for the money problem, I would not have resigned from my contract.

By the time we arrived in Turkey, it was mid-February, and only gave me a short time at home before I had to leave for the Philippines.

Dangerous times in the Philippines

# Chapter Sixteen
## Part 1

The Philippines is the 12 th most populated country in the world and has over 17,000 islands. Unfortunately, it also sits on the 'Ring of Fire,' and suffers from numerous earthquakes and volcanic eruptions. Still, as I lived in Turkey, I was not too worried when I arrived in Manila airport in 1998.

Like my previous visit, I found the mass of people waiting across the road from the arrivals area intimidating. Thankfully, among the jostling crowd, I spotted my new colleague Rob. After pushing through the crowd, Rob and I shook hands. On the drive into town, he said I would be staying at the Mandarin Hotel until I had found suitable accommodation. This I thought would be a great way to start my new contract. Once checked-in and leaving my case in my room, Rob drove me to his apartment.

As we walked in, Mary, his wife, greeted me with a broad smile. "Welcome back, Colin, it good to see you again, and I'm looking forward to meeting your wife when she arrives."

"Thank you. I'm sure it will please Jen to meet you as well." Rob and Mary lived in an apartment on the fourteenth floor of an eighteen-story apartment block. I found it furnished and much better than I expected. Given this, I knew Jen would enjoy living here. After a brief chat, we went out for dinner, then Rob drove me back to my hotel.

The next morning, I still felt jet-lagged when Rob came to take me to the project site. It took aback me to find it right next door to the hotel.

On my arrival, construction works were only up to the ninth floor. Once completed, at 52 stories, it would tower over all the other nearby buildings. At twice the height of the Hyatt and the Westin Hotel, it would be the tallest building I had ever worked on. At the site, Rob led me to a small room he used as an office. It contained just two basic looking desks and two plastic chairs. Although not what I was used to having as an office, my place would be on-site.

The joint owners of the project employed Rob and I as advisors. Our job was to check and make up reports on anything we deemed unacceptable quality. Once issued to the prime contractor and the joint owners, they would decide to either perform our recommendations or ignore them.

In the afternoon, Rob took me to the client's office and introduced me to the director in charge of the project. He apologised for not being able to meet me on my previous visit, with my accepting his apology.

After two nights in the hotel, Rob said I would meet Lourdes, a woman member of our office staff the next morning. To my delight, he said she would be showing me an apartment. "It is only a short distance from my apartment block," he said. "But unlike mine, it's only nine floors high."

When I met Lourdes in the apartment foyer, the glistening white marble walls and flooring impressed me. Knowing Lourdes, a waiting doorman allowed us to go upstairs in the lift. On exiting it, it surprised me to find myself inside the apartment entrance hall. As we walked around, I whistled in appreciation. The apartment looked fabulous, being large, well-furnished, with gleaming light-coloured marble flooring. There were two bedrooms, each with an en-suite bathroom, with the lounge/dining room large enough for a game of football. It also had a good-sized kitchen and a separate maid's area. Rob having explained that maids were not expensive, with it typical to have one. This I knew would delight Jen when she arrived.

Lourdes explained that I was fortunate in being offered this apartment. It had only become available after one of our managers became transferred to another country. This was like a dream come true. I had never received such a beautiful company apartment in any of my contracts.

On leaving the apartment, I went back and checked out of the hotel. When I moved into the apartment that afternoon, I wore a huge smile of satisfaction. Not only was it a fabulous apartment, but Linda, the maid who had worked for our manager, was available if required. I met her two days later, with my delighted when she agreed to work for me.

A week after I arrived in Manila, they delivered the goods I had sent over from Malaysia.

At work, I soon found Rob and I were wasting our time in making up our reports. The prime contractor never seemed to take any notice of them. Talking to Rob about this, he shrugged. "This is what we have to put up with on this project." "This was not good. I was used to having action taken to remedy any complaints I made. Still, with my being well paid and living in a rent free luxury apartment, I had to grin and accept it.

As construction works continued, the number of floors climbed upwards. However, with it only concrete works, it kept Rob busy., leaving me little to do, so I used to accompany Rob during his inspections.

On the social side, things good. Rob took me to a quiz night at the 'Prince of Wales' pub, known as the P.O.W. Here I met a number of British expats who also worked in Manila. Among them were Jane, and Glen, who worked for my company on another local project. There was also Peter and Frances, Mike, and Sue, plus another couple, Alan, and Joanna. Everyone proved friendly, and we all got on well together. Without Jen, quiz nights were the highlight of my social life, with my time spent with friends enjoyable.

A month after my arrival, Jen arrived. She, like me, felt intimidated by the crowd waiting outside the arrivals area. After a warm embrace, Jen relaxed as a company driver drove us to our apartment block. Although impressed when greeted by our doorman, when Jen stepped out of the lift and into our glitzy apartment foyer, her face beamed with delight. "Wow! Now, this is really something." She waved a hand. This is a world of difference from the apartment we had in Malaysia."

I chuckled. "Yes, it is. Oh, did I tell you we have a maid who's also a fabulous cook?"

Jens eyebrows shot up. "What! You are joking!" She exclaimed.

Shaking my head, I said. "Just a minute, I'll call her. Linda, would you come here, please?"

The next minute Linda walked in. "Afternoon, Madam, I'm pleased to meet you." From that moment on, Linda was not only a maid; but part of our family.

The next morning, I took Jen out for a walk around the central shopping area that included the vast Glorietta Shopping Mall and several other large stores. As we did, Jen commented on the thousands of people thronging the streets. "This is much busier than Surabaya in Indonesia." She shook her head. "I can't believe how many people there are here."

I grinned. "If you look closer, you'll see most are young. The average age here is under twenty-one."

With the Glorietta Mall so crowded; we had difficulty finding somewhere to have lunch. On leaving the Mall, we stood outside with a crowd of people awaiting a traffic police officer to stop the traffic. The minute he did, a surge of humanity swept us across the road.

As we stepped on to the pavement, Jen grabbed my arm. "Oh! My handbag is open." After a quick check, in a trembling voice, she said. "My reading glasses have gone. Someone must have taken them while we were waiting for the traffic to stop." Fortunately, nothing else was missing, and Jen had brought a spare pair of with her. From then on, Jen kept her handbag around her neck and in front of her.

When I later mentioned this to Rob, he apologised. "Sorry, I should have warned you to be careful when out with Jen. Handbag theft is a big problem here."

On quiz night, I took Jen to the P.O.W., where I introduced her to the gang. When I told them what had happened to Jen's handbag, one girl nodded. "It's not only a problem, it's an enormous problem." She then went on to said, "Never leave your bag on a chair when you go to order drinks or go to the bathroom. If you do, it will have gone when you return." She shook her head. "I know from experience, after having my handbag stolen."

"Thanks for the warning," Jen said. "I'll be more careful from now on." She then retold how a thief had stolen her handbag in Malaysia.

"You were lucky," one girl said. "A girl, who had the strap of her handbag over her head, had it snatched by a man on the back of a passing motorbike. As she couldn't let it go, they dragged her along the road before the man let go." She shuddered, then added, "The poor woman is now a paraplegic."

"Oh my God, that's terrible!" Jen exclaimed.

"Yes, it is, so be warned. If someone grabs your handbag; let it go."

One of my favourite places to go for both entertainment and food was the Hobbit House. It was a unique restaurant, being owned, run, and managed by dwarfs. With it advertised as the only such place in the world. I first went there with Jane and Glyn.

As they had not said, it surprised me when a dwarf served me. It proved an unusual experience, and I enjoyed the evening so much; it became the first of my frequent visits.

I took Jen there one evening without telling her about the dwarfs. She was delighted to see them, but on hearing the music played by a group named Lampang Alley, she was even more pleased. Apart from an American harmonica player, the group were all Filipinos. We especially liked listening to the lead singer, who had such a powerful voice; he didn't need to use a microphone. He could sing ballads and rock music with incredible feeling. On the nights the group played, the restaurant became packed, and unless you had booked a table, you could not get in. Even if not eating, the glee of listening to the group's music made it worthwhile to sit there.

Even though the restaurant is usually crowded, the dwarfs had no issues serving. We found them friendly and happy to have their photo taken with customers. A picture taken with them was a successful souvenir to remind you of being in such a unique restaurant.

One sad thing about the Hobbit House was the young children who used to sleep outside. On my first visit, seeing large pieces of cardboard on the pavement, I thought it rubbish left lying around. To my disbelief, Jane informed me, it was used to cover the children who slept there.

When Jen and I first took a trip to Greenhills, an out-of-town shopping centre, the enormous amount of traffic amazed us. It included large numbers of Jeepneys that are particular to the Philippines. These vary in size from small jeeps to large mini-buses, all of which are painted in bright colours. With a variety of hanging decorations stuck on the windscreen and windows, they are a fantastic sight.

Another amazing sight were the countless single-decker buses packed with passengers. Because of the black, evil-smelling exhaust fumes, they emitted; most countries would ban them. At night, hundreds of these buses formed a continuous stream of traffic on the main highway. With, each bus jam-packed with workers on their way home, this type of situation has to be seen to be believed.

Although I found the on-site work boring, the social life was much better than on any of my previous overseas contracts. Jen and I had a lot of fun on quiz nights, with the competition between the various groups serious. However, whether we won or lost, we enjoyed the company.

At one time, Jane, a friend of ours, took Jen to see her house. On her return, Jen told me of her shock while going there. "When we reached the main road." Jane said, '*Look up, we have to cross here.*' "With a continuous flow of traffic, I thought she was joking. Then, when she grabbed my hand, and we walked out into the traffic, it petrified me. I thought for sure we would get knocked down and killed, but to my amazement, we somehow managed to cross without incident."

Jen was in rapture as she continued. "Jane and her husband David, known as Wal, have a beautiful swimming pool at their house. With chairs and tables set up under what is part of the roof, it's where they entertain guests." She paused, then said. "Although they live in a village, it is not what you might think. It comprises many detached houses set inside a high walled perimeter fence. It also has strict security at the various gates leading into the village. Jane told me that before you're allowed in, a security guard asked who you are visiting. They then call to ask if you may enter. If the answer is no, the security guard turns you away. Even taxis could not enter the village unless you had previously given their details to the gate."

Impressed, I said. "Wow! Now that's what I call security."

From that initial meeting, we became firm friends with Jane and Wal. We spent a lot of time with them in Manila, as well as after they left.

During our first year in Manila, Jen and I enjoyed a fabulous social life. We dined out with friends at various restaurants and attended dinner parties at their houses. In return, we held dinner parties at our apartment. With Linda being such a successful cook, we always received compliments about the meals she served.

Apart from dinner parties, we also attended several balls. As neither Jen nor I had never done so before, we found them a fantastic experience. Given this, I made use of the Tuxedo I had made in Indonesia for the hash dinner party.

Before we knew it, December was upon us. Jen and I flew back to England to spend Christmas with our two daughters and grandchild.

After returning to Manila on my own in early January, I attended a 1960-70s party at a friend's house. I've always felt the music from that time was the best, so I enjoyed a successful evening.

A week after Jen returned to Manila, our daughter Kim, arrived for a holiday. She was fortunate, as Jen and I were about to leave for a free weekend at the Shangri-la Hotel in Cebu. We had won this during a raffle at a ball we attended the previous year. Luckily, we arranged for Kim to accompany us. After all, we couldn't leave her alone just after her arrival. At Cebu, we spent a relaxing and enjoyable weekend at the hotel, away from the hustle and bustle of Manila. Also, the air was fresh, a far cry from back in the city.

On our return to the airport, we found our flight delayed for five hours. Still, this was not too much problem. We had enjoyed a successful weekend, plus, it cost little for Kim to join us. It also made a pleasant break for Kim, who on her return home, would start work for the season as a tour rep .

A few weeks after Kim left, Jen and I attended 'The Glitter Ball,' where despite the mediocre music, the ball lived up to its name. The women, including Jen, looked fantastic in a variety of glittering ball gowns, with the men, including yours truly, elegant in tuxedos and wearing bow ties.

While Jen was back in England, Jane surprised me. "Colin, I know Jen is due back in two days, but the girls and I have planned a trip to the island of Boracay next weekend. Do you think she would like to join us? It's unfortunate, but I have to know now, as I'm making the bookings for flight and accommodation."

As I knew all the girls were friendly, I had no hesitation in said, "That sounds successful. Please book Jen in. If she were here, I know she would accept in a flash."

Jane flashed a smile. "You're right, and I'm sure Jen will be happy that you accepted on her behalf. Tell her we will leave on Friday morning. Oh, she won't need much to wear; it's just a basic beach resort."

My decision to book Jen on the trip without first asking if it would interest her might seem absurd, but I knew she would be delighted at my doing so. On the evening Jen arrived back, her eyes opened wide with delight when I told her.

"Oh, that sounds fantastic!" She exclaimed. "Thank you so much."

When I left for work that morning, Jen wore a big smile. She was bubbling with excitement about going on holiday with a bunch of girls, and not a husband in sight.

# Part 2

On her return, Jen was full of it, and told me all of what they had done. "The trip over to the island was an adventure in itself," she said. "My first surprise was seeing the fuselage of our plane as it came into land on a grass runway. With it covered in pictures of flowers, it took me back to the Hippy Days." Then, on leaving the airport, instead of taxis, our transport to the beach was by motorcycle and sidecar."

"What! You are joking?" I said.

"No! nevertheless, after my initial nerves, I found the Motorcycle ride an experience. Nevertheless, I was pleased to find it only a short distance to the beach. Here we boarded a boat fitted with what Jane told me were outriggers, which with about twenty passengers was full. Nevertheless, about a half-hour later, we came in sight of a long sandy beach. All I could see were a few buildings set back among a line of palm trees. As I stood gazing towards the shore, Jane nudged me. '*Well, here we are. Welcome to Boracay.*'

It looked fabulous, even better than Bali. To my surprise, the boat stopped a short distance from the shore. The captain said, '*OK everyone, this is as close as we can get. From here, you have to walk ashore.*" He chuckled. "*Don't worry, though; the water is shallow and warm.*'

I thought he was joking, but then some passengers jumped over the side into the knee-deep water. Holding their bags high, they started wading towards the beach. You know me; I was frightened I would fall over in the water. When I told the captain my concern, he said, 'No problem, I'll give you a piggyback to the beach.' Before I could say anything, he jumped overboard. After I scrambled onto his back, he carried me up to the beach."

I chuckled. "So," I said, "it sounds like you had a good start to your holiday."

"Yes, and things only got better. Our accommodation was in chalets set on the beautiful, clean, soft, white sandy beach. What with that and the different shades of the blue sea, it's a fantastic place. Apart from in films, I've never seen such an amazing place. After changing into our swimsuits, we went exploring. We called in at one bar where they had live music. By the time we left, it was late." She sighed in cheerful remembrance. "There is nothing to do at Boracay, so we spent our time eating and drinking at several of the bars lining the beach. Anyway, I've had a fabulous time, so thank you so much for arranging for me to go with the girls. They are a great bunch."

About a week after Jen's return, our friends Glyn and Jane, invited us to join them on a trip to Crocodile Island. This Glyn said, obtained its name from its silhouette that looks like a crocodile. To reach the island, we first had to fly to Cebu, and then take a boat across to the island. Although none of us had any idea what would be on the island, it would be an adventure. However, little did we know what a dangerous experience it would prove to be.

At Cebu, we took a taxi down to the seashore where we found a boat waiting to take us over to the island. It's called a 'Banka,' and fitted with large outriggers, as, Jen had earlier mentioned. With the only shelter on the boat, a small central cabin, it looked like boats seen in films about the South Pacific.

Our trip over to the island took thirty minutes, where on arrival, a man greeted us. He then led us to a where concealed among the palm trees lining the beach, he said our meals would be served. With our accommodation in timber chalets, Jen and I were pleased when given one on the beautiful, soft sand. Glyn and Jane were a few yards back on the edge of a trail. This we later found, wound its way along the coastline, amid swaying palm trees.

To my surprise, they constructed both chalets and furniture from bamboo, with the chalets blending in well with the surroundings. Additionally, they used roll down bamboo window blinds instead of glass in the windows, and they covered the openings with mosquito nets.

After walking first in one direction, and then the other way down the trail, we realised there was nothing on the island. Still, we thought it not a problem, and could enjoy the peace of the island, with neither the sound of man nor beast disturbing the tranquillity. Just to sit relaxing on the sandy beach was enough. Another bonus, although nothing special, the meals served were both filling and tasty.

One morning, as we sat on a wall by the jetty, we noticed a large Banka approaching the island. As it grew nearer, I felt puzzled to see it loaded down with what looked like palm trees. However, as the boat drew closer, I could see it was not palm trees, but hundreds of palm fronds. Once tied to the jetty, the men put down a gangplank and started to offload them.

When I asked one man what the fronds were for, he said, "They are to replace the damaged roofs of the chalets." It seems this happened during a recent typhoon that had swept across the island.

After a few glorious days of chilling out on the island, we set off on our return trip to the mainland.

Because of heavy rain, we all sat huddled up inside the small cabin. The boat became buffeted and rocked this way and that as it strained to make headway through the churning seas. About half an hour later, when I glanced behind us, I was shocked by what I saw. The island was still in sight. Because of its low silhouette, it should have been invisible. I also noticed the waves were higher than I expected. It explained why we were not making much progress. My surprise turned to horror when I saw one of the crew climb overboard. To my astonishment, he started a slow and perilous way out to the outrigger. With the seas crashing over it, it was a dangerous thing to attempt. As I watched this frightening scene, with considerable difficulty, the man reached the outrigger. I sighed with relief. The man would have been swept away with no prospect of being rescued if he had lost his grip on the way. His loss would then have put all on board in extreme danger.

Although unable to see what he did, he must have released the locking fastenings holding the outrigger in place. After fighting his way back on board, he and the other crew member slowly dragged the outrigger towards the edge of our violently rocking boat. Once secured in place, the boat's engine that had been idle while the man worked on the outrigger—was re-started. Without the drag of the outrigger, we slowly but surely started making better progress through the surging waves. After what then seemed like a lifetime, we reached the shore.

Compared to our trip over, our terrifying journey back from the island had taken one and a half hours. I only hoped I would not have to endure such a trip again. Thankfully, once back at the airport, our flight back to Manila was uneventful.

Ine evening, Peter, and Frances invited Rob and Caroline plus Jen and me to their house for an egg decoration contest. It being something neither Jen nor I had done before. Using various bits and pieces to add arms, legs, and glasses, etc., we made up a variety of designed eggs. It's amazing what you can do to an ordinary egg, to turn it into something strange and unusual. For sure, it made for an entertaining evening.

During a phone call with my son-in-law Niko, he told me of his idea of extending the line of silver items he sold at a local market. When I told him about the variety of silver objects one could buy here, he was interested. After making enquiries, I found two companies that made silver items for export. I later visited their factories to see what, and how much they made cost. Plus, of course, the quality. The designs and quality of artistry looked excellent, so I phoned and informed Niko. He said this sounded good, but with the addition of shipping charges, he could not sell them at a profit. I agreed with his thoughts so bought a few pieces to show him an example of what was on offer. When I later gave them to Niko, his eyes lit up. After he put them on sale with his other silver items, he sold them a short time later. Regrettably, there was no feasible solution to avoid the shipping costs.

With the Philippines offering a diverse selection of inexpensive products, it is worthwhile to explore import-export possibilities.

While attending a client's meeting, they informed me that Chito, a Filipino architect and I would be going to Holland and then Germany. In Holland, we would check out the factory that was supplying the timber flooring for our project. In Germany, we would and visit Poggenpohl, the luxury kitchen supplier. This was great news. Not only would it enable me to get off-site for a while, but I would also visit two countries I had never visited.

The following Monday, because of Chito having a prior arrangement, I flew alone to Holland. On my arrival, I found Toby, a senior designer involved with our project, waiting to meet me. A driver then took us to the factory where we met Tom, the owner. As we walked inside, I stopped in my tracks. Instead of using an automated system for manufacture the boards as expected, they were using a standard routing machine. This was not good.

On checking a selection of boards, we found them well below the quality and color range agreed upon earlier. To make matters worse, one container of boards was already on its way to Manila. Toby told Tom to inspect the thousands of stacked boards before loading them into another container. He clarified that the quality and colour must match the agreed, signed sample boards.

After spending the night in a hotel, the next day, Toby and I met Chito at the airport, where after a brief discussion, Toby left to return to Hong Kong.

As I expected, although Chito was far from pleased with the situation at Tom's factory, it was too late to change things. On our way to the factory, Chito informed me there had been a change of plans. Because of a public holiday in Germany, we could not visit the Poggenpohl factory until the Sunday. It then pleased me when he said, "Instead, we will fly to Munich and spend a few days with my brother and his wife.

After a brief talk with Tom, a driver took us to the hotel where I stayed the previous night. The next morning after a further discussion with Tom, a driver drove us to the airport. At Munich, Chito's brother met and then drove us to his home. It turned out that the town was in a quiet area, several hours away from the airport. Here I enjoyed several days with Chito's brother and his wife.

On leaving them, we flew to Hanover, where we visited the Poggenpohl factory. This we found a far cry from Tom's factory, it being fully automated, and spotlessly clean. On inspection, the quality of manufactured units impressed us, being first class. After spending the night in a hotel, we returned for another inspection. Once completed, a driver took us to the airport for our return to Manila.

Because of the change of plans, after I had left Manila, I had to purchase a ticket to fly back to Munich. Later, whereas Chito only had a brief wait before catching a flight to Manila, I, had a KLM ticket. With no flights available until the next day, after spending the night in a hotel, the next morning I flew back to Manila.

The trip had proved interesting, especially in Germany where I enjoyed my visit to the small town near where Chito's brother lived. With a beautiful old church and streets full of quaint looking houses, I found it attractive.

Once back on the site, Chito and I raised our concerns about the quality of the timber plank boards we had seen at the factory. However, Tom, who was in attendance, assured us he had put stricter controls in place regarding quality. This, however, we later found to be incorrect.

One weekend, Jen and I attended the 'Queens Ball,' where apart from enjoying a successful evening, we also won a raffle prize. It being a night for two at the five-star Peninsula Hotel in Makati. We found the afternoon high tea so delicious; we went there every so often for a treat. I thought it novel to be served by servers wearing crisp black and white outfits. They served up dainty cups of tea, along with a selection of small cakes, displayed on a tiered cake stand. It being how a typical old-fashioned English Afternoon Tea was served.

At one time, Jen and I took part in an organised treasure hunt. This involved participants searching for clues hidden in and around one of the walled-in villages. Because of its size, although we travelled around in cars, it still took all afternoon to complete. I am sure that the village residents must have wondered why a series of vehicles were passing by in front of their houses. Nevertheless, we enjoyed a successful day, with our team winning first prize.

During a dinner party at our apartment, along with several friends, we also invited Tunca from the Turkish Embassy. Thanks to Linda, the evening proved a successful success. It also proved the start of a relationship with the Embassy. This proved helpful when we required new residence permits for our return home to Turkey. It being necessary, as because of our long- time away, we had let our old ones lapse.

At a quiz night one evening, we were delighted to win both the first and second prizes. Our evening became spoiled; however, when Caroline, my employer's wife, came in. We were shocked when she informed us that our Asia director had died. I had met him several times and thought him a genuine type of person, who always appeared to be in good health.

About a month later, Caroline called in to see us. She was bubbling with excitement. "I have news and news. They have promoted Rob to take over as JLI, Asia director."

Although Jen and I were happy for Rob, we also felt sad. Because of our Asian head office being in Hong Kong, Rob, and Caroline would be moving there.

# Part 3

At one time, I didn't feel well, so I went to the doctor. To my surprise, he said my blood pressure and cholesterol were higher than usual. Given this, I started to take daily walks around the small park opposite our apartment block. Jen also informed Linda, who cut down on what she considered unhealthy foods. In fairness, I think my problem arose from the amount of food and drink I was consuming. This I'm sure this was due in part to the number of dinner parties and balls we attended.

One Sunday, a group of us went to Sonia's Secret Garden for lunch. We had heard it was an experience not to be missed. To our surprise, there was no menu. Instead, you ate whatever dish Sonia had chosen to make that day. Also, because of the vegetarian restaurant set-up in part of her home, Sonia only accepted confirmed bookings. We leaned that Sonia grew virtually everything she served. When we went there, it was winter, with a strong wind blowing. With the restaurant primarily outdoors, we were pleased when Sonia provided thick jumpers and windproof jackets for all those in need of them. These were much appreciated, as without them, we would not have enjoyed the time spent eating and talking with Sonia. For sure, we found dining at Sonia's Secret Garden an experience. So, should you ever be in the area, it's something I recommend you try.

On one trip back to Turkey, with my luggage well overweight, I had to pay a £45 excess charge. From experience, I have found it all depends on the person at the check-in desk, as to whether you get charged or not.

While at home in Turkey, Anita, Niko, and the kids arrived for a holiday. A few days later, while Jen stayed with Anita and the kids, Niko and I flew up to Kirsehir. We went there to meet Ugur, my old friend from Uçgün, who wanted to discuss a possible business venture. After meeting us at the airport, he drove us to a hotel in Cappadocia where we spent the night. On the way, Ugur spoke about his idea of our taking over the running of a hotel. This I thought could prove interesting, and would make a change from traveling the world.

The next morning, we had a meeting with the head of the Kirsehir Belidiye (council). During this, he informed us there was another group interested in taking over the hotel. As Ugur spoke little English, Niko who had come to interpret, told me what they discussed.

On leaving the Belidiye, we went to see the hotel. Although a good size, the hotel had not undergone modernisation for years. As such, it would cost a sum of money to update. In return, however, whoever they awarded the running of the hotel would receive a five-year contract. Without such an extended deal, it would not have been a viable venture.

One of the Belidiye conditions for awarding the hotel, they wanted ideas on how to attract more business to the area. As I fancied the idea of running the hotel, I made up a list of things I thought would help us obtain the contract. I gave this to Ugur, who then drove us to the airport.

On the way back to Kemer, Niko told me he was unconvinced about the hotel being an idea. However, as we did not obtain the contract, I never discovered if he was right or wrong.

A short time after our return home, Niko, and Anita bought a tree to plant over Ashley's grave in the garden, which Jen and I considered a sympathetic gesture. Because of ill health, we had to put Ashley down, with his passing leaving Jen and I devastated.

A week after I arrived back in Manila, my friend Talat phoned me from Turkey. To my surprise, he was going to attend a trade exhibition in China and asked if I would like to join him for the weekend. If so, I could stay with him at his hotel. With it only a short flight from Manila, and the fare inexpensive, I accepted. We planned to meet at the arrivals area in Hong Kong, then fly on to Guangzhou where the exhibition was being held. Talat was attending the fair, as he and his partner had a fabric factory in Istanbul. They supplied clothing to numerous shops in Turkey and also had the copyright to several of their own brands.

As I stood awaiting Talat's arrival, I spotted him approaching, but then he disappeared. Ongoing to investigate, I found him standing inside one of the nearby smoking booths. As a smoker on a non-smoking long-haul flight, he must have felt desperate for a smoke. On finishing his cigarette and coming outside, his face lit up at seeing me standing there.

He chuckled. "Sorry, Colin, but I needed that."

"No problem," I said. I chuckled. Still, I had wondered where you disappeared."

After going to departures, and a short wait, we flew on to Guangzhou. On arrival, we took a taxi to the hotel, then once checked in, we went to the exhibition hall.We found it enormous and packed with hundreds of stands. All kinds of clothing, hats, boots, and everything in between were on offer. What impressed me the most was the remarkably low prices. At one stall selling sandals like the ones I wore; they were the equivalent of £11, while mine had cost around £35. Had I not seen the prices asked, I would never have believed it possible to buy goods so inexpensive. It was a real eye-opener.

The following day at the exhibition, Talat purchased large quantities of various items. The next morning, we flew back to Hong Kong., where after thanking Talat for attending the exhibition, we said our goodbyes. He went to join the other Turkish entrepreneurs for the flight back to Turkey, while I went to check in for my return flight to Manila.

At the desk, I became shocked when an official informed me that I didn't have a visa to enter the Philippines. This news hit me hard. Without a permit, I could not re-enter the country. After insisting I had a valid visa, they summoned a supervisor. On checking, she confirmed I had no visa in my passport. Given this, she said I could not take my flight to Manila. Only after my pleading and saying I had a permit, did she finally relent. "Alright, I will let you fly, but if you cannot enter the country, you will have to pay for a flight back here."

I felt so relieved on hearing this; I could have kissed her. After thanking her multiple times, I checked in and caught my flight to Manila. No sooner had we landed and off the plane, I called our office and spoke to Lourdes. "Lourdes, its Colin. I'm in Manila airport and have a problem. When I went to check-in at the Hong Kong airport, they told me I didn't have a visa. Only after some persuasion did a supervisor agree to let me board the plane."

"Colin, we renewed your visa a few months ago."

"That's what I thought, but despite checking through my passport several times, we couldn't find it."

"Alright, where are you now?"

"I'm standing in the corridor on the way to passport control."

"Right, stay there. I'll check and call you back."

I then stood anxiously, awaiting her call. As soon as my phone rang, I answered it.

"Colin, if you look on page 34, you will find your visa."

With trembling fingers, I checked through my passport. Initially, I couldn't find the page, but then found two pages were stuck together. With care, I opened them. I then breathed an enormous sigh of relief to see my missing visa.

"Oh, thank you, Lourdes," I explained about the stuck pages, then with a spring in my walk, I passed through customs.

One weekend, Jen and I took a trip out to Greenhills Shopping Centre, which as usual we found packed. People were pushing and shoving while going upstairs on a narrow escalator. When I got off at the top and turned to talk to Jen, to my surprise, she was only halfway up. As she reached the top, I said, "I thought you were behind me."

She turned back and snapped at me. "It was those stupid girls. One was afraid to get on, with everyone pushed up against her."

On looking to see who she meant, I became suspicious. I had seen this same group of girls standing near us several times when we stopped to look in shop windows. It made me uneasy. I had a feeling about these girls. After a short time looking around, we went back down. No sooner had we done so, when a minute later, I noticed the same bunch of girls stood nearby.

"That's it, we're leaving," I said. "Those girls are following us."

On the way back to town, we decided to call in at the 'Outback' an Australian restaurant franchise outlet for lunch. Here the meals were, substantial, filling, and the prices reasonable.

As we walked upstairs to sit down, Jen said, "I'm going to the bathroom, you order for me."

Before a server arrived to take our order, Jen reappeared from the bathroom. I noticed she looked close to tears, so asked. "What on the earth's the matter? You look terrible."

"Look! " she said, turned her handbag that was hanging over her shoulder towards me. "I've just seen it."

I gasps. Someone had split her bag open from top to bottom. "What's gone?" I asked.

"Only my purse. As we were going to Greenhills, I didn't take anything else with me."

I thought for a minute, then nodded. "I know who did this. Do you remember the girl you said was afraid to step on the escalator? She was not afraid; she only pretended to be. It allowed the girl behind you to push up against you. That's when she slashed your handbag open," I shrugged. " Given what happened, I was right to leave when we did." I chuckled. "Still, it's a job you were not carrying much money or anything of value with you."

Jens' eyebrows flared. "Never mind the money!" She retorted. "I liked this handbag. Now it's ruined."

When massive demonstrations broke out against the then-President, it split the country into two camps. Those who supported him, and those against. Things came to a head one day when both sides of the main highway became packed with thousands of supporters squaring up against each other. The situation became so tense; it only needed a spark to set off a frenzy of violence between them. Thankfully, the President agreed to step down from power. Without a doubt, his doing so saved the deaths and injuries of a great many people.

From what I can remember, only one man, a police officer, lost his life during this terrifying situation. This incident became the first case that coined the words 'People Power.'

Jen told me one day that Idris, one of our Turkish friends, had asked if he could visit us for a holiday. After I agreed, the following week I went to pick him up from the airport. When Idris appeared, my surprise was evident. He only carried a plastic shopping bag. When I asked where his case was, he replied, "I never brought one. Things are so cheap here; I can buy whatever I need." During his two weeks with us, because of his buying numerous items, Idris had to buy a suitcase to take them back to Turkey.

Shortly before his return to Turkey, we all went to the Hobbit House for dinner. After a successful evening, we returned to our apartment around 1.30 am. While saying goodnight to Idris, there came a sudden loud bang. Then, before anyone of us could ask what happened, the room started to shake. The movement started slight, but then accelerated in tempo. As I clung tight to Jen, she called out in alarm, "What's happening?"

I laughed when Idris calmly replied, "Don't worry! It's only an earthquake; we can all die together."

Jen's eyebrows shot up to her hairline. As she started to answer Idris, the shaking stopped. "Are you mad!" she exclaimed, "I don't want any of us to die, especially in an earthquake."

As the shaking stopped, on looking out the window, I noticed numerous people were going into the park opposite.

The next morning, Rob told me what happened to them after the earthquake struck. "Because of concerns about aftershocks, we were told to evacuate the building and head to the park. Here we joined other residents from different apartment blocks, who like us were instructed to leave their apartments."

> "That's strange," I said. "We were never told to leave ours." I shrugged. "Perhaps it was because our building is only nine floors high, whereas yours and others are all over sixteen."

On talking to friends who lived a short distance from our apartment, I had to smile when they told me what happened to them when the earthquake occurred. "*We were asleep, and woke to find the bed shaking across the floor.*"

As he and his wife were no lightweights, I could well imagine the shock of their terrifying experience.

From what we later heard; we were fortunate. The earthquake had only lasted a short time. On the news, it said that had it continued another ten seconds, it would have resulted in significant destruction.

Although fortunate to escape unharmed, the experience of going through an earthquake is not one I recommend.

A week after Idris had returned to Turkey, Jen and I went to Balikpapan, a large souvenir shop,. Here we checked out the cost of the wooden bars they sold. These wooden bars were unusual because they were made from the base of a tree. Once polished, it looked similar to mahogany. Sections of the thick roots acted as a solid base. The polished top being formed from a natural cut of the trunk. In this way, no two bars were the same. They looked so unique; that on seeing them, they became an instant talking point. Unfortunately, when we went to buy one, we could not find one without damage or wormholes. Therefore, with deep disappointment, we did not buy one.

In early December Jen and I attended a carol service in the grounds of the British Embassy. We found it well attended with various people joining in the singing, and proved to be the start of the festive season. Once in full swing, we found it a pleasure to walk around the streets strewn with a vast amount of lights and decorations. However, this was nothing compared to what we found when visiting friends in various villages. It amazed us to see the fabulous decorative displays set-up in gardens and outside numerous houses. These included brightly lit reindeers, sledges, and Father Christmases of all different sizes. The entire neighborhood was filled with houses covered in colorful lights and decorations, each trying to outshine the other. Never had we seen such a fantastic display of decorations. We misjudged it because of the forthcoming millennium celebrations. However, friends informed us this was a typical occurrence during the Christmas season in the Philippines.

Jen, and I celebrated Christmas at a large party held at Jane and Wal's house. The evening was a successful success, with Jane, a fantastic cook, served up a meal fit for a king. To round things off, there was plenty to drink, including some excellent champagne.

What with the warm weather and a large swimming pool, numerous people enjoyed a refreshing swim.

We enjoyed a fabulous Christmas evening,

# Part 4

On New Year's Eve, along with Rob, Caroline, David, and Jackie Bosher, we checked into the Mandarin Hotel. They were putting on a party to celebrate the New Millennium. Ongoing up to our rooms, we were far from pleased. Although our floor was supposed to be for adults only, we found children running around. No doubt their parents had paid extra to have their children with them on this once in a lifetime experience.

In the ballroom where dinner would be served, we found numerous tables established. On stage were two groups who would provide the evening's entertainment. Given the speciality of the night, both young and old packed the dance floor all out enjoying themselves.

Only the table service spoiled the evening, it, with our kept waiting long after people coming in after us had been served. As a result, Rob had a server fetch a manager to our table. When he arrived, Rob complained about the poor service. He told the manager that his company frequently booked guests into the hotel and it had deeply disappointed him. The manager was most apologetic, and said the problem was because of the numerous people being served.

When the countdown reached midnight, we toasted each other with champagne, a perfect way to see in the New Millennium. Then, we went outside and watched a fantastic fireworks display. It felt good stood among crowds of people singing and enjoying themselves, with it an evening I shall never forget.

The next evening, along with Rob and Caroline, Jen and I went to a Japanese restaurant for dinner. Here I watched in fascination as a chef behind a Tepanyaki counter set to work. He cut up meat, fish, and vegetables in the blink of an eye, and then cooked them.

433

To my amazement, in a matter of minutes, he served up a variety of steaming hot, and tasty dishes. As this was the first time I had ever witnessed or eaten food served this way, I found it an experience.

The Turkish Ambassador to his residence to welcome Beste, who had just arrived to assume her position as the new ambassador invited one evening, Jen and. We later invited her and Halit, another Turkish friend, to dinner at our apartment. Halit we found, had recently taken over a company specialising in exporting household effects. Given this, we discussed the possibility of shipping things back to Turkey. Because of our previous problem, we were dubious about doing so, but Halit assured us things had changed. Plus, his brother, who lived in Istanbul, would help us if the need required.

One evening, Jen and I went to see 'Miss Saigon' at a theatre in town. We found it an incredible experience, with both actors and scenery proving to be first class. As we enjoyed it so much, when Kim came out the following month, we took her to see the show. Afterwards, Kim said she had seen the show in London years earlier, but here the sound effects with the helicopter were much better.

On 'Burns Night,' our friend Alistair invited us to join him and his wife Elle for a celebration supper at his club. It being the first time I had tasted Haggis, the traditional Scottish delicacy. This I found tasty, and not as expected, but no doubt the whiskey poured over it helped improve the taste.

A few weeks later, Chris and Karen invited Jen and me to their house for a party. On our arrival, as Chris was a Royal Naval Attaché, we found diplomats from various countries in attendance. During a talk with some of them, a woman standing with us said she worked at the British Embassy in Ankara. When Jen heard this, she dropped a bombshell.

"Oh! Then you must know B—J—S." Initially, there was shocked silence, and then everyone burst out laughed. For me, however, it had been embarrassing.

While Jen was back in Turkey, I received an invitation to an evening at the Turkish Embassy, so dressed in my tuxedo, I attended. To my surprise, the first person I met waiting to go inside was not wearing a dinner suit. Instead, he wore a traditional Filipino dress shirt. When we entered, I became even more surprised. Apart from the servers, no one else wore a tuxedo. I mistakenly assumed it was a black-tie event. It did, however, cause me amusement, as while stood there, two ladies asked which country I represented. No doubt it disappointed them when I said, "I am not a diplomat, just a guest in a tuxedo."

On another evening, Mike, one of my friends, invited me to join him at a golf driving range. After watching him for a while, I borrowed one of his clubs and took a few swings at the ball. Although I had never swung a golf club before, to my surprise, some of my swings propelled the ball (to me) a distance. As a result, I then accompanied Mike to the driving range every week. I had considered learning to play golf while in Malaysia, but the lessons were so expensive, I did not. However, as costs here were much lower, I booked lessons from one of the golf pros. During one lesson, he told me he had a second-hand set of clubs for sale. As they looked okay, and were I thought a reasonable price, I bought them.

When Kim returned for another holiday; she was again fortunate. Along with Mike and his wife Suzanne, Jen and I, had booked to go to Boracay for the weekend. After a few calls, I managed to arrange for for Kim to join us.

As we walked out to board our plane to Cebu, I stopped dead in amazement. The plane, embellished with a variety of large coloured flowers, looked like something left over from the Hippy Days.

Jen laughed. "This is like the one I flew on with the girls." After boarding, another strange event occurred. While going through the list of safety procedures the air hostesses made jokes. It being something Jen had not mentioned.

On our arrival at Cebu, as Jen had said, our transport to the beach was by motorbike and sidecar. After the experience of the plane and transportation to the beach, our boat trip to the island was uneventful.

Jen was over the moon when we arrived at Boracay. This time, as I was with her, she had no problem in stepping off the boat and into the water. Holding her hand, we waded up to the beach.

It delighted Kim when informed her chalet was on the gleaming soft white sand. Although ours were further inland, they were still on the sand.

I soon found that everything Jen had said about Boracay to be true. The sand was pure white, and the sea in a variety of shades of blue. Given this, it was obvious why Boracay is classed as one of the best beaches in the world. We had such a successful time; there we felt sad to leave at the end of our four-day holiday.

At the airport, an announcement said our plane would be late arriving. Once it did, and all the passengers had disembarked, we expected to board. However, there was, a problem. As we watched, a man who until then, had been cleaning the airport, walked out to the plane carrying a pair of steps. He climbed up to one engine and removed the cowling. Then, for the next two hours, the man—who must have been a mechanic—worked on the engine. Eventually, he replaced the cowling, climbed down, and removed the steps.

The pilot then switched on the engine, which as it fired, sent a puff of smoke shooting out from the exhaust. It then disappeared as the engine built up power. After a few minutes, the pilot must have been satisfied that all was well, so he shut down the power. Only then were we allowed to board the plane. By the time we took off, we had been at the airport for four hours. Although I felt concerned about our flight, we arrived safely back in Manila.

While Kim stayed with us, she loved getting up, and Linda asking what she wanted for breakfast. So, it was unexpected when she suddenly told us, "You two aren't in touch with reality

Puzzled, I asked. "What do you mean? Are you referring to our having a maid? As here in the Philippines, it's normal. Numerous people even have a nanny to look after the children." I chuckled. "I agree that were we living in the UK; it would be abnormal for us to have a maid."

Although Jen and I thought her remark funny, not once did Kim tell Linda she would get her own breakfast.

Apart from going to the driving range with Mike, I also played golf with Wal, his son Jonathan, and Alistair. Despite being only fourteen, Jonathan could hit a ball incredible distances. Whereas Wal, Alastair and myself were complete novices. I found it amazing to watch Jonathan tee off. He would glance at where he wanted the ball to go, then with a blur of arms, whack. The crisp sound was a sure sign the ball had travelled a successful distance.

Sometimes, we would play at Intramuros, which being in Manila, was easy to reach. Although not a big course, it had large sized ponds to negotiate. As a result, I usually lost several balls while hitting one over the water. However, it added more fun to the game. At this course, there were girls you could pay to carry a large golf umbrella to protect you from the fierce sun. This being something that none of us found necessary.

Before the installation of the external window cladding, two Americans arrived on-site. One named Jimmy was the employer, while John, his friend, would be in charge of the insulation works.

I soon found both men, along with Janet, Jimmy's wife, to be friendly.

One evening, Jimmy invited me to join them at a golf driving range. On watching, I thought neither needed any practice. Later, a short time after taking lessons with another club pro, Jimmy invited me to play a game with him and John. Although nervous and far from good, I enjoyed myself. Both Jimmy and John were helpful and offered advice on how to improve my game. From then on, I played golf every weekend with them on a variety of golf courses.

Although most were out of town, this proved not a problem, as Jimmy would drive us to whatever we were going to play. Because of traffic, we always played early when it was lighter. However, by the time we finished playing and had lunch, our trip back usually took twice as long.

As I now played golf every week, Jen bought me a set of second-hand Ping golf clubs. With these, I could play reasonably well. However, during one game with the boys, I lost sixteen balls, all that I had. In my defence, this was because of the roughness of the course. If you hit off the fairways, there was little chance of finding the ball. Thanks to a local man out selling golf balls he recovered, I bought some and able to finish the game.

Although I enjoyed playing with Jimmy and John, I found that Jimmy changed moods in a flash. The first time I witnessed this, it shocked me. After taking what I thought a good shot, Jimmy went mad. He mouthed off and threw his club onto the grass. John, however, took no notice of Jimmy's antics. He just shrugged as if to say okay. Now let's get on with the game.

Until I started playing golf with the boys, I never knew how fabulous many of the clubhouses were. Some were luxurious , with restaurants that provided meals ranging from snacks to five-course menus. What with this and beautiful marble clad changing rooms, you would think you were entering a five-star hotel. As such, I found it an incredible experience to visit them.

At one time, a friend took the three of us to the Highlands Golf Course that got its name because of being way up a steep hillside. To my amazement, a funicular ran from the second course up to the highest one. However, because of a typhoon blowing we could not play on that course, so instead, we played the middle one. Even then, because of the high winds; we could only play nine holes. Regardless, it was an incredible experience to attempt playing golf under such conditions, where apart from us, only two other crazy golfers were playing.

# Part 5

The following week, a typhoon struck Manila, with all works suspended until it passed. These are typical in this part of the world and at times cause tremendous loss of life and damage to property. Although typhoons are not what I call fun, it's something the local people have to put up with.

At one time, a friend introduced Jen to a Mrs Santos. She was a jeweller who could make all kinds of high-quality gold jewellery. If you gave her a design, she could make it to perfection. Apart from making Jen several pieces, she made a fabulous ring for me in the design of an eagle head, with sapphires fitted as its eyes. Although not to everyone's taste, I liked both the result and the cost.

After being on-site for around one year, a director from the prime contractor came to talk with me. To my astonishment, he suggested his company's quality control team worked with ours.

"That's not possible," I exclaimed. "You don't have a QC team."

"What! Of course, we do;" he said. "It's essential on a project this size."

I chuckled at his statement. "I couldn't agree more," I said. "but strange as it seems, you don't have one."

His eyebrows shot up in alarm, when I explained that JLI were the only people on the site conducting quality control works. Shortly afterwards, Rob and I were asked to attend a meeting with our employer, Rob M. As a result, the prime contractor would form a Q.C team to collaborate with JLI. After some persuasion, I accepted the role as head of the group. I had initially refused the position and suggested Rob took it. However, with the project now about interiors, my experience of working on high-class projects made me more suitable.

Based on my strong recommendation; a short time afterwards, two JLI men joined us. Chris, accompanied by his fiancée Carol, specialised in preparing and updating snagging lists on the computer. This, on a project the size of ours, it would keep him more than busy. The other, a man named Derek, was around my age. He would look after MEHP works, which involved the various service installations. Because of all the ongoing activities on-site, our team found ourselves more than busy.

With everything set-up on the site, Jen and I set off to go to Turkey for a holiday. As Bong, our driver drove us to the airport; Jen, (who usually handled our tickets) asked to look at them. No sooner had I passed them to her when she exploded. "You stupid! We should be at the airport now." Before I could speak, she continued. "The flight leaves at 16.00, not 6 pm!"

I could not believe I had made such a mistake, but on looking, I found she was right. I called out, "Bong; put your foot down; we are really late."

However, because of heavy traffic, this was easier said than done. Nevertheless, Bong managed to cover the remaining distance to the airport in record time. With Jen and I each carrying a large case and a hand carry, we rushed to the check-in desk. To our surprise and relief, the check-in desk attendant allowed us to check-in.

Once through passport control, on trembling legs, we somehow managed to run to the departure gate. To our amazement, we found the passengers for our flight still sat there. Our plane had not yet arrived. We had been fortunate, as had it been on time, we would have missed our flight.

After spending a glorious holiday in Turkey, I flew back to Manila, while Jen stayed to start work for Dr Cemal at his hospital in Kemer. On arrival, it shocked me to hear about a bomb that had gone off in Glorietta, injuring twelve shoppers. With the centre always packed, it was a miracle the bomb had not killed anyone.

When I heard about yet another public holiday coming up, this for five days, I decided to take a trip to Punto Galario. One of my friends had told me that it was an excellent place to chill out.

To reach it, however, turned out far from straightforward. I first had a three-hour bus trip, followed by a two-hour ferry trip over to the island. Even then, this was not the end of my journey. I then had to take a fifteen-minute ride on a small Banka to the actual resort. As a crew member tied it up to a wobbling floating jetty, my first impression was the place looked great. Although the beach consisted of only a narrow strip of sand, I found it clean and soft. Also, to my delight, my accommodation was in a cabin a short distance back from the beach.

The next day, it surprised me to find that apart from small cafes lining the shoreline, there was nothing else. When I inquired about this at one café, a man said, "Tourists only come here for diving." I found this to be big business, with several of the cafes strung out along the beach acting as dive shops.

Still, despite the lack of facilities, it did not bother me at all. I enjoyed having a muted drink in one bar, where I usually ate a freshly cooked meal. I also liked to read a book while relaxing in a hammock established on the sand outside my cabin. The peace and muted being a world away from the hustle and bustle of Manila. I enjoyed being there, and felt sad when it was time to return to Manila.

About a year later, I returned to Punto Galario. This time, the trip to the island proved nothing short of terrifying. It all started when Chris invited me to join him, and a bunch of his diving friends for a weekend there.

When we set off to go over to the Island, it was dark, with a slight swell on the water. However, no sooner had we left the shore when the waves increased in size. Then, as the wind grew stronger, the waves ploughing into the boat caused it to dip and sway alarmingly. Given this, they gave everyone a life-jacket, with all who could get below in the cabin area, did.

While sat near the doorway, talking to one of the men's wives, her husband ducked his head into the cabin. To my shock and horror, I heard him said, "If the boat starts going down, get out over the stern."

"What's going on?" I whispered in alarm. "Are we going to sink?"

He forced a grim smile. "All being well, no, but it's best to take precautions." He then explained how one boat crossing in similar conditions had sunk. "All those below in the cabin drowned, they could not get out in time." He shrugged. "Now you know why I said what I did; it's best to be prepared."

As a non-swimmer, I found his news unnerving. Nevertheless, even if I could swim, with the rough seas and strong winds, I didn't fancy my chances of survival. The others on board were mostly divers; and would stand a much better chance than me.

When we eventually reached the island, the seas were too rough to allow our boat to get close to the jetty. Seeing this, two of the men jumped over into the shallow water. They then pushed the boat to the dock, where a crew member tied it up. I, for one, felt relieved to have made it across to the island without mishap.

Only when we walked into the small pension (guest house) where we were going to stay did we discover just how fortunate we had been?

"Well," the receptionist exclaimed, "we didn't expect to see you tonight. Because of the bad weather, no boats are allowed to cross. Yours is the last one across tonight."

After we arrived, I heard a lot of familiar singing coming from the pension next door. It was the sound of hash songs, something I had not heard since leaving Malaysia. Ongoing across, I found the patio packed full of hashers, all wearing a variety of printed hash shirts. On asking what was going on, one said they had come for an Inter-Islands hash run the next morning. I felt disappointed, as due to not having my trainers, I could not take part.

Still, felt pleased when they told me I could pay a handful and join them for tomorrow's run. The money also covered coupons that allowed me to have a drink in several bars that evening. I was happy to pay, as apart from that, I also received a commemoration T-Shirt. After putting it on, I blended in well with the other hashers. After a drink in their bar, we went out to enjoy ourselves at several more bars, with my feeling felt great being back among a bunch of hashers once again.

Come the morning; the wind had dropped, with it now a bright and sunny day. Along with a crowd of boisterous hashers, I climbed into one of a long line of waiting Jeepneys. These would take us to the other side of the island where the run would start. Our ride involved driving up a steep, unsurfaced muddy trail, with several hairpin bends to negotiate. Because of the rough surface, it was dangerous, with the ride down the other side almost as bad. Cries of alarm rang out as one jeepney started to slide on the muddy trail. Thankfully, none slide off over the edge, and we all arrived safely at the beach.

I was bubbling with excitement when I joined the sizeable crowd of hashers who were already there. The group I joined ,being only part of those awaiting the run to begin. As the horn sounded the off, the crowd set off. They had just left when, to my surprise, one of my hash friends from Indonesia appeared. Before I could speak to him, he dashed off, catching up with the others.

When I saw him after the run, it shocked me to see his legs were a mass of bloody cuts. I approached him and pointing to his bleeding legs; I asked, "What happened?"

He grinned. "Oh, hi, Moses, good to see you," he said.

According to hash rules, I must use my official hash name, Moses, when I meet a fellow hasher.

He then explained. "As I set off late, I decided to try a shortcut to catch up." He laughed, "Unfortunately, I ran into a barbed wire fence and got tangled up in it." Still, apart from that, it was a run. Nevertheless, I'll see you later. I have to go and clean my legs before the down- downs."

As he walked off, I wandered down to where some hashers were standing. As I drew closer, I noticed what appeared to be two cows being barbecued. Because of the numerous hashers present, this being necessary to feed them all. After several hours talking, drinking and eating with some of the group, I then returned to my side of the island. Although unable to run, I felt fortunate to be on the island at the same time as the Inter Islands Hash. It proved to be the highlight of the weekend.

Thankfully, unlike coming over, our boat trip back to the mainland proved uneventful.

A few weeks later, I received a call from Nic of Richmond Int, the company I had worked for in Malaysia. To my delight, he said there was a contract for me in Morocco. However, I heard no more about it for several months. I then received an e-mail from Louise at Richmond's head office in London. To my delight, she said I was being considered for the post and would contact me once she had more positive news.

On phoning Jen back in Turkey, it shocked me to hear that the temperature was over 50°C. This was incredible, as I had never known it as hot as this in Kemer. Given the extreme heat, the government had closed all official buildings for two days. Jen also told me that various temperature gauges left outside were exploding, as the temperature was more than they could take.

While driving around Manila, not far from the project site, I gasped in shock. Lining both sides of the railway track, were small ramshackle huts made from bits of cardboard, plywood, and rusty tin sheets. With them covered in all kinds of rubbish, the entire scene looked terrible. What made this so incredible, it was near the financial district of Makati. It highlighted the vast distance between the rich and the poor.

Another unpleasant sight were children around five years old begging for money. I thought it pitiful to see children so young out on the streets when they should have been at school. If stopped in traffic near them, I usually gave them coins.

As the children always looked hungry, instead of giving money, one of our friends gave a tin of food. It shocked her when the young beggar threw it away. Apparently, many of these children work under the control of an adult, who collects the money they raise. No doubt the children only receive a small portion of what they hand in. If so, it would explain why the boy discarded the tin of food. His only interest was money.

. Many of these children work under the control of an adult, who collects the money they raise. No doubt the children only receive a small portion of what they hand in. It would explain why the boy discarded the tin of food. His only interest was money.

# Part 5

On seeing a brochure advertising a resort further down the coast, Jen who had returned from Turkey made us a booking. From the pamphlet, the resort appeared ideal, but as they say, all that glitters is not gold. After Bong dropped us off at the resort reception office, I arranged for him to return and pick us up on Sunday evening.

The receptionist made us welcome , then gave us the keys to our room. As we walked inside, we gasped in horror. The room gave the impression of not being redecorated for numerous years. The wallpaper had tears and stains, and the wardrobe resembled a relic from a sunken ship. Checking the bathroom, I found the toilet, washbasin, and bath all stained. It looked a disgusting sight.

Exasperated, I said. "They have got to be joking. There's no way we're going to sleep here. Wait here, while I will go back to the reception and tell them." Then I stomped back to the reception office.

"That room!" I exclaimed. "We are not going to sleep there."

To my surprise, the receptionist said, "Sorry about that; use this room." She then handed me another room key.

I thanked her and returned to where Jen stood waiting. I waved the key. "OK, we have another room. Let's see what this one's like."

When I unlocked the door and we walked in, I was furious. The room was as bad as the previous one.

"Right! That's it. Now I'm really annoyed. If they think they can get away with giving us rooms like this, they are sadly mistaken. If Bong is still here, we will return to Manila. This is unbelievable! Could you tell me why on earth are they putting us in rooms as bad as this?"

I then stormed out to seek Bong, but to my dismay, he had left, which made me even angrier. By the time I walked into reception, I was fit to burst and ready to explode. I yelled at the woman sitting behind the desk.

"What is going on here? Both the rooms you offered us are disgusting. I wouldn't even let my dog sleep in such terrible conditions." Before she could respond, I said, 'If my driver had not already left, we would be out of here in a shot. This place looks nothing like your brochure."

The woman, whom I hadn't met before, apologized for the rooms we received. She offered us a new one in a different section of the hotel, which she believed we'd enjoy. "It is in another section of the hotel, which you will like. As for the state of this place, I can only agree. When first built, the resort used to be an upmarket place, but since then has been in decline. My company is now improving things." Before I could comment, she added. "Because of your justified complaints, I will refund your booking fee."

Although news, it did not make up for the disappointment of our having wasted an entire weekend.

For Jen's birthday, I arranged a surprise party at Jane and Wal's apartment. When we walked in, Jen thought we were having dinner with them. She then squealed with delight on finding it packed with many of our friends. When Jen asked if Caroline would come, Jane hugged her, then said, "They live in Hong Kong, so they couldn't come."

Jen was visibly upset. Caroline had been her best friend in Manila since they first met. Despite this, as every other of her friends was there, Jen soon cheered up. A short time later, Jane asked all the girls to gather around Jen. She wanted to take a photo. As one went to sit next to Jen, someone said, "Sorry, but that chair's taken."

Jen recognised the voice and gasped in shock. As she turned around, a pair of arms wrapped around her. The voice said, "You didn't think for one minute that I would miss your party, did you?"

It was Caroline. Jen burst into tears of happiness. "Oh! You don't know how happy I am; you're here. I've missed you since you went to Hong Kong."

Wearing a beaming smile, Jane, said, "See, some of us can keep a secret. I knew all along Caroline would be here."

That Caroline had come over, especially for her birthday was the best present Jen could have. The evening was a successful success. Jane provided plenty of tasty snacks and more than enough to drink.

For my 60$^{th}$ birthday a few weeks later, Jen had told me we were going to meet Jane and Wal in the evening, then have dinner out. On entering their apartment, I found it packed with many of our friends. I thought Jen might lay on something special for me, but it still came as a shock to find numerous friends there. Because of all those invited, Jane had brought in an outside caterer that made it a birthday to remember.

Then a few days later, Jen and I flew over to England to spend Christmas with Anita, Niko, and their children. We were pleased to see them, with our all having a successful time. Despite not cooking for some time, Jen prepared a delicious Christmas Day dinner. With a 14lb Turkey and a variety of delicious fresh vegetables, it was a proper feast. To our surprise, the next morning, we found it had snowed during the night. Although it looked great, Anita's house was in a valley. Given this, Niko could not go work. Instead, he and I took the dogs for a walk in the nearby fields. It felt successful breathing in the crisp air as we tramped through the snow. The two dogs enjoyed playing around and leaving trails as they ran back and forth.

Although we enjoyed New Year's Eve together, it was much quieter than the previous one in the Philippines.

After returning to Manila the following week, I found work on the site now in full swing. They completed the swimming pool and much of the landscape work, with the project looking, as expected, upmarket.

Health-wise, things were not so rosy for me. A short time after returning, I felt ill and went to see a doctor. After various checks, he confirmed that I had a touch of food poisoning. As a result, it kept me off work for a few days.

Apart from finding a doctor in Manila, I also found an excellent dentist. He performed several repairs, with my pleased with both results and cost.

I know people feel nervous about receiving medical care when abroad. Personally, I have received excellent medical treatment in several countries outside the UK and satisfied with both the results, and cost

As a way of keeping fit, I signed up at the Mandarin Hotel gym. With it next to the site, I used to go there during my lunch break. I enjoyed running on the hash, so I exercised on a treadmill. No doubt this helped when I later had a test on a treadmill in hospital. On completion, the doctor said that no one my age had ever managed to run on the eleven settings. Given my result, he told me I would never have a heart problem. Unfortunately, his statement later proved incorrect.

The following month, Rob asked if I would extend my contract. I had done so for three months prior. After he agreed to my request for a holiday in between, I decided to stay until the end of June. I thought this would work out well, as Jen had promised Dr Cemal, she would return to help him in his new hospital. Therefore, she would stay in Turkey after our scheduled flight back the following month. Although unhappy with my decision, I told Jen a promise was a promise.

During the next month, Jen and I talked with Jane about Kim's eyes. Jane expressed her satisfaction with the operation she had underwent. As a result, when Kim came out on holiday, Jane took her to see if she was acceptable or not. To our delight, Kim's' results were excellent, so she had the eye operation. During a routine check-up a few weeks afterwards, all seemed okay. However, Kim was told she should have another check-up in a month's time. Although it meant she would have to stay on longer in Manila, Kim was more than happy to do so.

During this time, the annual 'Anza Ball' occurred. As Derek, was on his own, he agreed to accompany Kim. Like all the balls Jen and I had attended, this one proved no exception. Come the end of the evening, Jen, and I were tired, so we decided to return home. Derek however, took Kim out for a drink. The next morning, it shocked me when Derek told me what happened after we left.

"While having a drink in a bar, someone stole my wallet. It ruined the evening, as Kim and I had to go to a police station to report the theft. It then took several hours before we could leave."

In the evening, when I spoke to Kim about her ruined evening. To my surprise, she said, "I don't know what you are talking about. I must have had too much to drink at the ball, as I have no recollection of Derek losing his wallet."

Nodding, I said. "Yes, I thought you had a bit much. Look, although you're a big girl, you must be careful when you're out."

Just before Jen left Manila for the last time, Jane arranged a farewell party for her. Although a successful evening, it was also sad. Jen had loved her time in the Philippines and did not want to leave. She told all our friends that I was sending her home. On hearing this, I agreed it was true. I then explained how Dr Cemal had been awaiting Jen's return for the past three months.

This they admitted put a different slant on what Jen told them. I also explained what she would be doing at the hospital.

"Jen is not just going to work there. Apart from the doctors, she will run the hospital. It is something Jen always wanted to do. She enjoyed working in his old hospital. This one, however, is brand new and much larger."

At the check-in for our flight home, because we had various bits and pieces we had bought in the Philippines, we had a lot of baggage. To our amazement and delight, we did not have to pay for any excess luggage.

On our arrival at Antalya, Fethi, one of our Turkish friends, was there to drive us home. To our dismay, ongoing inside, the electric supply was not working, but came back on later.

It came as a shock to discover Ahmed our friend and neighbour had moved to Antalya without telling us. During our several phone calls, he had not mentioned his intention. We then found he had rented his house to a young couple, who we found friendly, and like us, dog lovers.

In the meantime, back in Manila, Kim had another eye check-up, which showed she needed what they called a top-up. Once done, Kim could then dispense with her old bottle topped glasses. It made her look much different.

My return to Manila differed from before. With Jen not there and Kim leaving, I would soon be on my own. Wal and Jane were back from Botswana. As his company was posting him there, they had gone to check things out. Although good to hear all about their trip, I felt sad when a short time later, they packed up and left.

Along with them, several other friends also left. It meant my attending various farewell parties. As a result, I felt on a countdown until it was time for my departure.

A short time after Kim left to start work as a tour rep in England, Chris informed me Rob had resigned. This was not too unexpected, as both sections of works he controlled were completed. Rob and Mary then left the following month.

While talking on the phone with Niko back in England, he surprised me when he mentioned about our going into business. He said he had found a place he wanted to buy and use as a barber shop. With Niko an experienced barber and working as one in England, I thought his idea could prove profitable. After saying I was interested, I then called Jen. After a long chat, we agreed we should discover more about Nikos' idea. During a later talk with Niko, after he detailed the costs involved, I decided to accept his proposal. I told him that on my return to Turkey; I would arrange to transfer the money he needed to buy the shop.

It was about this time when Linda told me she would leave; as she was getting married. Although Linda's news was not good for me, I felt pleased for her. Linda had proved not only an excellent maid, but someone Jen and I regarded as family. We had offered to take Linda to Turkey and work with us, but to our disappointment, she declined.

Linda had told us that after going with one family to Japan, her employer had offered to find her a suitable husband. She had refused, as she wanted to marry a Filipino like herself. As this was now what she was going to do, I wished her well. I said I hoped her husband would prove as good as she was. Just before she left, Linda found me a replacement maid, for which I was grateful. Although I could handle the cooking, I needed someone to clean and tidy the apartment.

It must have been the time for getting married for the following week; I received a surprise message. Chris and Carol had married while on holiday in El Salvador. I thought this successful news. They were a lovely couple.

Over the next few months, there was no news from Richmond International about the project in Morocco. Given this, I contacted several companies regarding a new contract, but with no success. On talking to Jim, he said there might be an opening for me with his company in Hong Kong. Therefore, I felt the future could work out okay.

The Roxas project had been the longest of my career. Jen and I had enjoyed an incredible social life in the Philippines.

Not long before I left the Philippines, I attended a ball held to celebrate the Queen's birthday. Although I had a time with some of my friends, without Jen being there, it was not the same.

The British Consulate extended an invitation for me to attend a security meeting about a week before my return to Turkey. On attending, I found many people there to hear a talk on security issues. The speakers included the British Consul and senior officials from two major English security companies.

To my surprise, I found the meeting held because of several people being kidnapped and held for ransom. I felt shocked when I learned that some had been kidnapped from outside the hotel next to the project site. If that was not bad enough, worse was to follow. The kidnappers targeted Chinese-English individuals because their families often paid the ransom without involving the police. In one case where they did not pay, the kidnappers established a video camera, then taped the victim, having one of his fingers cut off. As a result, the family then paid without further delay. Those present gasped in horror upon hearing this. It made me think more about my safety. Until then, I had given little thought about it when out late at night.

During the meeting, they advised us to never use the same route back and forth to work every day. Also, could we trust our drivers? At the end of the session, I turned to a woman sat next to me. "If I had just arrived in Manila with a young family and told what we were tonight, I would think twice about staying," I said. In this respect, I felt even happier about leaving the Philippines.

Instead of flying straight home to Turkey, I had decided to break up the long flight with a brief holiday in Thailand. This idea came about while enquiring about flights back to Turkey. A friend suggested I take a break in Thailand, as to my surprise; I could then get an inexpensive flight back to Turkey.

When I spoke to the travel agent in Thailand he recommended, I found by doing so, the cost was less than a direct flight to Turkey.

On later talking with my employer Rob, he agreed the company would allow me to do as I planned. As a result, the money saved on a direct flight home would pay for my hotel stay in Thailand.

Three weeks before leaving the Philippines, Halit's men came to pack the various items to be shipped back to Turkey. He assured us that these items would be delivered to our home in approximately one month. Because of my break in Thailand, I thought they would arrive around the same time as me. In this, however, I was to be badly mistaken.

After dropped off at the airport for my flight to Thailand, I went inside to check-in. When I discovered my flight was delayed, I felt dismayed. After awaiting an hour with all the other passengers, a coach took us to the Dusit Hotel back in town. They informed us that we would spend the night here and then offered us food. However, while eating, there was a change of plans. We would be returning to the airport. A short time after our arrival and checking in, we boarded our plane, then took off.

Upon my arrival in Bangkok, a waiting driver escorted me to the travel agent's office, where I received my flight ticket to Turkey. With this in hand, I could then relax. By the time I arrived at the hotel I had booked, it was late, so after a shower, I went to bed.

The next morning, while on a tour of the city, our coach stopped outside a large jewellery mall. Inside I found the prices reasonable, so bought a sapphire ring for both Kim and Anita, plus one for Jen. I also purchased a gold dragon pendant and chain for myself. On leaving there, we then called in at a tailor advertising suits made in 24 hours. Although I didn't need a suit, there were also many special offers. With the reasonable prices; I ordered a pair of slacks, a sports coat, and a couple of shirts. These they said, would be delivered to my hotel the next evening.

The next morning, I took a river trip. After a taxi took me to where boats were offering trips, I picked one and climbed aboard. Apart from cruising for miles along the river and up some canals, we called in at the 'Grand Palace.' I thought it a fantastic, and filled with a great variety of beautiful statues and carvings. From here we then visited 'Wat Arum' that I also found interesting. By the time we returned to the start of the tour, I felt exhilarated. Never had I seen such beautiful buildings.

A delivery person brought the items of clothing I had ordered to my room in the evening. On trying them on, I found they fitted perfectly. To my surprise and delight, I also received a present of several silk ties. Given this, I thought it a perfect finish to my brief holiday, as apart from the things I had bought, it had cost little money.

The next morning, I set off back to Turkey. On my arrival in Istanbul, I was far from pleased when I had to wait five hours for my flight down to Antalya. However, thanks to my friend Vedat checking on flight schedules, he was there to meet me.

On the drive to my house, we called in at the hospital where Jen worked., with my delighted to see her smiling face once again.

In the evening, although tired, I felt good to be back home.

As our things had not arrived from Manila as expected, I contacted Halit. When he called me back, I was stunned when he said, "The crate containing your goods was stuck in Singapore. I'm now getting it sent on to Turkey A.S.A.P."

Although they arrived in Istanbul several weeks later, this delay was nothing compared to the nightmare we then had. Even with the help of Turkish friends, we had successful difficulty in getting our goods out of customs. At one point, the customs threatened to send them back to Manila. In total, apart from waiting several months before the delivery, I also had to pay around £2,000. This being more than the value of the goods we had shipped.

When I later set about seeking a new contract, I wondered where my next adventure would occur. Little did I know that I would end up living alongside royalty, on a long, beautiful sandy beach in North Africa!

Moroccan adventure

# Chapter Seventeen

After being back in Turkey for several months, I had all but given up on hearing any more about the Morocco project. Then, on checking my e-mail one day, I found one from Louise. She apologised for the delay and asked me to call and speak with Sue, the designer in charge of the project. After talking on the phone, we later met up in London. Sue emphasised that the project, a five-star hotel complex, was in a desolate location, with no shops, bars, or restaurants nearby. She then surprised me when she said, "Oh, did I mention the project is situated next to the King of Morocco's palace?"

I laughed. "That's not a problem. I've worked on several palaces, so I know about security issues."

Sue gave me a sideways glance, "I am not saying you might meet him," she shrugged. "I've been there numerous times without seeing him. Anyway, your sole purpose on the site is to ensure quality and design issues are as RI specifications." She gave a grim smile."At present, things are not going as we expected." She frowned displeasure. "You will soon find out what I mean when you arrive. Anyway, with your help, we're hoping things will improve."

This didn't sound too good, but after working in the Philippines, I didn't think it would prove too much of a problem.

In the course of our talk, I had the impression Sue felt concerned about my ability to work in such a secluded location. She had mentioned this aspect several times. I smiled. "Don't worry," I said. "I'm used to working on my own, and the isolation won't be a problem. It will give me a chance to catch up on my reading."

Although due to begin work on the project several months earlier, I did not fly out to Morocco until mid-February. On arriving in Casablanca late one evening, an awaiting driver drove me to the Sheraton Hotel, where I would stay the night. I'd then meet up with Sue for breakfast.

The next morning, after Sue gave me an update on the latest situation on the site, a driver drove us too the site. From talking with Sue, I knew it was halfway between Casablanca and Rabat.

On our arrival, the design of the hotel complex impressed me. It was in typical Moroccan style, with the outside finished in gleaming white stucco. After a driver dropped off at the site office, Sue indicated the King of Morocco's Palace. It was right next door. A high-security wall ran down to the sea, with a stone jetty extending out past the edge of the beach.

With the hotel complex set on the edge of a beautiful, long, wide, and sandy beach, it looked a fabulous location. The sea seemed too rough for swimming, but as I didn't swim, it would not be a problem.

As we walked through the site, Sue introduced me to a Mr Muller, the French site engineer. To my amazement, Sue said that due to there being no project manager, Mr Muller was in charge of the site. I thought this most unusual, as on projects of this size, it was standard practice to have one. After a brief chat, he accompanied us to meet Mr Dich, the hotel manager. As we walked into his office, he stood up. "Welcome to Morocco, Colin."

"Thank you," I replied, "it good to be here."

During a talk that followed, Mr. Dich pleased me by saying he would help me in any way he could. Sue then took me on tour around the complex. This I found consisted of numerous buildings, spread out over a large area.

Sue said that my first job was to make up a list of everything not up to the quality I expected for a five-star hotel. Unfortunately,

I could see there were numerous things unacceptable. First, was the marble floor tiling. There were significant differences in the shades of the tiles, with some badly stained. I considered it unacceptable. Another area of concern was the rough and uneven wall plaster. From my initial inspection, a great deal of work required rectifying.

During the next few days, Sue and I went through the various design drawings. As for my accommodation, Sue said I could stay in one of the ten hotel suites that were set just above the beach. However, she advised against it. On seeing my puzzled expression, Sue explained. "Although they're comfortable and fully furnished, if you live on the site, you could find yourself working 24/7." Nevertheless, I felt pleased when Sue said I could stay at the Sheraton until I found somewhere suitable.

After Sue left to return to London, I talked to Mr Dich about finding accommodation. He proved most helpful and later drove me along the road that ran past the hotel and palace. About two miles from the site, he stopped at a hotel, situated above the edge of the beach.

"Right, Colin, you go and see what you think of this place. From here, we will then go on to see a few more hotels. You can then decide which one you prefer."

After I had checked the hotel and several others, I felt disappointed. None of them were particularly good. However, after deciding the 'Kasbah Hotel' was the best, I booked in there. Although plainly furnished, with the hotel on a low cliff above the beach, it offered excellent views out to sea and along the coastline

For the next few days, a driver picked me up from the hotel, drove me to the site, then home again in the evening. Come the Saturday morning, however, after waiting half an hour and still no car, although two miles, I decided to walk.

Nevertheless, come the evening, I made sure a driver took me back to my hotel. I found it muted and peaceful, with the restaurant serving a variety of tasty meals. Unfortunately, my peace and tranquillity only lasted until that weekend. Then, many of the rooms became filled with local people coming to enjoy time on the beach. To my extreme disappointment, I found the walls between the rooms were far from soundproof. As a result, the noise coming through made it difficult to sleep.

On the Monday, after I informed Mr Dich of this, he took me to look at a furnished villa that was close to the site. Here he said I would have the whole top floor to myself. Although the primary rooms were modern and well furnished, the kitchen was old and of poor quality. Nevertheless, as I thought the lounge and bedroom good, I decided to move in.

Come the evening, Mr Dich drove me to a supermarket on the outskirts of Rabat. It was, he said, where he and his wife shopped. After stocking up with a week's supply of groceries, he drove me back to my new home.

A few days after moving in, I had major electrical problems with both the security shutters and the wiring in the kitchen. After an electrician came and checked, he said he could not rectify the issues. Given this, I thought it best to move into one of the hotel suites on the site.

On informing Mr Dich of my decision, he took me to look at one. As I walked in, my eyes lit. The room was well-furnished and looked comfortable. Plus, only a few meters away were steps leading down to the sandy beach. It looked so good, I moved in later. The next morning I decided to go for a jog. After walking through the deep, soft sand until it became firmer, I then set off at a steady pace. Just breathing in the fresh sea air and looking at the waves curling in up to the sand made me feel good. As I enjoyed the exercise, I then used to jog every morning before breakfast.

During the weekdays the beach became deserted, but at weekends became packed, so I made sure to finish my jog early.

During my first ten days on-site, I inspected all the various areas and made up a detailed report of all the defects I had seen. Although the marble flooring was a significant source of concern, it was not practical to have it all taken up and replaced. I suggested a compromise, where we could keep the marble flooring if we replaced the badly stained tiles and re-polished all the floors. Although it would involve a lot of time, there were no other acceptable alternatives. Another concern arose when I found wardrobes installed in areas without the marble flooring being laid. This was unbelievable, as they left the unprotected closets surrounded by piles of construction materials. I put this down to not having a project manager on-site. Had there been one, this situation could never have happened.

After compiling my report, Jamala, Mr Dich's secretary, faxed a copy to Sue at the UK office. I also gave a copy to Mr Muller and Mr Dich. A few days later, I was pleased to hear that Omar, the project architect, had accepted my report. He agreed with my recommendations about the marble flooring.

For the first three weeks on-site, I did not have the use of a car, as per my contract. Nevertheless, after talking with Mr Dich, he provided me with a car and driver who would take me wherever I wanted during the weekend. After a few times of finding him not available, Mr Dich arranged for me to have my own vehicle. This then enabled me to go out for lunch or a meal in the evenings.

During Sundays, my day off work, I usually drove to Rabat, where I enjoyed wandering through the old city. I found some alleyways were incredibly narrow. Given this, I'm sure people living in the houses could lean out their windows and shake hands with their neighbours.

However, I liked the bazaar most, where I spent hours searching the shops for bargains. In one shop, I found numerous different fossils for sale. After haggling with the owner, as I thought they would make unique presents for my friends, I bought some.

On the site, Mr Dich's chief admin manager, a Moroccan named Azziz, proved both friendly and helpful. One morning, he asked, "Colin, would you like to have fish for lunch?"

As I usually made do with just a snack, I replied, "That would great, but where can we get it?"

He gave a knowing smile. "Come to the office at lunchtime, and I will show you," he said.

When Azziz later led me down to the beach, I felt puzzled. Despite jogging along this beach every day, I had never seen a café. After walking along the seashore for fifteen minutes, we rounded a bend I had not reached before. To my surprise, I found fishing boats lying on the sand. They must have come in with their catch on the high tide and would go out again on the next one

As we walked between the boats, I noticed several of the fishermen had fish laid out for sale. Although Azziz glanced at several, he kept walking. On coming to one man, Azziz greeted him, then picked out a few fish that he handed to the man. It left me puzzled when he walked off carrying the fish.

Azziz noticed my expression, for he smiled and said, "Follow me." He led me up the beach to a small, decrepit looking café. To my surprise, there was no kitchen. Instead, there was a gas ring perched on a small table behind an old counter unit. The seating area consisted of several rickety wooden tables and chairs established under a few worn out advertising umbrellas. As we sat down at one table, I felt anxious about eating in such dingy conditions. I wondered how safe it would be to eat.

Azziz could see I looked uncomfortable, for he chuckled. "Don't worry what this place looks like," he said, "the lunch here is excellent. After you buy the fish from one of the fishermen, he weighs, cleans it, and then brings it here to be cooked. You'll agree that you cannot eat fish more freshly caught than here."

After a brief wait, a man came out carrying a tray. Balanced on it were two plates of fish and chips, a dish of salad, and a bowl of freshly cut bread. Although the place would never pass a health inspection, the food tasted delicious. On finishing our meal, I asked Azziz the cost. It then shocked me to learn how inexpensive it was. After this, we ate there several times a week. The fish was so mouthwatering; I looked forward to going there for lunch.

Another place Azziz took me to was a small village about three miles from the site on the main road that runs between Casablanca and Rabat. On my first visit, Azziz took me to a small market area. To my surprise, among stalls selling clothing, was a little open-air butchers' shop where hanging from a rail looked like a side of beef. Azziz said something to the butcher, who carved off a chunk of meat. He weighed it, then took to a small café next door. As I watched, a man using an old hand operated mincer ground the meat. Once mixed with various herbs, he made it into meatballs. These he cooked in an old, battered frying pan, then served them with a small portion of rice and salad. Again, like at the beach, the meal proved both tasty and inexpensive.

While in the village one day, I noticed a large horse-drawn cart waiting at the side of the road. On enquiring about it, Azziz grinned. "There are no buses, so the cart takes people around to the nearby areas."

After lunch there one day, Azziz took me to a restaurant for coffee. He introduced me to a young man who he said, was Yusuf. "He is Jamal's brother and the manager of the café."

Yusuf, who spoke excellent English, shook my hand and made me welcome. The cappuccino he made tasted excellent, so from then on, we went to Yusuf's for a coffee. Not only did their cappuccino taste good, but also looked the way one should.

At work, the only activity ongoing was being performed by a French company. Once they had completed the areas, an Italian company would then come in. Their job being to install the interior fittings to the restaurant and piano bar, plus all the guest room furniture. On his arrival, I found their manager, a young man named Marco, both friendly and helpful. Unfortunately, although he had worked on luxurious power yachts, he had no experience in fitting out a hotel.

However, with Marco on-site, I had someone to talk to, who proved excellent company . Whenever we went to the Rose Marie restaurant, where I had most of my meals, Marco brightened up my day and made life more enjoyable.

While in Mr Dich office one day, Jamala invited Marco and I to dinner at her house. Although unexpected, we were both pleased to accept. Without Jamala taking us, we would never have found her house that was in an area of Casablanca I had never visited. Once inside, Jamala introduced us to her mother, father, and her younger brother and sister. Although her parents didn't speak English, both her brother and sister did. Therefore, via them, we could converse with their parents while Jamala prepared dinner. This turned out to be a typical Moroccan meal, comprising meat, vegetables, and a mixture of spices. All of which were cooked together in a large earthenware pan, then served with an enormous pile of savoury rice. The meal tasted delicious. Later, at the end of a pleasant and enjoyable evening, after Jamala directed us back to the main road, we returned to the hotel.

After Marco complained about a bad back, I accompanied him to the hospital for an examination. After spending the night there, he returned to Italy the next day for specialised treatment.

Throughout the numerous meetings I attended, I consistently emphasized the insufficient number of workers on-site. I said that to complete the project within the scheduled time frame, they must bring in more men. The reply I received was always the same: "We will get more resources." However, they never backed up these words with action. On talking with Mr Muller about this, he said the problem, "Is because of a shortage of finances." Whatever the reason, works were proceeding at a snail's pace.

In mid-March, I received a disturbing telephone call from my companies head office. They were advising that they had not received payments for my services. Given this, they had given the client one week's notice to rectify this situation. If they did not receive the money due for their invoices, they would withdraw me from the site. This situation disturbed me, and I hoped they would resolve it.

In the mean-time, after breaking one of my teeth, Mr Dich recommended I went to a dentist in Rabat. Although apprehensive, my fears were dissolved when I discovered he had modern equipment. On completion, I felt pleased with both treatment, and the price charged.

At one time, when a Saudi Prince came to stay for a two-week holiday in one of the ten completed suites. Then, because of security concerns, I moved to a suite further away from his. I later heard the prince's visit helped the finances of the project more than when a group of Saudi princesses stayed for five weeks. This it seems, was because of the large number of people who attended the numerous parties the prince held.

All was quiet on the site one day when I heard shouting and screaming coming from the beach. Ongoing to investigate, I spotted a speedboat drifting towards the rough stone jetty wall of the Palace. With its engine stopped, it was being swept along by the surging waves. As I watched in fascination, one wave larger than the others crashed into the boa, it turned over, throwing the two occupants into the water.

No sooner had this happened, when a crowd of people on the beach sprang into action. To my amazement, they formed a human chain out into the water. Because of the strong wind and wave action, this proved no simple task. However, despite being battered, and the chain breaking several times, they managed to reach the men. Once bundled back along the chain of people and up onto the beach, an enormous cheer rose. If the people had not formed the chain, the two men might have drowned or suffered severe injuries when washed against the jagged rocks of the jetty.

Soon afterwards, another speedboat appeared. With great difficulty, one of the two men on board managed to grab a rope attached to the drifting boat. Once secured, they towed the overturned boat clear of the rocks. Once again, those standing on the beach applauded their action. It had been an exhilarating experience watching this desperate action unfold, with my relieved at seeing the men saved.

One Sunday afternoon, Azziz took me to visit his parents at their home. They made me welcome, with our spending an enjoyable afternoon and evening. When it became time for Azziz and me to leave, I turned to embrace his father and thank him for his hospitality. To my shock and embarrassment, our heads crashed into each other. The sudden sharp blow, caused both of us to stagger back holding our heads. I felt terrible. It ruined what, until then, had been a pleasant time. I profusely offered my apologies to Azziz's father who brushed them aside said, "It's not a problem just an accident."

I, however, felt foolish and embarrassed. So on the way back to the hotel, I asked Azziz to call his father and convey my sincerest apologies. He said he would, but thought it unnecessary.

When Sue returned to the site in mid-May, she witnessed what I had been telling her about the slow rate of progress on the project. After taking her on a tour, she also felt disappointed.

During Sue's visit, she had agreed I could return to Turkey for a break. Therefore, after spending the day with Sue, a driver took me to the Sheraton Hotel. Here I would spend the night, then early the next morning, I would take a taxi to the airport. The next morning, all started okay, until the cab began slowing down, before coming to a halt. I then spent an anxious fifteen minutes until the driver managed to restart the engine. Fortunately, we arrived at the airport in time for me to catch my flight to Frankfurt, where I would change planes for the one on to Turkey.

At the airport, I checked the indicator board for my flight and went to the specified gate. However, when the time came to board, I grew concerned when the gate remained closed. On rechecking the indicator board, it shocked me to learn the gate number had changed. Fortunately, the new gate was close to where I had been waiting, so I went to and boarded my flight to Turkey.

Although this had been a bit of concern, my trip back to Morocco was far from straightforward. Upon reaching Frankfurt and proceeding to the departures area, I discovered that my flight to Morocco was delayed. Approximately forty minutes later, an announcement said the plane was ready to board. I handed my boarding pass to an official at the gate who checked, ripped it in two and gave me the stub.

Once onboard, I could not find my seat number, so I went to a flight attendant and explained my problem.

On showing her my ticket stub, her puzzlement turned to shock and disbelief. Her eyebrows shot up in alarm. "You're on the wrong plane! This plane doesn't go to Morocco! How on earth did you manage to board?" Not expecting this news, my expression said it all.

"I showed my boarding pass at the gate. They checked it and gave me back the section I have now."

"I can't understand how it happened," she said, "but you must leave this plane now."

I left and backtracked up to the boarding area. A quick check revealed there were two Air France flights leaving from adjacent gates. The one I should have gone through, being next to the one I had used.

I showed my boarding pass stub and explained to the check-in attendant what had happened. She too appeared shocked at the mix-up, but then allowed me to board the plane.

Had there been an empty seat with a corresponding number when I boarded the wrong plane, both myself and the flight attendants would have found ourselves in deep trouble.

When I later talked with friends about this incident, one laughs and said, "It could only happened to you."

Strange, but no one I have ever spoken to had heard of such a mishap.

Back on the site, I felt pleased to find more works were ongoing. However, there were still not enough personnel to boost progress towards the early completion of the project.

A short time later, because of continual problems in getting their invoices paid, my company terminated my contract. This was a successful pity, as I would have liked to have seen the hotel completed and operating. From what I had seen, it would have looked fabulous.

When I left Morocco, I did not know it would prove to be my last working contract. Despite everything, my positive mindset led to an incredible career in various countries across the Middle East, Far East, and North Africa. Plus, I'd visited many fantastic locations at either none or little cost.

Readers will agree that the experiences, events, and people I met during my travels are something one usually only reads about in adventure books.

For me, however, this was living, not just life. I can't think of a better way to see the world than by being paid to do so.

For those who have read my story, I hope it gives you the confidence to succeed in your life. Whenever you feel down, remember these words. "Positive thoughts produce positive results, negative ones, negative results."

**Also by this author**

**An Expat's Experiences of Living in Turkey.**

Covering over 25 years of the author's life living in Turkey. This captivating memoir covers how he and his late wife came to be in Turkey, and having a house built. It also mentions how Colin ended up flying back to England on a stretcher. Plus, how after his wife died, at age 72, he met and married a wonderful Turkish lady three years younger than him.

**For the Greater Good.**

When Jeff hears that his brother died in police custody in Yemen, a country racked by civil war, he flies in seeking answers. However, before he realizes, he finds himself involved in a plot to assassinate the self-proclaimed president. It seems he is a threat not only to his own country, but to world peace. Using his skills as a black ops specialist, Jeff goes about resolving this situation...

**A Dangerous Love Affair.**

When an inspiring author finds himself involved with a famous erotic writer, their love gets put to the test by her vengeful ex. It results in a perilous mission to save her, as he is prepared to do whatever it takes to put an end to the budding romance—including murder.

**Impending Disaster.**

Three friends survive a plane crash on top of a mountain. While making their way down to town, they uncover a dangerous situation. As a result, they must reach the town in time to sound the alarm.

**Desperation Rules the Day.**

Over his head in gambling debts, Nathan accepts a large sum of money to allow two containers aboard his ship. Little does he know, he's now become an accomplice in an Iran-backed terrorist plot set to cause mass devastation on Independence Day.

**Never Pull the Tiger's Tail.**

The President has asked Jeff Stone, who leads an anti-terrorist organization, to look into the recent bombing attempt on the Golden Gate Bridge. Traveling to Panama with a colleague, they start an investigation into a series of rocket launchers in two shipping containers.

**Terror Holiday.**

When Simon books a dream holiday in Istanbul, Turkey for his family, a military coup on their doorstep is the last thing anyone expected. Stranded by the crisis, the family worries for their safety and hopes to make it through the holiday.

**Fatal Love.**

When Melissa married Ian, she expected the same loving and sexual relationship as they had before they married. However, Ian changes and has no interest in either sex or Melissa. After Ian dies in a traffic accident, Melissa meets Steve. They enjoy making love with Melissa happy when they later marry,. Unfortunately, Steve has kept a dark secret from her that almost leads to her death.

**Suzy's Dilemma.**

Suzy's life changes for the better when she meets Vincent, a man who, like her, loves sex. When she finds out she is pregnant, Vincent is delighted and proposes marriage. Caught between keeping the baby or having an abortion, Suzy has to decide what to do.

**It Happened in Barcelona**

After Peter's wife dies in a traffic accident, he can no longer live in the barn conversion house that he and his late wife had designed. Later, while talking with friends, one suggests he moves to Spain.

After Peter moves there with his faithful dog Sam, he ends up with what had been missing during his previous life in England.

**An Unforgettable Cruise.**

When Ashley's husband dies in a plane crash, it releases her from a loveless marriage. Later, while on a luxury cruise she meets Stephan. He not only rekindles her desire for sex, but makes her happy and contented. After a brief engagement, they marry, and while on honeymoon in St Petersburg, experience a frightening situation.

**Accidental Death.**

A story about John, a teenager who after joining the army and catches the eye of Dexter, the leader of a secret anti-terrorist group. After years of clandestinely eliminating terrorists, John's life takes a dramatic turn when he saves a young woman's life in South Africa.

### About the author

Colin Guest, who resides in Turkey, began his working life with a five-year apprenticeship as a joiner/shopfitter in Plymouth, Devon. Early on, he travelled around England on a variety of projects, before working on two contracts abroad. A back injury in 1982 ended any labour-intensive work, reducing Colin's earning potential. After a discussion with his wife, Colin became an expat worker. During the next nineteen years, he worked on high-class interior-fit-outs spread through the Middle, Far East, and North Africa. As a result, Colin lived a life most only dream. His writing career began after his wife died in 2007, The idea being to motivate people to think positive in difficult situations. An optimistic attitude, that from experience, Colin believes will help you climb back into the driving seat of life.

In 2024, Colin started to write film scripts, these being much different from writing stories.

## Social media contacts

Website: www.colinguestauthor.com
     Goodreads: www.goodreads.com/author/show/9857414
     Blog: www.turkmed.wordpress.com[1]
     Twitter: www.twitter.com/Tigermanguest
     Facebook: www.facebook.com/tigerman55[2]
     Instagram: www.instagram.com/tigerman101[3]

     Email:      guestcolin992@      gmail.com      & tigermanpress@gmail.com

     interest: www.pininterest.com/colinguest9

---

1.      http://www.turkmed.wordpress.com

2.      http://www.facebook.com/tigerman55

3.      http://www.instagram.com/tigerman101

LinkedIn: www.linkedin.com/in/colin-john-guest

Did you love *Follow in the Tigerman's Footprints*? Then you should read *A Dangerous Love Affair*[4] by Colin Guest!

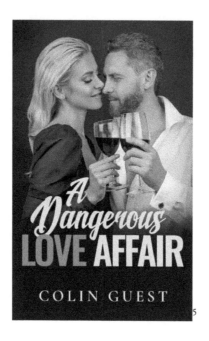

**Since falling in love with Tara, from seemingly life-threatening accidents in London to kidnapping and a deadly encounter high in the Italian Alps, John's life has been in danger.**

Read more at https://www.colinguestauthor.com.

---

4. https://books2read.com/u/4jwGvX

5. https://books2read.com/u/4jwGvX

# Also by Tigerman

Follow in the Tigerman's Footprints

Watch for more at https://www.colinguestauthor.com.

# Also by Colin Guest

**1**
Desperation Rules the Day
Suzy's Dilemma

**Standalone**
Desperation Rules the Day
An Unforgettable Cruise
A Dangerous Love Affair
An Expats Experiences of Living in Turkey
Terror Holiday
It Happened in Barcelona
Impending Disaster
Fatal Love
Accidental Death
Follow in the Tigerman's Footprints

Watch for more at https://www.colinguestauthor.com.

# About the Author

Colin Guest is English, now retired and living in Istanbul. He has written eleven books, including memoirs, thrillers and romance stories. His latest book is Unforgettable Cruise, a romance story. Colin is passionate about wild animals and has adopted a tiger for the past twelve years.

Read more at www.colinguestauthor.com.

Milton Keynes UK
Ingram Content Group UK Ltd.
UKHW011909060524
442290UK00001B/89